Applied Meta-Analysis for Social Science Research

Methodology in the Social Sciences
David A. Kenny, Founding Editor
Todd D. Little, Series Editor

This series provides applied researchers and students with analysis and research design books that emphasize the use of methods to answer research questions. Rather than emphasizing statistical theory, each volume in the series illustrates when a technique should (and should not) be used and how the output from available software programs should (and should not) be interpreted. Common pitfalls as well as areas of further development are clearly articulated.

SPECTRAL ANALYSIS OF TIME-SERIES DATA
Rebecca M. Warner

A PRIMER ON REGRESSION ARTIFACTS
Donald T. Campbell and David A. Kenny

REGRESSION ANALYSIS FOR CATEGORICAL MODERATORS
Herman Aguinis

HOW TO CONDUCT BEHAVIORAL RESEARCH OVER THE INTERNET:
A BEGINNER'S GUIDE TO HTML AND CGI/PERL
R. Chris Fraley

CONFIRMATORY FACTOR ANALYSIS FOR APPLIED RESEARCH
Timothy A. Brown

DYADIC DATA ANALYSIS
David A. Kenny, Deborah A. Kashy, and William L. Cook

MISSING DATA: A GENTLE INTRODUCTION
*Patrick E. McKnight, Katherine M. McKnight, Souraya Sidani,
and Aurelio José Figueredo*

MULTILEVEL ANALYSIS FOR APPLIED RESEARCH: IT'S JUST REGRESSION!
Robert Bickel

THE THEORY AND PRACTICE OF ITEM RESPONSE THEORY
R. J. de Ayala

THEORY CONSTRUCTION AND MODEL-BUILDING SKILLS:
A PRACTICAL GUIDE FOR SOCIAL SCIENTISTS
James Jaccard and Jacob Jacoby

DIAGNOSTIC MEASUREMENT: THEORY, METHODS, AND APPLICATIONS
André A. Rupp, Jonathan Templin, and Robert A. Henson

APPLIED MISSING DATA ANALYSIS
Craig K. Enders

ADVANCES IN CONFIGURAL FREQUENCY ANALYSIS
Alexander A. von Eye, Patrick Mair, and Eun-Young Mun

PRINCIPLES AND PRACTICE OF STRUCTURAL EQUATION MODELING,
THIRD EDITION
Rex B. Kline

APPLIED META-ANALYSIS FOR SOCIAL SCIENCE RESEARCH
Noel A. Card

Applied Meta-Analysis
for Social Science Research

Noel A. Card

Series Editor's Note by Todd D. Little

THE GUILFORD PRESS
New York   London

© 2012 The Guilford Press
A Division of Guilford Publications, Inc.
72 Spring Street, New York, NY 10012
www.guilford.com

Printed in the United States of America

This book is printed on acid-free paper.

Last digit is print number: 9 8 7 6 5 4 3 2 1

Library of Congress Cataloging-in-Publication Data
Card, Noel A.
    Applied meta-analysis for social science research / Noel A. Card;
Series editor's note by Todd D. Little.
        p. cm. — (Methodology in the social sciences)
    Includes bibliographical references and index.
    ISBN 978-1-60918-499-5 (hbk.: alk. paper)
    1. Social sciences—Statistical methods.   2. Social sciences—
Methodology.   3. Meta-analysis.   I. Title.
    HA29.C286 2011
    300.72—dc23
                                                    2011019332

For my family—Jeanet, Gabby, and Angie

Series Editor's Note

I am particularly proud and happy to introduce you to Noel Card and his wonderful resource *Applied Meta-Analysis for Social Science Research*. The reason that I am so enthusiastic is that I have a close professional and personal relationship with Noel spanning some 10-plus years now. Noel overlapped with me for a number of years at the University of Kansas before he moved to his current position at the University of Arizona. During this time, I have seen Noel develop into one of the very finest pedagogically gifted quantitative scholars of our day. His honors include an early career award from the Society for Research in Child Development. He is also a member of the Society of Multivariate Experimental Psychology (SMEP), a limited-membership society devoted to the advancement of multivariate methods as applied in the social and behavioral sciences. Noel's election to SMEP at such a young age speaks volumes about his ability and accomplishments.

When I became the Series Editor of the Methodology in the Social Sciences series, one of the first books I sought was a comprehensive book on meta-analysis written in the accessible style of this series. I approached Noel about writing this book knowing that he was the absolute best person to write it. To begin, Noel has had a long-standing passion for meta-analysis, and he has honed his pedagogy for quantitative synthesis techniques by regularly teaching the University of Kansas Summer Institutes in Statistics ("Stats Camps"; *www.Quant.ku.edu*) course on meta-analysis. Couple his dogged determination to understand all that is meta-analysis with his gifted ability to communicate quantitative methods to a diverse audience and you have a recipe for a perfect book: a desk reference for those who are familiar with meta-analysis and an all-in-one learning tool to use in classes at both the undergraduate or graduate level. Noel's coverage is both broad and deep and not tainted by preferences or restricted by a particular software focus. As a resource work, Noel's book covers many topics that others avoid, but Noel integrates these topics so seamlessly that you'll wonder which topics are lacking in the other books (e.g., calculating appropriate and unique effect sizes, thoroughly handling artifact corrections, evaluating publication bias with bias alternative analytic representations, evaluating advanced statistical models of the assembled data, and so on). In each chapter, Noel provides thoughtful and helpful advice on the key issues as well as offers alternative tactics. He carefully presents the pros and cons of each alternative and issue. As you read, you will immediately hear him reaching out to you and guiding your understanding of the material. His "voice" as he writes is assuring and clear, light-hearted yet authoritative. He deftly introduces a topic or idea at the ground level and moves you step by step up the rungs of understanding to the very top of where the field currently resides.

Throughout Noel's book you will find a number of appealing pedagogical features. For those who are not comfortable with equations, for example, Noel is very careful to explain the concepts in clear, simple language and in equation form. He also annotates the equations so that beginners can learn how to "read" a statistical equation. Equations are useful only when you the reader can follow them. Noel makes sure you can follow them—primarily as a supplement to the accompanying narrative. To illustrate all of the key points throughout the book, Noel uses ample real data examples that he's discovered in his own meta-analytic work. Noel also has very thoughtfully selected and annotated some recommended readings that you will find at the end of each chapter.

You can see from the table of contents that the coverage is complete. You will discover when you read each topic that Noel does not assume that you have prior knowledge nor does he offend the seasoned expert. His motivation is genuine: He provides a comprehensive yet accessible work that will advance scientific practice of quantitative synthesis in the social, behavioral, and educational sciences. His many examples provide solid grounding for and concrete clarifications of the concepts. Noel's book is about as close to a "page turner" as you can get.

TODD D. LITTLE
At 30,000 feet between
Houston and Kansas City;
University of Kansas
Lawrence, Kansas

Preface and Acknowledgments

In some sense, I began this book over 10 years ago, when I was a graduate student at St. John's University. During this period of reading and trying to draw conclusions from the research literature on childhood aggression and victimization (my first area of substantive interest), I became discouraged by the lack of accumulation of science, as evidenced by the discrepant conclusions drawn in (narrative) reviews of the literature and the numerous studies conducted and published in what seemed an absence of knowledge of the existing literature. During this time, I became motivated to find a better way to summarize and synthesize the research literature in my particular field.

I soon was introduced to meta-analysis as a potential solution, and it did not take long before I was convinced of its value. I began reading all I could about this methodology and had the good fortune to attend a workshop by Robert Rosenthal in the summer of 2004. Since that time, I have become increasingly interested and immersed in meta-analysis through publishing meta-analyses within my substantive area, teaching graduate classes and workshops on the topic, and collaborating with researchers on their own meta-analyses. So, when Todd D. Little, Editor of The Guilford Press's Methodology in the Social Sciences series, approached me in 2007 about the possibility of writing a book, I was eager for the opportunity and believed I was ready to do so.

The key phrase of the last sentence is " ... believed I was ready to do so." During the last 3 years of writing this book, I have learned that the methods of meta-analysis are both broad and deep, and that this is a continuously evolving methodology. In this book, I have tried to capture each of these qualities in presenting this methodology to you. First, I have tried to cover the full breadth of meta-analysis, covering every aspect of the process of planning, conducting, and writing a meta-analytic review. Second, I have delved into the depth of meta-analysis when I believe that more advanced methods are valuable, aiming to present this material in the least technical manner I can. Finally, I have tried to present the state of the art of meta-analysis by covering recent advances that are likely to be valuable to you. In balancing these sometimes competing demands of coverage, I have consistently thought back to when I was preparing my first meta-analyses to consider what is the most important material for beginning users of meta-analysis techniques to know. The result, I hope, is that this book will help you learn about and then use what I believe is an invaluable tool in the advancement of science.

Fortunately, I had many people supporting me during the writing of this book. First and foremost, I want to thank C. Deborah Laughton (Publisher, Methodology and Statistics, at Guilford) and Todd D. Little (Series Editor). Both provided the perfect balance of patience and prompting, listening and advice giving, and—above all—sincere friendship throughout the writing of this book. I also thank C. Deborah for securing input from a number of expert reviewers and am grateful to these reviewers for their thoughtful and constructive feedback: Adam Hafdahl, ARCH Statistical Consulting, LLC; Mike Cheung, Department of Psychology, National University of Singapore; Blair Johnson, Department of Psychology, University of Connecticut; Soyeon Ahn, Department of Educational and Psychological Studies, University of Miami; Jody Worley, Department of Human Relations, University of Oklahoma; Robert Tett, Department of Psychology, University of Tulsa; John Norris, Department of Second Language Studies, University of Hawaii; Brad Bushman, Institute for Social Research, University of Michigan; Meng-Jia Wu, School of Education, Loyola University; Tania B. Huedo-Medina, Department of Psychology, University of Connecticut; and Jeffrey Valentine, Department of Educational and Counseling Psychology, University of Louisville. I am also thankful to the many individuals who provided prepublication copies of their writings on meta-analysis, which was necessary to ensure that the material presented in this book is up to date. This book also benefited from feedback from students in a class at the University of Arizona (spring 2010) and two workshops (2009 and 2010) in an ongoing course I teach at the University of Kansas Summer Institutes in Statistics (affectionately known as "Stats Camps"; see *quant.ku.edu/StatsCamps/overview.html*). The students in these classes provided invaluable feedback and reactions to the material that greatly improved the pedagogical value of this book. Finally, I am most grateful to the support of my family throughout this process.

Contents

PART II. THE BUILDING BLOCKS: CODING INDIVIDUAL STUDIES

PART III. PUTTING THE PIECES TOGETHER: COMBINING AND COMPARING EFFECT SIZES

Applied Meta-Analysis for Social Science Research

Part I

The Blueprint

Planning and Preparing a Meta-Analytic Review

1

An Introduction to Meta-Analysis

Meta-analysis, also called quantitative research synthesis, is a powerful approach to summarizing and comparing results from empirical literature. The goal of this book is to provide you, the reader, with information to conduct and evaluate meta-analytic reviews.

1.1 THE NEED FOR RESEARCH SYNTHESIS IN THE SOCIAL SCIENCES

Isaac Newton is known to have humbly explained his success: "If I have seen further it is by standing upon the shoulders of giants" (1675; from Columbia World of Quotations, 1996). Although the history of science suggests that Newton may have been as likely to kick his fellow scientists down as he was to collaboratively stand on their shoulders (e.g., Boorstin, 1983, Chs. 52–53; Gribbin, 2002, Ch. 5), this statement does eloquently portray a central principle in science: That the advancement of scientific knowledge is based on systematic building of one study on top of a foundation of prior studies, the accumulation of which takes our understanding to ever increasing heights. A closely related tenet is replication—that findings of studies are confirmed (or not) through repetition by other scientists.

Together, the principles of orderly accumulation and replication of empirical research suggest that scientific knowledge should steadily progress. However, it is reasonable to ask if this is really the case. One obstacle to this progression is that scientists are humans with finite abilities to retain, organize, and synthesize empirical findings. In most areas of research, stud-

3

ies are being conducted at an increasing rate, making it difficult for scholars to stay informed of research in all but the narrowest areas of specialization. I argue that many areas of social science research are in less need of further research than they are in need of organization of the existing research. A second obstacle is that studies are rarely exact replications of one another, but instead commonly use slightly different methods, measures, and/or samples.[1] This imperfect replication makes it difficult (1) to separate meaningful differences in results from expectable sampling fluctuations, and (2) if there are meaningful differences in results across studies, to determine which of the several differences in studies account for the differences in results.

An apparent solution to these obstacles is that scientists systematically review results from the numerous studies, synthesizing results to draw conclusions regarding typical findings and sources of variability across studies. One method of conducting such systematic syntheses of the empirical literature is through meta-analysis, which is a methodological and statistical approach to drawing conclusions from empirical literature. As I hope to demonstrate in this book, meta-analysis is a particularly powerful tool in drawing these sorts of conclusions from the existing empirical literature. Before describing this tool in the remainder of the book, in this chapter I introduce some terminology of this approach, provide a brief history of meta-analysis, further describe the process of research synthesis as a scientific endeavor, and then provide a more detailed preview of the remainder of this book.

1.2 BASIC TERMINOLOGY

Before further discussing meta-analysis, it is useful to clarify some relevant terminology. One clarification involves the distinction of meta-analysis from primary or secondary analysis. The second clarification involves terminology of meta-analysis within the superordinate category of a literature review.

1.2.1 Meta-Analysis versus Primary or Secondary Analysis

The first piece of terminology to clarify are the differences among the terms "meta-analysis," "primary analysis," and "secondary analysis" (Glass, 1976). The term "primary analysis" refers to what we typically think of as data analysis—when a researcher collects data from individual persons, companies, and so on,[2] and then analyzes these data to provide answers to the research questions that motivated the study. The term "secondary analysis" refers to re-analysis of these data, often to answer different research questions or to answer research questions in a different way (e.g., using alternative analytic approaches that were not available when the data were originally analyzed). This secondary data analysis can be performed either by the original researchers or by others if they are able to obtain the raw data from the researchers. Both primary and secondary data analysis require access to the full, raw data as collected in the study.

In contrast, meta-analysis involves the statistical analysis of the results from more than one study. Two points of this definition merit consideration in differentiating meta-analysis from either primary or secondary analysis. First, meta-analysis involves the *results* of studies as the unit of analysis, specifically results in the form of effect sizes. Obtaining these effect sizes does not require having access to the raw data (which are all-too-often unavailable), as it is usually possible to compute these effect sizes from the data reported in papers resulting from the original, primary or secondary, analysis. Second, meta-analysis is the analysis of results from *multiple* studies, in which individual studies are the unit of analysis. The number of studies can range from as few as two to as many as several hundred (or more, limited only by the availability of relevant studies). Therefore, a meta-analysis involves drawing inferences from a sample of studies, in contrast to primary and secondary analyses that involve drawing inferences from a sample of individuals. Given this goal, meta-analysis can be considered a form of literature review, as I elaborate next.

1.2.2 Meta-Analysis as a Form of Literature Review

A second aspect of terminological consideration involves the place of meta-analysis within the larger family of literature reviews. A literature review can be defined as a synthesis of prior literature on a particular topic. Literature reviews differ along several dimensions, including their focus, goals, perspective, coverage, organization, intended audience, and method of synthesis (see Cooper, 1988, 2009a). Two dimensions are especially important in situating meta-analysis within the superordinate family of literature reviews: focus and method of synthesis. Figure 1.1 shows a schematic representation of how meta-analysis differs from other literature reviews in terms of focus and method of synthesis.

Meta-analyses, like other research syntheses, focus on research outcomes (not the conclusion reached by study authors, which Rosenthal noted are "only vaguely related to the actual results" (1991, p. 13). Reviews focusing on research outcomes answer questions such as "The existing research shows

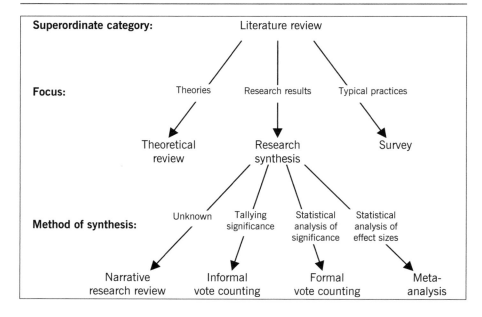

FIGURE 1.1. Relation of meta-analysis to other types of literature reviews.

X" or "These types of studies find X, whereas these other types of studies find Y." Other types of literature reviews have different foci. Theoretical reviews focus on what theoretical explanations are commonly used within a field, attempt to explain phenomena using a novel theoretical alternative, or seek to integrate multiple theoretical perspectives. These are the types of reviews that are commonly reported in, for example, *Psychological Review*. Survey reviews focus on typical practices within a field, such as the use of particular methods in a field or trends in the forms of treatment used in published clinical trials (e.g., Card & Little, 2007, surveyed published research in child development to report the percentage of studies using longitudinal designs). Although reviews focusing on theories or surveying practices within the literature are valuable contributions to science, it is important to distinguish the focus of meta-analysis on research outcomes from these other types of reviews.

However, not all reviews that focus on research outcomes are meta-analyses. What distinguishes meta-analysis from other approaches to research synthesis is the method of synthesizing findings to draw conclusions. The methods shown in the bottom of Figure 1.1 can be viewed as a continuum from qualitative to quantitative synthesis. At the left is the narrative review. Here, the reviewer evaluates the relevant research and somehow draws conclusions. This "somehow" represents the limits of this qualitative, or narrative, approach to research synthesis. The exact process of how the reviewer draws conclusions is unknown, or at least not articulated, so there is considerable room for subjectivity in the research conclusions reached. Beyond just the potential for subjective bias to emerge, this approach to synthesizing research taxes the reviewer's ability to process information. Reviewers who attempt to synthesize research results qualitatively tend to perceive more inconsistency and smaller magnitudes of effects than those performing meta-analytic syntheses (Cooper & Rosenthal, 1980). In sum, the most common method of reviewing research—reading empirical reports and "somehow" drawing conclusions—is prone to subjectivity and places demands on the reviewer that make conclusions difficult to reach.

Moving toward the right, or quantitative direction, of Figure 1.1 are two vote-counting methods, which I have termed informal and formal. Both involve considering the significance of effects from research studies in terms of significant positive, significant negative, or nonsignificant results, and then drawing conclusions based on the number of studies finding a particular result. Informal (also called conventional) vote counting involves simply drawing conclusions based on "majority rules" criteria; so, if more studies find a significant positive effect than find other effects (nonsignificant or significant negative), one concludes that there is a positive effect. A more formal vote-counting approach (see Bushman & Wang, 2009) uses statistical analysis of the expected frequency of results given the type I error rates (e.g., Given a traditional type I error rate of .05, do significantly more than 5% of studies find an effect?). Although vote-counting methods can be useful when information on effect sizes is unavailable, I do not discuss them in this book for two reasons (for descriptions of these vote-counting methods, see Bushman & Wang, 2009). First, conclusions of the existence of effects (i.e., statistical significance) can be more powerfully determined using meta-analytic procedures described in this book. Second, conclusions of significance alone are unsatisfying, and the focus of meta-analysis is on effect sizes that provide information about the *magnitude* of the effect.[3]

At the right side of Figure 1.1 is meta-analysis, which is a form of research synthesis in which conclusions are based on the statistical analysis of effect sizes from individual studies.[4] I reserve further description of meta-analysis for the remainder of the book, but my hope here is that this taxonomy makes clear that meta-analysis is only one approach to conducting a literature review. Specifically, meta-analysis is a quantitative method of synthesizing empirical research results in the form of effect sizes. Despite this specificity, meta-analysis is a flexible and powerful approach to advancing scientific knowledge, in that it represents a statistically defensible approach to synthesizing empirical findings, which are the foundation of empirical sciences.

1.3   A BRIEF HISTORY OF META-ANALYSIS

In this section, I briefly outline the history of meta-analysis. My goal is not to be exhaustive in detailing this history (for more extensive treatments, see Chalmers, Hedges, & Cooper, 2002, Hedges, 1992, and Olkin, 1990; for a history intended for laypersons, see Hunt, 1997). Instead, I only hope to provide a basic overview to give you a sense of where the techniques described in this book have originated.

There exist several early individual attempts to combine statistically results from multiple studies. Olkin (1990) cites Karl Pearson's work in 1904 to synthesize associations between inoculation and typhoid fever, and several similar approaches were described from the 1930s. Methods of combining probabilities advanced in the 1940s and 1950s (including the method that became well known as Stouffer's method; see Rosenthal, 1991). But these approaches saw little application in the social sciences until the 1970s (with some exceptions such as work by Rosenthal in the 1960s; see Rosenthal, 1991).

It was only in the late 1970s that meta-analysis found its permanent place in the social sciences. Although several groups of researchers developed techniques during this time (e.g., Rosenthal & Rubin, 1978; Schmidt & Hunter, 1977), it was the work of Gene Glass and colleagues that introduced the term "meta-analysis" (Glass, 1976) and prompted attention to the approach, especially in the field of psychology. Specifically, Smith and Glass (1977) published a meta-analysis of the effectiveness of psychotherapy from 375 studies, showing that psychotherapy was effective and that there is little difference in effectiveness across different types of therapies. Although the former finding, introduced by Glass, would probably have been received with little disagreement, the latter finding by Smith and Glass was controversial and prompted considerable criticism (e.g., Eysenck, 1978). The controversial nature of Smith and Glass's conclusion seems to have had both positive and negative consequences for meta-analysis. On the positive side, their convincing approach to the difficult question of the relative effectiveness of psychotherapies likely persuaded many of the value of meta-analysis. On the negative side, the criticisms of this particular study (which I believe were greater than would have been leveled against meta-analysis of a less controversial topic) have often been generalized to the entire practice of meta-analyses. I describe these criticisms in greater detail in Chapter 2.

Despite the controversial nature of this particular introduction of meta-analysis to psychology, the coming years witnessed a rapid increase in this approach. In the early 1980s, several books describing the techniques of meta-analysis were published (Glass, McGraw, & Smith, 1981; Hunter, Schmidt, & Jackson, 1982; Rosenthal, 1984). Shortly thereafter, Hedges and Olkin (1985) published a book on meta-analysis that was deeply rooted in traditional statistics. This rooting was important both in bringing formality and perceived statistical merit to the approach, as well as serving as a starting point for subsequent advances to meta-analytic techniques.

The decades since the introduction of meta-analysis to the social sciences have seen increasing use of this technique. Given its widespread use in social science research during the past three decades, it appears that meta-analysis is here to stay. For this reason alone, scholars need to be familiar with this approach in order to understand the scientific literature. However, understanding meta-analysis is valuable not only because it is widely used; more importantly, meta-analysis is widely used because it represents a powerful approach to synthesizing the existing empirical literature and contributing to the progression of science. My goal in the remainder of this book is to demonstrate this value to you, as well as to describe how one conducts a meta-analytic review.

1.4   THE SCIENTIFIC PROCESS OF RESEARCH SYNTHESIS

Given the importance of research syntheses, including meta-analyses, to the progression of science, it is critical to follow scientific standards in their preparation. Most scientists are well trained in methods and data-analytic techniques to ensure objective and valid conclusions in primary research, yet methods and data-analytic techniques for research synthesis are less well known. In this section, I draw from Cooper's (1982, 1984, 1998, 2009a) description of five[5] stages of research synthesis to provide an overview of the process and scientific principles of conducting a research synthesis. These stages are formulating the problem, obtaining the studies, making decisions about study inclusion, analyzing and interpreting study results, and presenting the findings from the research synthesis.

As in any scientific endeavor, the first stage of a literature review is to formulate a problem. Here, the central considerations involve the question that you wish to answer, the constructs you are interested in, and the population about which you wish to draw conclusions. In terms of the questions answered, a literature review can only answer questions for which prior literature exists. For instance, to make conclusions of causality, the reviewer will need to rely on experimental (or perhaps longitudinal, as an approximation) studies; concurrent naturalistic studies would not be able to provide answers to this question. Defining the constructs of interest seems straightforward but poses two potential complications: The existing literature may use different terms or operationalizations for the same construct, or the existing literature may use similar terms to describe different constructs. Therefore, you need to define clearly the constructs of interest when planning the review. Similarly, you must consider which samples will be included in the literature review; for instance, you need to decide whether studies of unique populations (e.g., prison, psychiatric settings) should be included within the review. The advantages of a broad approach (in terms of constructs and samples) are that the conclusions of the review will be more generalizable and may allow for the identification of important differences among studies. However, a narrow approach will likely yield more consistent (i.e., more homogeneous, in the language of meta-analysis) results, and the quantity of literature that must be reviewed is smaller. Both of these features might be seen as advantages or disadvantages, depending on the goals (e.g., to identify average effects versus moderators) and ambition (in terms of the number of studies one is willing to code) of the reviewer.

The next step in a literature review is to obtain the literature relevant for the review. Here, the important consideration is that the reviewer is exhaustive, or at least representative, in obtaining relevant literature. It is useful to conceptualize the literature included as a sample drawn from a population of all possible studies. Adapting this conceptualization (and paralleling well-known principles of empirical primary research) highlights the importance of obtaining a representative sample of literature for the review. If the literature reviewed is not representative of the extant research, then the conclusions drawn will be a biased representation of reality. One common threat to all literature reviews is publication bias (also known as the file drawer problem). This threat is that studies that fail to find significant effects (or that find effects counter to what is expected) are less likely to be published, and therefore less likely to be accessible to the reviewer. To counter this threat, you should attempt to obtain unpublished studies (e.g., dissertations), which will either counter this threat or at least allow you to evaluate the magnitude of this bias (e.g., evaluating whether published versus unpublished studies find different effects). Another threat is that reviewers typically must rely on literature written in a language they know (e.g., English); this excludes literature written in other languages and therefore may exclude most studies conducted in other countries. Although it would be impractical to learn every language in which relevant literature may be written, you should be aware of this limitation and how it impacts the literature on which the review is based. To ensure the transparency of a literature review, the reviewer should report the means by which potentially relevant literature was searched and obtained.

The third, related, stage of a literature review is the evaluation of studies to decide which should inform the review. This stage involves reading the literature obtained in the prior stage (searching for relevant literature) and drawing conclusions regarding relevance. Obvious reasons to exclude works include investigation of constructs or samples that are irrelevant to the review (e.g., studies involving animals when one is interested in human behavior) or failure of the work to provide information relevant to the review (e.g., it treats the construct of interest only as a covariate without providing sufficient information about effects). Less obvious decisions need to be made for works that involve questionable quality or methodological features different from other studies. Including such works may improve the generalizability of the review but at the same time may contaminate the literature basis or distract from your focus. Decisions at this stage will typically involve refining the problem formulated at the first stage of the review.

The fourth stage is the most time-consuming and difficult: analyzing and interpreting the literature. As mentioned, there exist several approaches to how reviewers draw conclusions, ranging from qualitative to informal or formal vote counting to meta-analysis. For a meta-analysis, this stage involves systematically coding study characteristics and effect sizes, and then statistically analyzing these coded data. As I describe later in this book (Chapter 2) there are powerful advantages to using a meta-analytic approach.

The final stage of the literature review is the presentation of the review, often in written form. Although I suspend detailed recommendations on reporting meta-analyses until later in the book, a few general guidelines should be considered here. First, we should be transparent about the review process and decisions taken. Just as empirical works are expected to present sufficient details so that another researcher could replicate the results, a well-written research synthesis should provide sufficient detail for another scholar to replicate the review. Second, it is critical that the written report answers the original questions that motivated the review, or at least describes why such answers cannot be reached and what future work is needed to provide these answers. A third, related, guideline is that we should avoid a simple study-by-study listing. A good review synthesizes—not merely lists—the literature. Meta-analysis provides a powerful way of drawing valuable information from multiple studies that goes far beyond merely listing their individual results.

1.5   AN OVERVIEW OF THE BOOK

1.5.1   Organization of the Book

The five stages of research synthesis guide the organization of this book. Chapter 2 describes the stage of formulating a problem for meta-analysis, and Chapter 3 describes both stages two (searching the literature) and three (deciding which studies should be included) of a meta-analytic review. I mentioned that the fourth stage, analyzing and interpreting the literature, is the most time-consuming and challenging, and I have therefore devoted the majority of the book (Chapters 4 to 12) to this topic. Specifically, Chapter 4 offers suggestions for coding study characteristics, and Chapters 5 to 7 describe the coding and correction of various types of effect sizes. Chapters 8 to 12 cover various topics in analyzing effect sizes, including ways of computing average effect sizes, analyzing variability in effect sizes across studies, and evaluating the threat of publication bias. Finally, Chapter 13 addresses the final stage of conducting a meta-analysis by offering advice on presenting the results of a meta-analysis. Collectively, these chapters should provide enough information for you to conduct a meta-analytic review from beginning to end—from conceptualization to publication.

In each chapter, I offer my advice on what I consider the "practical matters" of performing a meta-analysis. These include topics that are often not discussed in other books on meta-analysis, but that I have learned through my own experience in conducting, publishing, consulting for, and reviewing others' meta-analytic reviews. These topics include advice on managing the potentially overwhelming amount of information of a meta-analysis, how much information you should code from studies, whether it is useful to use specific meta-analysis software programs, selecting from multiple models for meta-analysis, and linking meta-analytic results with theory. Because these are topics not often written about, it is likely that some may disagree with my recommendations. At the same time, this advice represents what I wish I had known when I first began learning about and conducting meta-analytic reviews, and I offer it with the hope that it will help new meta-analysts.

1.5.2   Example Meta-Analysis

To illustrate many of the steps in conducting a meta-analytic review, I will rely on a meta-analytic review my colleagues and I have published (Card, Stucky, Sawalani, & Little, 2008). The paper reported results of several interrelated meta-analyses comparing two forms of aggression among children and adolescents: direct aggression (a.k.a. overt aggression), which includes behaviors such as hitting, pushing, teasing, and calling other kids mean names; and indirect aggression (a.k.a. relational, social, or covert aggression), which includes behaviors such as gossiping, hurtful manipulation of relationships, and excluding a peer from activities. In this paper, we considered gender differences in each of these forms of aggression, the magnitude of correlation between these two forms, and how strongly correlated each form is to various aspects of psychosocial adjustment. My goal in presenting these results is not to illustrate the substantive conclusions, but rather to provide a consistent, ongoing example throughout the book.

1.6 PRACTICAL MATTERS: A NOTE ON SOFTWARE AND INFORMATION MANAGEMENT

Conducting a meta-analytic review is usually a substantial undertaking. I do not mean that the statistical analyses are daunting; in fact, one of my goals is to show you that the statistical analyses for a basic meta-analysis are fairly straightforward. However, the process of exhaustively searching and collecting the literature, of reading and coding studies, and of analyzing and reporting results requires a substantial amount of time and effort.

One way to reduce this burden, or at least to avoid adding to it, is through organization. Let me make one point clear: My first practical suggestion to beginning meta-analysts is to be extremely organized throughout the process. Some examples of this organization, which I expand upon throughout this book, are to keep detailed records of literature searches, to have a well-organized system for keeping copies of studies evaluated for the meta-analysis, and—if working with a team of researchers—to ensure that all individuals are following the same system of organizing, coding, and the like. Carefully conducting a meta-analysis requires a lot of work, and you certainly want to avoid doubling (or tripling) that work by repetition due to poor organization, or even worse, not being able to adequately describe this work when reporting your findings.

To aid in this organization, you should use a good spreadsheet program (such as Microsoft Excel or a comparable program). Although early meta-analysts relied on hundreds of notecards, the capacities of modern spreadsheets to store, sort, and search for information makes their use a necessity for the modern meta-analyst. Along with a good spreadsheet program, you will need basic statistical analysis software to conduct a meta-analysis.

Any program that can conduct weighted general linear model analyses (e.g., weighted regression analyses) will suffice, including SPSS and SAS.

At this point, I have only recommended that you use standard spreadsheet and basic statistical analysis software. Are there special software packages for meta-analysis? Yes, there exist a range of freely downloadable as well as commercial packages for conducting meta-analyses, as well as sets of macros that can be used within common statistical packages.[6] I do not attempt to describe these programs in this book (interested readers can see Bax, Yu, Ikeda, & Moons, 2007, or Borenstein, Hedges, Higgins, & Rothstein, 2009, Ch. 44). I do not describe these software options because, as I state later in this book, I do not necessarily recommend them for the beginning meta-analyst. These meta-analysis programs can be a timesaver after one learns the techniques and the software, and they are certainly useful in organizing complex data (i.e., meta-analyses with many studies and multiple effect sizes per study) for some more complex analyses. However, the danger of relying on them exclusively—especially when you are first learning to conduct meta-analyses—is that they may encourage erroneous use when you are not adequately familiar with the techniques.

1.7 SUMMARY

In this chapter, I have introduced meta-analysis as a valuable tool for synthesizing research, specifically for synthesizing research outcomes using quantitative analyses. I have provided a very brief history and overview of the terminology of meta-analysis, and described five stages of the process of conducting a meta-analytic review. Finally, I have previewed the remainder of this book, which is organized around these five stages.

1.8 RECOMMENDED READINGS

Cooper, H. M. (1998). *Synthesizing research: A guide for literature reviews*. Thousand Oaks, CA: Sage.—This book provides an encompassing perspective on the entire process of meta-analysis and other forms of literature reviews. It is written in an accessible manner, focusing on the conceptual foundations of meta-analysis rather than the data-analytic practices.

Hunt, M. (1997). *How science takes stock: The story of meta-analysis*. New York: Russell Sage Foundation.—This book provides an entertaining history of the growth of meta-analysis, written for an educated lay audience.

NOTES

1. A common misperception is that lack of replicability is more pervasive in social than in natural sciences. However, Hedges (1987) showed that psychological research demonstrates similar replicability as that in physical sciences.

2. What is called the "unit of analysis," or fundamental object about which the researcher wishes to draw conclusions.

3. Bushman and Wang (2009) describe techniques for estimating effect sizes using vote-counting procedures. However, this approach is less accurate than meta-analytic combination of effect sizes and would be justifiable only if effect size information was not available in most primary studies.

4. Some authors (e.g., Cooper, 1998, 2009a) recommend limiting the use of the term "meta-analysis" to the statistical analysis of results from multiple studies. They suggest using terms such as "systematic review" or "research synthesis" to refer to the broader process of searching the literature, evaluating studies, and so on. Although I appreciate the importance of emphasizing the entire research synthesis process by using a broader term, the term "meta-analysis" is less cumbersome and more recognizable to most potential readers of the review. For this reason, I use the term "meta-analysis" (or "meta-analytic review") in this book, though I focus on all aspects of the systematic, quantitative research synthesis.

5. Cooper (2009a) has recently expanded these steps by explicitly adding a step on evaluating study quality. I consider the issue of coding study quality and other characteristics in Chapter 4.

6. For instance, David Wilson makes macros for SPSS, SAS, and Stata on his website: *mason.gmu.edu/~dwilsonb/ma.html*.

2

Questions That Can and Questions That Cannot Be Answered through Meta-Analysis

The first step of a meta-analysis, like the first step of any research endeavor, is to identify your goals and research questions. Too often I hear beginning meta-analysts say something like "I would like to meta-analyze the field of X." Although I appreciate the ambition of such a statement, there are nearly infinite numbers of research questions that you can derive—and potentially answer through meta-analysis—within any particular field. Without more specific goals and research questions, you would not have adequate guidance for searching the literature and deciding which studies are relevant for your meta-analysis (Chapter 3), knowing what characteristics of the studies (Chapter 4) or effect sizes (Chapters 5–7) to code, or how to proceed with the statistical analyses (Chapters 8–10). For this reason, the goals and specific research questions of a meta-analytic review need to be more focused than "to meta-analyze" a particular set of studies.

After describing some of the common goals of meta-analyses, I describe the limits of what you can conclude from meta-analyses and some of the common critiques of meta-analyses. I describe these limits and critiques here because it is important for you to have a realistic view of what can and cannot be answered through meta-analysis while you are planning your review.

2.1   IDENTIFYING GOALS AND RESEARCH QUESTIONS FOR META-ANALYSIS

In providing a taxonomy of literature reviews (see Chapter 1), Cooper (1988, 2009a) identified the goals of a review to be one of the dimensions on which reviews differ. Cooper identified integration (including drawing generalizations, reconciling conflicts, and identifying links between theories of disciplines), criticism, and identification of central issues as general goals of reviewers. Cooper noted that the goal of integration "is so pervasive among reviews that it is difficult to find reviews that do not attempt to synthesize works at some level" (1988, p. 108). This focus on integration is also central to meta-analysis, though you should not forget that there is room for additional goals of critiquing a field of study and identifying key directions for future conceptual, methodological, and empirical work. Although these goals are not central to meta-analysis itself, a good presentation of meta-analytic results will usually inform these issues. After reading all of the literature for a meta-analysis, you certainly should be in a position to offer informed opinions on these issues.

Considering the goal of integration, meta-analyses follow one of two[1] general approaches: combining and comparing studies. Combining studies involves using the effect sizes from primary studies to collectively estimate a typical effect size, or range of effect sizes. You will also typically make inferences about this estimated mean effect size in the form of statistical significance testing and/or confidence intervals. I describe these methods in Chapters 8 and 10. The second approach to integration using meta-analysis is to compare studies. This approach requires the existence of variability (i.e., heterogeneity) of effect sizes across studies, and I describe how you can test for heterogeneity in Chapter 8. If the studies in your meta-analysis are heterogeneous, then the goal of comparison motivates you to evaluate whether effect sizes found in studies systematically differ depending on coded study characteristics (Chapter 4) through meta-analytic moderator analyses (Chapter 9).

We might think of combination and comparison as the "hows" of meta-analysis; if so, we still need to consider the "whats" of meta-analysis. The goal of meta-analytic combination is to identify the average effect sizes, and meta-analytic comparison evaluates associations between these effect sizes and study characteristics. The common component of both is the focus on effect sizes, which represent the "whats" of meta-analysis. Although many different types of effect sizes exist, most represent associations between two variables (Chapter 5; see Chapter 7 for a broader consideration). Despite this simplicity, the methodology under which these two-variable associations were obtained is critically important in determining the types of research questions that can be answered in both primary and meta-analysis. Concurrent associations from naturalistic studies inform only the degree to which the two variables co-occur. Across-time associations from longitudinal studies (especially those controlling for initial levels of the presumed outcome) can inform temporal primacy, as an imperfect approximation of causal relations. Associations from experimental studies (e.g., association between group random assignment and outcome) can inform causality to the extent that designs eliminate threats to internal validity. Each of these types of associations is represented as an effect size in the same way in a meta-analysis, but they obviously have different implications for the phenomenon under consideration. It is also worth noting here that a variety of other effect sizes index very different "whats," including means, proportions, scale reliabilities, and longitudinal change scores; these possibilities are less commonly used but represent the range of effect sizes that can be used in meta-analysis (see Chapter 7).

Crossing the "hows" (i.e., combination and comparison) with the "whats" (i.e., effect sizes representing associations from concurrent naturalistic, longitudinal naturalistic, quasi-experimental, and experimental designs, as well as the variety of less commonly used effect sizes) suggests the wide range of research questions that can be answered through meta-analysis. For example, you might combine correlations between X and Y from concurrent naturalistic studies to identify the best estimate of the strength of this association. Alternatively, you might combine associations between a particular form of treatment (as a two-group comparison receiving versus not receiving) and a particular outcome, obtained from internally valid experimental designs, to draw conclusions of how strongly the treatment causes improvement in functioning. In terms of comparison, you might evaluate the extent to which X predicts later Y in longitudinal studies of different duration in order to evaluate the time frame over which prediction (and possibly causal influence) is strongest. Finally, you might compare the reliabilities of a particular scale across studies using different types of samples to determine how useful this scale is across populations. Although I could give countless other examples, I suspect that these few illustrate the types of research questions that can be answered through meta-analysis. Of course, the particular questions that are of interest to you are going to come from your own expertise with the topic; but considering the possible crossings between the "hows" (combination and comparison) and the "whats" (various types of effect sizes) offers a useful way to consider the possibilities.

2.2 THE LIMITS OF PRIMARY RESEARCH AND THE LIMITS OF META-ANALYTIC SYNTHESIS

Perhaps no statement is more true, and humbling, than this offered as the opening of Harris Cooper's editorial in *Psychological Bulletin* (and likely stated in similar words by many others): "Scientists have yet to conduct the flawless experiment" (Cooper, 2003, p. 3). I would extend this conclusion further to point out that no scientist has yet conducted a flawless study, and even further by stating that no meta-analyst has yet performed a flawless review. Each approach to empirical research, and indeed each application of such approaches within a particular field of inquiry, has certain limits to the contributions it can make to our understanding. Although full consideration of all of the potential threats to drawing conclusions from empirical research is beyond the scope of this section, I next highlight a few that I think are most useful in framing consideration of the most salient limits of primary research and meta-analysis—those of study design, sampling, methodological artifacts, and statistical power.

2.2.1 Limits of Study Design

Experimental designs allow inferences of causality but may be of questionable ecological validity. Certain features of the design of experimental (and quasi-experimental) studies dictate the extent to which conclusions are valid (see Shadish, Cook, & Campbell, 2002). Naturalistic (a.k.a. correlational) designs are often advantageous in providing better ecological validity than experimental designs and are often useful when variables of interest cannot, or cannot ethically, be manipulated. However, naturalistic designs cannot answer questions of causality, even in longitudinal studies that represent the best nonexperimental attempts to do so (see, e.g., Little, Card, Preacher, & McConnell, 2009).

Whatever limits due to study design that exist within a primary study (e.g., problems of internal validity in suboptimally designed experiments, ambiguity in causal influence in naturalistic designs) will also exist in a meta-analysis of those types of studies. For example, meta-analytically combining experimental studies that all have a particular threat to internal validity (e.g., absence of double-blind procedures in a medication trial) will yield conclusions that also suffer this threat. Similarly, meta-analysis of concurrent correlations from naturalistic studies will only tell you about the association between X and Y, not about the causal relation between these constructs. In short, limits to the design that are consistent across primary studies included in a meta-analysis will also serve as limits to the conclusions of the meta-analysis.

2.2.2 Limits of Sampling

Primary studies are also limited in that researchers can only generalize the results to populations represented by the sample. Findings from studies using samples homogeneous with respect to certain characteristics (e.g., gender, ethnicity, socioeconomic status, age, settings from which the participants are sampled) can only inform understanding of populations with characteristics like the sample. For example, a study sampling predominantly White, middle- and upper-class, male college students (primarily between 18 and 22 years of age) in the United States cannot draw conclusions about individuals who are ethnic minority, lower socioeconomic status, females of a different age range not attending college, and/or not living in the United States.

These limits of generalizability are well known, yet widespread, in much social science research (e.g., see Graham, 1992, for a survey of ethnic and socioeconomic homogeneity in psychological research). One feature of a well-designed primary study is to sample intentionally a heterogeneous group of participants in terms of salient characteristics, especially those about which it is reasonable to expect findings potentially to differ, and to evaluate these factors as potential moderators (qualifiers) of the findings. Obtaining a heterogeneous sample is difficult, however, in that the researcher must typically obtain a larger overall sample, solicit participants from multiple settings (e.g., not just college classrooms) and cultures (e.g., not just in one region or country), and ensure that the methods and measures are appropriate for all participants. The reality is that few if any single studies can sample the wide range of potentially relevant characteristics of the population about which we probably wish to draw conclusions.

These same issues of sample generalizability limit conclusions that we can draw from the results of meta-analyses. If all primary studies in your meta-analysis sample a similar homogeneous set of participants, then you should only generalize the results of meta-analytically combining these results to that homogeneous population. However, if you are able to obtain a collection of primary studies that are diverse in terms of sample characteristics, even if the studies themselves are individually homogeneous, then you can both (1) evaluate potential differences in results based on sample characteristics (through moderator analyses; see Chapter 9) and (2) make conclusions that are generalizable to this more heterogeneous population. In this way, meta-analytic reviews have the potential to draw more generalizable conclusions than are often tractable within a primary study, provided you are able to obtain studies collectively consisting of a diverse range of participants. However, you should keep in mind the limits of the samples of studies included in your meta-analysis and be cautious not to extrapolate beyond these limits. Most meta-analyses contain some limits—intentional (specified by inclusion/exclusion criteria; see Chapter 3) or unintentional (required by the absence or unavailability—e.g., written in a language that you do not know—of primary research with some populations)—that limit the generalizability of conclusions.

2.2.3 Limits of Methodological Artifacts

Researchers planning and conducting primary studies do not intentionally impose methodological artifacts, but these often arise. These artifacts, described in detail in Chapter 6, can arise from imperfect measures (imperfect reliability or validity), sampling homogeneity (resulting in direct or indirect restriction of ranges among variables of interest), or poor data-analytic choices (e.g., artificial dichotomization of continuous variables). These artifacts typically[2] attenuate, or diminish, the effect sizes estimated in primary studies. This attenuation leads to lower statistical power (higher rates of type II error) and underestimation of the magnitude—and potentially the importance—of the results.

These artifacts can be corrected in the sense that it is possible to estimate the magnitude of "true" effect sizes disattenuated for these artifacts. In primary studies, this is rarely done, with the exception of those using latent variable analyses to correct for unreliability (see, e.g., Kline, 2005). This correction for attenuation of effect sizes is more common in meta-analyses, though the practice is somewhat controversial and varies across disciplines (see Chapter 6). Whether or not you correct for certain artifacts in your own meta-analyses should guide the extent to which you view these artifacts as potential limits (by attenuating your effect sizes and potentially introducing less meaningful heterogeneity).

2.2.4 Limits of Statistical Power

Statistical power refers to the probability of concluding that an effect exists when it truly does. The converse of statistical power is type II error, or failing to conclude that an effect exists when it does. Although this concept of statistical power is rooted in the Null Hypothesis Significance Testing framework (which is problematic, as I describe in Chapter 5), statistical power is also relevant in other frameworks such as reliance on point estimates and confidence intervals in describing results (i.e., low statistical power leads to large confidence intervals).

The statistical power of a primary study depends on several factors, including the type I error rate (i.e., α) set by the researcher, the type of analysis performed, and the magnitude of the effect size within the population. However, because these other factors are typically out of the researcher's control,[3] statistical power is dictated primarily by sample size, where larger sample sizes yield greater statistical power. When planning primary studies, researchers should conduct power analyses to guide the number of participants needed to have a certain probability (often .80) of detecting an effect size of a certain magnitude (for details see, e.g., Cohen, 1969; Kraemer & Thiemann, 1987; Murphy & Myors, 2004).

Despite the potential for power analysis to guide study design, there are many instances when primary studies are underpowered. This might occur because the power analysis was based on an unrealistically high expectation of population effect size, because it was not possible to obtain enough participants due to limited resources or scarcity of appropriate participants (e.g., when studying individuals with rare conditions), or because the researcher failed to perform a power analysis in the first place. In short, although inadequate statistical power is not a problem inherent to primary research, it is plausible that in many fields a large number of existing studies do not have adequate statistical power to detect what might be considered a meaningful magnitude of effect (see, e.g., Halpern, Karlawish, & Berlin, 2002; Maxwell, 2004).

When a field contains many studies that fail to demonstrate an effect because they have inadequate statistical power, there is the danger that readers of this literature will conclude that an effect does not exist (or that it is weak or inconsistent). In these situations, a meta-analysis can be useful in combining the results of numerous underpowered studies within a single analysis that has greater statistical power.[4] Although meta-analyses can themselves have inadequate statistical power, they will generally[5] have greater statistical power than the primary studies comprising them (Cohn & Becker, 2003). For this reason, meta-analyses are generally less impacted by inadequate statistical power than are primary studies (but see Hedges & Pigott, 2001, 2004 for discussion of underpowered meta-analyses).

2.3 CRITIQUES OF META-ANALYSIS: WHEN ARE THEY VALID AND WHEN ARE THEY NOT?

As I outlined in Chapter 1, attention to meta-analysis emerged in large part with the attention received by Smith and Glass's (1977) meta-analysis of psychotherapy research (though others developed techniques of meta-analysis at about the same time; e.g., Rosenthal & Rubin, 1978; Schmidt & Hunter, 1977). The controversial nature of this meta-analysis drew criticisms, both of the particular paper and of the process of meta-analysis itself. Although these criticisms were likely motivated more by dissatisfaction with the results than the approach, there has been some persistence of these criticisms toward meta-analysis since its early years. The result of this extensive criticism, and efforts to address these critiques, is that meta-analysis as a scientific process of reviewing empirical literature has a deeper appreciation of its own limits; so this criticism was in the end fruitful.

In the remainder of this section, I review some of the most common criticisms of meta-analysis (see also, e.g., Rosenthal & DiMatteo, 2001; Sharpe, 1997). I also attempt to provide an objective consideration of the extent, and under what conditions, these criticisms are valid. At the end of this section, I place these criticisms in perspective by noting that many apply to *any* literature review.

2.3.1 Amount of Expertise Needed to Conduct and Understand

Although not necessarily a critique, I think it is important first to address a common misperception I encounter: that meta-analysis requires extensive statistical expertise to conduct. Although very advanced, complex methods exist for various aspects of meta-analysis, most meta-analyses do not require especially complicated analyses. The techniques might seem rather obscure or complex when one is first reading meta-analyses; I believe that this is primarily because most of us received considerable training in primary analysis during our careers, but have little if any exposure to meta-analysis. However, performing a basic yet sound meta-analysis requires little more expertise than that typically acquired in a research-oriented graduate social science program, such as the ability to compute means, variances, and perhaps perform an analysis of variance (ANOVA) or regression analysis, albeit with some small twists in terms of weighting and interpretation.[6]

Although I do not view the statistical expertise needed to conduct a sound meta-analysis as especially high, I do feel obligated to make clear that meta-analyses are not easy. The time required to search adequately for and code studies is substantial (see Chapters 3–7). The analyses, though not requiring an especially high level of statistical complexity, must be performed with care and by someone with the basic skills of meta-analysis (such as provided in Chapters 8–11). Finally, the reporting of a meta-analysis can be especially difficult given that you are often trying to make broad, authoritative statements about a field (see Chapters 13–14). My intention is not to scare anyone away from performing a meta-analysis, but I think it is important to recognize some of the difficulty in this process. However, needing a large amount of statistical expertise is not one of these difficulties for most meta-analyses you will want to perform.

2.3.2 Quantitative Analysis May Lack "Qualitative Finesse" of Evaluating Literature

Some complain that meta-analyses lack the "qualitative finesse" of a narrative review, presumably meaning that it fails to make creative, nuanced conclusions about the literature. I understand this critique, and I agree that some meta-analysts can get too caught up in the analyses themselves at the expense of carefully considering the studies. However, this tendency is certainly not inherent to meta-analysis, and there is certainly nothing to preclude the meta-analyst from engaging in this careful consideration.

To place this critique in perspective, I think it is useful to consider the general approaches of qualitative and quantitative analysis in primary research. Qualitative research undoubtedly provides rich, nuanced information that has contributed substantially to understanding in nearly all areas of social sciences. At the same time, scientific progress would be limited if we did not also rely on quantitative methods and on methods of analyzing these quantitative data. Few scientists would collect quantifiable data from dozens or hundreds of individuals, but would instead use a method of analysis consisting of looking at the data and "somehow" drawing conclusions about central tendency, variability, and co-occurrences of individual differences. In sum, there is substantial advantage to conducting primary research using both qualitative and quantitative analyses, or a combination of both.

Extending this value of qualitative and quantitative analyses in primary research to the process of research synthesis, I do not see careful, nuanced consideration of the literature and meta-analytic techniques to be mutually exclusive processes. Instead, I recommend that you rely on the advantages of meta-analysis in synthesizing vast amounts of information and aiding in drawing probabilistic inferential conclusions, but also using your knowledge of your field where these quantitative analyses fall short. Furthermore, meta-analytic techniques provide results that are statistically justifiable (e.g., there is an effect size of a certain range of magnitude; some type of studies provide larger effect sizes than another type), but it is up to you to connect these findings to relevant theories in your field. In short, a good meta-analytic review requires *both* quantitative methodology and "qualitative finesse."

2.3.3 The "Apples and Oranges" Problem

The critique known as the "apples and oranges problem" was first used as a critique against Smith and Glass's (1977) meta-analytic combination of studies using diverse methods of psychotherapy in treating a wide range of problems among diverse samples of people (see Sharpe, 1997). Critics charge that including such a diverse range of studies in a meta-analysis yields meaningless results.

I believe that this critique is applicable only to the extent that the meta-analyst wants to draw conclusions about apples *or* oranges; if you want to draw conclusions only about a narrowly defined population of studies (e.g., apples), then it is problematic to include studies from a different population (e.g., oranges). However, if you wish to make conclusions about a broad population of studies, such as all psychotherapy studies of all psychological disorders, then it is appropriate to combine a diverse range of studies. To extend the analogy: combining apples and oranges is appropriate if you want to draw conclusions about fruit; in fact, if you want to draw conclusions about fruit you should also include limes, bananas, figs, and berries! Studies are rarely identical replications of one another, so including studies that are diverse in methodology, measures, and sample within your meta-analysis has the advantage of improving the generalizability of your conclusions (Rosenthal & DiMatteo, 2001). So, the apples and oranges critique is not so much a critique about meta-analysis; rather, it just targets whether or not the meta-analyst has considered and sampled studies from an appropriate level of analysis.

In considering this critique, it is useful to consider the opportunities for considering multiple levels of analysis through moderator analysis in meta-analysis (see Chapter 9). Evoking the fruit analogy one last time: A meta-analysis can include studies of all fruit and report results about fruit; but then systematically compare apples, oranges, and other fruit through moderator analyses (i.e., do results involving apples and oranges differ?). Further moderator analyses can go further by comparing studies involving, for example, McIntosh, Delicious, Fuji, and Granny Smith apples. The possibility of including diverse studies in your meta-analysis and then systematically comparing these studies through moderator analyses means that the apples and oranges problem is easily addressable.

2.3.4 The "File Drawer" Problem

The "file drawer" problem is based on the possibility that the studies included in a meta-analysis are not representative of those that have been conducted because studies that fail to find significant or expected results are hidden away in researchers' file drawers. Because I devote an entire chapter to this problem, also called publication bias, later in this book (Chapter 11), I do not treat this threat in detail here. Instead, I briefly note that this is indeed a threat to meta-analysis, as it is to any literature review. Fortunately, meta-analyses typically use systematic and thorough methods of obtaining studies (Chapter 3) that minimize this threat, and meta-analytic techniques for detecting and potentially correcting for this bias exist (Chapter 11).

2.3.5 Garbage In, Garbage Out

The critique of "garbage in, garbage out" is that the meta-analysis of poor quality primary studies only results in conclusions of poor quality. In many respects this critique is a valid threat, though there are some exceptions. First, we can consider what "poor quality" (i.e., garbage) really means. If studies are described as being of poor quality because they are underpowered (i.e., have low statistical power to detect the hypothesized effect), then meta-analysis can overcome this limitation by aggregating findings from multiple underpowered studies to produce a single analysis that is more powerful. If studies are considered to be of poor quality because they contain artifacts such as using measures that are less reliable or less valid than is desired, or if the primary study authors used certain inappropriate analytic techniques (e.g., artificially dichotomizing continuous variables), then methods of correcting effect sizes might help overcome these problems (see Chapter 6). For these types of "garbage" then, meta-analyses might be able to produce high-quality findings.

There are other types of problems of study quality that meta-analyses cannot overcome. For instance, if all primary studies evaluating a particular treatment fail to assign participants randomly to conditions, do not use double-blind procedures, or the like, then these threats to internal validity in the primary studies will remain when you combine the results across studies in a meta-analysis. Similarly, if the primary studies included in a meta-analysis are all concurrent naturalistic designs, then there is no way that meta-analytic combination of these results can inform causality. In short, the design limitations that consistently occur in the primary studies will also be limitations when you meta-analytically combine these studies.

Given this threat, some have recommended that meta-analysts exclude studies that are of poor study quality, however that might be defined (see Chapter 4). Although this exclusion does ensure that the conclusions you reach have the same advantages afforded by good study designs as are available in the primary studies, I think that uncritically following this advice is misguided for three reasons. First, for some research questions, there may be so few primary studies that meet strict criteria for "quality" that it is not very informative to combine or compare them; however, there may be many more studies that contain some methodological flaws. In these same situations, it seems that the progression of knowledge is unnecessarily delayed by stubborn unwillingness to consider all available evidence. I believe that most fields benefit more from an imperfect meta-analysis than no meta-analysis at all, provided that you appropriately describe the limits of the conclusions of your review. A second reason I think that dogmatically excluding poor quality studies is a poor choice is that this practice assumes that certain imperfections of primary studies result in biased effects, yet does not test this assumption. This leads to the third reason: Meta-analyses can evaluate whether systematic differences in effect sizes emerge from certain methodological features. If you code the relevant features of primary studies that are considered "quality" within your particular field (see Chapter 4), you can then evaluate whether these features systematically relate to differences in the results (effect sizes) found among studies through moderator analyses (Chapter 9). Having done this, you can (1) make statements about how the differences in *specific aspects* of quality impact the effect sizes that are found, which can guide future design of primary studies; (2) where differences are found, limit conclusions to the types of studies that you believe produce the most valid results; and (3) where differences are not found, have the advantage of including all relevant studies (versus a priori excluding a potentially large number of studies).

2.3.6 Are These Problems Relevant Only to Quantitative Reviews?

Although these critiques were raised primarily against the early meta-analyses and have since been raised as challenges primarily against meta-analytic (i.e., quantitative) reviews, most apply to all types of research syntheses. Aside from the first two I have reviewed (meta-analyses requiring extensive statistical expertise and lacking in finesse), which I have clarified as being generally misconceptions, the remainder can be considered as threats to all types of research syntheses (including narrative research reviews) and often all types of literature reviews (see Figure 1.1). However, because these critiques have most often been applied toward meta-analysis, we have arguably considered these threats more carefully than have scholars performing other types of literature reviews. It is useful to consider how each of the critiques I described above threatens both quantitative and other literature reviews (considering primarily the narrative research review), and how each discipline typically manages the problem.

The "apples and oranges" problem (i.e., inclusion of diverse types of studies within a review) is potentially threatening to both narrative and meta-analytic review. However, my impression is that meta-analyses more commonly attempt to draw generalized conclusions across diverse types of primary studies, whereas narrative reviews more often draw fragmented conclusions of the form "These types of studies find this. These other types of studies find this." If practices stopped there, then the apples and oranges problem could more fairly be applied to meta-analyses than other reviews. However, meta-analysts usually perform moderator analyses to compare the diverse types of studies, and narrative reviews often try to draw synthesized conclusions about the diverse types of studies. Given that both types of reviews typically attempt to draw conclusions at multiple levels (i.e., about fruits in general and about apples and oranges in particular), the critique of focusing on the "wrong" level of generalization—if there is such a thing, versus just focusing on a different level of generalization than another scholar might choose—is equally applicable to both. However, both the process of drawing generalizations across diverse studies and the process of comparing diverse types of studies are more objective and lead to more accurate conclusions (Cooper & Rosenthal, 1980) when performed using meta-analytic versus narrative review techniques.

The "file drawer" problem—the threat of unpublished studies not being included in a review, and the resultant available studies being a biased representation of the literature—is a threat to all attempts to draw conclusions from this literature. In other words, if the available literature is biased, then this bias affects any attempt to draw conclusions from the literature, narrative or meta-analytic. However, narrative reviews almost never consider this threat, whereas meta-analytic reviews routinely consider it and often take steps to avoid it and/or evaluate it (indeed, there exists an entire book on this topic; see Rothstein, Sutton, & Borenstein, 2005b). Meta-analysts typically make greater efforts to systematically search for unpublished literature (and studies published in more obscure sources) than do those preparing narrative reviews (Chapter 3). Meta-analysts also have the ability to detect publication bias through comparison of published and available unpublished studies, funnel plots, or regression analyses, as well as the means to evaluate the plausibility of the file drawer threat through failsafe numbers (see Chapter 11). All of these capabilities are absent in the narrative review.

Finally, the problem of "garbage in, garbage out"—that the inclusion of poor quality studies in a review leads to poor quality results from the review—is a threat to both narrative and meta-analytic reviews. However, I have described ways that you can overcome some problems of the primary studies in meta-analysis (low power, presence of methodological artifacts), as well as systematically evaluate the presumed impact of study quality on results, that are not options in a narrative review.

In sum, the problems that might threaten the results of a meta-analytic review are also threats to other types (e.g., narrative) of reviews, even though they are less commonly considered in other contexts. Moreover, meta-analytic techniques have been developed that partially or fully address these problems; parallel techniques for narrative reviews either do not exist or are rarely considered. For these reasons, although you should be mindful of these potential threats when performing a meta-analytic review, these threats are not limited—and are often less of threats—in a meta-analytic relative to other types of research reviews.

2.4   PRACTICAL MATTERS: THE RECIPROCAL RELATION BETWEEN PLANNING AND CONDUCTING A META-ANALYSIS

My placement of this chapter on identifying research questions for meta-analysis before chapters on actually performing a meta-analysis is meant to correspond to the order you would follow in approaching this endeavor. As with primary research, you want to know your goals and research questions, as well as potential limitations and critiques, of your meta-analysis before you begin.

However, such an ordering is somewhat artificial in that it misses the often reciprocal relation between planning and conducting a meta-analytic review. At a minimum, someone planning a meta-analysis almost certainly has read empirical studies in the area that would likely be included in the review, and conclusions that the reader takes from these studies will undoubtedly influence the type of questions asked when planning the meta-analysis.

Beyond this obvious example, I think that much of the process of conducting a meta-analysis is less linear than is typically presented, but more of an iterative, back-and-forth process among the various steps of planning, searching the literature, coding studies, analyzing the data, and writing the results. I do not view this reality as problematic; although we should avoid the practice of "HARKing" (Hypothesizing After Results are Known; Kerr, 1998), we do learn a lot during the process of conducting the meta-analysis that can refine our initial questions. Next, I briefly describe how each of the major steps of searching the literature, coding studies, analyzing the data, and writing the results can provide reasons to revise our initial plans of the meta-analysis.

As I discuss in detail in Chapter 3, an important step in meta-analysis is specifying inclusion/exclusion criteria (i.e., what type of studies will be included in the literature) and searching for relevant literature. This process should be guided by the research questions you wish to answer, but the process might also change your research questions. For example, finding that there is little relevant literature to inform your meta-analysis research questions—either too few studies to obtain a good estimate of the overall effect size or too little variation over levels of moderators of interest—might force you to broaden your questions to include more studies. Conversely, finding that so many studies are relevant to your research question that it is not practical to include all of them might cause you to narrow your research question (e.g., to a more limited sample, type of measure, and/or type of intervention).[7]

Research questions can also be modified after you begin coding studies (see Chapters 4–7). Not only might your careful reading of the studies lead you to new or modified research questions, but also the more formal process of coding might necessitate changes in your research questions. If studies do not provide sufficient information to compute effect sizes consistently, and it is not possible to obtain this information from study authors, then it may be necessary to abandon or modify your original research questions. If your research questions involve comparing studies (i.e., moderator analyses), you may have to alter this research question if the studies do not provide adequate variability or coverage of certain characteristics. For example, if you were interested in evaluating whether an effect size differs across ethnic groups, but during the coding of studies found that most studies sampled only a particular ethnic group, then you would not have adequate variability across the studies and would have to abandon this particular research question (or else modify it in some way to make it more tractable).

Analyzing the data (see Chapters 8–12) is probably where the most modifications to original study questions will occur. Although you should thoroughly investigate your original research questions, and you should avoid entirely exploratory "fishing expeditions," you will invariably form new research questions during the data analysis phase. Some of these new questions will be formed as you learn answers to your original questions (e.g., "Having found this, I wonder if ...?"), whereas other questions will come from simply looking at the data (e.g., thinking about why a particular study, or set of studies, has discrepant effect sizes). Although both approaches are post hoc, the latter is certainly more exploratory—and therefore more likely to capitalize on chance—than the former. However, both approaches to creating new research questions are valuable, as long as you are upfront about their source when presenting and drawing conclusions from your meta-analysis (see Chapter 13).

As is true of analyzing the data, the process of writing your results may lead to refinement of research questions or even the development of new ones. Furthermore, the process of presenting your findings to colleagues—through either conference presentations or the peer review process—is likely to generate further refinement and creation of research questions.

2.5 SUMMARY

As with any research endeavor, it is important to identify the research questions you wish to answer when you are planning your meta-analysis. To facilitate generating and shaping these questions, I have described the primary methods of meta-analysis as combination and comparison across studies, with the focus being on one of a variety of effect sizes. I have also compared potential limitations of primary research and meta-analysis to offer perspective on the ways that meta-analysis can (and cannot) improve upon existing primary studies. In addition, I have discussed some of the common criticisms of meta-analysis; although most of these are either inaccurate or else applicable to both meta-analytic and narrative reviews, early recognition of these criticisms can help you avoid some of these charges. Finally, I have described how formulating research questions for meta-analysis is a reciprocal process. Although you should identify research questions during the planning stage, it is likely that these will be modified or appended throughout the process of conducting a meta-analysis.

2.6 RECOMMENDED READINGS

Hall, J. A., Tickle-Degnen, L., Rosenthal, R., & Mosteller, F. (1994). Hypotheses and problems in research synthesis. In H. Cooper & L. V. Hedges (Eds.), *The handbook of
research synthesis* (pp. 17–28). New York: Russell Sage Foundation.—This chapter
provides a brief overview of some of the critical considerations in formulating problems
for a meta-analytic review.

Pan, M. L. (2008). *Preparing literature reviews: Qualitative and quantitative approaches*
(3rd ed.). Glendale, CA: Pyrczak.—This very accessible and brief book provides
pragmatic advice for students preparing a literature review. Chapter 2 describes ways
to identify potential topics for review. The book as a whole is probably most useful for
undergraduate or early graduate students.

NOTES

1. Rosenthal (1991) identified a third general approach called aggregate analysis.
   This approach evaluates some characteristics of the studies in relation to some
   mean value. For example, Rosenthal (1991) cited an analysis by Underwood
   (1957) evaluating a methodological feature of 14 learning studies (number of
   lists participants had to learn prior to the list of interest) with the mean values
   of participants in those 14 studies (mean amount of material recalled from the
   list of interest). This type of aggregate analysis represents a special case of meta-
   analysis in which the effect size is a single variable (in this example, a mean; see
   Chapter 7, Section 7.1) rather than the more typical effect size representing an
   association between two variables (see Chapter 5). Associations of this single
   variable with study characteristics represent what I have described as moderator analyses in Chapter 9 (though the term "moderator analysis" is not accurate
   when the effect size is a single variable, these same techniques apply). Given that
   the aggregate analysis described by Rosenthal (1991) represents a special case of
   the more general meta-analytic approach I describe in this book, I do not consider it a third, unique goal of meta-analysis.

2. The single exception to this statement is that primary studies that have overly
   heterogeneous samples (e.g., sampling extreme cases) can suffer expansion of
   range of variables of interest, which leads to overestimation of effect sizes.

3. Strictly speaking, the researcher can modify each of these factors, though it is
   typically difficult to do so. Type I error rates are arbitrary, yet most fields have
   such entrenched standards (most often $\alpha = .05$) that deviations are met with skepticism. The researcher is of course free to choose from a range of data-analytic
   strategies, but generally there is little variability in this decision because all
   researchers will choose the approach that provides the highest statistical power.
   Finally, special design limitations, such as intentionally sampling homogeneous

populations to reduce extraneous variance in between-group comparisons, can impact the population effect size; but this effect size is generally considered to exist independent of the researcher's control.

4. Two important caveats to this claim merit consideration. First, it is necessary for the collection of underpowered studies to have enough methodological similarities if they are to be considered reasonable replications of one another (Halpern et al., 2002). Second, some underpowered studies will still yield statistically significant results because they, by chance alone, happen to estimate a particularly large effect size that achieved statistical significance, whereas other underpowered studies will yield more typical effect sizes that fail to achieve statistical significance. If the former are more likely to be published (or otherwise included in your meta-analysis) than the latter, then meta-analytic combination of this biased sample of underpowered effect sizes will lead to overestimates of the effect size in your meta-analysis. This possibility has led to suggestions that you exclude underpowered studies from meta-analyses (Kraemer, Gardner, Brooks, & Yesavage, 1998). Although I view the categorical exclusion of all underpowered studies as being problematic in areas of research where there are few adequately powered studies, the possibility of underpowered studies being systematically biased does indicate the importance of thorough literature reviews (especially for unpublished studies; see Chapter 3), the value of conducting analyses to detect publication bias (see Chapter 11), and the need for caution in interpreting meta-analyses of underpowered studies.

5. A meta-analysis using fixed-effects analysis (see Chapter 8) will always have greater statistical power in determining the mean effect size than will any one of the multiple studies included. Meta-analyses using random-effects models (Chapter 9) can have lower statistical power than a single primary study if substantial population heterogeneity in effect sizes exists.

6. I should make clear that basic meta-analytic techniques require only this level of prerequisite knowledge, but there are some more advanced meta-analytic techniques that require understanding of matrix algebra and multivariate statistics. Most of the material in this book is accessible for readers with basic graduate-level training, though I also include—with appropriate warning—some of this more advanced material.

7. In principle, it is acceptable to identify a large sample of studies and randomly sample a more tractable number of studies. In practice, however, nearly all meta-analyses that are published include all identified studies in the coding and analyses, which means that many readers expect you to include all available studies in your meta-analysis.

3

Searching the Literature

After articulating one or more research questions for your meta-analysis (Chapter 2), the next step is to locate the studies that will provide information to answer these questions (as described in subsequent chapters on coding and analysis). Unlike narrative reviews that are typically unsystematic in their searching of the literature (or at least typically do not articulate this process), the field of meta-analysis has devoted considerable attention to practices of searching and retrieving relevant literature.

In this chapter, I describe how it is useful to conceptualize the studies in your meta-analysis as a sample of a larger population (Section 3.1) and how this conceptualization leads to explicit criteria of which type of studies should be included versus excluded from your meta-analysis (Section 3.2). I will then describe various methods of searching for relevant literature, considering the advantages and disadvantages of each (Section 3.3). I conclude the chapter by describing the importance of "reality checking" your search (Section 3.4) and the practical matter of creating a meta-analytic database (Section 3.5). The steps involved in a literature search as described in this chapter are summarized in Figure 3.1.

3.1 DEVELOPING AND ARTICULATING A SAMPLING FRAME

Given that meta-analysis uses the individual study as its unit of analysis, it is useful to think of your meta-analysis as consisting of a sample of studies, just as primary analyses sample people or other units (e.g., families, businesses)

34

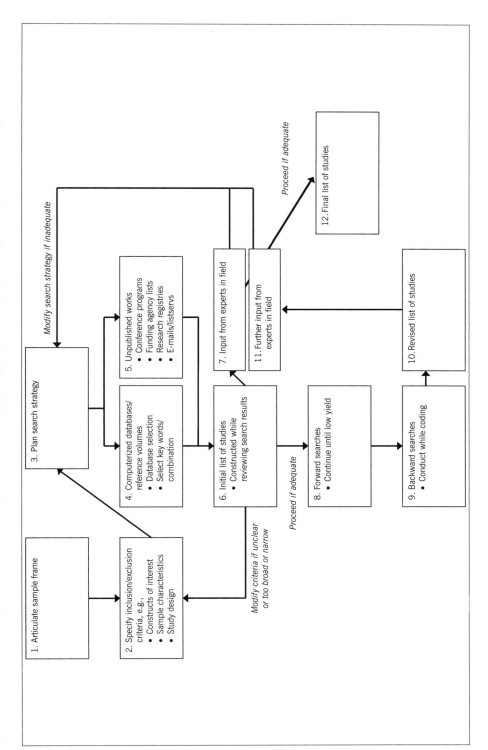

FIGURE 3.1. Basic steps of searching the literature.

comprising its sample. In primary analyses, we typically wish to make inferences to a larger population that is represented by the sampled individuals; in meta-analysis, we typically wish to make inferences to a larger population of possible studies from the sample of studies included in our review. In both cases, we want our sample to be representative of this larger population, as opposed to a biased (nonrepresentative) set.

To illustrate the importance of obtaining an unbiased sample of studies, we can consider the threat of publication bias (discussed in further detail in Chapter 11). The top of Figure 3.2 displays a hypothetical population of effect sizes, with the horizontal (x) axis representing the effect sizes obtained in studies of this population and the vertical (y) axis representing the frequency that studies yield this effect size.[1] We see that the mean effect size in this population is somewhere around 0.20 and that there is a certain amount of deviation around this mean due to either sampling fluctuation or unspecified (random) differences. The bottom part of this figure shows the distribution of a biased sample of studies drawn from this population. I have used arrows of different width to represent the likelihood of studies from the population being included in this sample. The arrows to the right are thick to represent studies with large effect sizes being very likely to be included in the sample (i.e., very likely to be found in a search), whereas the arrows to the left are thin to represent studies with small effect sizes being very unlikely to be included in the sample (i.e., likely not found in a search). We can see that this differential likelihood of inclusion by effect sizes results in a biased sample. If you were to meta-analyze studies from this sample, you would find a mean effect size somewhere around 0.30 rather than the 0.20 found in the population. Thus, analysis of this biased sample of studies leads to biased results in a meta-analysis.

The goal of searching and retrieving the literature for a meta-analytic review is to obtain a representative, unbiased collection of studies from which inferences can be made about a larger population of studies. Meta-analyses differ from primary analyses in that your goal is typically to obtain *all* of the studies comprising this population as it currently exists.[2] Whether or not you are successful in obtaining all available studies (and it is not possible to know with certainty that you have), it is still appropriate to consider this set of studies as a sample, from which you might draw inferences about a larger population including studies you did not locate or studies performed in the future (assuming that these studies are part of the same population as those included in your meta-analysis).

This approach, in which you think of the studies included in your meta-analysis as a sample from a population to which you wish to make inferences, has two important implications. First, this conceptualization properly frames the conclusions you draw from results after completing your meta-analysis; this is important in allowing you to avoid either understating or overstating the generalizability of your findings. Second, and more relevant during the planning stages of your review, this conceptualization should guide your criteria for which type of studies should or should not be included in your meta-analysis, as described next.

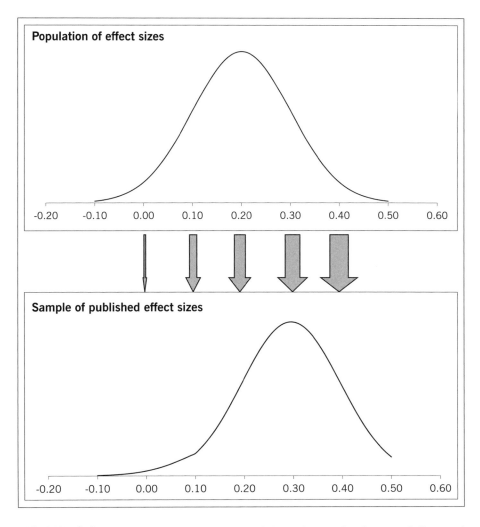

FIGURE 3.2. Hypothetical illustration of biased sample due to differential likelihood of including studies in a meta-analysis.

3.2 INCLUSION AND EXCLUSION CRITERIA

The inclusion criteria, and conversely the exclusion criteria, are a set of explicit statements about the features of studies that will or will not (respectively) be included in your meta-analysis. Ideally, you should specify these criteria before searching the literature so that you can then determine whether each study identified in your search should be included in your meta-analysis. Practically speaking, however, you are likely to find studies that are ambiguous given your initial criteria, so you will need to modify these criteria as these unanticipated types of studies arise.

3.2.1 The Importance of Clear Criteria

Developing an explicit set of inclusion and exclusion criteria is important for three reasons. First, as I noted earlier, these criteria should reliably guide which studies you will (or will not) include in your meta-analysis. This guidance is especially important if others are assisting in your search. Even if you are conducting the search alone, however, these criteria can reduce subjectivity that might be introduced if the criteria are ambiguous.

The second reason that explicit criteria are important is that these criteria define the population to which you can make conclusions. A statement of exclusion (i.e., an exclusion criterion) limits your conclusions *not* to involve this characteristic. For example, in the example meta-analysis I will present throughout this book (considering various effects involving relational aggression), my colleagues and I excluded samples with an average age of 18 years or older. It would therefore be inappropriate to attempt to draw any conclusions regarding adults from this meta-analysis. A statement of inclusion (i.e., an inclusion criterion) implies that the population is defined—at least in part—by this criterion. For example, a criterion specifying that included studies must use experimental manipulation with double-blind procedures would mean that the population is of studies with this design (and any other inclusion criteria stated).

The third reason that explicit criteria are important relates to the goal of transparency, which is an important general characteristic to consider when reporting your meta-analysis (see Chapter 13). Here, I mean that your inclusion/exclusion criteria should be so explicit that a reader could, after performing the same searches as you perform, come to the same conclusions regarding which studies should be included in your meta-analysis. To illustrate, imagine that you perform a series of searches that identify 100 studies, and based on your inclusion/exclusion criteria you decide that 60 should be included in your meta-analysis. If another person were to evaluate those same 100 studies using your inclusion/exclusion criteria, he or she should—if your criteria are explicit enough—identify the same 60 studies as appropriate for the review. To achieve this level of transparency in your meta-analysis, it is important to record and report the full set of inclusion/exclusion criteria you used.

3.2.2 Potential Inclusion/Exclusion Criteria

The exact inclusion/exclusion criteria you choose for your meta-analysis should be based on the goals of your review (i.e., What type of studies do you want to make conclusions about?) and your knowledge of the field. Nevertheless, there are several common elements that you should consider when developing your inclusion/exclusion criteria (from Lipsey & Wilson, 2001, pp. 18–23):

3.2.2.a Definitions of Constructs of Interest

The most important data in meta-analyses are effect sizes, which typically are some index of an association between X and Y.[3] In any meta-analysis of these effect sizes, it is important to specify criteria involving operational definitions of both constructs X and Y. Although it is tempting for those with expertise in the area to take an "I know it when I see it" approach, this approach is inadequate for the reader and for deciding which studies should be included. One challenge is that the literature often refers to the same (or similar enough) construct by different names (e.g., in the example meta-analysis, the construct I refer to as "relational aggression" is also called "social aggression," "indirect aggression," and "covert aggression"). A second challenge is that the literature sometimes refers to different constructs with the same name (e.g., in the example meta-analysis, several studies used a scale of "indirect aggression" that included such aspects as diffuse anger and resentment that were inconsistent with the more behavioral definition of interest). By providing a clear operational definition of the constructs of interest, you can avoid ambiguities due to these challenges.

3.2.2.b Sample Characteristics

It is also important to consider the samples used in the primary studies that you will want to include or exclude. Here, numerous possibilities may or may not be relevant to your review, and may or may not appear in the literature you consider. Some basic demographic variables to consider include gender (e.g., Will you include studies sampling only males or only females?), ethnicity (e.g., Will you include only representative samples, or those that sample one ethnic group exclusively?), and age (e.g., Will you include studies sampling infants, toddlers, children, adolescents, young adults, and/or older adults?). It is also worth considering what cultures or nationalities will be included. Even if you place no restrictions on nationality, you will need to exclude reports written in languages you do not know,[4] which likely precludes many studies of samples from many areas of the world. Beyond these examples, you might encounter countless others—for example, samples drawn from unique settings (e.g., detention facilities, psychiatric hospitals, bars), selected using atypical screening procedures (e.g., certain personality types), or based on atypical recruitment strategies (e.g., participants navigating to a website). Although it is useful if you can anticipate some of these irregular sample characteristics in advance, many will invariably arise unexpectedly and you will have to deal with these on a case-by-case basis.

3.2.2.c   Study Design

A third consideration for inclusion/exclusion criteria for almost every meta-analysis is the type of research design that included studies should have. Some obvious possibilities are to include only experimental, quasi-experimental, longitudinal naturalistic, or concurrent naturalistic designs. Even within these categories, however, there are innumerable possibilities. For example, if you are considering only experimental treatment studies, should you include only those with a certain type of control group, only those using blinded procedures, and so on? Among quasi-experimental studies, are you interested only in between-group comparisons or pre–post designs? Answers to these sorts of questions must come from your knowledge of the field in which you are performing the review, as well as your own goals for the meta-analysis.

3.2.2.d   Time Frame

The period of time from which you will draw studies is a consideration that may or may not be relevant to your meta-analysis. By "period of time," I mean the year in which the primary study was conducted, for which you might use the proxy variable year of publication (or completion, presentation, etc., for unpublished works). For many phenomena, it might be of more interest to include studies from a broad range of time and evaluate historic effects through moderator analyses (i.e., testing whether effect sizes vary regularly across time; see Chapter 9) rather than a priori excluding studies. However, in some situations it may make sense to include only those studies performed within a certain time period. These situations might include when you are only interested in a phenomenon after some historic changes (e.g., correlates of unprotected sex after the AIDS crisis) or when the phenomenon has only existed during a certain period of time (e.g., studies of cyberbullying have only been performed since the popularity of the Internet has increased).

3.2.2.e   Publication Type

The reporting format of the studies is another consideration for potential inclusion/exclusion criteria. Although including only published studies is generally considered problematic (due to the high possibility of publication bias; see Chapter 11), it is important to consider what types of reports will be included. Possibilities include dissertations, other unpublished written reports (e.g., reports to funding agencies), conference presentations, or information that the researcher provides you upon request.

3.2.2.f   Effect Size Information

Finally, a necessary inclusion criterion is that the studies provide sufficient information to compute an effect size.[5] In most situations, this will be information provided in the written report that allows you directly to compute an effect size (see Chapter 5). However, you should also consider whether you would include studies that provide only enough information to compute a lower-bound estimate (e.g., probability ranges such as $p < .05$, statements that results were nonsignificant; see Chapter 5). When studies do not report sufficient information to compute effect sizes, you should contact the study authors to request more information; here, a necessary inclusion criterion is that the authors supply this information.

3.2.3   Relative Advantages of Broad versus Narrow Inclusion Criteria

In developing inclusion/exclusion criteria, specifying both broad and narrow sets of criteria has notable advantages. By broad criteria, I refer to a set of criteria that include most possible studies and exclude few, whereas narrow criteria will exclude many studies and include few. Of course, these two choices represent end points along a continuum. Selecting a set of criteria that falls along this continuum has several implications for your meta-analysis.

Perhaps the most important consideration in weighing a broad versus narrow set of criteria is that of the population of studies about which you want to draw conclusions. Put simply: Would you prefer to make conclusions about a very specific, well-defined population, or would you rather make more generalizable conclusions about a potentially messy population (i.e., one with likely fuzzy boundaries, likely inconsistent representation in your sample of studies, and possibly undistinguished subpopulations)? Specific to the issue of study quality (see Chapter 4) is the question of whether you want to include only the most methodologically rigorous studies or are willing to include methodologically flawed studies (risking the "garbage in, garbage out" criticism described in Chapter 2). There is not a universal "right answer" to these questions, just as there is not a right answer to the issue of level of generalization to the "apples and oranges" problem described in Chapter 2. If you choose a narrow set of criteria, you should be cautious to draw conclusions only about this narrowly defined population. In contrast, if you choose a broad set of criteria, it is probably advisable to code for study characteristics that contribute to this breadth and to evaluate these as potential moderators of effect sizes (see Chapter 9).

A second consideration is the number of studies that will ultimately be included in your meta-analysis by specifying a broad versus narrow set of criteria. Broad criteria will result in a meta-analysis of more studies that are more diverse in their features, whereas narrow criteria will result in fewer studies that are more similar in their features. Having fewer studies will sometimes result in inadequate power to evaluate the average effect size (see Chapters 8 and 10), will usually preclude thorough consideration of study characteristics that account for differences in effect sizes (i.e., moderator analyses; see Chapter 9), and might even lead your audience to view your review as too small to be important to the field. In contrast, having more studies increases the amount of work involved in the meta-analysis (especially the coding of studies), perhaps to the point where a meta-analysis of the full collection of studies is impossible.[6] Therefore, one consideration is to specify inclusion/exclusion criteria that yield a reasonable number of studies given your research questions, your available time and resources, and typical practices in your field. This is not the only, or even primary, consideration, but it is a realistic factor to consider.

3.3 FINDING RELEVANT LITERATURE

After specifying inclusion/exclusion criteria, the next step is to begin searching for empirical studies that fit within this sampling frame. In searching for this relevant literature, you have many options, each with advantages and limitations over the others. Although it is not always necessary to use all of the options I list next, it is useful to consider at least most of them and how reliance on some but not others might bias the sample of studies you obtain for your meta-analysis.

Before describing these search options, it is useful to consider the concepts of recall and precision (see White, 2009). Recall is the percentage of studies retrieved from those that should be retrieved (i.e., the number of studies meeting your inclusion criteria that actually exist); it is a theoretical value that can never be known because you never know how many studies actually exist. Precision is the percentage of retrieved studies that are relevant (i.e., actually meet your inclusion criteria). Ideally, we would like both to be 100%, such that our search strategies yield every available study that meets our criteria and none that do not. In reality, we can never meet this goal, so you must balance the relative costs of one or the other being less than 100%. The cost of imperfect recall is that you will miss studies that should have been included, resulting in reduced statistical power and potentially biased results if the missed studies differ from those you included. The cost of imperfect precision is that we will waste our resources retrieving and reading studies that will not be included in our meta-analysis. Although this might not seem like a tremendous cost, it is if it means that you cannot complete your meta-analysis.[7] The goal of your search strategy should be to achieve high recall without diminishing precision beyond an unacceptable level, where "unacceptable" depends on your available resources and the expected benefits of increasing recall in terms of statistical power and reducing bias.

3.3.1   Electronic Databases

Modern electronic databases, available via the Internet through most university libraries (or available for subscription for others), have made the task of searching for relevant studies much easier than in the early days of meta-analysis. Electronic databases exist in many fields, such as economics (EconLit), education (ERIC), medicine (Medline), psychology (PsycINFO), and sociology (Sociological Abstracts), to name just a few. These databases often have wide coverage (though see cautions below) and therefore serve as one of the primary search tools in modern meta-analysis. In fact, these databases are typically the first searches performed by meta-analysts, and I would consider them necessary (though not sufficient) for your meta-analysis.

Despite their power and apparent simplicity, using electronic databases is a more complex process than might be initially apparent (see Reed & Baxter, 2009). I next describe three considerations in using these databases, attempting to consider these generically rather than focusing on any one database.

3.3.1.a   What Is Included and What Is Excluded?

The first question you should ask before using any electronic database is "What is included (and what is excluded) from this database?." Answering this question requires you to read the documentation of the databases you are considering; consulting with librarians in your topical area is invaluable, as they have considerable expertise on this question.

Some databases include dissertations and other unpublished works, whereas others do not. If the database you plan to use does not include dissertations, you should certainly supplement your search of this database with one that includes dissertations (such as Proquest dissertation and thesis database). If the database does not include other unpublished work, and your inclusion criteria allow for this work, then you will need to ensure that other search strategies will find these works. If the database does include unpublished works, you should investigate how these works are selected for inclusion; databases that include works unsystematically (e.g., primary study authors being willing to submit works to the database) should be treated cautiously as the sample of unpublished work may be biased.[8]

Another consideration is the breadth of published work included in the database. Prominent journals are more likely to be included than peripheral journals, and books by larger publishers are more likely to be included than those by lesser-known publishers. If it is plausible that the results (effect sizes) could differ in studies published in outlets included (e.g., prominent journals) versus excluded (e.g., periphery journals) in the database(s) you are using, then reliance on this database may yield a biased sample of studies.

3.3.1.b   Key Words

After researching the databases you will use to understand their coverage, you then search the databases for relevant studies. To perform this search, you generally enter key words, for which the search engine will return records containing these key words. Selection of appropriate key words goes far in increasing recall and precision, so you should consider these key words carefully and report them in your meta-analytic review.

A first consideration is the key words you select. You can select key words based on your knowledge of the literature in your area, by examining the key words specified in studies that you know contain data about the phenomenon of interest, and through thesauri available in some electronic databases. Your goal is to create a list of words or phrases that (1) are as specific to the phenomenon you are investigating as possible and (2) cover the range of terms used to describe the phenomenon. Considering the example meta-analysis involving associations of relational aggression with various other constructs (e.g., gender, peer rejection), our goal was to search for all studies of relational aggression. Terms such as "aggression" were too broad, as these would identify studies investigating constructs aside from that in which we were interested. Using the term "relational aggression" was more specific, but by itself would have been inadequate because different researchers use different terms for this construct. We ultimately developed a list of four terms to use in our search ("relational aggression," "social aggression," "indirect aggression," and "covert aggression") that represent the terms typically used by primary study authors investigating this construct.

Wildcard marks (e.g., "*" in PsycINFO) are useful in combination with key words. Wildcard marks are used in conjunction with a stem, specifying that the search engine returns all studies containing the specified stem followed by any characters where the wildcard mark is typed. For example, submitting the phrase "relational agg*" would return studies containing the phrases "relational aggression," "relational aggressor," and so on. Using wildcard marks can also return unexpected and unwanted findings, however, (e.g., the example stem and wildcard would also return any studies that used the phrase "relational aggravation"). These can generally be recognized quickly and skipped, or you can modify the wildcard search term or use the Boolean statement "not" as described next.

Boolean statements are a tremendous asset when you are searching electronic databases. These statements include "or," "and," and "not" in most databases. The use of "or" is especially valuable in combining alternative key words for the same construct; for example, we connected the four terms for the construct of interest using "or" in our example meta-analysis (i.e., the search phrase was: "relational aggression" or "social aggression" or "indirect aggression" or "covert aggression"). The logical statement "and" is useful for either limiting the studies returned or specifying two construct associations that are of interest in many meta-analyses. For example, in the example meta-analysis, we could have combined the above search (various key words for relational aggression combined using "or") with a phrase limiting the samples to childhood or adolescence ("child* or adolesc*") using the "and" statement.[9] Similarly, if we were only interested in studies reporting associations between relational aggression and peer rejection (one of the examples I use commonly throughout the book), we could have used "and" to link the phrases for relational aggression with a set of phrases for peer rejection. Finally, you can use the key word "not" either to exclude unwanted wildcard phrases (e.g., in the example above, I could specify "not 'relational aggravation'" to remove the unwanted studies using this term), or to specify exclusion criteria (e.g., specifying "not 'adult'").

3.3.1.c   Cautions

Electronic databases are incredibly powerful and time-efficient tools for searching for relevant studies, and I believe that every modern meta-analysis should use these databases. However, at least three cautions merit consideration.

First, as I described earlier, you should carefully consider what is *not* included in the electronic databases you use. If a database does not include (or if it has poor rates of inclusion) unpublished works or studies published in peripheral outlets, then reliance on this database alone would result in diminished recall. This diminished recall can threaten your meta-analysis by decreasing statistical power and, if the studies not included in the database systematically differ from those included (e.g., publication bias, Chapter 11), by producing biased results. To avoid these problems, you should identify alternative electronic databases and other search strategies that are likely to identify relevant studies not included in the electronic database you are using.

A related caution comes from the fact that most electronic databases are discipline specific. Although the databases vary in the extent to which they include works in related disciplines, this disciplinary specificity suggests that you should not rely on only a single database within your discipline. Many, if not most, phenomena that social scientists study are considered within multiple disciplines. For example, research on relational aggression might appear not only in psychology (e.g., in the PsycINFO database), but also in criminal justice, education, gender studies, medicine, public health, and sociology (to name just a few possibilities). I recommend that you consider searching at least one or two databases outside of your primary discipline to explore how much literature might be obtained from other disciplines.

A third caution in using electronic databases relates to their very nature: You perform a search and a list of studies is provided, but you have no idea how many potentially relevant studies were *not* provided. In other words, relying only on electronic databases provides no information about what studies were not identified in your search, so the possibility remains that some studies—and possibly even some very well-known studies—did not match your specified search criteria. You can address this problem in several ways. One possibility is to perform some additional searches within your selected database(s) that use broader terms (e.g., "aggression" rather than more specific terms such as "relational aggression") and visually scan results to see if any additional relevant studies could be identified with broader search criteria. Second, you can rely on additional search procedures besides the electronic database. I return to this topic of assessing the adequacy of your search (including the adequacy of electronic database searches) in Section 3.4.

3.3.1.d   Conclusions about the Use of Electronic Databases

Electronic databases of journal articles, books and chapters, and often some unpublished works exist in most social science disciplines. These searchable databases can provide an efficient method of searching for studies to include in your meta-analysis if you carefully consider the coverage of the databases you use and select appropriate key words along with wildcard marks and Boolean statements. These electronic databases should not be your only method of searching the literature, however, as several cautions need to be considered when using them. Nevertheless, the electronic databases are likely to be one of the primary ways you will search for studies, and every modern meta-analysis should use these tools.

3.3.2   Bibliographical Reference Volumes

Bibliographical reference volumes are printed works that provide information similar to electronic databases (e.g., titles, authors, abstracts), often listing studies by broad topics and/or including an index of key words. These volumes were frequently published by large research societies and were intended to aid literature searches in specific fields in much the same way that electronic databases now do in most fields. For example, the American Psychological Association published *Psychological Abstracts* from 1927 to 2006. In many fields, publication of these printed reference volumes has been discontinued in favor of online electronic versions (though exceptions may exist).

Searching these reference volumes is not nearly as convenient as searching electronic databases, and few meta-analysts currently rely on these volumes as their primary search instrument (though you are likely to see them used when you read older meta-analytic reviews). Nevertheless, there still may be instances when you would consider using these printed volumes. Specifically, if studies potentially relevant for your meta-analysis include older studies, and the electronic databases that you use have not yet incorporated all of these older studies, then it may be useful to consult these reference volumes to ensure that you do not systematically exclude these older studies.

3.3.3   Listings of Unpublished Works

As I mentioned briefly in Chapter 2, and describe in detail in Chapter 11, one of the most challenging threats to many meta-analyses is that of publication bias (a.k.a. the "file drawer problem"). The extent to which you can avoid and evaluate this threat depends on your searching for and including unpublished studies in your meta-analysis. I have already mentioned the value of searching electronic databases that include dissertations as one method of obtaining unpublished studies. Next I list three additional listings that might allow you to find more unpublished studies. For each, I suggest searching with the same careful rigor I suggested for searching electronic databases.

3.3.3.a   Conference Programs

A potentially valuable way to find unpublished studies is to search the programs of academic conferences in which relevant work is likely to be presented. Dedicated meta-analysts often have shelves of these programs, though even this idea is becoming antiquated as more conference programs are archived and searchable online. In this approach, you search the titles of presentations listed in conference books (larger conferences typically have at least crude indices) and request copies of these works from authors (whose contact information is usually listed in these books).

From my experience, it is usually possible to identify a large number of unpublished works by searching conference programs; however, retrieving copies of these presentations for coding can be more difficult. Typically, you are better able to contact authors and more likely to receive requested presentations if you make your request shortly after the conference rather than several years later. Therefore, studies obtained through conference programs probably underrepresent older studies. Some other tips I have learned through experience include: (1) whenever you request a conference presentation, provide exact details such as the title of the presentation and the year and conference where it was presented; (2) contact coauthors if you do not receive a response from the first author, as some authors of the presentation may have graduated or left academia; (3) tell the author why you are requesting this information (I will elaborate on this piece of general advice below).

Although I think conference presentations are a valuable source of unpublished studies, there are some limitations and cautions to consider. First, your search for conference presentations should be systematic. If you decide to search the programs of a particular conference, you should make reasonable efforts to search the programs' books across a reasonable number of years (vs. the years you attended but not the years in between when you did not attend), and you should certainly search for works within the entire conference book (vs. just the presentations you happened to attend). Second, you should recognize that the response rate to your requests might be low (you should track this response rate as it might be useful to report), and you should consider the possibility that responses might be systematically related to effect sizes.[10] Finally, you should anticipate that conference presentations will often present information needed for study coding (Chapter 4) and effect size calculation (Chapters 5–7) in less detail than other formats (e.g., journal articles). It is still better to code what you can from these studies than not to consider them at all, and it is possible to request further information from study authors.

3.3.3.b Funding Agency Lists

Another valuable way to obtain unpublished studies is to search funding award listings from relevant funding agencies (e.g., National Institutes of Health, National Science Foundation, private foundations). Because funding decisions are made before results are known, studies obtained through this approach will not likely be subject to biases in findings of significance/non-significance. Furthermore, searching these listings is likely to yield studies that have been started but have not yet gone through the publication process (i.e., more recent studies).

3.3.3.c Research Registries

Some fields of clinical science have established listings in which researchers are expected to register a study before conducting it. To encourage registration, some journals will only publish results from studies registered prior to conducting the study. Such registries, by creating a listing of studies in advance of knowing the results, should yield a collection of results unbiased by the findings (e.g., nonsignificant or counterintuitive findings). If the field in which you are performing your meta-analysis has such registries, these will be a very valuable search avenue for obtaining an unbiased set of studies.

3.3.4 Backward Searches

After accumulating a set of studies for potential inclusion in your meta-analysis, you will begin the process of coding these studies (see Chapters

4–8). You should read these articles completely (vs. going straight for the method and results sections where most information you will code appears), searching for cited studies that might be relevant for your review that you did not identify through your other strategies. Similarly, you should carefully read prior reviews (narrative or meta-analytic) searching for potentially relevant studies.

This process of searching for relevant studies cited in the works you have found is referred to as "backward searching" (sometimes also called "footnote chasing"); that is, you are working from the studies you have "backward" in time to identify previously conducted studies cited in these works. This approach is especially useful in identifying older studies, whereas it is unlikely to identify newer studies that have not yet been cited. An important potential bias of this approach comes from the possibility that studies yielding certain "favorable" results (e.g., significant findings, effects favoring expectations) are probably more likely to be cited than studies with "unfavorable" results (e.g., null findings, counterintuitive findings).

Despite the potential biases of backward searches, I believe that they represent a valuable method of searching. My own experience is that many studies come from this approach even with what I consider quite thorough initial searches using other means. This approach is also valuable in identifying literature that might have been missed in other search approaches due to failures to use appropriate key words or to search literatures in other disciplines.

3.3.5 Forward Searches

Whereas backward searches attempt to find studies cited in the studies you have, forward searches attempt to find studies that cite the studies you have. Forward searches are often performed using special databases for this purpose (e.g., Social Science Citation Index), though some field-specific databases are incorporating this approach (e.g., the psychology database PsycINFO now has this capacity). To perform a forward search, you enter information for a study you know is relevant to the topic of your meta-analysis, and the search engine finds works that cite this study. Because these citing studies necessarily occur after the cited study, the search is moving "forward" in time and is more likely to find newer articles than a backward search.

There are various degrees of intensity in engaging in forward searches. A less intense approach is to identify several of the earliest and most seminal works on the topic, then perform forward searches to identify studies citing these seminal papers. At the other end of the spectrum, you could perform forward searches of all works that you have determined meet the inclusion criteria for your review.

Forward searches are likely to yield high recall, as it is unlikely that many relevant studies would fail to cite at least some of the seminal works in the area. However, my experience[11] is that forward searches are often quite low in precision. This is because many papers will cite a seminal work in an area when this area is of tangential interest to the paper.

3.3.6 Communication with Researchers in the Field

The final search approach that I will describe is to consult experts/researchers in the field in which you are performing your meta-analysis. This approach actually consists of several possibilities.

At a minimum, you should ask some experts to examine your inclusion/exclusion criteria and the list of studies you have identified, requesting that they note additional studies that should have been included. If you examine these suggested studies and some do meet your inclusion criteria, then you should not only include these studies, but also consider why your search strategy failed to identify these studies (and revise your search strategy accordingly). I recommend that you consult colleagues who have a somewhat different perspective in the field than your own (i.e., different "camps") to provide a unique perspective.

Another valuable approach to communicating with researchers is simply to e-mail those individuals who conduct research in the area of your meta-analysis, asking them if they have any additional studies on the topic. This effort can also vary in intensity, ranging from e-mailing just the most active researchers in the field to e-mailing every author of studies you have identified through other means. Although you will have to identify an approach that works best for you given your field and relationships with other researchers, some practices that I have found valuable are: (1) to clearly state why I am requesting studies (e.g., "I am conducting a meta-analytic review of the associations between X and Y"); (2) to provide a small number of the most critical inclusion criteria (e.g., "I am interested in obtaining studies involving children or adolescents"); and (3) to state the various ways that they could provide the requested information to me (e.g., "I would like the correlation between X and Y, but can compute this from most other statistics you might have available, such as t-tests, ANOVA results, or raw means and standard deviations. I am also happy to compute this correlation myself, if you are willing to share the raw data with the agreement that I will delete this data file after computing this correlation.").

A related but less targeted approach is to post requests on listservs, web-pages, or similar forums. Many of the same practices that are valuable when e-mailing are useful in such postings, though the standards of particular forums might necessitate briefer requests.

These communications with researchers are extremely valuable, though several considerations are important. First, my impression is that the response rates vary widely for different meta-analysts, with some receiving almost no responses but others receiving tremendous responses. I suspect that the factors that improve response rates include your ability to convince others that your request is important and worth their time, your ability to minimize the burden on the researchers, and the quality of relationships you have with these colleagues. A second consideration is the obvious fact that the more widespread your requests (i.e., numerous e-mails or public postings), the more people know that you are conducting this particular meta-analysis, which is a consideration in terms of the review process. Perhaps the most important consideration, however, is one that I believe means that you *absolutely must*, to at least some degree, involve colleagues in the area of your meta-analysis: Meta-analytic reviews synthesize the body of knowledge in an area of study and typically provide the foundation for the next wave of empirical study in this area. Thus, the research community has a vested interest in this process, and the meta-analyst has an obligation to consider their input. This statement does not mean that you need to send the initial draft of your meta-analysis to everyone in your field (you should not), nor that your review needs to support the conclusions of everyone in your field (your conclusions are hopefully empirically driven). Instead, by soliciting input from others in your field, whether by simply including the full body of their empirical results in your review or obtaining input from a smaller number of colleagues, your meta-analysis will benefit from this collective knowledge.

3.4 REALITY CHECKING: IS MY SEARCH ADEQUATE?

Regardless of what methods of searching the literature you rely upon, the most important question is whether your search is adequate. You can think of the adequacy of your search in three ways. First, is the sample of studies you have obtained representative of the population of studies, or is it instead biased (as illustrated in Figure 3.2)? Second, does the sample of studies you have obtained provide sufficient statistical power to evaluate the hypotheses you are interested in (or, similarly, does it provide sufficiently narrow confidence intervals of effect size estimates to be useful)? Third, would the typical scholar in my field find the sample of studies complete, or have I missed studies that obviously should be included? The first two questions directly affect the quality of the empirical conclusions of your meta-analysis and so are obviously important. The third question is less important to the conclusions drawn, but is pragmatically relevant to others' viewing of your review as adequate. This is a worthy consideration affecting both the likelihood of publication of your review and the impact it will have on your field.

The question of whether the sample you have obtained is an unbiased representation of the population is impossible to answer with certainty. However, there do exist methods of evaluating for the most likely bias—that of publication bias—which I describe in Chapter 11.

Probably the best way to answer all of these questions satisfactorily is to make every reasonable effort to ensure that your search is exhaustive—that is, to ensure that the sample of studies for your meta-analysis contains as close to all the studies that exist in the current population as possible. This goal is probably never entirely attainable, yet if you have made every effort to obtain all available studies, it is reasonable to conclude that you have come "close enough."[12] No one knows when "close enough" is adequate, and there is less empirical evidence to inform this decision than is desired, but I offer the following suggestions for your own consideration of this topic.

First, you should conduct an initial search using some combination of the methods described above that you expect will provide a reasonably thorough sample of studies. For example, you might decide to consult prior (narrative or meta-analytic) reviews in this area, search several electronic databases in which you believe relevant studies might exist (ensuring that these electronic searches include searches of unpublished studies such as dissertations), several listings of unpublished studies (i.e., conference programs, funding databases, and any research registries that exist in your field), and send out a request to authors via e-mail or listserv/website postings.

Second, you should create a list of studies obtained from these sources and ask some colleagues familiar with this research area to examine this list along with your inclusion/exclusion criteria. If they view it as complete, you have a good beginning. However, if they identify studies that are missing but should have been found, you should revise your search strategies (e.g., specifying different key words for electronic searches) and repeat the prior step.

The third suggestion is to take this list and begin forward and backward searches. You might start with forward searches, as this is less time-consuming. Here, you would start with a small number of the most seminal works in the area (in the absence of a clear idea of the seminal works, you might create a short list of the first studies and the studies published in the top journals in your field). After performing forward searches with these seminal works (spending considerable time reviewing the citing papers to ensure relevance, as these types of searches are usually low in precision), you probably will have identified some additional studies; if not, you can reasonably conclude that forward searching will not yield any additional studies. Then, you can begin performing forward searches with the remaining studies, perhaps starting with the oldest studies first, as these have existed for the longest time and have therefore had more opportunity to be cited. At some point, you will likely reach a point where forward searches of more articles no longer yield new articles, and you can stop forward searching.

At this point, you can begin coding studies (see Chapters 4–7). While doing so, you should also perform backward searches (i.e., reading the works carefully for citations to other potentially relevant studies). My experience is that I often find a considerable number of additional studies when I begin coding, but that this number quickly diminishes as I progress in coding studies. If you find that you are almost never identifying additional studies near the end of your coding, you can be reasonably confident that your search is approaching exhaustion.

Despite this confidence, I recommend two additional steps to serve as a reality check. First, sit down with a few years of journals that are likely to publish studies relevant to your meta-analysis, and simply flip through the tables of contents and potentially relevant studies.[13] If you do not find any additional articles, then this adds to your confidence that you have conducted an exhaustive search. However, if you do find additional articles, then you obviously need to revise your search procedures (if you find relevant articles, carefully consider why they were not found—e.g., did the authors use different key words or terminology than you used in your search?). The second step, if your flipping through the journals suggests the adequacy of your search, is to send the list of studies again to some experts in your field (preferably some who did not evaluate the initial list). If they identify studies you have missed, you should revise your search procedures; but if they do not, you can feel reasonably confident that your search is adequate.

My intention is not to be prescriptive in the process you should take in searching the literature. In fact, I think that the search process I described is more intensive than that used for most published meta-analyses. Nevertheless, I present these steps as a model of a process that I believe leaves little uncertainty that your search is "close enough" to exhaustive. Although there is no guarantee that you have obtained every study from the population, I believe that after taking these steps you have reached a point where more efforts are unlikely to identify additional studies and are therefore not worthwhile. I also believe that no other potential meta-analyst would be willing to engage in significantly greater efforts, so your search represents the best that is likely to be contributed to the field. Moreover, by consulting with experts in your field, you have ensured that your peers view the search as reasonable, which usually means that reviewers will have a favorable view during the review process, and readers will view it as adequate after it is disseminated. In sum, I believe that strategies similar to the one I have described can provide a high degree of confidence that your search is adequate.

3.5 PRACTICAL MATTERS:
BEGINNING A META-ANALYTIC DATABASE

Aside from perhaps persistence and patience, the most import virtue you can have for searching the literature for a meta-analysis is organization. As you have likely inferred, searching for studies is a time-intensive process, and you certainly do not want to add to this time by repeating work because of poor organization.

A good organizational scheme for the literature search will include several key components. First, you should have a clear, written statement of the inclusion/exclusion criteria that you will use in evaluating studies found through this search. Toward this end, it might be useful to record studies identified in your search that were excluded for one reason or another (recording why they were excluded). Second, you should have a clear list of methods for searching the literature, with enough details to replicate these searches. For example, you might have a list that begins:

> Step 1: Read the following review papers and chapters (listing these works).
> Step 2: Search the PsycINFO database using the following key words (listing the key words, including any wildcard marks and logical operations).
> Step 3: Search the ERIC database using the following key words (listing the same set of key words as the step 2 search, unless there is reason to use other key words or logical operations).

You then record the dates—and names, if multiple people are conducting the searches—of each search.

During the course of these searches, you will scan many titles and abstracts in an attempt to determine whether each study is relevant for your meta-analysis. I suggest that you be rather inclusive during this initial screening, retaining any studies that *might* meet your inclusion criterion. You should also retain any nonempirical works, such as reviews or theoretical papers; although these do not provide empirical results for your meta-analysis, it will be worthwhile to read them (1) to identify additional studies cited in these papers, and (2) to inform interpretation of results of your meta-analysis.

As you are identifying works that you will retain, it is critical to have some way of organizing this information. I use spreadsheets such as that shown in Table 3.1. (I have shown only four studies here, your spreadsheet will likely be much larger.) Although you should develop an approach that meets your own needs, this example spreadsheet contains several pieces of information that I recommend recording. The first column contains a number for each paper (article, chapter, dissertation, etc.) identified in the search. The number is arbitrary, but it is useful for filing purposes (as the number of papers becomes large, it is useful to file them by number rather than, e.g., author name). The next four columns contain citation information for the paper. This information is useful not only for citing the paper in your write-up, but in identifying repetitive papers during your multiple search strategies (for this purpose, having this information in a searchable spreadsheet is useful). The sixth column contains the abstract, which is useful if you want to search for specific terms within your spreadsheet. I recommend copying this information into your spreadsheet if it is electronically available, but it probably is not worth the time needed to type this in manually. The seventh column identifies where and when the paper was found; recording the date is important because (1) you might want to update the search near the completion of your meta-analysis, and (2) you should report the last search dates in your presentation of your meta-analysis. The two rightmost columns (columns eight and nine) contain information for retrieving and coding the reports. One column indicates whether you have the report, or the status of your attempt to retrieve it (e.g., the third paper notes that I had requested this dissertation through my university's interlibrary loan system). The last column will become relevant when you begin coding the studies (see Chapters 4–8). Here, I have recorded the person (BS = Brian Stucky, the second author on this paper) who coded this report and the date it was coded. Recording both pieces of information are valuable in case you later identify a problem in the coding (e.g., if one coder was making a consistent error) or if you revise the coding protocol (you then need to modify the coding of all studies coded before this change). In this column, I also record when studies are excluded for a particular reason; for instance, the fourth study was excluded because it used an adult sample (which was one of the specified exclusion criteria in this review).

TABLE 3.1. Example Spreadsheet for Organizing a Literature Search

Paper No.	Authors	Year	Title	Source	Abstract	Found in	Have	Entered
1	Crick and Grotpeter	1995	Relational aggression …	*Child Development, 66*(3), 710–722	Assessed a form …	PsycINFO (Nov. 2005)	Yes	BS, 12/1/05
2	Hawley, Little, and Card	2007	The allure of a mean friend …	*International Journal of Behavioral Development, 31*(2), 170–180	Recent theory …	PsycINFO (May 2007)	Yes	NC, 9/12/07
3	Blachman	2003	Predictors of peer …	Dissertation, University of California, Berkeley	Examined the role …	Proquest dissertation	Requested ILL	
4	Bailey and Ostrov	In press	Differentiating forms …	*Journal of Youth and Adolescence*	The purpose …	E-mail request	Yes	Adults

Note. The table lists Bailey and Ostrov as "in press" even though it was published in 2008. I left the date in the table as "in press," however, because the table is meant to show progress as it occurred during the time of this research (which was prior to this work being published).

Of course, you may use a different way of organizing information from your literature search. The point is that you should have *some* way of organizing information that clearly records important information and avoids any duplication of effort.

3.6   SUMMARY

One of the most important steps of a meta-analytic review is obtaining the sample of studies that will provide the data for your analyses. To define this sample, we need to specify a clear set of inclusion and exclusion criteria specifying what types of studies will and will not comprise this sample. We then search the literature for studies fitting these inclusion criteria. Several approaches to searching for literature exist, and I have described some of the more common methods. The goal of this search is to obtain an unbiased, typically exhaustive (i.e., complete) sample of studies.

3.7   RECOMMENDED READINGS

Reed, J. G., & Baxter, P. M. (2009). Using reference databases. In H. Cooper, L. V. Hedges, & J. C. Valentine (Eds.), *The handbook of research synthesis and meta-analysis* (2nd ed., pp. 73–101). New York: Russell Sage Foundation.—This chapter provides a very detailed, practical guide to using electronic databases, including forward search databases.

Hopewell, S., Clarke, M., & Mallett, S. (2005). Grey literature and systematic reviews. In H. R. Rothstein, A. J. Sutton, & M. Borenstein (Eds.), *Publication bias in meta-analysis: Prevention, assessment and adjustments* (pp. 49–72). Hoboken, NJ: Wiley.—This chapter describes several ways of identifying and retrieving studies that are more obscure than traditional journal articles, and discusses the biases potentially introduced by not including this literature.

NOTES

1. The details (e.g., effect sizes, distributions around the mean) of this example will become clearer as you read subsequent chapters. For now, you should just try to understand the gist of this example.

2. In principle, a meta-analysis does not need to include all studies that exist. Instead, you can select a random sample of all existing studies on which to perform your analyses, assuming the studies you have selected provide adequate

statistical power to evaluate your research questions. I view this type of random sampling as an extremely valuable approach to performing reviews in areas where there is so much empirical literature that a full meta-analysis is not practical. However, very few meta-analytic reviews use this random-sampling approach; nearly all attempt to be exhaustive in their inclusion of studies. Unfortunately, this typical practice of being exhaustive seems to have created a standard where meta-analytic reviews are expected to be exhaustive, and the random-sampling approach would likely draw criticism.

3. The importance of developing clear operational definitions of constructs is important regardless of effect sizes used, whether they are of single variables (e.g., means or proportions) or multivariate effect sizes (see Chapter 7).

4. If you are particularly interested in drawing cross-cultural conclusions and there exists adequate numbers of studies written in a tractable number of languages, it may be possible to hire translators. However, you should remember that coding studies is an intensive effort (see Chapters 4 and 5) that requires considerable technical expertise. Because it would be difficult to find someone with both multilingual and meta-analytic skills, and require considerable amounts of their time, this is not a viable alternative in the vast majority of cases. For this reason, restriction of populations of studies to those written in languages you know is often reasonable as long as you recognize this restriction.

5. This condition is necessary to include a study in your analyses. However, you should also consider whether the studies that report insufficient information differ in meaningful ways, with the most relevant possibility being that the results were nonsignificant. If you find that a considerable number of studies report insufficient information to compute effect sizes (and other efforts, such as contacting the authors, do not alleviate this problem), then you should report these studies in your report for transparency.

6. Here, performing the meta-analysis with a random sample of studies might be preferable to changing your inclusion/exclusion criteria, especially if doing so makes the population of studies of lesser interest. Footnote 2 of this chapter describes some of the challenges to this approach.

7. To illustrate this cost, consider my experience when publishing the example meta-analysis I use throughout this book: During this review process, one of the reviewers suggested that I "plow through" the approximately 30,000 studies that could be identified using a very general search term like "aggression." Assuming 10 minutes to review each study for possible inclusion (which is a conservative estimate), this process would have taken over two years of 40 hours/week reviewing. During this time, approximately 3,000 additional studies identified using this search term would have been added, thus requiring another 3 to 4 months of full-time reviewing. Furthermore, during the coding, analysis, and write-up of these results, a couple thousand more works would likely have been

added to the database. Although this reviewer was certainly trying to be helpful by ensuring high recall, this example illustrates that the cost of low precision can be substantial in making a meta-analysis impossible.

8. The use of nonacademic search engines (e.g., Google scholar) might be especially plagued by inconsistency in what works are included. I personally do not use these nonacademic search engines. If you do decide to use one, I recommend *not* using it as a primary search method, but rather as a check of the adequacy of your other search procedures (i.e., after searching for literature using other methods, does this nonacademic search engine uncover additional works that should have been included?).

9. We did not do so in the actual meta-analysis because the number of studies using samples outside of this age range was reasonably small.

10. To my knowledge, no one has evaluated this possibility empirically. I also suspect that factors unrelated to the effect sizes (e.g., length of time since the presentation, your persuasiveness and persistence in requesting presentations) are more influential with regard to response than the effect sizes. But this possibility of biased response should be kept in mind when response rates are low, and it might be worthwhile to evaluate this possibility (through, e.g., funnel plots or effect size–sample size correlations; see Chapter 11) among the conference presentation included in your meta-analysis.

11. I do not believe that anyone has evaluated this empirically.

12. I find it comforting to consider that, just as there has never been a flawless study (see quote by Cooper, 2003, in Chapter 2 of the present volume), there has never been—and never will be—a flawless meta-analysis. Although you might strive to obtain every study within your sample, there comes a point of diminishing returns where a tremendous amount of additional effort yields very few additional benefits. When this point is reached, your field benefits more from timely completion and dissemination of your meta-analysis than futile efforts to obtain additional studies.

13. This image might seem quaint to some readers. If you prefer, point-and-click your way through the online tables of contents of some relevant journals.

Part II

The Building Blocks

Coding Individual Studies

4

Coding Study Characteristics

Performing the simplest meta-analysis, in which the goal is simply to estimate a typical (mean) effect size and perhaps to make statistical inferences about this effect size (see Chapters 8 and 10), requires only that you code the effect sizes and sample sizes (to compute the standard errors of the effect sizes) from each study (see Chapter 5). If you wish to correct for artifacts to these effect sizes, it is also necessary to code information for these corrections such as the reliabilities and dichotomizations of variables comprising the effect sizes (see Chapter 6).

Performing this sort of simple meta-analysis may seem adequate if it answers all of your research questions. However, this approach would fail to provide information about why effect sizes might differ across studies, a question that might be a key motivator of the meta-analysis (see Chapter 2) or a valuable follow-up to observed heterogeneity (Chapter 8). Moderator analyses attempt to explain this heterogeneity among effect sizes by evaluating whether coded study characteristics systematically predict variation in effect sizes across studies (see Chapter 9). To perform these moderator analyses, it is necessary that you code relevant study characteristics that might be useful in predicting variation in effect sizes across studies.

In addition to coding study characteristics for moderator analyses, thorough coding of these characteristics is important simply for describing the research basis for your meta-analysis. In other words, what does the sample of studies from which you draw your conclusions look like? This description is useful both in describing the population to which you can make conclusions (see Chapter 3 for a discussion of conceptualizing samples and populations of studies) and in identifying gaps within the research. For example, does your meta-analysis rely primarily on studies using a particular measure or type of measure to the exclusion of others, or certain types of samples to the neglect of others? Answers to these questions inform both the extent to which you can generalize your conclusions and where it might be valuable to perform future primary research.

In short, almost every meta-analysis will benefit from careful coding of study characteristics, whether you use them for performing moderator analyses or for describing the sample of studies. In this chapter, I first describe considerations in selecting study characteristics to code (Section 4.1) and then turn to the specific topic of coding study quality (Section 4.2). I next describe the important step of evaluating coding decisions (Section 4.3). Finally, I provide practical suggestions for developing a coding protocol to guide the coding of studies (Section 4.4).

4.1   IDENTIFYING INTERESTING MODERATORS

Decisions about which study characteristics to code need to be heavily informed by your knowledge of the content area in which you are performing a meta-analytic review. Nevertheless, I describe two sets of general considerations that I believe apply to meta-analytic reviews across fields: considering the research questions you are interested in and considering coding certain specific aspects of studies.

4.1.1   Considering Research Questions of Interest

Just as planning a primary research study requires you to select variables based on your research questions, planning a meta-analysis requires that you base your decisions about which study characteristics to code on the research questions that you wish to answer. If your research questions are exclusively about average effect sizes across studies (i.e., combining studies), then you might not need to code much beyond effect sizes, sample sizes, and information for any artifact corrections you wish to make. I qualify this statement by noting that it is still valuable to be able to provide basic descriptive information about this sample of studies to inform the generalizability of your review. Nevertheless, the number of study characteristics that you will need to code to address this research question adequately is small.

In contrast, if at least some of your research questions involve comparing studies (i.e., identifying whether studies with certain features yield larger effect sizes than studies with other features), then it will be much more important to code many study characteristics. Obviously, if you put forth a research question about a specific characteristic moderating effect sizes (e.g., do studies with this characteristic yield larger effect sizes than studies without this characteristic?), then it will be necessary to code this specific characteristic. However, you should also consider what study characteristics might commonly co-occur with the characteristic you are interested in, and code these. For example, if you are interested in investigating whether studies with certain types of samples yield different effect sizes (e.g., children vs. adults), you should carefully consider the other study characteristics that are likely to differ across these types of samples (e.g., studies of adults might frequently rely on self-reports, whereas studies of children might frequently rely on parent reports, observations, etc.). If you fail to code these other study characteristics, then you cannot empirically rule out the possibility that your results involving the coded study characteristic of interest are not really due to these co-occurring characteristics. In contrast, if you do code these characteristics, then you are able to evaluate empirically such competing explanations (see Chapter 9).

As a more extreme version of research questions involving specific moderators, some meta-analysts aim to predict *all* heterogeneity in effect sizes by coded study characteristics. Although this goal tends to be quite exploratory, and you would therefore view the findings of moderation by specific characteristics cautiously, it nevertheless is a goal you might consider. If so, then you will necessarily code a large number of study characteristics; specifically, you will code any study characteristics that meet two conditions. First, the study characteristics are consistently reported in many or even most studies; this is necessary to avoid a preponderance of missing data when you evaluate the coded characteristic as a moderator. The second condition is that the study characteristic varies across at least some studies; this variability across studies is necessary for the study characteristic to covary with effect sizes. You would then enter these coded study characteristics into some large predictive model (e.g., forward stepwise regression) to explore relations between them and variation in effect sizes.

4.1.2 Considering Specific Aspects of Studies

As I mentioned, the exact study characteristics you code will depend on your research questions and be informed by your knowledge of the topic area. Nevertheless, four general types of characteristics should be considered in any meta-analysis in the social sciences: characteristics of the sample, measurement, design, and source (see also Lipsey, 2009; Lipsey & Wilson, 2001, pp. 83–86). These are summarized in Table 4.1.

TABLE 4.1. Summary of Study Characteristics to Consider Coding

Broad aspect	Narrow aspects	Examples
Sample characteristics	Sampling procedures	Sampling from unique settings, representative sample, country
	Demographic features	Gender composition, ethnic composition, socioeconomic status, age, IQ
Measurement characteristics	Sources of information	Self-report, other reporter (e.g., spouse, parent, teacher), observations
	Measurement process	Covert versus overt observations, timed versus untimed performance
	Specific measures used	Specific measure, original versus short forms, translations
Design characteristics	Type of design	Experimental, quasi-experimental, pre–post comparisons, regression discontinuity
	Specific design features	Type of control group, length of longitudinal time span
Source characteristics	Publication status	Published versus unpublished, publication quality
	Year of study	Year of publication, year of data collection
	Funding	Funded versus unfunded, source of funding
	Researcher characteristics	Discipline, gender, ethnicity
Study quality	Internal validity	Use of random assignment, condition concealment, attrition
	External validity	Use of random sampling procedures, samples based on specific subpopulations
	Construct validity	Reliability of measures (for correction rather than exclusion or moderator analyses), relevant measurement characteristics (described above)

4.1.2.a Sample Characteristics

Potentially relevant characteristics of the sample that you might consider include aspects of the sampling procedure and the demographic features of the sample. For instance, you might code sampling procedures such as whether the sample was drawn from unique settings (e.g., from a university setting, some sort of clinical setting, a correctional facility, or specific other settings relevant to the area), whether the study attempted to draw a sample representative of a larger population (e.g., a nationally representative sample) versus relying on a convenience sample, and the country from which the sample was drawn. Potentially relevant demographic features to consider include the gender or ethnic composition of the sample, the mean socioeconomic status or age of the sample, or any other potentially relevant descriptors (e.g., average IQ). Although you will not necessarily code all of these possible characteristics, either because you do not believe they are relevant or because the primary studies do not consistently report these features, I believe that most meta-analyses in the social sciences should at least consider coding some sample characteristics.

4.1.2.b Measurement Characteristics

In many areas of social science, there exist multiple approaches to measurement and multiple specific measures of the variables that comprise your effect sizes. For this reason, you may want to code the measurement characteristics of either or both variables comprising your effect size. Potential aspects that can be coded include both the source of information (e.g., self-report; some other reporter such as a spouse, parent, or teacher; observations by the researcher) and specific features of the measurement process (e.g., covert versus overt observations, timed versus untimed performance on a test). In areas where a small number of measurement instruments are widely used, you might also consider coding the specific measure used. In survey research, you might code whether the original version of an instrument, a shortened form, or a translated form of the scale was used. These suggestions represent just a few of the possibilities you might consider. A thorough knowledge of the strengths and limitations about measurement processes and specific measures in your field will be extremely influential in guiding your decisions about the measurement characteristics you might decide to code.

4.1.2.c Design Characteristics

You might also consider coding both broad and narrow characteristics of the designs of studies included in your meta-analysis. At the broad level, you might code, for example, whether studies used experimental group comparisons, quasi-experimental group comparisons, single-group pre–post comparisons, or regression discontinuity designs. At a narrower level, you could consider specific design features; for example, if you were conducting a meta-analysis of treatment studies, you might code various aspects of the control groups (e.g., no contact, attention only, treatment as usual, placebo).

4.1.2.d   Source Characteristics

Finally, in some instances coding characteristics of the research report itself may be valuable. As described in Chapter 11, you should always code whether or not the report is published (and potentially more nuanced codes such as publication quality) to evaluate evidence of publication bias. There may be instances when it is useful to code the year of publication (or year of presentation for conference presentations, year of defense for dissertation, etc.), which might serve as a proxy for the year the data was collected.[1] Evaluation of this year as a moderator might illuminate historic trends in the effect sizes across time. It might also be useful to evaluate whether or not studies were funded, or perhaps the specific sources of funding, if you suspect that these factors could bias the results. A fourth set of source characteristics to consider are the potentially relevant characteristics of the researchers themselves (e.g., discipline, gender, ethnicity). Evaluating these in relation to effect sizes might indicate either the presence of uncoded methodological features (related to, e.g., disciplinary styles) or systematic differences in results potentially caused by biases of the researchers (e.g., different magnitudes of gender differences found by male versus female researchers).

4.2 CODING STUDY "QUALITY"

Some have recommended that meta-analysts code for study quality and then either (1) include only studies meeting a certain level of quality or (2) evaluate quality as a moderator of effect sizes.[2] This recommendation is problematic, in my view, because it assumes (1) that "quality" is a unidimensional construct and (2) that we are always interested in whether this overarching construct of "quality" directly relates to effect sizes. I believe that each of these assumptions is inaccurate, as I describe next.

4.2.1   The Multidimensional Nature of Study Quality

Study quality can be defined in many ways (see Valentine, 2009; for an example scoring instrument see Valentine & Cooper, 2008). At a broad level, you can consider quality in terms of study validity, specifically internal, external, construct, and statistical conclusion validity (Cook & Campbell, 1979; Shadish et al., 2002). Of course, within each of these four broad levels, there exist numerous specific aspects of studies contributing to the validity (and hence, quality). For example, internal validity is impacted by whether or not random assignment was used, the comparability of groups in quasi-experimental designs both initially and throughout the study, and the rates of attrition (to name just a few influences). Even more specifically, many fields of research have adapted—whether explicitly or implicitly—certain empirical practices that many researchers agree contribute to higher or lower quality of studying the phenomenon of interest (for a summary of three explicit sets of criteria, see Valentine, 2009).

If you believe that these numerous features of studies reflect an underlying dimension of study quality, then you would expect these various features to co-occur across studies. For example, studies that have certain features reflecting internal validity should have other features reflecting internal validity, and studies with high internal validity should also have high external, construct, and statistical conclusion validity. Whether or not these co-occurrences exist in the particular collection of studies in your meta-analysis is both a conceptual and an empirical question. Conceptually, do you expect that the various features are reflections of a unidimensional quality construct in this area of study? Empirically, do you find substantial and consistent positive correlations among these features across the studies in your meta-analysis? If both of these conditions hold, then it may be reasonable to conceptualize an underlying (latent) construct of study quality (see left side of Figure 4.1). However, my impression is that in most fields, the conceptual argument is doubtful and the empirical evaluation is not made.

4.2.2   Usefulness of Moderation by Study Quality versus Specific Features

If you cannot provide conceptual and empirical support for an underlying "quality" construct leading to manifestations of different aspects of quality across studies, I believe that it becomes more difficult to describe some phenomenon of "quality." Nevertheless, even if such a construct that produces consistent variation in features across studies does not exist, the collection of these features might still define something meaningful that could be termed "quality." This situation is displayed on the right side of Figure 4.1. The difference between these two situations—one in which the features of the studies reflecting quality can be argued, conceptually and empirically, to co-occur (left) versus one in which the concept of quality is simply defined by these features—parallels the distinction between reflective versus formative indicators (see Figure 4.1 and, e.g., Edwards & Bagozzi, 2000; Howell, Breivik, & Wilcox, 2007; MacCallum & Browne, 1993). However, this approach would also suffer the same problems of formative measurement (e.g., Howell et al.,

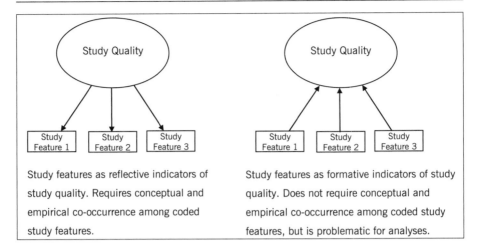

FIGURE 4.1. Conceptualizing study features as reflective versus formative indicators of study quality.

2007), including difficulties in defining the construct if some of the formative indicators differentially relate to presumed outcomes. In terms of meta-analytic moderator analyses (see Chapter 9), the problem arises when some study features might predict effect sizes at a magnitude—or even direction—differently than others. This situation will lead to a conceptual change in the definition of the "study quality" construct; more importantly, this situation obscures your ability to detect which specific features of the studies are related to variation in effect sizes across studies. I argue that it is typically more useful to understand the specific aspects of study quality that relate to the effect sizes found, rather than some broader, ill-defined construct of "study quality."

4.2.3 Recommendations for Coding Study Quality

In sum, I have argued that (1) the conditions (conceptual unidimensionality and empirically observed substantial correlations) in which study features might be used as reflective indicators of a "study quality" construct are rare, and (2) attempting simply to combine the conceptually multidimensional and empirically uncorrelated (or modestly correlated) features as formative indicators of a "study quality" construct are problematic. This does *not* mean that I suggest not considering study quality. Instead, I suggest coding the various aspects of study quality that are potentially important within your field and evaluating these as multiple moderators of the effect sizes among your studies.

My recommendation to code, and later analyze (see Chapter 9), individual aspects of study quality means that you must make decisions about what aspects of study quality are important enough to code.[3] These decisions can be guided by the same principles that guided your decision to code other potential moderators (see Section 4.1). Based on your knowledge of the area in which you are performing a meta-analysis, you should consider the research questions you are interested in and generally consider coding at least some of the aspects of study quality contributing to internal, external, and construct validity.[4] My decision to organize coding around these aspects of validity follows Valentine (2009), and these possibilities are summarized in the bottom of Table 4.1.

4.2.3.a Internal Validity

Internal validity refers to the extent to which the study design allows conclusions of causality from observed associations (e.g., association between group membership and outcome). The most important influence on internal validity is likely the study design, with experimental (i.e., random assignment) studies providing more internal validity than quasi-experimental studies (such as matched naturally occurring groups, regression continuity, and single-subject designs; see Shadish et al., 2002). However, other study characteristics of studies might also impact internal validity. The degree to which condition is concealed to participants—also known as the "blinding" of participants to condition—impacts internal validity. For example, studies comparing a group receiving treatment (e.g., medication, psychotherapy) to a control group (e.g., placebo, treatment as usual) can have questionable internal validity if participants know which group they are in. Similarly, studies that are "double blind," in that the researcher measuring the presumed outcome is unaware of participants' group membership, are considered more internally valid in some areas of research. Finally, attrition—specifically selective and differential attrition between groups—can impact internal validity, especially in studies not using appropriate imputation technique (see Schafer & Graham, 2002).

4.2.3.b External Validity

External validity refers to the extent to which the findings from a particular study can be generalized to different types of samples, conditions, or different ways of measuring the constructs of interest. However, attention to external validity focuses primarily on generalization to other types of samples/participants. The most externally valid studies will randomly sample participants from a defined population (e.g., all registered voters in a region, all schoolchildren in the United States). In many, if not most, fields, this sort of random sampling is rare. So, it is important for you to determine what you consider a reasonably broad level of generalization in the research context of your meta-analysis, and code whether studies achieve this or focus on a more limited subpopulation (and likely the specific types of subpopulations).[5] Fortunately, meta-analytic aggregation of individual studies with limited external validity can lead to conclusions that have greater external validity (see Chapter 2), provided that the studies within the meta-analysis collectively cover a wide range of relevant sample characteristics (see Section 4.1.2.a above on coding these characteristics).

4.2.3.c   Construct Validity

Construct validity refers to the degree to which the measures used in a study correspond to the theoretical construct the researchers intend to measure. The heading of "construct validity" is often used to refer to a wider range of measurement properties, including both the reliability and validity of the measure. I suggest coding the reliability of the measures comprising the two variables for potential effect size corrections (see Chapter 6). I do not support decisions to exclude studies with measures below a certain threshold reliability given that any choice of the threshold is arbitrary and because reliability scores reported in a study are imperfect parameter estimates (e.g., it is very plausible that two studies with identical sampling procedures from the same population, same methodology, and using the same measures could obtain slightly different estimates of internal consistency, perhaps with one at 0.78 and the other at 0.82 around an arbitrary 0.80 cutoff). It is more difficult to make such clear recommendations regarding the validity of the measures. Certainly, you should have a clear operational definition of the constructs of interest that can guide decisions about whether a study should or should not be included in your meta-analysis (see Chapter 3). Beyond this, it is possible to correct for imperfect validity (see Chapter 6), at least in situations where you have a good estimate of the correlation (i.e., validity coefficient) between the measure used in the study and some "gold standard" for the construct. Probably the safest approach is to treat this issue as an empirical question, and code relevant measurement characteristics (see Section 4.1.2.b) for use as potential moderators of study effect sizes.

4.2.3.d   Conclusions Regarding Coding Aspects of Quality

This consideration of study "quality" in terms of aspects of validity highlights the range of potential characteristics you can code for your meta-analysis. Given this range, I have treated the issue of coding study "quality" similarly to that of coding study characteristics (see Section 4.1), and do not see these aspects of "quality" holding a greater value than any other study characteristics.

At the same time, you should be aware of the "garbage in, garbage out" criticism (see Chapter 2), and consider this critique in light of the goals and intended audience of your meta-analysis. If your goal is to inform policy or practice, and the intended audience consists primarily of individuals who want clear, defensible answers (e.g., policymakers), then I suggest that you use aspects of study quality primarily as inclusion/exclusion criteria (see Chapter 3) in selecting studies (assuming that enough studies meet these inclusion criteria so as to provide a reasonably precise effect size estimate). In contrast, if your goal is to inform understanding of a phenomenon, and the intended audience is primarily individuals comfortable with nuanced, qualified conclusions (e.g., scientists), then I suggest coding these aspects of study quality for analysis as potential moderators of effect sizes (see Chapter 9). Perhaps a middle ground between these two recommendations is to code and evaluate moderation by various aspects of study quality, but to base policy or practice recommendations on results from higher-quality studies when these aspects are found to moderate effect sizes. Regardless of how these aspects of study quality are used (i.e., as inclusion/exclusion criteria versus coded moderators), I believe that a focus on specific aspects of study qualities is preferable to a single code intended to represent an overall "quality" construct.

4.3   EVALUATING CODING DECISIONS

Once you have decided what study characteristics to code, the next step, of course, is to do it—to carefully read obtained reports and to record information about the studies. The information recorded is that regarding both the study characteristics you have decided to code (see previous two sections) and the effect sizes. I defer discussion of computing effect sizes until Chapter 5, but the same principles of evaluating coding decisions of effect sizes apply as for coding study characteristics that I describe in this section.

Two important qualities of your coding system are the related concepts of transparency and replicability (Wilson, 2009). In addition to these qualities, it is also important to consider the reliability of your coding.

4.3.1   Transparency and Replicability of Coding

When writing or otherwise presenting your meta-analysis, you should provide enough details of the coding process that your audience knows exactly how you made coding decisions (transparency) and, at least in principle, could reach the same decisions as you did if they were to apply your coding strategy to studies included in your meta-analysis (replicability). To achieve these principles of transparency and replicability, it is important to describe fully how each study characteristic is quantified.

Some study characteristics are coded in a straightforward way; the characteristics that require little or no judgment decisions on the part of the coder are sometimes termed "low inference codes" (e.g., Cooper, 2009b, p. 33). For example, coding the mean age of the sample will usually involve simply recording information stated in the research reports. You should fully describe even such simple coding (e.g., that you recorded age in years). In my experience, however, even such seemingly simple study characteristics yield complexities. For example, a study might report an age range (from which you might record the midpoint) or a proxy such as grade in school (from which you might estimate a likely age). Ideally, your original coding plan will have ways of determining a reasonable value from such information, or you might have to make these decisions as the unexpected decisions arise. In either case, it is important to report these rules to ensure the transparency of your coding process.[6]

When study characteristics are less obvious (i.e., high inference coding, in which the coder must make judgment decisions), it is critical to fully report the coding process to ensure transparency and replicability (and this process should already be written to ensure reliability of coding; discussed next in Section 4.3.2). For example, if you have decided to code for types of measures or designs of the studies, you should report the different values for this categorical code and define each of the categories. During the planning stages, you should consider whether it is possible to reduce a high inference code into a series of more specific low inference codes.[7]

4.3.2   Reliability of Coding

One way to evaluate empirically the replicability of your coding system is to assess the reliability of independent efforts of coding the same studies. You can evaluate this reliability either between coders (intercoder reliability) or within the same coder (intracoder reliability; Wilson, 2009).

Intercoder reliability is assessed by having two coders from the coding team independently code a subset of overlapping studies. The coders should be unaware of which studies each other is coding because an awareness of this fact is likely to increase the vigilance of coding and therefore provide an overestimate of the actual reliability. The number of doubly coded studies should be large enough to ensure a reasonably precise estimate of reliability. Lipsey and Wilson (2001, p. 86) recommended 20 to 50 studies, and your decision to choose a number within this range might depend on your perception of the level of inference of the coding. If your protocol calls for low inference coding, then a lower number should suffice in confirming intercoder agreement, whereas higher inference coding would necessitate a higher number of overlapping studies to more precisely quantify this agreement.

Intracoder agreement is assessed by having the same person code a subset of studies twice. Because it is likely that the coder will be aware of previously coding the study, it is not possible to conceal the studies used to assess this reliability. However, if the coder is unaware during the first coding trials of which studies they will recode (e.g., a random sample of studies is selected for recoding after the initial coding is completed), the overestimation of reliability is likely reduced. One reason for assessing intracoder agreement is to evaluate potential "drift"—changes in the coding process over time that could come about from the coding experience, increasing biases from "expecting" certain results and/or fatigue. A second reason is that it is not possible to assess intercoder agreement. This inability to assess intercoder agreement is certainly a realistic possibility if you are conducting the meta-analysis alone and you have no colleagues with sufficient expertise or time to code a subset of studies. Intracoder agreement is not a perfect substitute for intercoder agreement because one coder might hold potential biases or consistently make the same coding errors during both coding sessions. However, it can serve as reasonable evidence of reliability if efforts are made to ensure the independence of the coding sessions. For example, the coder should work with unmarked copies of the studies (not with copies containing notes from the previous coding), and the coding sessions should be separated by as much time as practical.

Using either an intercoder or intracoder approach, it is useful to report the reliability of each coded study characteristic (i.e., each study characteristic, artifact correction, and effect size), just as you would report the reliability for each variable in a primary study. It is deceptive to report only a single reliability across codes, as this might obscure important differences in coding reliability across study characteristics (Yeaton & Wortman, 1993). Several indices are available for quantifying this reliability (see Orwin & Vevea, 2009), three of which are agreement rates, Cohen's kappa, and Pearson correlation.[8]

4.3.2.a Agreement Rate

The most common index is the agreement rate (AR), which is simply the proportion of studies on which two coders (or single coder on two occasions) assign the same categorical code (Equation 4.1; from Orwin & Vevea, 2009, p. 187):

Equation 4.1: Computing agreement rate (AR)

$$AR = \frac{\text{No. of agreements}}{\text{No. of studies}}$$

- No. of agreements is the number of studies in which two coders provided the same categorical coding for this study characteristic.
- No. of studies is the number of studies that both coders provided score for this study characteristic.

The agreement rate is simple and intuitive, and for these reasons is the most commonly reported index of coding reliability. At the same time, there are limitations to this index; namely, it does not account for base rates of coding (i.e., some values are coded more often than others) and the resulting chance levels of agreement.

4.3.2.b Cohen's Kappa

An alternative index for reliability of categorical codes is Cohen's kappa (κ), which does account for chance level agreement depending on base rates for coding. Kappa is estimated using Equation 4.2 (from Orwin & Vevea, 2009, pp. 187–188):

Equation 4.2: Computing agreement rate (AR)

$$\kappa = \frac{P_O - P_E}{1 - P_E}$$

- P_O is the observed proportion agreement (defined as AR in Equation 4.2).
- P_E is the expected (chance) proportion agreement, derived from base rates (contingency table marginal sums) $= \frac{1}{n^2}\sum_{i=1}^{C}(n_{i\bullet}n_{\bullet i})$
- C is the number of categories.
- n is the number of observations (i.e., number of studies coded by both coders).
- $n_{i\bullet}$ is the number of studies coded at category i (i.e., base rate of this code) for first coder.
- $n_{\bullet i}$ is the number of studies coded at category i (i.e., base rate of this code) for second coder.

Cohen's kappa is a very useful index of coding reliability for study characteristics with nominal categorical levels. When used with ordinal coding, it has the limitation of not distinguishing between "close" and "far" disagreements (e.g., a close agreement might be two coders recording 4 and 5 on a 5-point ordinal scale, whereas far disagreement might be two coders recording 1 and 5 on this scale). However, ordinal coding can be accommodated by using a weighted kappa index (see Orwin & Vevea, 2009, p. 188). The major limitation of using kappa is that it requires a fairly large number of studies to produce precise estimates of reliability. Although I cannot provide concrete guidelines as to how many studies is "enough" (because this also depends on the distributions of the base rate), I suggest that you use either the upper end of Lipsey and Wilson's recommendations (i.e., about 40 to 50 studies) or all studies in your meta-analysis if it is important to obtain a precise estimate of coding reliability in your meta-analysis.

4.3.2.c   Pearson Correlation

When study characteristics are coded continuously or on an ordinal scale with numerous categories, a useful index of reliability is the Pearson correlation (r) between the two sets of coded values. One caveat is that the correlation coefficient does not evaluate potential mean differences between coders/ coding occasions. For example, two coders might exhibit a perfect correlation between their recorded scores of mean ages of samples, but one coded the values in years and the other in months. This discrepancy would obviously be problematic in using the coded study characteristic "mean age of sample" for either descriptive purposes or moderator analyses. Given this limitation of the correlation coefficient, I suggest also examining difference scores, or equivalently, performing a repeated-measures (a.k.a. paired samples) t-test to ensure that such discrepancies have not emerged.

4.4   PRACTICAL MATTERS: CREATING AN ORGANIZED PROTOCOL FOR CODING

Once you have decided what study characteristics to code, the next step is to plan to code them (likely coding effect sizes at the same time, as described in Chapter 5). The guidance for this coding comes from a coding protocol, which consists of both the interface coders used to record information from the studies as well as a coding manual providing instructions for this coding process (see Wilson, 2009). Through using this coding protocol, your goal is to create a usable database for later meta-analyses. There are several considerations for each aspect, which I describe next.

4.4.1 Coding Interface

Considering first the interface coders use to record information, three options include using paper forms that coders complete, using a computerized form to collect this information, or coding directly into the electronic format to be used for analyses. Part of an example paper coding form (from a meta-analysis of the association between relational aggression and peer rejection described throughout this book; Card et al., 2008) is shown in Figure 4.2.

Using paper forms would require coders to write information into predefined questions (e.g., "Sample age in years: _____"), which would then be transferred into an electronic database for analyses. The advantages of this approach are (1) that coders need training only in the coding process (guided by the manual of instructions described in Section 4.4.2) rather than procedures for entering data into a computer, and (2) the information is checked for plausibility when entered into the computer.

A computerized form would present the same information to coders but would require them to input the coded data electronically, perhaps using a relational database program (e.g., Microsoft Access). This type of interface would require only a small amount of training beyond using paper forms and would reduce the time (and potentially errors) in transferring information from paper to the electronic format. However, this advantage is also a disadvantage in that it bypasses the check that would occur during this entry from paper forms.

A third option with regard to a coding interface is to code information directly into an electronic format (e.g., Microsoft Excel, SAS, SPSS) later used for analysis. This option is perhaps the most time-efficient of all in reducing the number of steps, but it is also the most prone to errors. I strongly discourage this third method if multiple coders will be coding studies.

4.4.2 Coding Manual

A coding manual is a detailed collection of instructions describing how information reported in research reports is quantified for inclusion in your meta-analysis. Creating a detailed coding manual serves three primary purposes. First, this coding manual provides a guide for coders to transfer information in the study reports to the coding interface (e.g., paper forms). As

---

Date coded: **4/25**   Date entered into database: **5/10**

Initials: **BS**   Initials: **NC**

Study identifier

1. Study #: **104**

2. Study authors: **Crick & Grotpeter**

3. Year: **1995**

Sample characteristics

4. Sample size (*N*): **491**

5. Sample age (years): **Not reported**

6. Sample grade(s): **3-6 (128 3ʳᵈ grade, 126 4ᵗʰ grade, 126 5ᵗʰ grade, 111 6ᵗʰ grade)**

7. Proportion male: **.52**

8. Proportion ethnic minority: **.40**

9. Unique characteristics of sample: **public school sample**

Measurement

10. Aggression—source of information: **peer nomination**

11. Aggression—name of scale: **author created**

12. Rejection—source of information: **peer nominations**

13. Rejection—name of scale: **Classified by Coie et al. criteria**

. . .

FIGURE 4.2. Part of an example study coding form. This example shows part of a coding form for a meta-analysis of associations between relational aggression and peer rejection (see Card et al., 2008). This coding form, used in conjunction with a detailed coding manual, requires coders to record information from studies that is later entered into a computerized database.

such, it should be a clear set of instructions for coding both "typical" studies and more challenging coding situations. Second (and relatedly), this coding manual aims to ensure consistency across multiple reporters[9] by providing a clear, concrete set of instructions that each coder should study and have at hand during the coding process. Third, this coding manual serves as documentation of the coding process that should guide the presentation of the meta-analysis or be made available to others to ensure transparency of the coding (see beginning of this section).

With regard to the coding manual, the amount of instruction for each study characteristic coded depends on the level of inference of the coding: low-inference coding requires relatively little instruction, whereas high-inference coding requires more instruction. In addition, the coding manual is most often a work in progress. Although an initial coding manual should be developed before beginning the coding, ambiguities discovered during the coding process likely will force ongoing revision.

Turning again to the example coding form of Figure 4.2, we should note that this form would be accompanied by a detailed coding manual that all coders have been trained in and have present while completing this form. To provide illustrations of the type of information that might be included in such a manual, we can consider two of the coded study characteristics. First, item 5 (mean age) might be accompanied by the rather simple instruction "Record the mean age of the sample in years." However, even this relatively simple (low-inference) code requires fairly extensive elaboration: "If study analyzed a subset of the data, record the mean age of the subset used in analyses. If study reported a range of ages but not the mean, record the midpoint of this range." My colleagues and I also had to change the coding protocol rather substantially when we found that many studies failed to report ages, but did report the grades in school of participants. This led us to add the "grade" code (item 6) along with instructions for entering this information in the database: "If sample age is not reported in the study, then an estimated age can be entered from grade using the formula Age = Grade + 5."[10] A second study characteristic shown in Figure 4.2 that illustrates typical instruction is item 10 (aggression—source of information). The coding manual for this item specifies the choices that should be coded (self-report, peer nomination, peer rating, teacher report, parent report, researcher observations, or other) and definitions of each code.

4.4.3 Database for Meta-Analysis

The product of your coding should be an electronic file with which to conduct your meta-analysis. Table 4.2 provides an example of what this database might look like (if complete, the table would extend far to the right to include other coded study characteristics, coded effect sizes [Chapter 5], information for any artifact corrections [Chapter 6], and several calculations for the actual meta-analysis [Chapters 8–10]). Although the exact variables (columns) you include will depend on the study characteristics you decide to code, the general layout of this file sould be considered. Here, each row represents a single coded study, and each column represents a coded study characteristic.

TABLE 4.2. Partial Example of Database of Coded Study Characteristics

Study No.	Authors	Year	Sample size (N)	Sample age[a]	Sample grade	Male	Ethnic minority	Sample notes ...
368	Blachman	2003	228	9.2	NR	.00	.47	
104	Crick & Grotpeter	1995	491	**9.4**	3-6	.52	.40	
91	Crick et al.	1997	65	4.5	Pre	.52	.27	
431	Geiger	2003	458	8.0	3	.46	.26	
528	Hawley et al.	2007	929	14.7	7-10	.44	.19	German; included ...
94	Henington	1996	904	7.4	2-3	.51	.51	
11	Johnson	2003	74	6.0	Kind	.55	.65	
95	Leff	1995	151	**9.5**	4-5	.00	.33	
49	Miller	2001	150	8.0	3	.00	.44	
584	Murray-Close & Crick	2006	590	**9.0**	4	.50	.71	
389	Nelson et al.	2005	180	4.8	Pre	.52	.14	Headstart ...
551	Ostrov	NA[b]	139	3.6	Pre	.41	.42	
548	Ostrov & Crick	2007	132	4.1	Pre	.48	.25	
261	Ostrov et al.	2004	60	4.6	Pre	.52	.20	
310	Pakaslahti & Keltikangas-Järvinen	1998	839	14.5	8.0	.51	NR	Finland
122	Phillipsen et al.	1999	262	8.7	3-6	.49	.50	Included only ...
98	Rys & Bear	1997	266	9.5	3,6	.50	.36	
141	Salmivalli et al.	2000	209	15.5	9	.43	NR	Finland
93	Tomada & Schneider	1997	314	9.0	3-4	.53	NR	Italy
55	Werner	2000	881	**8.0**	3	.49	.37	
259	Werner & Crick	2004	517	8.0	2-4	.38	.45	
204	Zalecki & Hinshaw	2004	228	9.0	NR	.00	.47	Summer camp ...

[a]Values of age that are **bold and italicized** were estimated from sample grade.
[b]Article was under review during the preparation of this meta-analytic review. It has subsequently been published as Ostrov (2008).

4.5 SUMMARY

In this chapter, I have described the process of coding study characteristics. This process spans from the initial planning stages, in which you consider the characteristics that are most informative to your research questions, to the coding itself, in which you strive to extract and quantify information from the study reports. Potentially interesting study characteristics to code include features of the sample, measurement, design, and the source itself. Study quality is another important consideration, though I recommend coding for specific aspects of quality rather than some single dimension. It is important that your coding process is transparent and replicable; the process should also be reliable across coders or within the same coder, and I have described methods of evaluating this reliability. Finally, after deciding which study characteristics to code, the coding protocol will guide this coding process.

4.6 RECOMMENDED READINGS

Orwin, R. G., & Vevea, J. L. (2009). Evaluating coding decisions. In H. Cooper, L. V. Hedges, & J. C. Valentine (Eds.), *The handbook of research synthesis and meta-analysis* (2nd ed., pp. 177–203). New York: Russell Sage Foundation.—This chapter provides a thorough description of the sources of coding errors, ways to assess coder reliability, and uses of this information in analyses.

Valentine, J. C. (2009). Judging the quality of primary research. In H. Cooper, L. V. Hedges, & J. C. Valentine (Eds.), *The handbook of research synthesis and meta-analysis* (2nd ed., pp. 129–146). New York: Russell Sage Foundation.—This chapter describes the aspects of studies that collectively comprise "study quality," as well as the relative advantages of excluding poor quality studies versus assessing coded quality features as moderators.

Wilson, D. B. (2009). Systematic coding. In H. Cooper, L. V. Hedges, & J. C. Valentine (Eds.), *The handbook of research synthesis and meta-analysis* (2nd ed., pp. 159–176). New York: Russell Sage Foundation.—This chapter provides thorough guidance in planning a coding strategy that is explicit and transparent.

NOTES

1. The year of publication is a crude proxy for the year the study was conducted, as it does not account for likely inconsistencies across studies in the lag between data collection and publication. However, year of publication is almost always avail-

able, whereas the year of data collection is often not reported. Closer approximations of the year that data were collected might come from coding the dates the report was submitted for publication (which is reported in some journals), though this date will not reflect previous submissions of the work elsewhere or the variability in lag between data collection and submission. If accurately coding the year of data collection is critical in your meta-analysis, the best approach is to follow two steps. First, code the year of publication and the year of data collection for all studies reporting this information, contacting study authors who do not report year of data collection for this information. Second, based on the likely complete data for year of publication and the partially complete information for year of data collection that you are able to obtain, impute the missing values of year of data collection (see, e.g., Schafer & Graham, 2002 for a description of imputation approaches). If your review includes various formats and methods of coding year (e.g., year of conference presentation, year of defense), it will be useful to include the format as a predictor in the imputation model.

2. A third recommendation is to give greater weight to studies of higher than lower quality. This recommendation is problematic in my view because there is no singularly defensible magnitude for these weights. For instance, if the quality of studies is rated on a 3-point scale (1 = low quality, 2 = medium quality, 3 = high quality) and these ratings are used as weights, then this weighting would assume that high-quality studies deserve three times the weight as low-quality studies; but this choice is as arbitrary as weighing them twice or four times as heavily. Furthermore, these weights would need to be multiplied by the weights due to the standard errors of effect sizes from studies (i.e., the inverse of these standard errors squared; see Chapter 8), but this would make it impossible to draw statistically defensible (1) inferences about the mean effect size of your meta-analysis or (2) conclusions about the heterogeneity of effect sizes (see Chapter 8). In short, any weighting by study quality is arbitrary, and I strongly recommend against this practice.

3. Or, alternatively, are important enough to serve as inclusion/exclusion criteria. As with other study features, the decision to exclude studies with certain problems of quality, or to code these qualities and evaluate them as moderators of effect sizes, depends on your interest in empirically evaluating the impact of study quality, your desire to draw conclusions about a homogeneous versus heterogeneous population of studies, and the number of studies that would be included in your meta-analysis (see Chapter 3).

4. I do not describe the fourth broad type of validity, statistical conclusion validity, for two reasons. First, primary studies typically do not provide sufficient information regarding threats to this aspect of validity. Second, even if it were possible to code, the associations of these threats with effect sizes are likely small and of little interest. One exception to these statements is the problem of artificial dichotomization of continuous variables, an unfortunately common practice

that substantially impacts the statistical conclusion validity (see e.g., Hunter & Schmidt, 1990; MacCallum, Zhang, Preacher, & Rucker, 2002). However, it is better to correct for (see Chapter 6), rather than code, this artificial dichotomization.

5. Methods of correcting effect sizes that are biased by range restriction (or range enhancement) are described in Chapter 6.

6. Practically, it will not always be reasonable to report the many nuanced decisions for some study characteristics, owing to page limits or limits in the likely audience's interest in these minutiae. In these situations, it would be well to improve brevity or readability at the expense of transparency. However, I would recommend creating a complete documentation of these coding rules and study-by-study decisions that you can make available to interested readers.

7. This recommendation is another reason for coding aspects of study features (lower inference codes) rather than an overall study quality (a high-inference code), as I described in Section 4.2.

8. An additional approach is to quantify reliability with the intraclass correlation. This approach has certain advantages, including the ability to model between-rater variance and more realistic modeling of agreement across three or more coders (Orwin & Vevea, 2009). However, computing the intraclass correlation is more complicated than the three methods described in this chapter, and I believe that you will find the approaches I describe adequate if your goal is simply to evaluate and report the agreement of coding. Interested readers can consult Orwin and Vevea (2009, pp. 190–191) and the references cited in this work.

9. This coding manual is just as important if you are coding the studies yourself as it is if you have multiple coders. The coding process will very likely take an extended period of time, get interrupted by other demands, and so on. In these situations it is critical that you have a coding manual that can be used to retrain yourself (i.e., ensure consistency of coding across time), just as it is for training multiple coders.

10. For the particular study (Crick & Grotpeter, 1995) shown in Figure 4.2, in which exact subsample sizes per grade were reported, we estimate grade as the weighted average, $Age = [128(3+5) + 126(4+5) + 126(5+5) + 111(6+5)]/(128 + 126 + 126 + 111)$.

5

Basic Effect Size Computation

Effect sizes represent the most important information that you will extract from included studies. As such, carefully computing effect sizes from reported results is critical. In this chapter, I describe three common indices for representing effect sizes: *r* (Pearson correlation coefficient), *g* (one form of standardized mean difference), and *o* (odds ratio). I also describe how you can compute each from information commonly provided in empirical reports, such as reports of actual effect sizes, inferential statistics (e.g., *t*-tests), descriptive data, and statements of statistical significance. I then demonstrate how you can compare and transform among these three indices of effect sizes. Finally, I discuss a practical matter in computing effect sizes: using available effect size calculators within programs for conducting meta-analysis.

5.1 THE COMMON METRICS: CORRELATION, STANDARDIZED MEAN DIFFERENCE, AND ODDS RATIO

5.1.1 Significance Tests Are Not Effect Sizes

Before describing what effect sizes are, I describe what they are not. Effect sizes are not significance tests, and significance tests are not effect sizes. Although you can usually derive effect sizes from the results of significance tests, and the magnitude of the effect size influences the likelihood of finding statistically significant results (i.e., statistical power), it is important to distinguish between indices of effect size and statistical significance.

Imagine that a researcher, Dr. A, wishes to investigate whether two groups (male versus female, two treatment groups, etc.) differ on a particular variable X. So she collects data from five individuals in each group ($N = 10$). She finds that Group 1 members have scores of 4, 4, 3, 2, and 2, for a mean of 3.0 and (population estimated) standard deviation of 1.0, whereas Group 2 members have scores of 6, 6, 5, 4, and 4, for a mean of 5.0 and standard deviation of 1.0. Dr. A performs a t-test and finds that $t_{(8)} = 3.16$, $p = .013$. Finding that Group 2 was significantly higher than Group 1 (according to traditional criteria of $\alpha = .05$), she publishes the results.

Further imagine that Dr. B reads this report and is skeptical of the results. He decides to replicate this study, but collects data from only three individuals in each group ($N = 6$). He finds that individuals in Group 1 had scores of 4, 3, and 2, for a mean of 3.0 and standard deviation of 1.0, whereas Group 2 members had scores of 6, 5, and 4, for a mean of 5.0 and standard deviation of 1.0. His comparison of these groups results in $t_{(4)} = 2.45$, $p = .071$. Dr. B concludes that the two groups do not differ significantly and therefore that the findings of Dr. A have failed to replicate.

Now we have a controversy on our hands. Graduate student C decides that she will resolve this controversy through a definitive study involving 10 individuals in each group ($N = 20$). She finds that individuals in Group 1 had scores of 4, 4, 4, 4, 3, 3, 2, 2, 2, and 2, for a mean of 3.0 and standard deviation of 1.0, whereas individuals in Group 2 had scores of 6, 6, 6, 6, 5, 5, 4, 4, 4, and 4, for a mean of 5.0 and a standard deviation of 1.0. Her inferential test is highly significant, $t_{(18)} = 4.74$, $p = .00016$. She concludes that not only do the groups differ, but also the difference is more pronounced than previously thought!

This example illustrates the limits of relying on the Null Hypothesis Significance Testing Framework in comparing results across studies. In each of the three hypothetical studies, individuals in Group 1 had a mean score of 3.0 and a standard deviation of 1.0, whereas individuals in Group 2 had a mean score of 5.0 and a standard deviation of 1.0. The hypothetical researchers' focus on significance tests led them to inappropriate conclusions: Dr. B's conclusion of a failure to replicate is inaccurate (because it does not consider the inadequacy of statistical power in the study), as is Student C's conclusion of a more pronounced difference (which mistakenly interprets a low p value as informing the magnitude of an effect). A focus on effect sizes would have alleviated the confusion that arose from a reliance only on statistical significance and, in fact, would have shown that these three studies provided perfectly replicating results. Moreover, if the researchers had considered effect sizes, they could have moved beyond the question of *whether* the two groups differ to consider also the question of *how much* the two groups differ. These limitations of relying exclusively on significance tests have been the subject of much discussion (see, e.g., Cohen, 1994; Fan, 2001; Frick, 1996; Harlow, Mulaik, & Steiger, 1997; Meehl, 1978; Wilkinson & the Task Force on Statistical Significance, 1999), yet this practice unfortunately persists.

For the purposes of most meta-analyses, I find it useful to define an effect size as an index of the direction and magnitude of association between two variables.[1] As I describe in more detail later in this chapter, this definition includes traditional measures of correlation between two variables, differences between two groups, and contingencies between two dichotomies. When conducting a meta-analysis, it is critical that effect sizes be comparable across studies. In other words, a useful effect size for meta-analysis is one to which results from various studies can be transformed and therefore combined and compared. In this chapter I describe ways that you can compute the correlation (r), standardized mean difference (g), or odds ratio (o) from a variety of information commonly reported in primary studies; this is another reason that these indexes are useful in summarizing or comparing findings across studies.

A second criterion for an effect size index to be useful in meta-analysis is that it must be possible to compute or approximate its standard error. Although I describe this importance more fully in Chapter 8, I should say a few words about it here. Standard errors describe the imprecision of a sample-based estimate of a population effect size; formally, the standard error represents the typical magnitude of differences of sample effect sizes around a population effect size if you were to draw multiple samples (of a certain size N) from the population. It is important to be able to compute standard errors of effect sizes because you generally want to give more weight to studies that provide precise estimates of effect sizes (i.e., have small standard errors) than to studies that provide less precise estimates (i.e., have large standard errors). Chapter 8 of this book provides further description of this idea.

Having made clear the difference between statistical significance and effect size, I next describe three indices of effect size that are commonly used in meta-analyses.

5.1.2 Pearson Correlation

The Pearson correlation, commonly represented as r, represents the association between two continuous variables (with variants existing for other forms, such as r_{pb} when one variable is dichotomous and the other is continuous, ϕ when both are dichotomous). The formula for computing r (the sample estimate of the population correlation, ρ) within a primary data set is:

Equation 5.1: Computing *r*

$$r = \frac{\sum(x_i - \bar{x})(y_i - \bar{y})}{(N-1)s_x s_y} = \frac{\sum Z_X Z_Y}{N}$$

- x_i and y_i are scores of individual i on the two variables.
- $\bar{x}$ and $\bar{y}$ are the sample means of the two variables.
- N is the sample size.
- s_x and s_y are the population estimated standard deviations of the two variables.
- Z_X and Z_Y are standardized scores, computed as $Z_X = (x_i - \bar{x})/s_x$.

The conceptual meaning of positive correlations is that individuals who score high on X (relative to the sample mean on X) also tend to score high on Y (relative to the sample mean on Y), whereas individuals who score low on X also tend to score low on Y. The conceptual meaning of negative correlations is that individuals who score high on one variable tend to score low on the other variable. The rightmost portion of Equation 5.1 provides an alternative representation that illustrates this conceptual meaning. Here, Z scores (standardized scores) represent high values as positive and low values as negative, so a preponderance of high scores with high scores (product of two positive) and low scores with low scores (product of two negative) yields a positive average cross product, whereas high scores with low scores (product of positive and negative) yield a negative average cross product.

You are probably already familiar with the correlation coefficient, but perhaps are not aware that it is an index of effect size. One interpretation of the correlation coefficient is in describing the proportion of variance shared between two variables with r^2. For instance, a correlation between two variables of $r = .50$ implies that 25% (i.e., $.50^2$) of the variance in these two variables overlaps. It can also be kept in mind that the correlation is standardized, such that correlations can range from 0 to ± 1. Given the widespread use of the correlation coefficient, many researchers have an intuitive interpretation of the magnitude of correlations that constitute small or large effect sizes. To aid this interpretation, you can consider Cohen's (1969) suggestions of $r = \pm .10$ representing small effect sizes, $r = \pm .30$ representing medium effect sizes, and $r = \pm .50$ representing large effect sizes. However, you should bear in mind that the typical magnitudes of correlations found likely differ across areas of study, and one should not be dogmatic in applying these guidelines to all research domains.

In conclusion, Pearson's r represents a useful, readily interpretable index of effect size for associations between two continuous variables. In many meta-analyses, however, r is transformed before effect sizes are combined or compared across studies (for contrasting views see Hall & Brannick, 2002; Hunter & Schmidt, 2004; Schmidt, Hunter, & Raju, 1988). Fisher's transformation of r, denoted as Z_r, is commonly used and shown in Equation 5.2.

Equation 5.2: Fisher's transformation of r

$$Z_r = \frac{1}{2}\ln\left(\frac{1+r}{1-r}\right)$$

- Z_r is Fisher's transformation of r.
- r is the correlation coefficient.

The reason that r is often transformed to Z_r in meta-analyses is because the distribution of sample r's around a given population ρ is skewed (except in sample sizes larger than those commonly seen in the social sciences), whereas a sample of Z_rs around a population Z_r is symmetric (for further details see Hedges & Olkin, 1985, pp. 226–228; Schulze, 2004, pp. 21–28).[2] This symmetry is desirable when combining and comparing effect sizes across studies. However, Z_r is less readily interpretable than r both because it is not bounded (i.e., it can have values greater than ±1.0) and simply because it is unfamiliar to many readers. Typical practice is to compute r for each study, convert these to Z_r for meta-analytic combination and comparison, and then convert results of the meta-analysis (e.g., mean effect size) back to r for reporting. Equation 5.3 converts Z_r back to r.

Equation 5.3: Converting Z_r back to r

$$r = \frac{e^{2Z_r} - 1}{e^{2Z_r} + 1}$$

- r is the correlation coefficient.
- Z_r is Fisher's transformation of r.

Although I defer further description until Chapter 8, I provide the equation for the standard error here, as you should enter these into your meta-analytic database during the coding process. The standard error of Z_r is shown in Equation 5.4.

Equation 5.4: Standard error of Z_r

$$SE_{Z_r} = \frac{1}{\sqrt{N-3}}$$

- N is the sample size of the study.

This equation reveals an obvious relation inherent to all standard errors: As sample size (N) increases, the denominator of Equation 5.4 increases and so the standard error decreases. A desirable feature of Z_r is that its standard error depends only on sample size (as I describe later, standard errors of some effects also depend on the effect sizes themselves).

5.1.3   Standardized Mean Difference

The family of indices of standardized mean difference represents the magnitude of difference between the means of two groups as a function of the groups' standard deviations. Therefore, you can consider these effect sizes to index the association between a dichotomous group variable and a continuous variable.

There are three commonly used indices of standardized mean difference (Grissom & Kim, 2005; Rosenthal, 1994).[3] These are Hedges's g, Cohen's d, and Glass's index (which I denote as g_{Glass}),[4] defined by Equations 5.5, 5.6, and 5.7, respectively:

Equations 5.5–5.7: Computing standardized mean differences

5.5: Hedges's g: $g = \dfrac{M_1 - M_2}{s_{pooled}}$

5.6: Cohen's d: $d = \dfrac{M_1 - M_2}{sd_{pooled}}$

5.7: Glass's index: $g_{Glass} = \dfrac{M_1 - M_2}{s_1}$

- M_1 and M_2 are the means of Groups 1 and 2.
- s_{pooled} is the pooled estimate of the population standard deviation.
- sd_{pooled} is the pooled sample standard deviation.
- s_1 is the estimate of the population standard deviation from Group 1 (control group).

These three equations are identical in consisting of a raw (unstandard-ized) difference of means as their numerators. The difference among them is in the standard deviations comprising the denominators (i.e., the standardiza-tion of the mean difference). The equation (5.5) for Hedges's g uses the pooled estimates[5] of the population standard deviations of each group, which is the familiar $s = \sqrt{(x_i - \bar{x})^2/(n-1)}$. The equation (5.6) for Cohen's d is similar but instead uses the pooled sample standard deviations, $sd = \sqrt{(x_i - \bar{x})^2/n}$. This sample standard deviation is a biased estimation of the population standard deviation, with the underestimation greater in smaller than larger samples. However, with even modestly large sample sizes, g and d will be virtually identical, so the two indices are not always distinguished.[6] Often, people describe both indices as Cohen's d, although it is preferable to use precise terminology in your own writing.[7]

The third index of standardized mean difference is g_{Glass} (sometimes denoted with Δ or g'), shown in Equation 5.7. Here the denominator consists of the (population estimate of the) standard deviation from one group. This index is often described in the context of therapy trials, in which the control group is said to provide a better index of standard deviation than the therapy group (for which the variability may have also changed in addition to the mean). One drawback to using g_{Glass} in meta-analysis is that it is necessary for the primary studies to report these standard deviations for each group; you can use results of significance tests (e.g., t-test values) to compute g or d, but not g_{Glass}. Reliance on only one group to estimate the standard deviation is also less precise if the standard deviations of the two populations are equal (i.e., homoscedastic; see Hedges & Olkin, 1985). For these reasons, meta-analysts less commonly rely on g_{Glass} relative to g or d. On the other hand, if the population standard deviations of the groups being compared differ (i.e., heteroscedasticity), then g or d may not be meaningful indexes of effect size, and computing these indexes from inferential statistics reported (e.g., t-tests, F-ratios) can be inappropriate. In these cases, reliance on g_{Glass} is likely more appropriate if adequate data are reported in most studies (i.e., means and standard deviations from both groups).[8] If it is plausible that heteroscedastic-ity might exist, you may wish to compare the standard deviations (see Shaf-fer, 1992) of two groups among the studies that report these data and then base the decision to use g_{Glass} versus g or d depending on whether or not (respectively) the groups have different variances.

Examining Equations 5.5–5.7 leads to two observations regarding the standardized mean difference as an effect size. First, these can be either posi-tive or negative depending on whether the mean of Group 1 or 2 is higher. This is a desirable quality when your meta-analysis includes studies with potentially conflicting directions of effects. You need to be consistent in considering a particular group (e.g., treatment vs. control, males vs. females) as Group 1 versus 2 across studies. Second, these standardized mean differences can take on any values. In other words, they are not bounded by ± 1.00 like the correlation coefficient r. Like r, a value of 0 implies no effect, but standardized mean differences can also have values greater than 1. For example, in the hypothetical example of three researchers given earlier in this chapter, all three researchers would have found $g = (3 - 5)/1 = -2.00$ if they considered effect sizes.

Although not as commonly used in primary research as r, these standardized mean differences are intuitively interpretable effect sizes. Knowing that the two groups differ by one-tenth, one-half, one, or two standard deviations (i.e., g or d = 0.10, 0.50, 1.00, or 2.00) provides readily interpretable information about the magnitude of this group difference.[9] As with r, Cohen (1969) provided suggestions for interpreting d (which can also be used with g or g_{Glass}), with $d = 0.20$ considered a small effect, $d = 0.50$ considered a medium effect, and $d = 0.80$ considered a large effect. Again, it is important to avoid becoming fixated on these guidelines, as they do not apply to all research situations or domains. It is also interesting to note that transformations between r and d (described in Section 5.5) reveal that the guidelines for interpreting each do not directly correspond.

As I did for the standard error of Z_r, I defer further discussion of weighting until Chapter 8. However, the formulas for the standard errors of the commonly used standardized mean difference, g, should be presented here:

Equation 5.8: Standard error of g

$$SE_g = \sqrt{\frac{n_1 + n_2}{n_1 n_2} + \frac{g^2}{2(n_1 + n_2)}} \approx \frac{4 + g^2}{N_{total \ (equal \ sample \ sizes)}}$$

- n_1 and n_2 are the sample sizes of Groups 1 and 2.
- N_{total} is the total sample size of the study (assuming equal sample size per group).

I draw your attention to two aspects of this equation. First, you should use the first equation when sample sizes of the two groups are known; the second part of the equation is a simplified version that can be used if group sizes are unknown, but it is reasonable to assume approximately equal group sizes. Second, you will notice that the standard errors of estimates of the standardized mean differences are dependent on the effect size estimates themselves (i.e., the effect size appears in the numerators of these equations). In other words, there is greater expected sampling error when the magnitudes (positive or negative) of standardized mean differences are large than when they are small. As discussed later (Chapter 8), this means that primary studies finding larger effect sizes will be weighted relatively less (given the same sample size) than primary studies with smaller effect sizes when results are meta-analytically combined.

Before ending this discussion of standardized mean difference effect sizes, it is worth considering a correction that you should use when primary study sample sizes are small (e.g., less than 20). Hedges and Olkin (1985) have shown that g is a biased estimate of the population standardized mean differences, with the magnitude of overestimation becoming nontrivial with small sample sizes. Therefore, if your meta-analysis includes studies with small samples, you should apply the following correction of g for small sample size (Hedges & Olkin, 1985, p. 79; Lipsey & Wilson, 2001, p. 49):

Equation 5.9: Small sample adjustment of g

$$g_{adjusted} = g - \frac{3g}{4(n_1 + n_2) - 9}$$

- n_1 and n_2 are the sample sizes of Groups 1 and 2.

5.1.4   Odds Ratio

The odds ratio, which I denote as o (OR is also commonly used), is a useful index of effect size of the contingency (i.e., association) between two dichotomous variables. Because many readers are likely less familiar with odds ratios than with correlations or standardized mean differences, I first describe why the odds ratio is advantageous as an index of association between two dichotomous variables.[10]

To understand the odds ratio, you must first consider the definition of odds. The odds of an event is defined as the probability of the event (e.g., of scoring affirmative on a dichotomous measure) divided by the probability of the alternative (e.g., of scoring negative on the measure), which can be expressed as odds = $p / (1 - p)$, where p equals the proportion in the sample (which is an unbiased estimate of population proportion, Π) having the characteristic or experiencing the event. For example, if you conceptualized children's aggression as a dichotomous variable of occurring versus not occurring, you could find the proportion of children who are aggressive (p) and estimate the odds of being aggressive by dividing by the proportion of children who are not aggressive $(1 - p)$. Note that you can also compute odds for nominal dichotomies; for example, you could consider biological sex in terms of the odds of being male versus female, or vice versa.

The next challenge is to consider how you can compare probabilities or odds across two groups. This comparison actually indexes an association between two dichotomous variables. For instance, you may wish to know whether boys or girls are more likely to be aggressive, and our answer would indicate whether, and how strongly, sex and aggression are associated. Several ways of indexing this association have been proposed (see Fleiss, 1994). The simplest way would be to compute the difference between probabilities in two groups, $p_1 - p_2$ (where p_1 and p_2 represent proportions in each group; in this example, these values would be the proportions of boys and girls who are aggressive). An alternative might be to compute the rate ratio (sometimes called risk ratio), which is equal to the proportion experiencing the event (or otherwise having the characteristics) in one group divided by the proportion experiencing it in the other, $RR = p_1 / p_2$. A problem with both of these indices, however, is that they are highly dependent on the rate of the phenomenon in the study (for details, see Fleiss, 1994). Therefore, studies in which different base rates of the phenomenon are found (e.g., one study finds a high prevalence of children are aggressive, whereas a second finds that very few are aggressive) will yield vastly different differences and risk ratios, even given the same underlying association between the variables. For this reason, these indices are not desirable effect sizes for meta-analysis.

The phi (ϕ) coefficient is another index of association between two dichotomous variables. It is estimated via the following formula (where ϕ is the estimated population association):

Equation 5.10: Computing ϕ

$$\hat{\phi} = \frac{n_{00}n_{11} - n_{01}n_{10}}{\sqrt{n_{0\bullet}n_{1\bullet}n_{\bullet 0}n_{\bullet 1}}}$$

- n_{00} is the number of participants who scored negative on dichotomous variables X and Y.
- n_{01} is the number of participants who scored negative on X and positive on Y.
- n_{10} is the number of participants who scored positive on X and negative on Y.
- n_{11} is the number of participants who scored positive on X and Y.
- $n_{0\bullet}$ and $n_{1\bullet}$ are the total number of participants who scored negative and positive (respectively) on X (i.e., the marginal sums).
- $n_{\bullet 0}$ and $n_{\bullet 1}$ are the total number of participants who scored negative and positive on Y.

Despite the lack of similarity in appearance between this equation and Equation 5.1, ϕ is identical to computing r between the two dichotomous variables, X and Y. In fact, if you are meta-analyzing a set of studies involving associations between two continuous variables in which a small number of studies artificially dichotomize the variables, it is appropriate to compute ϕ and interpret this as a correlation (you might also consider correcting for the attenuation of correlation due to artificial dichotomization; see Chapter 6).

However, ϕ (like the difference in proportions and rate ratio) also suffers from the limitation that it is influenced by the rates of the variables of interest (i.e., the marginal frequencies). Thus studies with different proportions of the dichotomies can yield different effect sizes given the same underlying association (Fleiss, 1994; Haddock, Rindskopf, & Shadish, 1998). To avoid this problem, the odds ratio (o) is preferred when one is interested in associations between two dichotomous variables. The odds ratio in the population is often represented as omega (ω) and is estimated from sample data using the following formula:

Equation 5.11: Computing odds ratio, o

$$o = \frac{n_{00} n_{11}}{n_{01} n_{10}}$$

- n_{00} is the number of participants who scored negative on X and Y.
- n_{01} is the number of participants who scored negative on X and positive on Y.
- n_{10} is the number of participants who scored positive on X and negative on Y.
- n_{11} is the number of participants who scored positive on X and Y.

Although this equation is not intuitive, it helps to consider that it represents the ratio of the odds of Y being positive when X is positive $[(n_{11}/n_{1\bullet}) / (n_{10}/n_{1\bullet})]$ divided by the odds of Y being positive when X is negative $[(n_{01}/n_{0\bullet}) / (n_{00}/n_{0\bullet})]$, algebraically rearranged.

The odds ratio is 1.0 when there is no association between the two dichotomous variables, ranges from 0 to 1 when the association is negative, and ranges from 1 to positive infinity when the association is positive. Given these ranges, the distribution of sample estimates around a population odds ratio is necessarily skewed. Therefore, it is common to use the natural log transformation of the odds ratio when performing meta-analytic combination or comparison, expressed as ln(o). The standard error of this logged odds ratio is easily computed (whereas computing the standard error of an untransformed odds ratio is more complex; see Fleiss, 1994), using the following equation:

Equation 5.12: Standard error of ln(o)

$$SE_{\ln(o)} = \sqrt{\frac{1}{n_{00}} + \frac{1}{n_{01}} + \frac{1}{n_{10}} + \frac{1}{n_{11}}}$$

- n_{00} is the number of participants who scored negative on X and Y.
- n_{01} is the number of participants who scored negative on X and positive on Y.
- n_{10} is the number of participants who scored positive on X and negative on Y.
- n_{11} is the number of participants who scored positive on X and Y.

5.2   COMPUTING r FROM COMMONLY REPORTED RESULTS

You can compute r from a wide range of results reported in primary studies. In this section, I describe how you can compute this effect size when primary studies report correlations, inferential statistics (i.e., t-tests or F-ratios from group comparisons, χ^2 from analyses of contingency tables), descriptive data, and probability levels of inferential tests. I then describe some more recent approaches to computing r from omnibus test results (e.g., ANOVAs with more than two groups). Table 5.1 summarizes the equations that I describe for computing r, as well as those for computing standardized mean differences (e.g., g) and odds ratios (o).

5.2.1   From Reported Correlations

In the ideal case, primary reports would always report the correlations between variables of interest. This reporting certainly makes our task much easier and reduces the chances of inaccuracies due to computational errors or rounding imprecision. When studies report correlation coefficients, these are often in a tabular form.

TABLE 5.1. Summary of Equations for Computing Effect Sizes from Results of Primary Studies

	Pearson r	Hedges's g	Odds ratio (o)
Definitional formula	$$\dfrac{\sum (x_i - \bar{x})(y_i - \bar{y})}{(N-1)s_x s_y}$$	$$\dfrac{M_1 - M_s}{s_{pooled}}$$	$$\dfrac{n_{00}\, n_{11}}{n_{01}\, n_{10}}$$
Independent t-test with unequal group sizes	$$\sqrt{\dfrac{t^2}{t^2 + df}}$$	$$\dfrac{t\sqrt{n_1 + n_2}}{\sqrt{n_1 n_2}}$$	N/A
Independent t-test with equal group sizes	"	$$\dfrac{2t}{\sqrt{N}}$$	N/A
Independent F-ratio with unequal group sizes	$$\sqrt{\dfrac{F_{(1,df)}}{F_{(1,df)} + df}}$$	$$\sqrt{\dfrac{F_{(1,df)}(n_1 + n_2)}{n_1 n_2}}$$	N/A
Independent F-ratio with equal group sizes	"	$$2\sqrt{\dfrac{F_{(1,df)}}{N}}$$	N/A
Dependent (repeated-measures) t-test	$$\sqrt{\dfrac{t^2_{dependent}}{t^2_{dependent} + df}}$$	$$\dfrac{t_{dependent}}{\sqrt{N}}$$	N/A
Dependent (repeated-measures) F-ratio	$$\sqrt{\dfrac{F_{repeated\,(1,df)}}{F_{repeated\,(1,df)} + df}}$$	$$\sqrt{\dfrac{F_{repeated\,(1,df)}}{N}}$$	N/A
2×2 (i.e., 1 df) contingency χ^2	$$\sqrt{\dfrac{\chi^2_{(1)}}{N}}$$	$$2\sqrt{\dfrac{\chi^2_{(1)}}{N - \chi^2_{(1)}}}$$	Reconstruct contingency table
Probability levels from significance tests	$$\dfrac{Z}{\sqrt{N}}$$	$$\dfrac{2Z}{\sqrt{N}}$$	Reconstruct contingency table

Although it may be tempting to simply identify this correlation within a table and consider the study coded, it is still important to read the text of the report carefully. This reading may reveal additional information not included in the table that may be of interest, such as other effect sizes or correlations separately for subgroups. The text (as well as notes to the tables) may also contain important information regarding the correlation itself, such as whether it was computed for only a subset of the data, was based on a smaller sample size due to pairwise deletion of missing data, or is actually a partial or semipartial correlation due to the control of some other variables.

Although you still need to carefully read studies reporting correlation coefficients, these are much easier to code accurately. Unfortunately, many studies do not report these correlations, so you must turn to other data to code effect sizes. The following can be considered options when studies fail to report actual correlations.

5.2.2 From Inferential Statistics

Primary studies will often report results of inferential tests without reporting actual effect sizes (despite recommendations against this practice). This situation can arise in several ways. First, the primary study may simply report the significance test of a correlation coefficient without reporting the coefficient itself; most commonly, studies report this significance as a t-test. Second, the authors of the primary study may have artificially dichotomized one of the variables to form two groups, then compared the groups using an independent sample t-test or an ANOVA reported as a one degree of freedom (in numerator) F-ratio. Artificially dichotomizing a continuous variable attenuates the effect size estimate (see Hunter & Schmidt, 1990; MacCallum et al., 2002), so you might not only compute r as described below but also consider correcting for this dichotomization using the approaches described in Chapter 6. A third situation is that the authors of the primary study dichotomized both variables involved in the correlation, then analyzed the data as contingency tables and reported a χ^2 statistic with one degree of freedom (a situation in which you would also want to consider corrections for dichotomization described in Chapter 6).

The following formulas allow us to compute correlations in each of these situations. When primary studies report a t-test value (either for the significance of the correlation or in comparing two groups), the following equation can be used (Rosenthal, 1991, 1994):

Equation 5.13: Computing *r* from *t*-test value

$$r = \sqrt{\frac{t^2}{t^2 + df}}$$

- *t* is the reported value of the *t*-test.
- *df* is the degrees of freedom of the test ($df = N - 2 = n_1 + n_2 - 2$).

Note that this equation provides either the positive or the negative square root, and it is important to take the value that reflects the direction of the effect in the same way across studies. For instance, if I am interested in the association between relational aggression and rejection, and compute *r* from a *t*-test comparing rejection in aggressive versus nonaggressive groups, I need to consider which group has a higher mean when computing the sign of *r* (positive if the aggressive group is more rejected and negative if the non-aggressive group is more rejected).

Primary studies might alternatively conduct an analysis of variance (ANOVA) between two groups. The resulting inferential statistic is an *F*-ratio with 1 degree of freedom in the numerator (i.e., $F_{(1,df)}$). Because this *F*-ratio is the same as the square of the parallel *t*-test, it follows that you can compute a correlation from this value with this equation:

Equation 5.14: Computing *r* from 1*df* *F*-ratio

$$r = \sqrt{\frac{F_{(1,df)}}{F_{(1,df)} + df}}$$

- *df* here is the degrees of freedom in the denominator (N – No. of groups), also referred to as the df_{error}.

As with the *t*-test, you must be sure to take either the positive or the negative square root, depending on the direction of mean differences.

Equations 5.13 and 5.14 are for use in converting tests of independent sample *t*-tests or *F*-ratios to *r*. An alternative, albeit less frequent, situation occurs when primary studies report these statistics for repeated-measures (a.k.a. within-subject) comparisons. For instance, a study might report levels of rejection for a sample of children who were aggressive at one time point but not at another. Some recommend against combining independent sample and repeated-measures results in the same meta-analysis (e.g., Lipsey & Wilson, 2001, state that these should be considered in separate meta-analyses). However, when you believe that the two methodologies address the same effect, you should also explore the moderator variable "type of methodology" (i.e., independent sample versus repeated measures). When computing r, you can use the same formulas (Equations 5.13 and 5.14) for either the independent sample or repeated-measures t-tests or F-ratios. This is not the case when computing standardize mean differences.

Primary studies might dichotomize both variables of interest and report results as a 2×2 contingency tables analysis with a reported χ^2 with 1 degree of freedom. The formula to convert this χ^2 into r is (Rosenthal, 1991, 1994):

Equation 5.15: Computing r from 1df chi-square (χ^2) value

$$r = \sqrt{\frac{\chi^2_{(1)}}{N}}$$

- N is the sample size.

As with computing r from the t-test or F-ratio, it is critical that you take the correct positive or negative square root. To determine which is correct, it is necessary to examine the reported contingency tables: A positive association is indicated if observed cell frequencies are higher than expected (under the null hypothesis of no association) in the major diagonal (if the contingency table is arranged with higher variable values as the lower row and right column), whereas a negative association is indicated if these frequencies are lower than expected. For example, you would consider aggression and rejection to be positively correlated if children who were aggressive and rejected and children who were not aggressive and not rejected occurred more frequently than expected.

5.2.3   From Descriptive Data

Often primary studies do not report all results that you are interested in as significance tests, but will instead provide descriptive data (often in a table) that can be used to compute r.

Primary studies may present descriptive data (means and standard deviations) for one variable based on two groups formed by dichotomizing the other variable (paralleling the case of reported t-tests or F-ratios described above). In this case, it is convenient to compute a standardized mean difference (using Equation 5.5), then transform these into r using Equation 5.26. As with computing r from t-tests and F-ratios, you should consider correcting for the attenuation of effect size due to the artificial dichotomization of the grouping variable (see Chapter 6).

It is also common for primary studies to report results in 2×2 contingency tables when both variables are dichotomized. In this situation, one can compute ϕ using Equation 5.8 and then interpret this ϕ as r. You should then correct this correlation for the dichotomization of both variables (see Chapter 6).

5.2.4 From Probability Levels of Significance Tests

In some situations, primary studies will not provide any other information other than results of significance tests. The first potential reason for this is simply inadequate reporting of results of a parametric inferential test (i.e., the authors report the statistical significance of a t-test, F-ratio, or χ^2 test of a contingency, but not the value itself). If the exact significance probability is reported for a t-test, two-group ANOVA, or 2×2 contingency analysis, one can simply find the corresponding t, F, or χ^2 value at that level of significance and then use Equation 5.13, 5.14, or 5.15 (respectively) to compute r.

A second reason why you might only have probabilities from a significance test is the primary study's report of probabilities from nontraditional inferential tests (e.g., nonparametric tests). In these situations in which other methods of computing effect size are unavailable, one can compute effect sizes from these significance tests. To do so, you first identify the exact probability, p, of the significance test and look up the standard normal deviate (i.e., Z) score corresponding to the given two-tailed p that is more extreme than this score (it is important to avoid confusion of this Z-score with the Fisher's transformation of r, denoted as Z_r, described earlier). For example, if a primary study reported a two-tailed (which is assumed if the study did not specify) $p = .032$, you would identify the one-tail p as .016 and the corresponding $Z = 2.14$. You can find this corresponding Z-score in tables in many introductory statistics books, although you need to be careful to correctly use these tables (e.g., many tables will list p as the proportion or percentage of the normal distribution between the mean and Z, so it is necessary to look up the Z associated with $0.50 - p$ or $50 - p$, for proportions and percentages, respectively). These tables are also often limited with very small values of p because they frequently do not list these extreme values with enough precision to accurately identify Z. For these reasons, it is often useful to find Z using a computer to identify the inverse of the standard normal cumulative distribution; you can use basic programs such as Microsoft Excel (using the "normsinv" function) to compute exact Z from p.

After computing Z, it is straightforward to compute the corresponding effect size given this value and sample size. The following equation converts Z to r for a given sample size N:

Equation 5.16: Computing *r* from *Z* value of statistical significance

$$r = \sqrt{\frac{Z^2}{N}}$$

- N is the sample size.

As when computing r from significance tests (t or F), it is important to take either the positive or negative square root from Equation 5.16 to represent the direction of the effect.

In all-too-many primary studies, researchers report a range of probability but not the exact probability (or associated t or F). For instance, it is not uncommon for primary studies to report that an association or comparison of groups was significant, and then only state that $p < .05$ (or some other value). In these instances, if the report provides no other information, you cannot compute an exact effect size. You then have two options. The option is to contact the study authors requesting more information, such as the actual effect size, inferential statistic (t or F), or exact significance probability (p). This option is certainly preferable in obtaining accurate effect sizes; unfortunately, it is not always possible because authors have retired, left academia, are unwilling to respond to your request, or for any other of numerous reasons. In these situations, the second option is to compute the best estimate of effect size given the reported results, which is typically the lower-bound effect size given the upper-bound probability. In other words, if a study reports that $p < .05$ (let's say for a sample size of $N = 100$), you can make the conservative assumption that $p = .05$ and then compute the associated Z (=1.96) and r (from Equation 5.16, $r = \sqrt{(1.96^2/100)} = .20$). It is important to recognize that this value of r is a lower-bound estimate of the actual effect size found in the primary study. To illustrate, if the true $p = .03$, $r = .22$, if $p = .01$, $r = .26$, if $p = .001$, $r = .33$, and if $p = .0001$, $r = .39$, and so on. In other words, if a study only reports that p from a test of significance test is less than some value (e.g.,

$p < .05$), you can only conclude that the effect size is greater than some value (e.g., $r > .20$). Common convention is to be conservative and conduct analyses using this minimum value.

A similar situation of inadequate reporting of data arises when primary studies report only that a particular effect is not statistically significant. In this situation, it is possible to compute a range of possible values of the effect size. To do so, you can compute the Z-score associated with the chosen a (assume $a = .05$ if not otherwise stated) and then apply Equation 5.15 to determine the maximum magnitude of r that would fail to yield a statistically significant effect given the sample size. You can conclude that the actual effect size of the study was greater than the negative r and less than the positive r. For example, if $N = 100$, you know that $-.20 < r < .20$. However, common convention is to take the smallest magnitude effect size—in other words, to assume $r = .00$.

Taking the minimal effect sizes from primary studies reporting only that the p is less than some value or that an effect size is not significant is clearly not an ideal situation. When this practice is used for a substantial number of studies, the result will be that the mean effect size will be biased toward smaller magnitude (and tests of heterogeneity and moderation also may be biased). The best way to avoid this problem would be to (1) carefully read primary studies for any other information from which effect sizes can be computed and (2) persistently seek further information from authors of the primary studies. If you are still forced to make lower-bound estimates of effect sizes for some studies, it is good practice to (1) report the percentage of included studies for which these lower-bound estimates were made; and (2) conduct a sensitivity analysis by comparing results obtained with these studies versus without them (e.g., conducting two sets of analyses including and excluding these studies, or else evaluating a dichotomous moderator variable identifying these studies; one hopes that the impact of these studies is trivial). Alternatively, if many effect sizes (or coded study characteristics) are missing, it might be useful to rely on more recent methods of missing data management (see Pigott, 2009). In Chapters 9 and 10, I describe a structural equation modeling (SEM) representation of meta-analysis that uses sophisticated full information maximum likelihood (FIML) methods of handling missing data (Cheung, 2008).

5.2.5 From Results of Omnibus Tests

The effect sizes of interest to meta-analysts typically involve associations between two variables. As illustrated earlier, this information is sometimes obtained from two group comparisons on a continuous variable (*t*-tests or *F*-ratios with 1 *df* in numerator). In contrast, some primary studies report results of omnibus tests involving differences among three or more groups (*F*-ratios with 2 or more numerator *df*s). Although exceptions might exist, these omnibus results are generally of little direct use within a meta-analysis. As Rosenthal (1991) poignantly stated, "only rarely is one interested in knowing … that somewhere in the thicket of *df* there lurk one or more meaningful answers to meaningful questions that we had not the foresight to ask of our data" (p. 13). In other words, you are more often interested in identifying the linear (or other specified form) relations between two variables or the magnitudes of differences between two specific groups, more so than whether a number of groups differ in some unspecified way. For example, you might be interested in the linear relation between aggression and rejection from results comparing rejection among children who are aggressive never, sometimes, or often, whereas the question of whether there are some differences among these groups (i.e., the omnibus ANOVA) is of less interest. Similarly, you might be interested in a specific comparison of psychosocial intervention versus control conditions from a three-level ANOVA of control, psychosocial intervention, and pharmacological intervention conditions. These situations require us to extract meaningful information (i.e., effect sizes) from less meaningful omnibus tests.

Techniques for computing effect sizes from these omnibus tests are described in detail by Rosenthal, Rosnow, and Rubin (2000), and I refer readers to this source for complete description. Here, I briefly outline the approach to computing *r* from descriptive data (i.e., means and standard deviations) or results of one-way ANOVAs with three or more groups. Procedures for managing repeated-measures and factorial ANOVAs are described in Rosenthal et al. (2000).

5.2.5.a   From Descriptive Statistics

The first situation I consider is when the primary study reports group sizes, means, and standard deviations from three or more groups. The first step in computing the linear association between the independent (i.e., grouping) and dependent (i.e., outcome) variables is to determine a set of contrast weights for the groups, denoted as λ_g for the g groups, such that these contrast weights sum to zero. The most typical choices of contrast weights are −1, 0, and 1 for three groups; −3, −1, 1, and 3 for four groups; and −2, −1, 0, 1, and 2 for five groups (contrast weights for more groups could be obtained through tables of orthogonal contrast codes, e.g., Cohen, Cohen, West, & Aiken, 2003, p. 215; Rosenthal et al., 2000, p. 153).[11]

After determining appropriate contrast weights (λ_g), the next step is to use these and the reported group sizes (n_g) and means (M_g) to compute the average squared deviation due to the linear contrast, $MS_{contrast}$:

Equation 5.17: Computing linear contrast ($MS_{contrast}$) from descriptive data

$$MS_{contrast} = \frac{\left(\sum \lambda_g M_g\right)^2}{\sum \dfrac{\lambda_g^2}{n_g}}$$

- λ_g are the contrast weights (see text).
- M_g are the group means.
- n_g are the group sample sizes.

Given this squared deviation due to the contrast, one can then evaluate the statistical significance of the linear contrast, if this is of interest. This statistical significance can be evaluated as the $F_{contrast}$, which has 1 df in the numerator and df_{error}, or $\Sigma(n_g - 1)$, in the denominator. Regardless of whether you are interested in the significance of this contrast, the next step is to compute $F_{contrast}$ as $MS_{contrast}$ divided by MS_{within}, where MS_{within} might be reported in the primary study or can be computed as the group-size weighted average of within-group variances, $\Sigma(n_g s_g^2)/\Sigma n_g$.

From this $F_{contrast}$, the final step to computing an effect size from this three or more group situation is to compute r (called $r_{effect\ size}$ by Rosenthal et al., 2000) using the following equation:

Equation 5.18: Computing r from $F_{contrast}$

$$r = \sqrt{\frac{F_{contrast}}{F_{between}\left(df_{between}\right) + df_{within}}}$$

- $F_{between}$ is the original omnibus test of group differences.
- $df_{between}$ is the degrees of freedom of the original omnibus test of group differences.

Because $F_{between}$ and $df_{between}$ are from the original omnibus test of group differences, primary studies typically report these values. If a study does not provide these values, you can easily compute these values from the reported sample sizes, means, and standard deviations.[12]

5.2.5.b   From df > 2 F-Ratio

Another common method of reporting results of comparisons of three or more groups in primary studies is to report the omnibus F-ratio. To compute an effect size from this F-ratio, the primary study must also report the means (but standard deviations are not necessary) of three or more groups. If the primary study does not report the means of the groups, it is not possible to compute an effect size indexing the association between the independent (grouping) and dependent (outcome) variables (note that simply using the formula for the two group ANOVAs, Equation 5.14, is not appropriate).

Computing r from reported means and an omnibus F-ratio is similar to the computation from means, standard deviations, and sample sizes described in the previous section. Specifically, you still (1) determine appropriate contrast weights (λ_g); (2) compute $MS_{contrast}$ using Equation 5.17; and (3) compute $F_{contrast}$ for use in subsequent computations as described earlier. The difference here is that you do not use the reported group standard deviations to compute MS_{within} (which is used to compute $F_{contrast}$). If this value is reported in an ANOVA table, you can easily obtain this value. Otherwise, you must compute this MS_{within} from the reported omnibus F-ratio, based on the fact that $MS_{within} = MS_{between}/F$. Although $MS_{between}$ will typically not be reported if an ANOVA table is not provided, this can be computed from the reported means from the G groups: $MS_{between} = \Sigma(M_g - GM)^2/G - 1$.

You then follow the same steps described in the previous section: (1) computing $F_{contrast}$ as $MS_{contrast}/MS_{within}$; (2) computing r using Equation 5.18. Thus, obtaining r from data where there are three or more groups is similar when studies report either descriptive statistics or results of an omnibus one-way ANOVA.

5.2.5.c   Final Words Regarding Computing r from Omnibus Tests

In this section, I provide only a brief overview of computing r from the results of omnibus tests reported in primary studies. Although the simple situations I have described will likely help in most situations, others that I have not described here may emerge. My recommendation to readers who commonly encounter these situations is to first consult the book by Rosenthal et al. (2000), which provides further details on computing r in situations I have described as well as others, including factorial designs and repeated-measures ANOVAs. These authors also describe alternative assignment of contrast weights that may be of interest.

If you encounter situations not described here or in Rosenthal et al. (2000), several options are available to you. First, I recommend consulting the literature for more recent treatments that might apply to this situation.

Computing effect sizes such as *r* from omnibus test results has only recently gained attention (due largely to the Rosenthal et al. book), and it is likely that more will be written on this topic. Second, you might be able to apply the logic of this approach to develop reasonable ways of computing a meaningful effect size from omnibus results. It seems safe to suggest that if you can (1) identify the amount of variance due to the desired effect (e.g., a linear relation between the independent and dependent variables) and (2) determine a direction of effect, then it is possible to compute an *r* that indexes this effect. A third option, of course, is to request further information from the authors of the primary studies. Although this approach might deprive you of the joys of discovering ingenious ways of computing an effect size, you should remember that this is usually the most straightforward and most accurate way of obtaining the desired information.

5.3 COMPUTING *g* FROM COMMONLY REPORTED RESULTS

As when computing *r*, you can compute standardized mean differences from a wide range of commonly reported information. Although I have presented three different types of standardized mean differences (*g*, *d*, and g_{Glass}), I describe only the computation of *g* in detail in the following. If you are interested in using g_{Glass} as the effect size in one's meta-analysis, the primary studies must report means and standard deviations for both groups; if this is the case, then you can simply compute g_{Glass} using Equation 5.7. If you prefer *d* to *g* (although, again, they are virtually identical with larger sample sizes), then you can use the methods described in this section to compute *g* and then transform *g* into *d* using the following equation with no loss of precision:

Equation 5.19: Computing *d* from *g*

$$d = g\sqrt{\frac{N}{df}}$$

- *N* is the sample size.
- *df* is the degrees of freedom.

5.3.1 From Descriptive Data

The most straightforward situation arises when the primary study reports means and standard deviations for both groups of interest. In this situation, you simply compute g directly from this information using Equation 5.5. For convenience, this equation is

$$g = \frac{M_1 - M_s}{s_{\text{pooled}}}$$ (Equation 5.5, reproduced)

5.3.2 From Inferential Tests

5.3.2.a Continuous Dependent Variables

As when computing r, it is possible to compute g from the result of independent sample t-tests or 1 df F-ratios (see below for dependent sample or repeated-measures tests). For the independent sample t-test, the relevant equation is:

Equation 5.20: Computing g from independent sample t-test

$$g = \frac{t\sqrt{n_1 + n_2}}{\sqrt{n_1 n_2}} \approx \frac{2t}{\sqrt{N}}$$

- t is the positive or negative value of the t-test.
- n_1 and n_2 are the sample sizes for Groups 1 and 2.
- N is the total sample size.

When these two group sizes are equal, this equation simplifies to the ratio on the right. In instances where the primary studies report the results of the t-test but not the sample sizes for each group (but instead only an overall sample size), this simplification can be used if the group sizes can be assumed to be approximately equal. Figure 5.1 (see similar demonstration in Rosenthal, 1991) shows the percentage underestimation in g when one incorrectly assumes that group sizes are equal. The x-axis shows the percentage of cases in the larger group, beginning at 50% (equal group sizes) to the left and moving to larger discrepancies in group size as one moves right. It can be seen that the amount of underestimation is trivial when groups are similar in size, reaching 5% underestimation at around a 66:34 (roughly 2:1) discrepancy in group sizes. The magnitude of this underestimation increases rapidly after this point, becoming what I consider unacceptably large when group sizes reach 3:1 or 4:1 (i.e., when 75–80% of the sample is in one of the two groups). If this unequal distribution is expectable (which might be determined by considering the magnitudes of group sizes in other studies reporting sample sizes by group), then it is probably preferable to use r as an

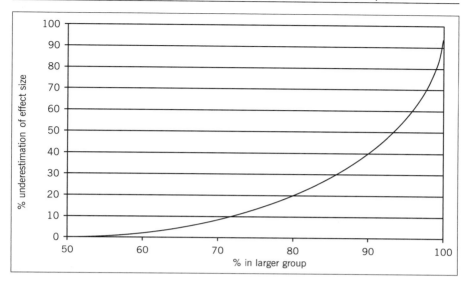

FIGURE 5.1. Underestimation of standardized mean difference when group sizes are assumed equal.

index of effect size given that it is not influenced by the magnitude of this unequal distribution.

As expected given the parallel between independent sample t-tests and two group ANOVAs, it is also possible to compute standardized mean differences from F-ratios with 1 df in the numerator using the following formulas:

Equation 5.21: Computing g from between-group F-ratio

$$g = \sqrt{\frac{F_{(1,df)}(n_1 + n_2)}{n_1 n_2}} \approx 2\sqrt{\frac{F_{(1,df)}}{N}}$$

- $F(1,df)$ is the F-ratio from a 1 df numerator (i.e., 2 group) ANOVA.
- df is the df in the denominator (i.e., error df).
- n_1 and n_2 are the sample sizes for Groups 1 and 2.
- N is the total sample size.

Because F-ratios are always positive, it is important that you carefully consider the direction of group differences and take the positive or negative square root of Equation 5.21, depending on whether Group 1 or 2 (respectively) has the higher mean.

Although computing r was equivalent whether the results were from independent (between-group) or dependent (repeated-measures) results, this is not the case when computing g. Therefore, it is critically important that you be sure whether the reported t or F values are from independent or dependent tests. If the results are from dependent, or repeated measures, tests, the following equations should be used:

Equation 5.22: Computing g from dependent (repeated-measures) tests

$$g = \frac{t_{dependent}}{\sqrt{N}} = \sqrt{\frac{F_{repeated\,(1,df)}}{N}}$$

- $t_{dependent}$ is the positive or negative value of the t-test for dependent means.
- $F_{repeated(1,df)}$ is the F-ratio from a repeated-measures ANOVA.
- N is the sample size.

Unlike Equations 5.20 and 5.21 for the independent sample situation in which there were separate formulas for unequal and equal group sizes, the dependent (repeated-measures) situation to which Equation 5.22 applies contains only an overall N, the size of the sample over time (or other type of repeated measures). It also merits mention that the same t or F values yield a standardized mean difference that is twice as large in the independent sample (between groups) than in the dependent (repeated-measures) situations, so a mistake in using the wrong formulas would have a dramatic impact on computed standardized mean effect size.

5.3.2.b   Dichotomous Dependent Variables

Primary studies might also compare two groups on the percentage or proportion of participants scoring affirmative on a dichotomous variable. This may come about either because the primary study authors artificially dichotomized the variable or because the variable truly is dichotomous. If the latter case is consistent across all studies, then you might instead choose the odds ratio as a preferred index of effect size (i.e., associations between a dichotomous grouping variable and dichotomous measure). However, there are also instances in which the standardized mean difference is appropriate in this situation, such as when the primary study authors artificially dichotomized the variable on which the groups are compared (in which case corrections for this artificial dichotomization might be considered; see Chapter 6), or when you wish to consider the dichotomous variable of the study in relation to a continuous variable of other studies (in which case it might be useful to consider moderation across studies using continuous versus dichotomous variables; see Chapter 10).

When two groups are compared on a dichotomous or dichotomized variable, you need to identify the 1 df χ^2 and direction of effect (i.e., which group has a higher percentage or proportion). This information might be reported directly, or you may need to construct a 2 × 2 contingency table from reported results. For instance, a primary study might report that 50% of Group 1 had the dichotomous characteristic, whereas 30% of Group 2 had this characteristic; you would use this information (and sample size) to compute a contingency table and χ^2. You then convert this χ^2 to g using the following equation:

Equation 5.23: Computing g from χ^2 of 2 × 2 contingency table

$$g = 2\sqrt{\frac{\chi^2_{(1)}}{N-\chi^2_{(1)}}}$$

- N is the sample size.

As with computing g from the F-ratio, it is critical that you take the correct positive or negative square root. The positive square root is taken if Group 1 has the higher percentage or proportion with the dichotomous characteristic, whereas the negative square root is taken if Group 2 more commonly has the characteristic.

5.3.3   From Probability Levels of Significance Tests

The practices of computing g from exact significance levels, ranges of significance (e.g., $p < .05$), and reports that a difference was not significant follow the practices of computing r described earlier. Specifically, you determine the Z for the exact probability (e.g., $Z = 2.14$ from $p = .032$), the lower-bound Z when a result is reported significant at a certain level (e.g., $Z = 1.96$ for $p < .05$), or the maximum Z when a result is reported as not significant (e.g., maximum $Z = \pm1.96$, although the conservative choice in this option is to assume $g = 0$), as described in Section 5.2.4. You then use the following equation to estimate the standardized mean difference from this Z: [13]

**Equation 5.24: Computing *g* from *Z* value
of statistical significance**

$$g = \frac{2Z}{\sqrt{N}}$$

- *N* is the sample size.

5.3.4   From Omnibus Test Results

Although you might consider the grouping variable to most appropriately consist of two levels (i.e., two groups), there is no assurance that primary study authors have all reached the same conclusion. Instead, the groups of interest may be subdivided within primary studies, resulting in omnibus comparisons among three or more groups. For example, you might be interested in comparing aggressive versus nonaggressive children, but a primary study might further subdivide aggressive children into those who are aggressive rarely versus frequently. Another example might be if you wish to compare a certain type of psychotherapy versus control, but the primary study reports results for three groups: control, treatment by graduate students, and treatment by doctoral-level practitioners. Studies might also report omnibus tests involving groups that are not of interest to a particular meta-analysis. For instance, a meta-analysis comparing psychotherapy versus control might include a study reporting outcomes for three different groups: control, psychotherapy, and medication. In each of these cases, it is necessary to reorganize the results of the study to fit the two-group comparison of interest. Next, I describe ways of doing so from reported descriptive statistics and *F*-ratios with *df* > 2.

5.3.4.a   From Descriptive Statistics

The simplest case is when studies report sample sizes, means, and standard deviations from three or more groups. Here, you can either select specific groups or else aggregate groups to derive data from the two groups of interest.

When you are interested in only two groups from among those reported in a study (e.g., interested in control and psychotherapy from a study reporting control, psychotherapy, and medication), it is straightforward to use the reported means and standard deviations from those two groups to compute

g (using Equation 5.5). When doing so, it is important to code the sample size, N (used to compute the standard error of the effect size for subsequent weighting), as the combined sample sizes from the two groups of interest ($N = n_1 + n_2$) rather than the total sample size from the study.

When the primary study has subdivided one or both groups of interest, you must combine data from these subgroups to compute descriptive data for the groups of interest. For example, when comparing psychotherapy versus control from a study reporting data from two psychotherapy groups (e.g., those being treated by graduate students versus doctoral-level practitioners), you would need to combine data from these two psychotherapy groups before computing g. Combining the subgroup sample sizes is straightforward, n_{group} = $n_{subgroup1} + n_{subgroup2}$. The group mean is also reasonably straightforward, as it is computed as the weighted (by subgroup size) average of the subgroup means, $M_{group} = (n_{subgroup1}M_{subgroup1} + n_{subgroup2}M_{subgroup2}) / (n_{subgroup1} + n_{subgroup2})$.

The combined group standard deviation is somewhat more complex to obtain in that it consists of two components: (1) variance within each of the groups you wish to combine and (2) variance between the groups you wish to combine. Therefore, to obtain a combined group standard deviation, you must compute sums of squared deviations (SSs) within and between groups. The SS_{within} is computed for each group g as $s_g^2*(n_g - 1)$, and then these are summed across groups. The $SS_{between}$ is computed as $\Sigma [(M_g - GM)^2 * n_g]$, (where GM is the grand mean of these two groups), summed over groups. You add the two SSs (i.e., SS_{within} and $SS_{between}$) to produce the total sum of squared deviations, SS_{total}. The (population estimated of the) variance for this combined group is then computed as $SS_{total} / (n_{combined} - 1)$ and the (population estimate of the) standard deviation ($s_{combined}$).

Combining more than two subgroups to form a group of interest is straightforward (e.g., averaging three or more groups). It may also be necessary to combine subgroups to form both groups of interest (e.g., multiple treatment and multiple control groups). Once you obtain the descriptive data (sample sizes, means, and standard deviations) for the groups of interest, you use Equation 5.5 to compute g.

5.3.4.b   From df > 2 F-Ratio

As when computing r, it is also possible to compute g from omnibus ANOVAs if the primary study reports the F-ratio and means from each group. Here, you follow the general procedures of selecting or aggregating subgroups as described in the previous section. Doing this for the sample sizes and reported means is identical to the approach described in Section 5.3.4.a. The only difference in this situation is that you must infer the within-group standard deviations from the results of the ANOVA, as these are not reported (if they are, then you can simply use the procedures described in the previous subsection).

Because omnibus ANOVAs typically assume equal variance across groups, this search is in fact for one standard deviation common across groups (equivalent to a pooled standard deviation). The MS_{within} of the ANOVA represents this common group variance, so the square root of this MS_{within} represents the standard deviation of groups, which are then used as described in the previous subsection (i.e., you must still combine the SSs within and between groups to be combined). If the primary study reports an ANOVA table, you can readily find this MS_{within} within the table. If the primary study does not report this MS_{within}, it is possible to compute this value from the reported means and F-ratio. As described earlier, you first compute the omnibus $MS_{between\text{-}omnibus} = \Sigma(M_g - GM)^2 / G - 1$ across *all* groups comprising the reported ANOVA (i.e., this $MS_{between\text{-}omnibus}$ represents the amount of variance between all groups in the omnibus comparison), and then compute $MS_{within} = MS_{between}/F$. As mentioned, you then take the square root of MS_{within} to obtain s_{pooled}, used in computing the SS_{within} of the group to be combined. It is important to note that you should add the $SS_{between}$ of *just the groups to be combined* in computing the SS_{total} for the combined groups, which is used to estimate the combined group standard deviation.

5.4 COMPUTING o FROM COMMONLY REPORTED RESULTS

When you are interested in computing the odds ratio (o, sometimes denoted by OR), or the association between two dichotomous variables, the range of typically reported data is usually more limited than that described in the previous two sections. In this section, I describe computing an odds ratio from three common situations: studies reporting descriptive data such as proportions or percentages in two groups, inferential tests (i.e., χ^2 statistic) from 2 × 2 contingency tables, and studies reporting only the significance of such a test. I also describe the less common situations of deriving odds ratios from research reports involving larger (i.e., $df > 1$) contingency tables or those analyzing continuous variables.

5.4.1 From Descriptive Data

The most straightforward way of computing o is by constructing a 2×2 contingency table from descriptive data reported in primary studies. Many studies will report the actual cell frequencies, making it simple to construct this table. Many studies will alternatively report an overall sample size, the sample sizes of groups from one of the two variables, and some form of prevalence of the second variable by these two groups. For example, a study might report that 50 out of 300 children are aggressive and that 40% of the aggressive children are rejected, whereas 10% of the nonaggressive children are rejected. This information could be used to identify the number of nonaggressive nonrejected children, $n_{00} = (300 - 50)(1 - 0.10) = 225$; the number of nonaggressive rejected children, $n_{01} = (300 - 50)(0.10) = 25$; the number of aggressive nonrejected children, $n_{10} = (50)(1 - 0.40) = 30$; and the number of aggressive rejected children, $n_{11} = (50)(0.40) = 20$.

After constructing this 2×2 contingency table, you can simply compute o from this information using Equation 5.11, which I reproduce as follows.

$$o = \frac{n_{00}n_{11}}{n_{01}n_{10}} \qquad \text{(Equation 5.11, reproduced)}$$

For example, given the cell frequencies of aggression and rejection described above, you could compute $o = (225*20)/(25*30) = 6.0$.

Special consideration is needed if one or more cells of this contingency table are 0. In this situation, it is advisable to add 0.5 to each of the cell frequencies (Fleiss, 1994). This solution tends to produce a downward bias in estimating o (Lipsey & Wilson, 2001, p. 54). Although the impact of having a small number of studies for which this is the case is likely negligible, this bias is problematic if many studies in a meta-analysis have small sample sizes (and 0 frequency cells). Meta-analysts for whom this is the case should consult Fleiss (1994) for alternative methods of analysis.

5.4.2 From Inferential Tests

Instead of fully reporting the contingency table (or descriptive data sufficient to reconstruct it), some studies might report a test of significance of this contingency, the χ^2 statistic. In this situation, it is important to ensure that the reported value is from a 1 df χ^2, meaning that it is from a 2×2 contingency table (see Section 5.4.4 for use of larger contingency tables). The χ^2 statistic by itself is not sufficient to compute o, however; it is also necessary to know the sample size and marginal proportions of this contingency. As described by Lipsey and Wilson (2001, pp. 197–198), values of the χ^2 statistic, overall sample size (N), and marginal proportions ($p_{0\bullet}$ and $p_{1\bullet}$ for the row, or variable 1, marginal proportions; $p_{\bullet 0}$ and $p_{\bullet 1}$ for the column, or variable 2, marginal proportions) allow you to identify the cell frequencies of a 2×2 contingency table. Specifically, you compute the frequency of the first cell using the following equation:

Equation 5.25: Computing cell frequencies to reproduce a contingency table

$$n_{00} = N\left(p_{0\bullet}.p_{\bullet 0} + \sqrt{\frac{\chi^2\, p_{0\bullet}.p_{1\bullet}.p_{\bullet 0}p_{\bullet 1}}{N}} \right)$$

- N is the overall sample size.
- χ^2 is the significance test of a 2×2 contingency.
- $p_{0\bullet}$ and $p_{1\bullet}$ are the row, or variable 1, marginal proportions.
- $p_{\bullet 0}$ and $p_{\bullet 1}$ are the column, or variable 2, marginal proportions.

It is important to use the correct positive or negative square root given the presence of a positive or negative (respectively) association between the two dichotomous variables.

Then you compute the remaining cells of the 2×2 contingency table using the following: $n_{01} = p_{0\bullet}N - n_{00}$; $n_{10} = p_{\bullet 0}N - n_{00}$; and $n_{01} = N - n_{00} - n_{01} - n_{10}$. You then use this contingency table to compute o as described in the previous section (i.e., Equation 5.11).

5.4.3   From Probability Levels of Significance Tests

Given the possibility of computing o from values of χ^2 (along with N and marginal proportions), it follows that you can compute o from levels of statistical significance of 2×2 contingency analyses. Given an exact significance level (p) and sample size (N), you can identify the corresponding χ^2 by either consulting a table of χ^2 values (at 1 df) or using a simple computer program like Excel ("chiinv" function).

Similarly, you can use a range of significance (e.g., $p < .05$) and sample size to compute a lower-bound value of χ^2 (i.e., assuming $p = .05$) and corresponding o. Given only a reported nonsignificant 2×2 contingency, you could compute the minimum (i.e., < 1.0) and maximum (i.e., > 1.0) values of

o from value of χ^2 at the type I error rate (e.g., $p = .05$), but a more conservative approach would be to assume $o = 1$ (null value for o). In both of these situations, however, it would be preferable to request more information (o or a contingency table) from the primary study authors.

5.4.4   From Omnibus Results

Some primary studies might report more than two levels of one or both variables that you consider dichotomous. For example, if you are considering associations between dichotomous aggression and dichotomous rejection statuses, you might encounter a primary study presenting results within a 3 (nonaggressive, somewhat aggressive, frequently aggressive) × 3 (nonrejected, modestly rejected, highly rejected) contingency table.

If these larger contingency tables are common among primary studies, this might be cause for you to reconsider whether the variables of interest are truly dichotomous. However, if you are convinced that dichotomous representations of both variables are best, then the challenge becomes one of deciding which of the distinctions made in the primary study are important or real and which are artificial. Given the example of the 3 × 3 aggression by rejection table, I might decide that the distinction between frequent aggression versus other levels (never and sometimes) is important, and that the distinction between nonrejected and the other levels (modestly and highly rejected) is important.

After deciding which distinctions are important and which are not, you then simply sum the frequencies within collapsed groups. Given the aggression and rejection example, I would combine frequencies of the never-aggressive nonrejected and the sometimes-aggressive nonrejected children into one group (n_{00}); combine the frequencies of never-aggressive modestly rejected, sometimes-aggressive modestly rejected, never-aggressive highly rejected, and sometimes-aggressive highly rejected children into another group (n_{01}); and so on. You could then use this reduced table to compute o as described above (Section 5.4.1).

5.4.5   From Results Involving Continuous Variables

If you find that many studies represent one of the variables under consideration as continuous, it is important to reconsider whether your conceptualization of dichotomous variables is appropriate. Presumably the representation of variables in studies as continuous suggests that there is an underlying continuity of that variable, in which case you should not artificially dichotomize this continuum (even if many studies in the meta-analysis do). You would then use a standardized mean difference (e.g., g) to represent the association between the dichotomous and continuous variable.

If you are convinced that the association of interest is between two truly dichotomous variables and that a primary study was simply misinformed in analyzing a variable as continuous, then an approximate transformation can be made. You would first compute g from this study, and then estimate $o = e^{\frac{g\pi}{\sqrt{3}}}$. This equation is derived from the logit method of transforming log odds ratios to standardized mean differences (Haddock et al., 1998; Hasselblad & Hedges, 1995; for a comparison of this and other methods of transforming o to standardized mean difference, see Sánchez-Meca, Marín-Martinez, & Chacón-Moscoso, 2003) and is not typically used to transform g to o. Again, I stress that the first consideration if you encounter continuous representations of dichotomies in primary studies is to rethink your decision to conceptualize a variable as dichotomous.

5.5 COMPARISONS AMONG r, g, AND o

I have emphasized the importance of basing the decision to rely on r, g, or o on conceptualizations of the association involving two continuous variables, a dichotomous and a continuous variable, or two dichotomous variables, respectively. At the same time, it can be useful to understand that you can compute values of one effect size from values of another effect size. For example, r and g can be computed from one another using the following formulas:

Equations 5.26 and 5.27: Converting between r and g

5.26: computing r from g: $r = \sqrt{\dfrac{g^2 n_1 n_2}{g^2 n_1 n_2 + (n_1 + n_2)df}}$

5.27: computing g from r: $g = \left(\dfrac{r}{\sqrt{1 - r^2}}\right)\sqrt{\dfrac{df(n_1 + n_2)}{n_1 n_2}}$

- n_1 and n_2 are the sample sizes of Groups 1 and 2.

Similarly, g and o can be computed from one another using the following equations:

Equations 5.28 and 5.29: Converting between g and o

5.28: computing g from o: $g = \dfrac{\sqrt{3}}{\pi}\ln(o)$

5.29: computing o from g: $o = e^{\frac{g\pi}{\sqrt{3}}}$

- p is the numeric value ≈ 3.14.

Finally, you can transform from o to r by reconstructing the contingency table (if sufficient information is provided), through intermediate transformations to g, or through one of several approximations of the tetrachoric correlation (see Bonett, 2007). An intermediate transformation to g or algebraic rearrangement of the tetrachoric correlation approximations also allows you to transform from r to o.

This mathematical interchangeability among effect sizes has led to arguments that one type of effect size is preferable to another. For example, Rosenthal (1991) has expressed preference for r over d (and presumably other standardized mean differences, including g) based on four features. First, comparisons of Equations 5.13 and 5.14 for r versus 5.20 and 5.21 for g reveal that it is possible to compute r accurately from only the inferential test value and degrees of freedom, whereas computing g requires knowing the group sample sizes or else approximating this value by assuming that the group sizes are equal. To the extent that primary studies do not report group sizes and it is reasonable to expect marked differences in group sizes, r is preferable to d. A second, smaller, argument for preferring r to g is that you use the same equations to compute r from independent sample versus repeated-measures inferential tests, whereas different formulas are necessary when computing g from these tests (see Equations 5.20 and 5.21 vs. 5.22). This should not pose too much difficulty for the competent meta-analyst, but consideration of simplicity is not trivial. A third advantage of r over standardized mean differences, according to Rosenthal (1991), is in ease of interpretation. Whether r or standardized mean differences (e.g., g) are more intuitive to readers is debatable and currently is a matter of opinion rather than careful study. It probably is the case that most scientists have more exposure to *r* than to *g* or *d*, but this does not mean that they cannot readily grasp the meaning of the standardized mean difference. The final, and perhaps most convincing, argument for Rosenthal's (1991) preference is that *r* can be used whenever *d* can (e.g., in describing an association between a dichotomous variable and a continuous variable), but it makes less sense to use *g* in many situations where *r* could be used (e.g., in describing an association between two continuous variables).

Arguments have also been put forth for preferring *o* to standardized mean differences (*g* or *d*) or *r* when both variables are truly dichotomous. The magnitudes of *r* (typically denoted with ϕ) or standardized mean differences (*g* or *d*) that you can compute from a 2×2 contingency table depend on the marginal frequencies of the dichotomies. This dependence leads to attenuated effect sizes as well as extraneous heterogeneity among studies when these effect size indices are used with dichotomous data (Fleiss, 1994; Haddock et al., 1998). This limitation is not present for *o*, leading many to argue that it is the preferred effect size to index associations between dichotomous data.

I do not believe that any type of effect size index (i.e., *r*, *g*, or *o*) is inherently preferable to another. What is far more important is that you select the effect size that matches your conceptualization of the variables under consideration. Linear associations between two variables that are naturally continuous should be represented with *r*. Associations between a dichotomous variable (e.g., group) and a continuous variable can be represented with a standardized mean difference (e.g., *g*) or *r*, with a standardized mean difference probably more naturally representing this type of association.[14] Associations between two natural dichotomies are best represented with *o*.

If you wish to compare multiple levels of variables in the same meta-analysis, I recommend using the effect size index representing the more continuous nature for both. For example, associations of a continuous variable (e.g., aggressive) with a set of correlates that includes a mixture of continuous and dichotomous variables (e.g., a continuous rejection variable and a dichotomous variable of being classified as rejected) could be well represented with the correlation coefficient, *r* (Rosenthal, 1991). Similarly, associations of a dichotomous variable (e.g., biological sex) with a set containing a combination of continuous (e.g., rejection) and dichotomous (e.g., rejection classification) variables could be represented with a standardized mean difference such as *g* (Sánchez-Meca et al., 2003). In both cases, it would be important to evaluate moderation by the type (i.e., continuous versus dichotomous) of correlate.

5.6 PRACTICAL MATTERS: **USING EFFECT SIZE CALCULATORS AND META-ANALYSIS PROGRAMS**

As I described in Chapter 1, several computer programs are designed to aid in meta-analysis, some of which are available for free and others for purchase. All meta-analytic programs perform two major steps: effect size calculation and effect size combination. Effect size combination (as well as comparison) is the process of aggregating results across studies, the topic of Chapters 8–10 later in this book. Effect size calculation is the process of taking results from each study and converting these into a common effect size, the focus of this chapter.

Relying on an effect size calculator found in meta-analysis programs to compute effect sizes (as well as to combine results across studies) can be a time-saving tool. However, I discourage beginning meta-analysts from relying on them. All of the calculations described in this chapter can be performed with a simple hand calculator or spreadsheet program (e.g., Excel), and the meta-analytic combination and comparison I describe later in this book can be performed using these spreadsheets or simple statistical analysis software (e.g., SAS or SPSS). In other words, I see little need for specific software when conducting a meta-analysis.

Having said both that these programs can save time but that I recommend not using them initially, you may wonder if I think that you have too much time on your hands. I do not. Instead, my concern is that these programs make it easy for beginning meta-analysts who are less familiar with the calculations to make mistakes. The value of struggling with the equations in this chapter is that doing so forces you to think about what the values mean and where to find them within the research report. The danger of using an effect size calculator is of mindless use, in which users put in whatever values they can find in the report that look similar to what the program asks for.

At the same time, I do not entirely discourage the use of these meta-analysis programs. They can be of great use in reducing the burden of tedious calculations *after you understand these calculations*. In other words, if you are just beginning to perform meta-analyses, I encourage you to compute some effect sizes by hand (i.e., using a calculator or spreadsheet program) as well as using one of these programs. Inconsistencies should alert you that either your hand calculations are inaccurate or that you are not providing the correct information to the program (or that the program is inaccurate, though this should be uncommon with the more commonly used programs). *After you have confirmed that you obtain identical results by hand and the program, then you can decide if using the program is worthwhile. I offer this same advice when combining effect sizes, which I discuss later in this book.

5.7 SUMMARY

In this chapter, I have described effect sizes as indices of association between two variables, a definition that is somewhat restricted but that captures the majority of uses in meta-analysis. I also emphasized that effect sizes are not statistical significance tests.

I also described three classes of effect sizes. Correlations (r) index associations between two continuous variables. Standardized mean differences (such as g) index associations between dichotomous and continuous variables. Odds ratios (o) are advantageous in indexing the associations between two dichotomous variables. I stressed that you should carefully consider the nature of the variables of interest, recognizing that primary studies may use other distributions (e.g., artificial dichotomization of a continuous variable). I also suggested that your conceptualization of the distributions of the variables of interest should guide your choice of effect size index. Finally, I considered the practical matter of using available effect size calculators in meta-analysis programs. Although you should be familiar enough with effect size computation that you can do so yourself, these effect size calculators can be a time-saving tool.

5.8 RECOMMENDED READINGS

Fleiss, J. H. (1994). Measures of effect size for categorical data. In H. Cooper & L. V. Hedges (Eds.), *The handbook of research synthesis* (pp. 245–260). New York: Russell Sage Foundation.—This chapter provides a thorough and convincing description of the use of *o* as effect size for associations between two dichotomous variables. This chapter does not provide much advice on estimating *o* from commonly reported data, so readers should also look at relevant sections of Lipsey and Wilson (2001).

Grissom, R. J., & Kim, J. J. (2005). *Effect sizes for research: A broad practical approach.* Mahwah, NJ: Erlbaum.—Although not specifically written for the meta-analyst, this book provides a thorough description of methods of indexing effect sizes.

Lipsey, M. W., & Wilson, D. B. (2001). *Practical meta-analysis.* Thousand Oaks, CA: Sage.—This short book (247 pages) provides a more thorough coverage than that of Rosenthal (1991), but is still brief and accessible. Lipsey and Wilson frame meta-analysis in terms of analysis of effect sizes, regardless of the type of effect size used. Although only part of one chapter (Chapter 4) is devoted to effect size computation, the authors include computational details in an appendix (Appendix B) and the second author provides an Excel worksheet through his website that is useful in computing *r* and *d*.

Rosenthal, R. (1991). *Meta-analytic procedures for social research* (revised ed.). Newbury Park, CA: Sage.—This book is a very short (153 pages) and accessible introduction to basic meta-analytic procedures. Chapter 2 provides an accessible introduction to the practice of computing effect sizes for meta-analysis, with a focus on the use of *r*.

NOTES

1. I should note here that this is a restrictive definition of an effect size, used for convenience here. In Chapter 7, I describe other types of effect sizes that expand this definition. For example, an effect size might be the mean or proportion of a single variable, or some relations among more than two variables (e.g., semi-partial correlations between two variables controlling for a third, internal consistencies of many items of a scale). However, this definition of effect sizes as indexing the association between two variables is the most widely used.

2. Although there is general support for this transformation (see, e.g., Alexander, Scozzaro, & Borodkin, 1989; Hedges & Olkin, 1985; James, Demaree, & Mulaik, 1986), readers should be aware that some experts (see Hunter & Schmidt, 2004, p. 83) recommend against using this transformation.

3. There has been some criticism of *g* and *d* (which also applies to g_{Glass}) as effect sizes. The main source of critique is that these effect size estimates are not robust to violations of normality assumptions (see Algina, Keselman, & Penfield, 2005). Several alternatives have been suggested including indices based on dominance statistics, Windsorized data, and bootstrapping. These alternatives do not seem viable for use in meta-analyses, however, because you typically do not have access to the primary data. Therefore, you will typically need to rely on *g* or *d* (or, less often, g_{Glass}) in computing standardized mean differences from information commonly reported in primary research. This necessity is probably not of too much concern for your meta-analysis given that the limits of traditional standardized mean differences lie primarily in the potential inaccuracy of confidence intervals rather than biases in point estimation. However, future quantitative research evaluating the impact of using nonrobust effect size estimates on conclusions of mean, confidence intervals, and heterogeneity drawn from meta-analyses is needed to support this claim.

4. Glass's (e.g., Glass, McGraw, & Smith, 1981) standardized mean difference has been represented by numerous symbols. Rosenthal (1991, 1994) has denoted this index using the Greek uppercase delta (Δ), although I avoid this practice because others use this symbol to denote a population parameter standardized mean difference. Hedges and Olkin (1985) use *g'* (in contrast to *g*) to denote Glass's standardized mean difference, which is clear, if not intuitive. Although it could

be argued that proliferation of more symbols is unnecessary, I use the symbol g_{Glass} for clarity.

5. Where "pooled estimates" refers to the combination of estimates from both groups, using

$$s_{\text{pooled}} = \sqrt{\frac{(n_1 - 1)s_1^2 + (n_2 - 1)s_2^2}{n_1 + n_2 - 2}}$$

for the pooled population estimate of standard deviation, or substituting sd for s when pooling sample standard deviations.

6. Both are considered estimators of the same population parameter, $(\mu_1 - \mu_2) / \sigma$. The difference in these two statistics is that d has a slight bias, whereas g is unbiased, in estimating this common population parameter.

7. It is also worth noting here that g and d also differ in that a correction exists for bias when estimating g from small samples that does not exist for d. I describe this small sample correction for g below.

8. Other effect size indices under conditions of heteroscedasticity have been proposed (see Grissom & Kim, 2001). However, these indices generally require access to raw data from primary studies, and those that do not require raw data have not been thoroughly enough studied to support their widespread use.

9. Alternatively, one could consider the standardized mean difference in reference to the standard normal cumulative distribution function (denoted by $\Phi(g)$, $\Phi(d)$, or $\Phi(g_{\text{Glass}})$) to determine the percentage of members of one group falling above the mean of the second group (Grissom & Kim, 2005; Hedges & Olkin, 1985). To put it in more comprehensible terms, one can look up the value of the standardized mean difference as a Z-score in a normal curve table to identify the percentage of the normal distribution that falls below (to the left of) that particular Z-score; this percentage represents the percentage of Group 1 members who are above the mean of Group 2. For example, a standardized mean difference of 0.75 implies that 77% of Group 1 members are above the mean of Group 2, whereas a standardized mean difference of −0.50 implies that 31% of Group 1 members are above the mean of Group 2. This interpretation assumes a normal distribution in both populations.

10. There is some evidence that an alternative index may be superior to the odds ratio. This alternative is to transform the natural log of the odds ratio, $\ln(o)$, to a standardized mean difference:

$$d_{\text{Cox}} = \frac{\ln(o)}{1.65}.$$

In a simulation study (Sánchez-Meca et al., 2003), d_{Cox} exhibited little bias, whereas $\ln(o)$ slightly underestimated associations, especially when the true (population) association was large. However, d_{Cox} has not yet been widely used by meta-analysts. Nevertheless, you might consider this alternative effect size if your meta-analysis indexes associations between dichotomous variables that you expect may be large.

11. Assignment of orthogonal contrast weights, in which successive values are equidistant, assumes that the groups themselves are equidistant with respect to the underlying continuous construct. For example, if we assigned contrast weights of −1, 0, and +1 to groups defined as "never," "sometimes," or "often" experiencing an event, this coding would assume that the amount of difference in the underlying group variable between "never" and "sometimes" is equal to the difference between "sometimes" and "often" groups. The extent to which this assumption is not valid will most likely attenuate the computed effect sizes using this technique. Of course, the meta-analyst might choose different contrast weights if there is reason to do so; the only restrictions on selecting contrast weights are that they make sense and that they sum to zero.

12. Using the equation $F_{between} = MS_{between}/MS_{within}$, where $MS_{between} = \Sigma(n_g(M_g - GM)^2)/df_{between}$ and $MS_{within} = \Sigma(n_g s_g^2)/\Sigma n_g$. The grand mean (GM) can be computed from group sizes and means as $GM = \Sigma(n_g M_g) / \Sigma n_g$. The other term needed is the numerator degrees of freedom of the omnibus test, or $df_{between}$ = number of groups − 1.

13. Lipsey and Wilson (2001) recommend using t rather than Z in this equation (where you would find the appropriate value of t given p and df). With small sample sizes, the use of t seems more appropriate when the significance level is from a test in which the t-distribution is the appropriate comparison distribution. However, with a large sample, the difference in values resulting from the use of Z versus t becomes negligible, and the use of Z is likely more flexible.

14. McGrath and Meyer (2006) have pointed out that r is affected by base rates (i.e., relative group sizes) of the dichotomous variable, whereas standardized mean differences are not. Specifically, more extreme group size discrepancies will diminish values of r but not standardized mean differences. Therefore, differences in base rates across studies might contribute to heterogeneity among r but not standardized mean differences. Based on this consideration, I believe that standardized mean differences (e.g., g) are preferable to r when one of the variables is dichotomous, especially if the distribution of this dichotomy is extreme (with one group more than 2 or 3 times more common) or variable across studies. However, Rosenthal (1991) maintains a preference for r.

6

Corrections to Effect Sizes

Several corrections can be made to the effect sizes described in Chapter 5. Some are made in order to produce more desirable statistical properties; for example, Fisher's transformation of r (to Z_r; Equation 5.2 in Chapter 5) and the log transformation of o (Section 5.1.4 in Chapter 5) aim to produce a more normal distribution of these effect sizes. Other corrections seek to alleviate biases that are known to exist under certain conditions. For example, the adjustment to g for small sample sizes (Equation 5.9) corrects for the systematic overestimation of effect sizes under these conditions.

In this chapter, I describe a specific family of corrections to effect sizes, often called artifact corrections (Hunter & Schmidt, 2004). These artifact corrections aim to correct for methodological features of primary studies that are known to bias (typically attenuate) effect sizes. The reasons for performing these corrections are twofold. First, the corrections provide a more accurate estimate of what effect sizes would have been if studies had not contained methodological imperfections. Second, the corrections may reduce heterogeneity (variability in effect sizes) across studies that is due to differences in methodological imperfections, thus allowing for the identification of more substantively interesting similarities or differences (i.e., moderators; see Chapter 9) across effect sizes. As promising as these reasons seem, there are critics of artifact correction. Next, I provide a brief overview of the arguments for and against artifact correction, and then describe several artifact corrections. Finally, I discuss some practical considerations in deciding whether (and how) to correct for artifacts in a meta-analysis.

6.1   THE CONTROVERSY OF CORRECTION

There is some controversy about correcting effect sizes used in meta-analyses for methodological artifacts. In this section I describe arguments for and against correction, and then attempt to reconcile these two positions.

6.1.1   Arguments for Artifact Correction

Probably the most consistent advocates of correcting for study artifacts are John Hunter (now deceased) and Frank Schmidt (see Hunter & Schmidt, 2004; Schmidt & Hunter, 1996; as well as, e.g., Rubin, 1990). Their argument, in a simplified form, is that individual primary studies report effect sizes among imperfect *measures* of constructs, not the constructs themselves. These imperfections in the measurement of constructs can be due to a variety of sources including unreliability of the measures, imperfect validity of the measures, or imperfect ways in which the variables were managed in primary studies (e.g., artificial dichotomization). Moreover, individual studies contain not only random sampling error (due to their finite sample sizes), but often biased samples that do not represent the population about which you wish to draw conclusions.

These imperfections of measurement and sampling are inherent to every primary study and provide a limiting frame within which you must interpret the findings. For instance, a particular study does not provide a perfect effect size of the association between X and Y, but rather an effect size of the association between a particular measure of X with a particular measure of Y within the particular sample of the study. The heart of the argument for artifact correction is that we are less interested in these imperfect effect sizes found in primary studies and more interested in the effect sizes between latent constructs (e.g., the correlation between construct X and construct Y).

The argument seems reasonable and in fact provides much of the impetus for the rise of such latent variable techniques as confirmatory factor analysis (e.g., Brown, 2006) and structural equation modeling (e.g., Kline, 2005) in primary research. Our theories that we wish to evaluate are almost exclusively about associations among constructs (e.g., aggression and rejection), rather than about associations among measures (e.g., a particular self-report scale of aggression and a particular peer-report method of measuring rejection). As such, it makes sense that we would wish to draw conclusions from our meta-analyses about associations among constructs rather than associations among imperfect measures of these constructs reported in primary studies; thus, we should correct for artifacts within these studies in our meta-analyses.

A corollary to the focus on associations among constructs (rather than imperfect measures) is that artifact correction results in the variability among studies being more likely due to substantively interesting differences rather than methodological differences. For example, studies may differ due to a variety of features, with some of these differences being substantively interesting (e.g., characteristics of the sample such as age or income, type of intervention evaluated) and others being less so (e.g., the use of a reliable versus unreliable measure of a variable). Correction for these study artifacts (e.g., unreliability of measures) reduces this variability due to likely less interesting differences (i.e., noise), thus allowing for clearer illumination of differences between studies that are substantively interesting through moderator analyses (Chapter 9).

6.1.2   Arguments against Artifact Correction

Despite the apparent logic supporting artifact correction in meta-analysis, there are some who argue against these corrections. Early descriptions of meta-analysis described the goal of these efforts as integrating the *findings* of individual studies (e.g., Glass, 1976); in other words, the synthesis of results was reported in primary studies. Although one might argue that these early descriptions simply failed to appreciate the difference between the associations between measures and constructs (although this seems unlikely given the expertise Glass had in measurement and factor analysis), some modern meta-analysts have continued to oppose artifact adjustment even after the arguments put forth by Hunter and Schmidt. Perhaps most pointedly, Rosenthal (1991) argues that the goal of meta-analysis "is to teach us better what *is*, not what might some day be in the best of all possible worlds" (p. 25, italics in original). Rosenthal (1991) also cautions that these corrections can yield inaccurate effect sizes, such as when corrections for unreliability yield correlations greater than 1.0.

Another, though far weaker, argument against artifact correction is simply that such corrections add another level of complexity to our meta-analytic procedures. I agree that there is little value in making these procedures more complex than is necessary to best answer the substantive questions of the meta-analysis. Furthermore, additional data-analytic complexity often requires lengthier explanation when reporting meta-analyses, and our focus in most of these reports is typically to explain information relevant to our content-based questions rather than data-analytic procedures. At the same time, simplicity alone is not a good guide to our data-analytic techniques. The more important question is whether the cost of additional data-analytic complexity is offset by the improved value of the results yielded.

6.1.3   Reconciling Arguments Regarding
Artifact Correction

Many of the critical issues surrounding the controversy of artifact correction can be summarized in terms of whether meta-analysts prefer to describe associations among constructs (those for correction) or associations as found among variables in the research (those against correction). In most cases, the questions likely involve associations among latent constructs more so than associations among imperfectly measured variables. Even when questions involve measurement (e.g., are associations between X and Y stronger when X is measured in certain ways than when X is measured in other ways?), it seems likely that one would wish to base this answer on the differences in associations among constructs between the two measurement approaches rather than the magnitudes of imperfections that are common for these measurement approaches. Put bluntly, Hunter and Schmidt (2004) argue that attempting to meta-analytically draw conclusions about constructs without correcting for artifacts "is the mathematical equivalent of the ostrich with its head in the sand: It is a pretense that if we ignore other artifacts then their effects on study outcomes will go away" (p. 81). Thus, if you wish to draw conclusions about *constructs*, which is usually the case, it would appear that correcting for study artifacts is generally valuable.

At the same time, one must consider the likely impact of artifacts on the results. If one is meta-analyzing a body of research that consistently uses reliable and valid measures within representative samples, then the benefits of artifact adjustment are likely small. In these cases, the additional complexity of artifact adjustment is likely not warranted. To adapt Rosenthal's (1991) argument quoted earlier, if what *is* matches closely with what *could be*, then there is little value in correcting for study artifacts.

In sum, although I do not believe that all, or even any, artifact adjustments are necessary in every meta-analysis, I do believe it is valuable to always consider each of the artifacts that could bias effect sizes. In meta-analyses in which these artifacts are likely to have a substantial impact on at least some of the included primary studies, it is valuable to at least explore some of the following corrections.

6.2   ARTIFACT CORRECTIONS TO CONSIDER

Hunter and Schmidt (2004; see also Schmidt, Le, & Oh, 2009) suggest several corrections to methodological artifacts of primary studies. These corrections involve unreliability of measures, poor validity of measured variables, artificial dichotomization of continuous variables, and range restriction of variables. Next I describe the conceptual justification and computational details of each of these corrections. The computations of these artifact corrections are summarized in Table 6.1.

Before turning to these corrections, however, let us consider the general formula for all artifact corrections. The corrected effect size (e.g., r, g, o), which is the estimated effect size if there were no study artifacts, is a function of the effect size observed in the study divided by the total artifact correction[1]:

Equation 6.1: General equation for artifact corrections

$$ES_{adjusted} = \frac{ES_{observed}}{a}$$

- $ES_{adjusted}$ is the adjusted (corrected) effect size.
- $ES_{observed}$ is the observed (uncorrected) effect size.
- a is the total correction for all study artifacts.

TABLE 6.1. Summary of Equations for Artifact Corrections

Artifact	Correction
Unreliability[a]	$a_{unreliability} = \sqrt{r_{xx}}$
Imperfect validity[a]	$a_{validity} = r_{XT}$
Artificial dichotomization[b]	$a_{dichotomization} = \dfrac{\phi(c)}{\sqrt{PQ}}$
Range restriction (direct)[c]	$a_{range} = \sqrt{u^2 + r^2(1 - u^2)}$
Range restriction (indirect)[c]	$u_T = \sqrt{\dfrac{u_X^2 - (1 - r_{xx})}{1 - (1 - r_{xx})}}$

[a]The correction for this artifact on both variables comprising the effect size is equal to the product of the correction on each variable.
[b]The correction for this artifact on both variables comprising the effect size is approximated by the product of the correction on each variable in many cases (see text for details).
[c]The correction for this artifact on both variables comprising the effect size requires special techniques described in the text.

Here, a is the total correction for all study artifacts and is simply the product of the individual artifacts described next (i.e., $a = a_1 * a_2 * \ldots$, for the first, second, etc., artifacts for which you wish to correct).[2] Each individual artifact (a_1) and the total product of all artifacts (a) have values that are 1.0 (no artifact bias) or less (with the possible exception of the correction for range restriction, as described below). The values of these artifacts decrease (and adjustments therefore increase) as the methodological limitations of the studies increase (i.e., larger problems, such as very low reliability, result in smaller values of a and larger corrections).

Artifact adjustments to effect sizes also require adjustments to standard errors. Because standard errors represent the imprecision in estimates of effect sizes, it makes conceptual sense that these would increase if you must make an additional estimate in the form of how much to correct the effect size. Specifically, the standard errors of effect sizes (e.g., r, g, or o; see Chapter 5) are also adjusted for artifact correction using the following general formula:

Equation 6.2: Equation for adjusting standard errors for artifact corrections

$$SE_{adjusted} = \frac{SE_{observed}}{a}$$

- $SE_{adjusted}$ is the adjusted standard error.
- $SE_{observed}$ is the observed (uncorrected) standard error.
- a is the total correction for all study artifacts.

The one exception to this equation is when one is correcting for range restriction. This correction represents an exception to the general rule of Equation 6.2 because the effect size is used in the computation of a, the artifact correction (see Equations 6.7 and 6.8). In this case of correcting for range restriction, you multiply a_{range} by $ES_{adjusted}/ES_{observed}$ prior to correcting the standard error.

6.2.1   Corrections for Unreliability

This correction is for unreliability of measurement of the variables comprising the effect sizes (e.g., variables X and Y that comprise a correlation). Unreliability refers to nonsystematic error in the measurement process (contrast with systematic error in measurement, or poor validity, described in Section 6.2.4).

Reliability, or the repeatability of a measure (or the part that is not unreliable), can be indexed in at least three ways. Most commonly, reliability is considered in terms of *internal consistency*, representing the repeatability of measurement across different items of a scale. This type of reliability is indexed as a function of the associations among items of a scale, most commonly through an index called Cronbach's coefficient alpha, α (Cronbach, 1951; see, e.g., DeVellis, 2003). Second, reliability can be evaluated in terms of agreement between multiple raters or reporters. This *interrater reliability* can be evaluated with the correlation between sets of continuous scores produced by two raters (or average correlations among more than two raters) or with Cohen's kappa (κ) representing agreement between categorical assignment between raters (for a full description of methods of assessing interrater reliability, see von Eye & Mun, 2005). A third index of reliability is the *test–retest reliability*. This test–retest reliability is simply the correlation (r) between repeated measurements, with the time span between measurements being short enough that the construct is not expected to change during this time. Because all three types of reliability have a maximum of 1 and a minimum of 0, the relation between reliability and unreliability can be expressed as reliability = 1 – unreliability.

Regardless of whether reliability is indexed as internal consistency (e.g., Cronbach's α), interrater agreement (r or κ), or test–retest reliability (r), this reliability impacts the magnitude of effect sizes that a study can find. If reliability is high (e.g., near perfect, or close to 1) for the measurement of two variables, then you expect that the association (e.g., correlation, r) the researcher finds between these variables will be an unbiased estimate of the actual (latent) population effect size (assuming the study does not contain other artifacts described below). However, if the measurement of one or both variables comprising the association of interest is low (reliability far below 1, maybe even approaching 0), then the maximum (in terms of absolute value of positive or negative associations) effect size the researcher might detect is substantially lower than the true population effect size. This is because the correlation (or any other effect size) between the two variables of interest is being computed not only from the true association between the two constructs, but also between the unreliable aspects of each measure (i.e., the noise, which typically is not correlated across the variables).

If you know (or at least have a good estimate of) the amount of unreliability in a measure, you can estimate the magnitude of this effect size attenuation. This ability is also important for your meta-analysis because you might wish to estimate the true (disattenuated) effect size from a primary study reporting an observed effect size and the reliability of measures. Given the reliability for variables X and Y, with these general reliabilities denoted as

r_{xx} and r_{yy}, you can estimate the corrected correlation (i.e., true correlation between *constructs* X and Y) using the following artifact adjustment (Baugh, 2002; Hunter & Schmidt, 2004, pp. 34–36):

Equation 6.3: Correction for unreliability

$$a_{\text{unreliability}} = \sqrt{r_{xx}r_{yy}}$$

- r_{xx} and r_{yy} are the reliability estimates of variables X and Y.

As described earlier (see Equation 6.1), you estimate the true effect size by dividing the observed effect size by this (and any other) artifact adjustment. Similarly, you increase the standard error (SE) of this true effect size estimate to account for the additional uncertainty of this artifact correction by dividing the standard error of the observed effect size (formulas provided in Chapter 5) by this (and any other) artifact adjustment (see Equation 6.2).

An illustration using a study from the ongoing example meta-analysis (Card et al., 2008) helps clarify this point. This study (Hawley, Little, & Card, 2007) reported a bivariate correlation between relational aggression and rejection of $r = .19$ among boys (results for boys and girls were each corrected and later combined). However, the measures of both relational aggression and rejection exhibited marginal internal consistencies ($\alpha_s = .82$ and .81, respectively), which might have contributed to an attenuated effect size of this correlation. To estimate the adjusted (corrected) correlation, I compute first $a_{\text{unreliability}} = \sqrt{r_{xx}r_{yy}} = \sqrt{.82 * .81} = .815$ and then $r_{\text{adjusted}} = \frac{r_{\text{observed}}}{a} = \frac{.19}{.815} = .23$. The standard error of Fisher's transformation of this uncorrected correlation is .0498 (based on $N = 407$ boys in this study); I also adjust this standard error to $SE_{\text{adjusted}} = \frac{.0498}{.815} = .0610$. This larger standard error represents the greater imprecision in the adjusted effect size estimated using this correction for unreliability.

This artifact adjustment (Equation 6.3) can also be used if you wish to correct for only one of the variables being correlated (e.g., correction for X but not Y). This may be the preference because the meta-analyst assumes that one of the variables is measured without error, because the primary studies frequently do not report reliability estimates of one of the variables, or because the meta-analyst is simply not interested in one of the variables.[3] If you are interested in correcting for unreliability in one variable, then you implicitly assume that the reliability of the other variable is perfect. In other words, correction for unreliability in only one variable is equivalent to substituting

1.0 for the reliability of the other variable in Equation 6.3, so this equation simplifies to the artifact correction being the square root of the reliability of the single variable.

Before ending discussion of correction for unreliability, I want to mention the special case of latent variable associations. These latent variable associations include (1) correlations between factors from an exploratory factor analysis with oblique factor rotation (e.g., direct oblimin, promax), and (2) correlations between constructs in confirmatory factor analysis models.[4] You should remember that these latent correlations are corrected for measurement error; in other words, the reliabilities of the latent variable are perfect (i.e., 1.0). Therefore, these latent correlations are treated as effect sizes already corrected for unreliability, and you should not further correct these effect sizes using Equation 6.3. This point can be confusing because many primary studies will report internal consistencies for these scales; but these internal consistencies are relevant only if the study authors had conducted manifest variable analyses (e.g., using summed scale scores) with these measures.

6.2.2   Corrections for Imperfect Validity

The validity of a measure refers to the systematic overlap between the measure and the intended construct (i.e., the thing the measure is meant to measure). It is important to distinguish between validity and reliability. Reliability, described earlier, refers to the repeatability of a measure across items, raters, or occasions; high reliability is indicated by different items, raters, or occasions of measurement having high correspondence (i.e., being highly correlated). However, reliability does not tell us whether we are measuring what we intend to measure, but only that we are measuring the same thing (whatever it may be) consistently. In contrast, validity refers to the consistency between the measure and the construct. For instance, "Does a particular peer nomination instrument truly measure victimization?", "Does a parent-report scale really measure depression?", and "Does a particular IQ test measure intelligence?" are all questions involving validity. Low validity means that the measure is reliably measuring something other than the intended construct. Reliability and validity are entirely independent phenomena: A scale can have high reliability and low validity, and another scale can have low reliability and high validity (if one assesses validity by correcting for attenuation due to unreliability, as in latent variable modeling; Little, Lindenberger, & Nesselroade, 1999).

You can conceptualize a measure's degree of validity as the disattenuated correlation between the measure and the construct. In other words, the validity of a measure (X) in assessing a construct (T) is r_{XT} when the measure is perfectly reliable. If the effect size of interest in your meta-analysis is the association between the true construct (T) and some other variable (Y; assuming for the moment that this variable is measured with perfect validity), then the association you are interested in might be represented as r_{TY} (you could also apply this correction to other effect sizes, but the use of correlations here facilitates understanding). Therefore, the observed association between the measure (X) and the other variable (Y) is equal to the product of the validity of the measure and the association of the construct with the other variable, $r_{XY} = r_{XT} * r_{TY}$. To identify the association between the construct (T) and the other variable (Y), which is what you are interested in, you can rearrange this expression to $r_{TY} = r_{XY}/r_{XT}$. In other words, the adjustment for imperfect validity in a study is:

Equation 6.4: Correction for imperfect validity

$a_{validity} = r_{XT}$

- r_{XT} is the validity coefficient.

Here, r_{XT} represents the validity coefficient or disattenuated (for measurement unreliability) correlation between the measure (X) and intended construct (T).

This adjustment is mathematically simple, yet its use contains two challenges. The first challenge is that this adjustment assumes that whatever is specific to the measure (X) that is not part of the construct (T) is uncorrelated with the other variable (Y). In other words, the reliable but invalid portion of the measure (e.g., method variance) is assumed to not be related to the other variable of interest (either the construct T_Y or its measure, X_Y). The second challenge in applying this adjustment is simply in obtaining an estimate of the validity coefficient (r_{XT}). This validity will almost never be reported in the primary studies of the meta-analysis (if a study contained this more valid variable, then you would simply use effect sizes from this variable rather than the invalid proxy). Most commonly, you need to obtain the validity coefficient from another source, such as from validity studies of the measure (X). When using the validity coefficient from other studies, however, you must be aware of both (unreliable) sampling error in the magnitude of this correlation and (reliable but unknown) differences in this correlation between the validity population and that of the particular primary study you are coding. For these reasons, I suspect that many fields will not contain adequate information to obtain a good estimate of the validity coefficient, and therefore this artifact adjustment may be difficult to use.

6.2.3   Corrections for Artificial Dichotomization

It is well known that artificial dichotomization of a variable that is naturally continuous attenuates associations that this variable has with others, yet this practice is all too common in primary research (see MacCallum et al., 2002). An important distinction is whether a variable is artificially dichotomized or truly dichotomous. When analyzing associations between two continuous variables (typically using r as an index of effect size; see Chapter 5), you might find that a primary study artificially dichotomized one of the variables in one of many possible ways, including median splits, splits at some arbitrary level (e.g., one standard deviation above the mean), or at some recommended cutoff level (e.g., at a level where a variable of maladjustment is considered "clinically significant"). Or you might find that the primary study dichotomized both variables of interest (again, through median splits, etc.). Finally, you might be interested in the extent to which two groups (a naturally dichotomous variable) differ on a continuous variable, which is dichotomized in some studies (e.g., the studies report the percentages of each group that have "clinically significant" levels of a maladjustment variable). In each of these cases, you need to recognize that the dichotomization of variables in the primary studies is artificial; that it does not represent the true continuous nature of the variable.

Corrections for one variable that is artificially dichotomized are straightforward. You need only to know the numbers, proportion, or percentages of individuals in the two artificial groups. Based on this information, the artifact adjustment for dichotomization of one variable is (Hunter & Schmidt, 1990; Hunter & Schmidt, 2004, p. 36; MacCallum et al., 2002):

Equation 6.5: Correction for artificial dichotomization

$$a_{\text{dichotomization}} = \frac{\phi(c)}{\sqrt{PQ}}$$

- P and Q are the proportions in each group.
- $\phi(c)$ is the normal ordinate at the point c.

The numerator, $\Phi(c)$, is the normal ordinate at the point c that divides the standard normal distribution into proportions P and Q. Because this value is unfamiliar to many, I have listed values of $\Phi(c)$, as well as the artifact adjustment for dichotomization of one variable ($a_{\text{dichotomization}}$), for various proportional splits in Table 6.2.

To illustrate this correction using the ongoing example (Card et al., 2008), I consider a study by Crick and Grotpeter (1995). Here, the authors artificially dichotomized the relational aggression variable by classifying children with scores one deviation above the mean as relationally aggressive and the rest as not relationally aggressive. Of the 491 children in the study, 412 (83.9%) were thus classified as not aggressive and 79 (16.1%) as relationally aggressive. The numerator of Equation 6.5 for this example is found in Table 6.2 to be .243. The denominator for this example is $\sqrt{.839 * .161}$ = .368. Therefore, $a_{\text{dichotomization}}$ = .243/.368 = .664 (accepting some rounding error), as shown in Table 6.2. For this example, the uncorrected correlation between relational aggression and rejection was .16 (computed from $F_{(1,486)}$ = 12.3) and the standard error of Z_r was .0453 (from N = 491). The adjustment for artificial dichotomization yields r_{adjusted} = .16/.664 = .24 and SE_{adjusted} = .0453/.664 = .0682. (Note that this adjustment is only for artificial dichotomization; we ultimately corrected for unreliability as well, which is why this effect size differs from that used in our analyses and used later.)

If both of two continuous variables are dichotomized, the correction becomes complex (specifically, you must compute a tetrachoric correlation; see Hunter & Schmidt, 1990). Fortunately, a simple approximation holds in most cases you are likely to encounter. Specifically, the artifact adjustment for two artificially dichotomized variables can be approximated by:

Equation 6.6: Approximation for dual dichotomization

$$a_{XY,\text{ dichotomization}} \approx a_{X,\text{ dichotomization}} \times a_{Y,\text{ dichotomization}}$$

- a_X and a_Y are the individual correction for dichotomization of X and Y.

In other words, the artifact adjustment for two variables is approximated by the product of each adjustment for the dichotomization of each variable. The feasibility of this approximation depends on the extremity of the dichotomization split and the corrected correlation (r_{adjusted}). Hunter and Schmidt (1990) showed that this approximation is reasonable when (1) one of the vari-

TABLE 6.2. Normal Ordinates and Artifact Corrections for Proportional Dichotomizations

Split	$\Phi(c)$	$a_{dichotomization}$	Split	$\Phi(c)$	$a_{dichotomization}$
.50 / .50	.3989	.7979	.25 / .75	.3178	.7339
.49 / .51	.3988	.7978	.24 / .76	.3109	.7279
.48 / .52	.3984	.7975	.23 / .77	.3036	.7215
.47 / .53	.3978	.7971	.22 / .78	.2961	.7148
.46 / .54	.3969	.7964	.21 / .79	.2882	.7076
.45 / .55	.3958	.7956	.20 / .80	.2800	.6999
.44 / .56	.3944	.7946	.19 / .81	.2714	.6917
.43 / .57	.3928	.7934	.18 / .82	.2624	.6830
.42 / .58	.3909	.7920	.17 / .83	.2531	.6737
.41 / .59	.3887	.7904	.16 / .84	.2433	.6637
.40 / .60	.3863	.7886	.15 / .85	.2332	.6530
.39 / .61	.3837	.7866	.14 / .86	.2226	.6415
.38 / .62	.3808	.7844	.13 / .87	.2115	.6290
.37 / .63	.3776	.7820	.12 / .88	.2000	.6156
.36 / .64	.3741	.7794	.11 / .89	.1880	.6010
.35 / .65	.3704	.7766	.10 / .90	.1755	.5850
.34 / .66	.3664	.7735	.09 / .91	.1624	.5674
.33 / .67	.3621	.7702	.08 / .92	.1487	.5480
.32 / .68	.3576	.7666	.07 / .93	.1343	.5262
.31 / .69	.3528	.7628	.06 / .94	.1191	.5016
.30 / .70	.3477	.7587	.05 / .95	.1031	.4732
.29 / .71	.3423	.7544	.04 / .96	.0862	.4398
.28 / .72	.3366	.7497	.03 / .97	.0680	.3989
.27 / .73	.3306	.7448	.02 / .98	.0484	.3458
.26 / .74	.3244	.7395	.01 / .99	.0267	.2679

ables has a median ($P = .50$) split and the corrected correlation is less than .70; (2) one of the variables has an approximately even split (.40 < P < .60) and the corrected correlation is less than .50; or (3) neither of the variables has extreme splits (.20 < P < .80) and the corrected correlation is less than .40. If any of these conditions apply, then this approximation is reasonably accurate (less than 10% bias). If the dichotomizations are more extreme or the corrected correlations are very large, then you should use the tetrachoric correlation described by Hunter and Schmidt (1990).

6.2.4   Corrections for Range Restriction

Estimates of associations between continuous variables are attenuated in studies that fail to sample the entire range of population variability on these variables. As an example (similar to that described by Hunter, Schmidt, & Le, 2006), it might be the case that GRE scores are strongly related to success in graduate school, but because only applicants with high GRE scores are admitted to graduate school, a sample of graduate students might reveal only small correlations between GRE scores obtained and some index of success (i.e., this association is attenuated due to restriction in range). This does not necessarily mean that there is only a small association between GRE scores and graduate school success, at least if we define our population as all potential graduate students rather than just those admitted. Instead, the estimated correlation between GRE scores and graduate school success is attenuated (reduced) due to the restricted range of GRE scores for those students about whom we can measure success. Aside from GRE scores and graduate school success, it is easy to think of numerous other research foci for which restriction of range may occur: Studies of correlates of job performance are limited to those individuals hired, educational research too often includes only children in mainstream classrooms, and psychopathology research might only sample individuals who seek psychological services. Combination and comparison of studies using samples of differing ranges might prove difficult if you do not correct for restrictions in range of one or both variables under consideration.

The first step in adjusting effect sizes for range restriction in one variable is to define some amount of typical (standard) deviation of that variable in the population and then determine the amount of deviation within the primary study sample relative to this reference population. This ratio of study (restricted) deviation to reference (unrestricted) standard deviation is denoted as $u = SD_{study}/SD_{reference}$ (Hunter & Schmidt, 2004, p. 37). With some studies, determining this u may be straightforward. For example, if a study reports the standard deviation of the sample on an IQ test (e.g., 10) with a known population standard deviation (e.g., 15), then we could compare the sample range on IQ relative to the population range (e.g., $u = 10/15 = 0.67$).

In other situations, the authors of primary studies select individuals scoring in the top or bottom of a certain percentile range (e.g., selection of those above the median of a variable for inclusion is equivalent to selecting the top 50th percentile). In these situations, it is possible to compute the amount that the range is restricted. Although such calculations are complicated (see Barr & Sherrill, 1999), Figure 6.1 shows the values of u given the proportion of individuals selected for the study. The *x*-axis of this figure represents the proportion of individuals included in the study (e.g., selection of all individuals above the 10th percentile means retention of 0.90 of participants). It can be seen that the less selective a study is (i.e., a higher proportion is retained, shown on the right side of the figure), the less restricted the range (i.e., *u* approaches 1), whereas the more selective a study is (i.e., a lower proportion is retained, shown on the left side of the figure), the more restricted the range (i.e., *u* becomes smaller). Note that the computations on which Figure 6.1 is based assume a normal distribution of the variable within the reference population and are only applicable with one-sided truncated data (i.e., the research selected individuals based on their falling above or below a *single* score or percentile cutoff).

In other situations, however, it may be difficult to determine a good estimate of the sample variability relative to that of the population. Although a perfect solution likely does not exist, I suggest the following: Select primary studies from all included studies that you believe do *not* suffer restriction of range (i.e., those that were fully sampled from the population to which you wish to generalize). From these studies, estimate the population (i.e., unrestricted) standard deviation by meta-analytically combining standard deviations (see Chapter 7). Then use this estimate to compute the degree of range restriction (*u*) among studies in which participants were sampled in a restrictive way.

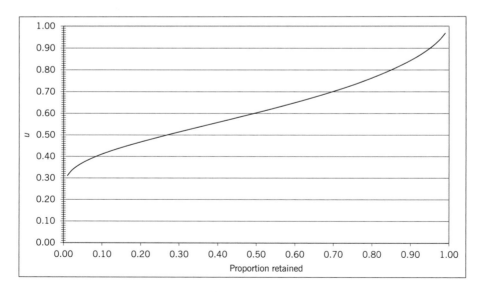

FIGURE 6.1. Restriction in range as a function of proportion of cases included in study.

The artifact adjustment for range restriction is based on this ratio of the sample standard deviation relative to the reference population standard deviation (as noted: $u = SD_{study}/SD_{reference}$) as well as the correlation reported in the study.[5] Specifically, this adjustment is (Hunter & Schmidt, 2004, p. 37):

Equation 6.7: Correction for range restriction

$$a_{Range} = \sqrt{u^2 + r^2(1 - u^2)}$$

- u is the degree of range restriction ($SD_{study}/SD_{reference}$).
- r is the correlation coefficient (see text for other effect sizes).

A unique aspect of this artifact adjustment for range restriction is that it can yield a values greater than 1.0 (in contrast to my earlier statement that these adjustments are always less than 1.0). The situation in which this can occur is when the sample range is *greater* than the reference population range (i.e., range *enhancement*). Although range enhancement is probably far less common than range restriction, this situation is possible in studies where individuals with extreme scores were intentionally oversampled.

A more complex situation is that of *indirect range restriction* (in contrast to the direct range restriction I have described so far). Here, the variables comprising the effect size (e.g., X and Y) were not used in selecting participants, but rather a third variable (e.g., Z) that is related to one of the variables of interest was used for selection. If (1) the range of Z in the sample is smaller than that in the population, and (2) Z is associated with X or Y, then the effective impact of this selection is that the range of X or Y in the sample is indirectly restricted. Continuing the example I used earlier, imagine that we are interested in the association between IQ (X) and graduate school success (Y). Although students might not be directly selected based on IQ, the third variable GRE (Z) is correlated with IQ, and we therefore have indirect restriction in the range of IQ represented in the sample.

This situation of indirect range restriction may be more common than that of direct range restriction that I have previously described (Hunter et al., 2006). It is also more complex to correct. Although I direct readers interested in a full explanation to other sources (Hunter & Schmidt, 2004, Ch. 3; Hunter et al., 2006; Le & Schmidt, 2006), I briefly describe this procedure. First, you need to consider both the sample standard deviation of the indirectly restricted variable (e.g., IQ, if GRE scores are used for selection and are associated with IQ) as well as the reliability of this restricted variable. You then compute an alternative value of u for use in Equation 6.7. Specifically, you compute this alternative ratio, denoted as u_T by Hunter and Schmidt (2004; Hunter et al., 2006, p. 106) using the following formula:

Equation 6.8: Alternative ratio for indirect range restriction

$$u_T = \sqrt{\frac{u_X^2 - (1 - r_{xx})}{1 - (1 - r_{xx})}}$$

- u_X is the ratio of observed to population standard deviation of the variable that is indirectly restricted (e.g., IQ).
- r_{xx} is the sample reliability estimate of that variable.

As mentioned, this alternative ratio u_T is then applied as u in Equation 6.7.

Another situation of range restriction is that of restriction on both variables comprising the effect size. In the example involving GRE scores and graduate school success, the sample may be restricted in terms of both selection on GRE scores (i.e., only individuals with high scores are accepted into graduate schools) *and* graduate school success (e.g., those who are unsuccessful drop out of graduate programs). This is an example of range restriction on both variables of the effect size, or double-range restriction (also called "doubly truncated" by Alexander, Carson, Alliger, & Carr, 1987). Although no exact methods exist for simultaneously correcting range restriction on both variables (Hunter & Schmidt, 2004, p. 40), Alexander et al. (1987) proposed an approximation in which one corrects first for restriction in range of one variable and then for restriction of range on the second variable (using the *r* corrected for range restriction on the first variable in Equation 6.7). Alexander et al. (1987) show that this approximation is generally accurate for most situations meta-analysts are likely to encounter, and Hunter and Schmidt (2004) report that this approximation can be used to correct for either direct or indirect range restriction.

6.3   PRACTICAL MATTERS: WHEN (AND HOW) TO CORRECT: CONCEPTUAL, METHODOLOGICAL, AND DISCIPLINARY CONSIDERATIONS

6.3.1   General Considerations

As I described earlier, one consideration in deciding whether to correct for artifacts is the expected magnitude of effects these artifacts have on the results. Given the numerous artifact adjustments described in the previous section, you might reasonably choose to correct only for those that seem most pressing within the primary studies being synthesized.

How pressing a particular type of artifact is within a meta-analysis is partly a conceptual question and partly an empirical question. First, you must consider the collection of primary studies in light of your conceptual expertise of the area. Relevant questions include the following: How valid are the measures within this research in relation to the construct I am interested in? How representative are the samples relative to the population about which I want to draw conclusions? Again, there is not a statistical answer to such questions; rather, these questions must be answered based on your understanding of the field.

In addition to conceptual considerations, you might also base conclusions on empirical grounds. Specifically, you can consider the data reported in primary studies to draw conclusions about the presence of important artifacts. For example, I recommend coding the internal consistencies of relevant measures within the primary studies, meta-analyzing these reliabilities (see Chapter 7), and determining (1) whether the collection of studies has generally high or low reliabilities of measures and (2) whether substantial variability exists across studies in these reliabilities. Similarly, if many studies use similar measures of a variable (i.e., with the same scale), then you could code and evaluate standard deviations across studies (see Chapter 7) to determine whether some studies suffer from restricted ranges. In short, for each of the potential artifacts described in the previous section, you should consider the available empirical evidence to determine whether this artifact is uniformly or inconsistently present in the primary studies being analyzed. If a particular artifact is uniformly present, then correcting for it will yield more accurate overall effect size estimates (among latent constructs). If a particular artifact is present in some studies but not in others (or present in differing degrees across studies), then correcting for this artifact will reduce less interesting (i.e., artifactual) variability across studies and allow for a clearer picture of substantively interesting variability in effect sizes.

6.3.2 Disciplinary Considerations

Whereas I view the conceptual and empirical considerations as most important in deciding whether and how to correct for artifacts, the reality is that these corrections are more common in some fields than in others. This means that one meta-analyst working within one field might be expected to correct for certain artifacts, whereas another meta-analyst working within another field might be met with skepticism if certain (or any) corrections were to be performed. These disciplinary practices are unfortunate, especially because they are more often due to those who are influential in a field more so than consideration of particular needs of a field. Nevertheless, it is useful to recognize the common practices within your particular field.

Notwithstanding recognition of these disciplinary practices, I want to encourage you to not feel restricted by these practices. In other words, do not base your decision to perform or not perform certain artifact corrections only on common practices within your field. Instead, carefully consider the conceptual and empirical basis for making certain corrections, and then use (or not) these corrections to obtain results that best answer your research questions.

6.4 SUMMARY

In this chapter I have described rationales for and against corrections of study artifacts, imperfections of primary studies that bias (typically attenuate) effect size estimates. I described methods of correcting for several types of artifacts: unreliability of measures, artificial dichotomization of continuous variables, range restriction, poor validity of measures, and covariation due to a third variable. Despite disciplinary differences in practices of artifact correction, I argue that the decision to correct or not to correct for certain artifacts should be based on conceptual and empirical grounds.

6.5 RECOMMENDED READINGS

Hunter, J. E., & Schmidt, F. L. (2004). *Methods of meta-analysis: Correcting error and bias in research findings* (2nd ed.). Thousand Oaks, CA: Sage.—This book provides a complete description of meta-analysis emphasizing the artifact corrections described in this chapter. The authors have been the most active advocates for artifact correction in the field of meta-analysis.

Schmidt, F. L., Le, H., & Oh, I.-S. (2009). Correcting for the distorting effects of study artifacts in meta-analysis. In H. Cooper, L. V. Hedges, & J. C. Valentine (Eds.), *The handbook of research synthesis and meta-analysis* (2nd ed., pp. 317–333). New York: Russell Sage Foundation.—This chapter represents a more concise overview of the practice of artifact correction in meta-analysis.

NOTES

1. By describing artifact corrections of effect sizes of individual studies, I am implicitly prescribing one of two possible methods of meta-analysis with artifact correction. Specifically, I am recommending that you correct the effect sizes of each individual study and use these corrected effect sizes in subsequent meta-analytic computations (described in Chapters 8–12). This approach is described in Hunter and Schmidt (2004, Ch. 3). My selection of this approach makes my subsequent description of combining and comparing effect sizes across studies more straightforward. However, it also requires that most studies provide sufficient information to make corrections (e.g., report internal consistency to correct for unreliability), and it may be necessary to substitute estimates of these corrections for studies that do not provide sufficient information (e.g., meta-analytically compute a mean reliability that is used for studies that do not report internal consistency). An alternative approach is to meta-analytically compute a distribution of uncorrected effect sizes across studies and distributions of corrections across studies. These techniques are more complex, yet may be useful when primary studies are inconsistent in reporting information needed to correct for artifacts. These techniques are described in Hunter and Schmidt (2004, Ch. 4).

2. An important caveat of this use of multiplicative combination of artifacts is that the artifacts are assumed to be independent of one another. Violations of this assumption can lead to inaccurate corrected effect sizes, including out-of-bounds effect sizes (e.g., r greater than 1.0).

3. I have arranged these reasons in what I consider the most to least justifiable. Not correcting for unreliability of one variable is acceptable if a convincing case can be made that it is highly reliably measured. Not correcting for reliability of one variable because primary studies do not report this reliability is weaker justification, though it is a reality you may have to deal with in some situations. It is likely that some studies in a meta-analysis will report reliability estimates, whereas others will not. In these cases it is preferable for you to seek reliability information from primary study authors. If it is still not possible to obtain reliability estimates for some studies in the meta-analysis, I recommend performing a meta-analysis of reliabilities among studies in the meta-analysis (see Chapter 7) and using either the mean reliability or an estimated reliability predicted by other study features. The final reason listed, not correcting for unreliability of one variable because you are not interested in the variable, is not acceptable. Expressing an interest in X but not Y ignores the fact that the association between these variables necessarily depends on the measurement properties (including reliability) of both variables, so unreliability in Y is going to adversely affect the association involving X, which you are interested in.

4. Latent correlations can also be found within structural equation models, or latent variable models that include directional (regression) paths. However, the

meta-analyst needs to be careful when determining latent correlations from such models. Although nondirection (i.e., bivariate) associations between exogenous (predictor) variables can be interpreted as latent correlations, nondirectional associations between endogenous variables (predicted variables) and directional associations cannot be interpreted as latent correlations. In these instances, the meta-analyst needs to derive the latent correlations through tracing rules, as described by Kline (2005) and Maruyama (1998).

5. When discussing range restriction, I focus on the use of r as the index of effect size. This is the most common situation, as range restriction is relevant only to continuous variables and is most often encountered in naturalistic studies. However, it is also possible to correct for range restriction of the continuous variable when considering standardized mean differences (e.g., g). For details regarding these corrections, see Hunter and Schmidt (2004) or Lipsey and Wilson (2001).

7

Advanced and Unique Effect Size Computation

Although the three effect sizes (r, g, or other standardized mean differences, and o) described in Chapter 5 are most commonly used, you are not restricted to these indices of two-variable associations in your meta-analysis. Instead, you should consider the broad range of potential effect sizes as answers to the research questions relevant to your review. In this chapter, I describe some less commonly used effect sizes that are useful for meta-analysis of single variables (i.e., means, proportions, and variances or standard deviations), effect sizes that retain the meaningful metric of the variables involved (i.e., unstandardized effect sizes), effect sizes from multivariate regression analyses, and a variety of different effect sizes that have received less consideration (e.g., scale reliabilities, longitudinal change scores). I then describe some of the challenges of using less common effect sizes in your meta-analysis, as well as some of the opportunities.

7.1 DESCRIBING SINGLE VARIABLES

There are relatively few instances of meta-analyzing single variables, yet this information could be potentially valuable. At least three types of information regarding single variables could be important: (1) the mean level of individuals on a continuous variable; (2) the proportions of individuals falling into a particular category of a categorical variable; and (3) the amount of variability (or standard deviation), in a continuous variable.

7.1.1   Mean Level on Variable

Meta-analysis of reported means on a single variable may have great value. One potential is that meta-analytic combination (see Chapters 8 and 9) allows you to obtain a more precise estimate of this mean than might be obtained in primary studies, especially when those primary studies have small sample sizes. Perhaps more importantly, meta-analytic comparison (see Chapter 10) allows you to identify potential reasons why means differ across studies (e.g., methodological differences such as condition or reporter; sample characteristics such as age or ethnicity). Thus, the meta-analysis of means of single variables has considerable value.

At the same time, there is also an important limiting consideration in the meta-analysis of means in that the primary studies must typically report this value in the same metric. For example, if one study measures the variable of interest on a 0–4 scale, whereas another uses a 1–100 scale, it usually does not make sense to combine or compare means across these studies.[1] Some exceptions can be considered, however. The first exception is if the different scales are due to the primary study authors scoring comparable measures in different ways, then it is usually possible to transform one of the scales to the metric of the other. For example, if two primary studies both use a 6-item scale with items having values from 1 to 5, one study may form a composite by averaging the items, whereas the other forms a composite by summing the items. In this case, it would be possible to transform one of the two means to the same scale of the other (i.e., multiplying the average by 6 to obtain the sum, or dividing the sum by 6 to obtain the average), and the means of the two studies could then be combined and compared. A second, more general exception is that it might usually be possible to transform studies using different scales into a common metric. From the example I provided of one study using a 0–4 scale and the other using a 1–100 scale, it is possible to transform a mean on one scale to an equivalent mean on the other using the following equation:

Equation 7.1: Transforming scores between two different scales

$$X_2 = \left[(X_1 - Min_1)\left(\frac{Max_2 - Min_2}{Max_1 - Min_1}\right)\right] + Min_2$$

- X_2 is the equivalent score on the second scale.
- X_1 is the score on the first scale that you wish to transform.
- Min_1 is the lowest possible score on the first scale.
- Max_1 is the highest possible score on the first scale.
- Min_2 is the lowest possible score on the second scale.
- Max_2 is the highest possible score on the score scale.

A caution in using different scales is that even if both studies use a common range of scores (e.g., 0–4), it is probably only meaningful to combine and compare means if the studies used the same anchor points (e.g., if one used response options of never, rarely, sometimes, often, and always, whereas the other used 0 times, once, 2–3 times, 4–6 times, and 7 or more times, it would make little sense to combine or compare these studies). This may prove an especially difficult obstacle if you are attempting to combine multiple scales in which scores from one scale are transformed to scores of another using Equation 7.1. This requirement of primary studies reporting the variable on the same—or at least a comparable—metric means that you will often include only studies using the same measure (e.g., a particular measure of depression, such as the Children's Depression Inventory; Kovacs, 1992) or else very similar measures (e.g., child- and teacher-reported aggression using parallel items and response options). I suspect that this rather restrictive requirement is the primary reason why meta-analysis of means is not more common. If you are using different but similar measures, or transformations to place values of different measures on a common scale, I highly recommend evaluating the measure as a moderator (see Chapter 9).

If you do have a situation in which the combination or comparison of means is feasible, computing this effect size (and its standard error) is straightforward. The equation for computing a mean is well known, but I reproduce it here:

Equation 7.2: Computing the mean ($\overline{X}$) from raw data

$$\overline{X} = \frac{\sum x_i}{N}$$

- x_i is scores of individual i.
- N is the sample size.

However, it is typically not necessary (or possible) for you to compute this mean, as this is usually reported within the primary study. Therefore, coding the mean, which is an effect size (of the central tendency of a single variable), is usually straightforward.

Occasionally, however, the primary studies will report frequency tables rather than means for variables with a small number of potential options. For example, a primary study might report the number or proportion of individuals scoring 0, the number or proportion scoring 1, and so on, on a measure that has possible options of 0, 1, 2, 3, and 4. Here, you can use these frequencies of different scores to re-create the raw data and then compute the mean from these data (using Equation 7.2). An easier way to compute this mean is using the following equivalent formula provided by Lipsey and Wilson (2001, p. 176), summing over all potential values of a variable:

Equation 7.3: Computing the mean ($\overline{X}$) from frequency data

$$\overline{X} = \frac{\sum xf}{\sum f}$$

- x is a potential value of the variable.
- f is the frequency (number, percentage, or proportion) of individuals with the value x.

Before ending my discussion of calculating the mean as an effect size, it is important to consider the standard error of this estimate of the mean (which is used for weighting in the meta-analysis; see Chapter 8). To compute the standard error of a study's estimate of the mean, you must obtain the (population estimate of the) standard deviation (s) and sample size (N) from that study, which are then used in the following equation:

Equation 7.4: Standard error of a mean ($SE_{\overline{X}}$)

$$SE_{\overline{X}} = \frac{s_X}{\sqrt{N}}$$

- s is the standard deviation of variable X.
- N is the sample size.

After computing the mean and standard error of the mean for each study, you can then meta-analytically combine and compare results across studies using techniques described later in this book (see Chapters 8–10).

7.1.2   Proportion of Individuals in Categories

Whereas the mean is a useful effect size for the typical score (i.e., central tendency) of a single continuous variable, the proportion is a useful effect size for a particular category of a categorical variable. For example, we may be interested in the proportion of children who are aggressive or the proportion of individuals who meet certain criteria for rejected social status, if we believe the meaningful conceptualization of aggression or rejection is categorical. In these cases, we are interested in the prevalence of an affirmative instance of a single dichotomous variable.[2]

This proportion is often either directly reported in primary studies (as either a proportion or percentage, which can be divided by 100 to obtain the proportion), or else can be computed from the reported frequency falling in this category (k) relative to the total sample size (N):

Equation 7.5: Computing the proportion (p)

$$p = \frac{k}{N}$$

- k is the number of individuals in the category of interest.
- N is the sample size.

This proportion works well as an effect size in many situations, but is problematic when proportions are far from 0.50.[3] For this reason, it is useful to transform proportions (p) into logits (l) prior to meta-analytic combination or comparison:

Equation 7.6: Computing logits (l) from proportions

$$l = \ln\left(\frac{p}{1-p}\right)$$

- p is the proportion of individuals in the category of interest.

This logit has the following standard error dependent on the proportion (p) and sample size (N) (Lipsey & Wilson, 2001, p. 40):

Equation 7.7: Standard error of a logit (SE_l)

$$SE_l = \sqrt{\frac{1}{Np} + \frac{1}{N(1-p)}}$$

- p is the proportion of individuals in the category of interest.
- N is the sample size.

Analyses would then be performed on the logit (l), weighted by the standard error (SE_l) as described in Chapters 8 through 10. For reporting, it is useful to back-transform results (e.g., mean effect size) in logits (l) back to proportions (p), using the following equation:

Equation 7.8: Transforming logits to proportions

$$p = \frac{e^l}{e^l + 1}$$

- p is the proportion of individuals in the category of interest.
- l is the logit transformation.

7.1.3   Variances and Standard Deviations

Few meta-analyses have used variances, or the equivalent standard deviation (the square root of the variance), as effect sizes. However, the magnitude of interindividual difference is a potentially interesting focus, so I offer this brief description of using these as effect sizes for meta-analysis.

The standard deviation, which is the square root of the variance, is calculated from raw data as follows:

Equation 7.9: Computing the standard deviation (s) or variance (s^2) from raw data

$$s_X = \sqrt{s_X^2} = \sqrt{\frac{\sum(X_i - \overline{X})^2}{N-1}}$$

- X_i is the score of individual i.
- $\overline{X}$ is the average of X across individuals.
- N is the sample size.

This equation is the unbiased estimate of population standard deviation (and the square root of variance) from a sample (versus a description of the sample variability, which would be computed using N rather than $N - 1$ in the denominator). This is also the statistic commonly reported in primary research. In fact, you will almost never need to calculate this standard deviation, as doing so requires raw data that are typically not available. Fortunately, standard deviations (or variances) are nearly always reported as basic descriptive information in primary studies.[4]

To meta-analytically combine or compare standard deviations (or variances) across studies, you must also compute the standard error used for weighting (see Chapter 8). The standard error of the standard deviation is a function of the standard deviation itself and the sample size (Pigott & Wu, 2008):

Equation 7.10: Standard error of the standard deviation (SE_s)

$$SE_s = \frac{s}{\sqrt{2N}}$$

- s is the (population estimate of the) standard deviation.
- N is the sample size.

The standard error of a variance estimate, as you might expect, is simply Equation 7.10 squared (i.e., $SE_{s^2} = s^2/2N$).

At this point, you may have concluded that meta-analysis of standard deviations (and therefore variances) is straightforward. To a large extent this is true, though three qualifiers should be noted. First, as with the mean, it is necessary that the studies included all use the same measure, or at least measures that can be placed on the same scale. Just as it would make little sense to combine means from studies' incomparable scales, it does not make sense to combine magnitudes of individual difference (i.e., standard deviations) from incomparable scales. Second, standard deviations are not exactly normally distributed, especially with small samples. Following the suggestion of Pigott and Wu (2008), I suggest that you do not attempt to meta-analyze standard deviations if many studies have sample sizes less than 25. A third consideration involves the possibility of diminished standard deviations due to ceiling or floor effects. Ceiling effects occur when most individuals in a study score near the top of the scale, and floor effects occur when most individuals score near the bottom of the scale. In both situations, estimates of standard deviation are lowered because there is less "room" for individuals to vary given the constraints of the scale. For example, if we administered a third-grade math test to graduate students, we would expect that most of them would score near the maximum of the test, and the real individual variability in math skills would not be captured by the observed variability in scores on this test. I suggest two strategies for avoiding this potential biasing effect: (1)

visually observe the means of studies and consider excluding those studies where the mean is close to the bottom or top of the scale, and (2) compute a correlation across studies between means and standard deviations—the presence of an association suggests a potential floor or ceiling effect, whereas the absence of association would suggest this bias is not present.[5]

7.2   WHEN THE METRIC IS MEANINGFUL: RAW DIFFERENCE SCORES

Paralleling the situation when you might want to meta-analyze means and standard deviations—that is, when included studies share a common (or comparable) scale for variable X—there may also be instances when we are interested in comparing two groups on a variable measured on a common scale across studies. For example, studies may all compare two groups on variable X using a common scale for X. Although Chapter 5 described the value of standardizing mean differences (e.g., g), in this situation of common scales across studies, it may be more meaningful to meta-analytically combine and compare studies on this common scale. In other words, it may sometimes be useful to retain the meaningful metric of the scale on which variables were measured in primary studies (see also Becker, 2003).

There are various circumstances in which you may prefer to compare two groups in terms of raw rather than standardized differences. For example, gender differences in height may be more meaningful when expressed as inches than as number of standard deviations. Similarly, the effectiveness of a weight-loss program might be more meaningful if expressed in pounds (e.g., the treatment group lost, on average, 10 pounds more than the control group). If you are meta-analytically combining or comparing studies that all use the same measure of the variable of interest (or at least measures that use the same scale), it is straightforward to use these raw, or unstandardized, differences as effect sizes.

The unstandardized mean is simply the raw difference in means between two groups (Lipsey & Wilson, 2001, p. 47):

Equation 7.11: Unstandardized mean difference (UM)

$UM = M_1 - M_2$

- M_1 is the mean of Group 1.
- M_2 is the mean of Group 2.

You probably recognize this equation from Chapter 5, where we discussed the various standardized mean differences (Equations 5.5 to 5.7). In Equation 7.11, however, there is no denominator involving some variant of the standard deviation. This standard deviation denominator of Equations 5.5 to 5.7 served to standardize the mean differences in terms of standard deviation units. Here, where the metric is meaningful, you do *not* wish to standardize this mean difference, but instead leave it in its unstandardized, or raw score, metric.

To estimate the standard error of this unstandardized mean difference (for weighting in your meta-analysis; see Chapter 8), you use the following equation (see Bond, Wiitala, & Richard, 2003; Lipsey & Wilson, 2001, p. 47):

Equation 7.12: Standard error of the unstandardized mean difference (SE_{UM})

$$SE_{UM} = s_p \sqrt{\frac{1}{n_1} + \frac{1}{n_2}} \approx \frac{2s_p}{\sqrt{N_{\text{total (equal sample size)}}}}$$

- s_p is the pooled standard deviation from both groups.
- n_1 and n_2 are the sizes of Groups 1 and 2.
- N_{total} is the total sample size of the study (assuming equal sample size per group).

Once you have computed unstandardized mean differences and associated standard errors for each study, it is then possible to meta-analytically combine and contrast these metrically meaningful effect sizes. However, Bond and colleagues (2003) discourage reliance on these traditional techniques and suggest more complicated procedures.[6] I suspect that their cautions are most appropriate when studies have small sample sizes and that the increase in precision from their more advanced techniques diminishes with larger sample sizes. However, further quantitative studies are needed to evaluate this claim. Regardless, their alternative formulas do not affect the computation of a mean effect size, but rather inferences about this effect size and heterogeneity. For now, I encourage you to consider the alternative formulas of Bond et al. (2003) if you are meta-analyzing unstandardized mean differences from studies with small sample sizes and your initial analyses of significance of the mean effect or test of heterogeneity are very close to your chosen level of statistical significance. In other cases, you may find the standard methods described in Chapter 8 more straightforward with little substantive impact on your results.

7.3   REGRESSION COEFFICIENTS AND SIMILAR MULTIVARIATE EFFECT SIZES

7.3.1   Regression Coefficients

In many areas of study, researchers are interested in associations of one variable (X), with another variable (Y) controlling for other variables (Zs). For example, education researchers might wish to understand the relation between ethnicity and academic success, controlling for SES. Or a developmental researcher might be interested in whether (and to what extent) children's use of relational aggression (e.g., gossiping about others, intentionally excluding someone from group activities) is associated with maladjustment, above and beyond their use of overt aggression (e.g., hitting, name calling, which is strongly correlated with relational aggression; see Card et al., 2008). In these cases, the central question involves the magnitude of unique, independent association between X and Y after controlling for Z (or multiple Zs).

In primary research, this situation is handled through multiple regression and similar techniques. Specifically, in these situations you would regress the presumed dependent variable (Y) onto both the predictor of interest (X) and other variables that you wish to control (one or more Zs). The well-known equation for this regression is (e.g., Cohen et al., 2003):

Equation 7.13: Multiple regression of Y onto X and Z

$Y = B_0 + B_1 X + B_2 Z + e$

- Y is the presumed dependent variable.
- X is the predictor variable of interest.
- Z is the variable one wishes to control.
- B_0 is the intercept, or implied value of Y when all predictors equal 0.
- B_1 is the regression coefficient of X, representing the unstandardized association of X with Y when Z is held constant.
- B_2 is the regression coefficient of Z, representing the unstandardized association of Z with Y when X is held constant.
- e is the error or residual term, representing the discrepancy between actual values and predicted values of Y.

Here, the regression coefficient of X (B_1) is of most interest. However, this value by itself is often less intuitive than several alternative indexes. The first possibility is the standardized regression coefficient, β_1, which is interpretably similar to the unstandardized regression coefficient but expressed according to a range from 0 (no unique association) to ±1 (perfect unique association).[7] If the X and Y variables are all measured according to a common scale, then the unstandardized regression coefficient may be meta-analyzed. But the more common situation of X and Y measured on different scales across different studies requires that we rely on the standardized regression coefficient. This standardized regression coefficient will often be reported in primary studies, but when only the component bivariate correlations are reported, you can rely on the following definitional formula (Cohen et al., 2003, p. 68) to compute this coefficient from correlations:

Equation 7.14: Computing standardized regression coefficients (β_1)

$$\beta_1 = \frac{r_{Y1} - r_{Y2}r_{12}}{1 - r_{12}^2}$$

- r_{Y1} is the correlation between the variable of interest (X) and Y.
- r_{Y2} is the correlation between the control variable (Z) and Y.
- r_{12} is the correlation between X and Z.

7.3.2   Semipartial Correlations

Another index of the unique association is the semipartial correlation (sr), which is the (directional) square root of the variance of X that does not overlap with Z with all of Y (vs. the partial correlation, which quantifies the variance of this nonoverlapping part of X relative to the part of Y that does not overlap with Z). Although sr is often reported, you may need to calculate it from bivariate correlations using the following definitional formulas (Cohen et al., 2003, pp. 73–74):

Equation 7.15: Computing semipartial (sr) correlations

$$sr_1 = \frac{r_{Y1} - r_{Y2}r_{12}}{\sqrt{1 - r_{12}^2}}$$

- r_{Y1} is the correlation between the variable of interest (X) and Y.
- r_{Y2} is the correlation between the control variable (Z) and Y.
- r_{12} is the correlation between X and Z.

As with r, it is preferable to transform sr using Fisher's Z transformation (Equation 5.2) before analysis and then back-transform average Z_{sr} to sr or pr for reporting.

7.3.3 Standard Errors of Multivariate Effect Sizes

Thus far, I have talked about three potential effect sizes for meta-analysis of associations of X with Y, controlling for Z. As I describe further in Chapter 8, it is also necessary to compute standard errors for each for potential use in weighting meta-analytic combination and comparison across studies. The following formulas provide the standard errors for these four effect sizes (Cohen et al., 2003):

Equation 7.16: Standard errors for independent effect sizes

$$SE_{B_1} = \frac{s_Y}{s_X} \sqrt{\frac{1}{1-R_1^2}} \sqrt{\frac{1-R_Y^2}{N-p-1}}$$

$$SE_{\beta_1} = \sqrt{\frac{1}{1-R_1^2}} \sqrt{\frac{1-R_Y^2}{N-p-1}}$$

$$SE_{Z_{sr}} = \frac{1}{\sqrt{N-p-2}}$$

- s_Y and s_X are the standard deviations of Y and X.
- R_X^2 is the variance in X predicted by other variables in the model (R_{XZ}^2 if there is only one control variable, Z).
- R_Y^2 is the variance in Y predicted in the model (by X and all Zs).
- N is the sample size.
- p is the number of predictors of Y (including X and all Zs).

Having described the computations of independent associations and their standard errors, I need to caution you about their potential use in meta-analysis. A critical limiting factor in using these effect sizes from multiple regression analyses is that every study should include the same covariates (Zs) in analyses from which results are drawn. In other words, it is meaningful to compare the independent association between X and Y only if every study included in our meta-analysis controls for the same Z or set of Zs. If different studies include fewer or more, or simply different, covariates, then it makes no sense to combine the effect sizes of the type described here (i.e., regression coefficients, semipartial or partial correlations) from these studies.

If different studies do use different covariates, then you have two options, both of which require access to basic, bivariate correlations among all relevant variables (Y, X, and all Zs). The first option is to compute the desired effect sizes (i.e., regression coefficients, semipartial or partial correlations) from these bivariate correlations for each study and then meta-analyze these now-comparable effect sizes. This requires that all included studies report the necessary bivariate correlations (or you are able to obtain these from the authors). The second option is to meta-analyze the relevant bivariate correlations from each study in their bivariate form and then use these meta-analyzed bivariate correlations as sufficient statistics for multivariate analysis. This option is more flexible than the first one in that it can include studies reporting some but not all bivariate correlations. I discuss this latter approach in more detail in Chapter 12.

7.3.4 Differential Indices

Differential indices capture the magnitude of difference between two correlations within a study. Although these differential indices are rarely used, they do offer some unique opportunities to answer specific research questions. Next, I describe differential indices for both dependent and independent correlations.

7.3.4.1 Differential Index for Dependent Correlations

Meta-analysis of partial and semipartial correlations answers questions of whether a unique association exists between two variables, controlling for a third variable. For example, I might consider semipartial correlations of the association of relational aggression with rejection, above and beyond overt aggression. A slightly different question would be whether relational or overt aggression was more strongly correlated to rejection (see Card et al., 2008). More generally, the differential index for dependent correlations indexes the direction and magnitude of difference of two variables' association with a third variable.

This differential index for dependent correlation, $d_{\text{dependent}}$, is computed in a way parallel to the significance test to compare differences between dependent correlations (see Cohen & Cohen, 1983, pp. 56–57). This effect size of differential correlation of two variables (A and B) with a third variable (Y) is computed from the three correlations among these variables (Card et al., 2008):

Equation 7.17: Differential index for dependent correlations
($d_{dependent}$)

$$d_{dependent} = \frac{(r_{AY}-r_{BY})\sqrt{(N-1)(1+r_{AB})}}{\sqrt{\frac{2(N-1)}{N-1}|R|+\bar{r}(1-r_{AB})^3}} \times \frac{1}{\sqrt{N-3}}$$

- r_{AY} is the correlation of A with Y.
- r_{BY} is the correlation of B with Y.
- r_{AB} is the correlation between A and B.
- N is the sample size.
- $|R|$ equals $1-r^2_{AY}-r^2_{BY}-r^2_{AB} + 2\,r_{AY}\,r_{BY}\,r_{AB}$.
- $\bar{r}$ equals $(r_{AY} + r_{BY})/2$.

This differential index will be positive when the correlation of A with Y is greater than the correlation of B with Y, zero when these two correlations are equal, and negative when the correlation of B with Y is larger. This differential correlation can be meta-analytically combined and compared across studies to draw conclusions regarding the extent (or under what conditions) one association is stronger than the other.

7.3.4.2   Differential Index for Independent Correlations

The differential index can also be used to meta-analytically compare differences between independent correlations, that is, correlations drawn from different populations. Independent correlations may emerge within a single primary study when the primary research reports effect sizes for different subgroups. For example, in our example meta-analysis of relational aggression and rejection (Card et al., 2008), we were interested in evaluating gender differences in the magnitude of associations between relational aggression and rejection. This question is really one of moderation (Is the relational aggression with rejection link moderated by gender?), but here we compute the moderating effect within each study and subsequently meta-analyze the effect.

This differential index for independent correlations parallels the significance test to compare differences between independent correlations (see Cohen & Cohen, 1983, pp. 54–55). Given separately reported correlations for subgroups A and B within a single primary study, we apply Fisher's transformation to each and then use the following equation to index the differential association for the two subgroups (Card et al., 2008):

Equation 7.18: Differential index for independent correlations ($d_{independent}$)

$$d_{independent} = \frac{2(Zr_A - Zr_B)}{\left(\sqrt{\dfrac{1}{n_A - 3} + \dfrac{1}{n_B - 3}}\right)(n_A + n_B - 4)}$$

- Zr_A is the Fisher's Z transformation of the correlation for subgroup A.
- Zr_B is the Fisher's Z transformation of the correlation for subgroup B.
- n_A is the number of participants in subgroup A in the study.
- n_B is the number of participants in subgroup B in the study.

This differential index for independent correlations will be positive when the correlation is more positive (i.e., stronger positive or weaker negative) for subgroup A than B, negative when the correlation is more negative (i.e., weaker positive or stronger negative) for subgroup A than B, and zero when groups A and B have the same correlation. Meta-analytic combination across multiple studies providing data for this index provides evidence of whether (and how strongly) subgroup classification moderates this correlation.

7.4 MISCELLANEOUS EFFECT SIZES

As I hope is becoming increasingly clear, you can include a wide range of options for effect sizes in your meta-analyses. Although this section on miscellaneous effect sizes could include dozens of possibilities, I limit my description to two that seem especially useful: scale internal consistency and longitudinal change scores.

7.4.1 Scale Internal Reliability

Internal consistency, or the internal reliability of a scale, indexes the magnitude to which items of a scale are homogeneous. The most widely used index of this internal consistency is Cronbach's alpha, a (Cronbach, 1951), which can be computed based on the number of items in α scale (j) and the average correlation among these items ($\bar{r}$):

**Equation 7.19: Computing Cronbach's alpha (α)
for internal consistency**

$$\alpha = \frac{j\bar{r}}{1+(j-1)\bar{r}}$$

- j is the number of items of the scale.
- $\bar{r}$ is the average correlation among items.

There are two situations in which you might be interested in meta-analyzing internal consistency. One situation was raised in Chapter 6—when I described the situation in which you wish to correct for unreliability but this estimate is not provided in some studies. In this situation, a meta-analytically derived mean or predicted variable (i.e., predicted by characteristics of the study) provides a reasonable estimate of internal consistency to use when correcting for the artifact of unreliability. A second situation is when the internal consistency is itself of interest. For instance, you might be interested in knowing the average internal consistency of a scale across multiple studies (i.e., the mean internal consistency), or you might be interested in the conditions under which internal consistency is higher or lower (i.e., moderator analyses across study characteristics). In both situations, meta-analysis of internal consistency estimates is valuable.

Although various methods of meta-analyzing reliability results have been proposed, I rely on the method described by Rodriguez and Maeda (2006) for Cronbach's alpha. This approach is relatively simple, and Cronbach's alpha is reported in most studies.[8] This method relies on a transformation of Cronbach's alpha as the effect size (Rodriguez & Maeda, 2006):

**Equation 7.20: Transformation of Cronbach's alpha
for meta-analysis**

$$ES_\alpha = \sqrt[3]{1-\alpha}$$

- α is the estimate of Cronbach's alpha in the study.

The standard error of this transformed internal consistency is a function of the number of items on the scale used in the study, the sample size, and the estimate of internal consistency itself (Rodriguez & Maeda, 2006):

Equation 7.21: Standard error of transformed Cronbach's alpha

$$SE_{ES_\alpha} = \sqrt{\frac{18J(N-1)(1-\alpha)^{\frac{2}{3}}}{(J-1)(9N-11)^2}}$$

- J is the number of items on the scale used in the study.
- N is the sample size of the study.
- α is the estimate of Cronbach's alpha in the study.

After computing the mean transformed internal consistency (as well as confidence interval limits or predicted values at different levels of moderators), you should back-transform results into the more interpretable Cronbach's alpha:

Equation 7.22: Back-transformation of Cronbach's alpha

$$\alpha = 1 - ES_\alpha^3$$

- α is the internal consistency Cronbach's alpha.
- ES_α is the transformed internal consistency found in the meta-analysis.

7.4.2 Longitudinal Change Scores

Longitudinal change is of central interest in many areas. In developmental science, much attention is given to change across age, which is often studied using naturalistic longitudinal designs (see Little et al., 2009). Longitudinal change is also relevant to experimental and quasi-experimental research; for instance, you might be interested in changes in some index of functioning from before to after an intervention. Given this empirical interest in longitudinal change, it follows that you may be interested in meta-analytically combining and comparing this change across studies.

We can consider longitudinal change scores as indexing a two-variable association between time (X) and the variable that is potentially increasing or decreasing (Y). Because most studies that you might potentially meta-analyze treat time as a categorical variable (e.g., Waves 1 and 2 of a survey, pre- and postintervention scores),[9] you can represent these change scores as either standardized mean change (e.g., g) or unstandardized mean change (if all studies use the same scale for the Y variable). Because it is more likely that you will want to meta-analyze studies using different measures of Y, I focus only on the standardized mean change here (for a description of unstandardized mean change, see Lipsey & Wilson, 2001, pp. 42–44).

The standardized mean change effect size is defined by the following formula (Lipsey & Wilson, 2001, p. 44):

Equation 7.23: Computing standardized mean change (g_{change})

$$g_{change} = \frac{M_2 - M_1}{\sqrt{\dfrac{s_1^2 + s_2^2}{2}}}$$

- M_1 and M_2 are the means at times 1 and 2.
- s_1 and s_2 are the standard deviations at times 1 and 2.

This equation is identical to that for the standardized mean difference (g) between independent groups shown in Chapter 5, if you recognize that the denominator is simply the pooled standard deviation across time. From this equation, you see that computing g_{change} from reported descriptive data is straightforward. One caveat is that you should be careful that the reported means and standard deviations at each time come from only the individuals who participated in both times. In other words, you need descriptive data from the nonattriting sample.[10]

Although most research reports will provide these descriptive data, you may find instances where they do not. If the primary study reports only a repeated-measures t-test or ANOVA (F-ratio), along with the correlation between Waves 1 and 2 (i.e., interindividual stability), you can use this information to compute g_{change} using the following equation (which was also provided in Chapter 5):

Equation 7.24: Computing g_{change} from repeated-measures inferential tests

$$g_{change} = \frac{t_{dependent}\sqrt{2(1-r)}}{\sqrt{N}} = \sqrt{\frac{F_{repeated(1,df)}\sqrt{2(1-r)}}{N}}$$

- t is the positive or negative value of the t-test for dependent means.
- $F(1,df)$ is the F-ratio from a repeated-measures ANOVA.
- N is the sample size.
- r is the correlation between Wave 1 and Wave 2 scores (i.e., interindividual stability of the variable).

When using these equations, you should be sure that you are assigning the correct sign to the effect size. I strongly recommend always using positive scores to represent increases in the variable over time and negative scores to represent decreases. These equations also allow us to compute g_{change} from probability levels—be they exact (e.g., $p = .034$) or minimum effect sizes from a range (e.g., $p < .05$). Here, you simply look up the associated t or F value given the reported level of significance and degrees of freedom.

In addition to the effect size g_{change}, we also need to compute the standard error of this estimate for weighting in our meta-analysis. As you would expect, the standard error is dependent on the sample size; but it is also dependent on the interindividual stability (r) of the variable across time. It is critical to find this information in the research report for accurately computing this standard error; if it is not provided, you should seek to obtain this information from the study authors. The equation for the standard error for g_{change} is (Lipsey & Wilson, 2001, p. 44):

Equation 7.25: Computing standard error for g_{change}

$$SE_{g_{change}} = \sqrt{\frac{2(1-r)}{N} + \frac{g_{change}^2}{2N}}$$

- r is the interindividual stability of the variable across the time studied.
- g_{change} is the standardized mean change effect size (see Equation 7.24).
- N is the sample size.

Before concluding this section on longitudinal change scores, I want to note that this approach is not limited only to longitudinal designs, even though that is where we are most likely to apply them. Instead, this approach can be used with any data that would typically be analyzed (in primary research) using paired-sample *t*-tests or two-group repeated-measures ANO-VAs. For example, this effect size would be appropriate in treatment studies where individuals are matched into pairs, and then randomly assigned to treatment versus control groups (see e.g., Shadish et al., 2002, p. 118). Similarly, this effect size would be useful when meta-analyzing dyadic data in which individuals are interdependently linked, such as studies considering differences between husbands and wives or between older and younger siblings (see Kenny, Kashy, & Cook, 2006). Although these types of studies are likely less common in most fields, you can keep these possibilities in mind.

7.5   PRACTICAL MATTERS: THE OPPORTUNITIES AND CHALLENGES OF META-ANALYZING UNIQUE EFFECT SIZES

7.5.1   The Challenges of Meta-Analyzing Unique Effect Sizes

Meta-analyzing unique effect sizes carries a number of challenges. In this section, I describe some challenges to meta-analyzing unique effect sizes. These challenges apply not only to the effect sizes I have described in this chapter, but to a nearly unlimited range of other advanced effect sizes that we might consider.

One challenge of using unique effect sizes in meta-analysis is that the primary studies might often fail to report the necessary data. When I described basic effect sizes in Chapter 5, I mentioned that these effect sizes are often reported, or else sufficient information to compute such effect sizes are typically reported. In this chapter, I have focused attention on some effect sizes that are likely to be commonly reported (e.g., internal consistency), but this information is still less likely to be reported in all relevant studies. If you are using unique effect sizes (either those I have described here or others), it will be important for you to contact authors of studies that could provide relevant data that are not reported. Often, you will need to give explicit instructions to these authors on how to compute these unique effects, which might be less familiar to researchers than more basic effect sizes (e.g., correlations).

A related challenge involves the inconsistencies in analytic methods and reporting of advanced effect sizes. Earlier in this chapter, I described this challenge when using independent effect sizes, such as regression coefficients or semipartial correlations from multiple regression analyses in which different studies include different predictors/covariates. We can also imagine how this inconsistency would pose obstacles to the use of other effect sizes. For example, imagine that you wanted to meta-analytically combine results of exploratory factor analyses, such as factor loadings and commonality. If you looked at the relevant literature, you would find tremendous variability in the use of principal components versus true factor analysis models, methods of extraction, the way authors determined the number of factors to extract or interpret, and methods of rotation. Given this diversity, it would be difficult, if not impossible, to attempt to meta-analytically combine these results. This example illustrates the challenge of meta-analyzing unique effect sizes from studies that might vary in their analytic methods and reporting.

As I will discuss further in Chapter 8, meta-analysis of an effect size involves not only obtaining an estimate of that effect size for each study, but also computing a standard error for each effect size estimate for weighting. In other words, it is not enough to simply be able to find sufficient data in the primary study to compute the effect size, but you must also determine the correct formula and find the necessary information in the study to compute the standard error. Some readers might agree that the equations just to compute effect sizes are daunting; the formulas to compute standard errors are usually even more challenging and are typically difficult to find in all but the most advanced texts (and in some cases, there is no consensus on what an appropriate standard error is). Furthermore, you typically need more information to calculate the standard errors than the effect sizes, and this information is more often excluded from reports (and more often puzzling to authors if you request this information). In short, you need to remember that, to use an advanced effect size in a meta-analysis, you must be able to compute both its point estimate and its standard error from primary studies.

7.5.2 Balancing the Challenges with the Opportunities of Meta-Analyzing Unique Effect Sizes

Although the use of unique effect sizes in meta-analysis poses several challenges, their use also offers several opportunities. Namely, if only unique effect sizes answer the questions you want to answer, then it is worth facing these challenges to answer these questions. How can you weigh the potential reward versus the cost of using unique effect sizes? Although this is a difficult question to answer, I offer some thoughts next.

First, I suggest asking yourself whether the question you want to answer in your meta-analysis (see Chapter 2) really requires reliance on unique effect sizes. Can your question be effectively answered using traditional effect sizes such as r, g, or o? Is it possible that the question you are asking is similar to one involving these unique effect sizes? If so (to the last question), you might consider coding both the basic and the unique effect sizes from the studies included; you then can attempt to proceed using the unique effect sizes, but can revert to the basic effect sizes if you have to. One special consideration involves questions where you are truly interested in multivariate effect sizes, such as independent associations from multiple regression-type analyses. In these situations, you may want to read Chapter 12 before proceeding, and decide whether you might better answer these questions through multivariate meta-analysis of basic effect sizes rather than through univariate meta-analysis of multivariate effect sizes.

Second, you will want to determine how readily available the necessary information is within the included effect sizes. It is invaluable to examine some of the primary studies that will be included in your planned meta-analysis to get a sense of what sort of information the authors report. When doing so, sample a few studies from different authors or research groups, as their reporting practices likely differ. If you find that the necessary information is usually reported, then this can be taken as encouragement to proceed with meta-analysis of unique effect sizes. However, if the necessary information is rarely or inconsistently reported, you need to assess whether you will be able to obtain this information. Consider both your own willingness to solicit this information from authors and the likely response you will get from them. If you think that the availability of this information will be inconsistent, then consider both (1) the expected total number of studies from which you could get the necessary information, and (2) the degree to which these studies are representative of all studies that have been conducted.

Finally, you need to realistically consider your own expertise with both meta-analysis and the relevant statistical techniques. If this is your first meta-analysis, I recommend against attempting to use unique effect sizes. Performing a good meta-analytic review of basic effect sizes is challenging enough, so I encourage you to get some experience using these before attempting to meta-analyze unique effect sizes (at a minimum, be sure to code both basic and unique effect sizes). If you feel ready to try to meta-analyze unique effect sizes, consider your level of expertise in that particular statistical area (i.e., that regarding the unique effect size). Do you feel you are fluent in computing the effect size from commonly reported information? Are you familiar with the relevant standard errors and believe you can consistently calculate these from reported information? Do you feel comfortable in guiding researchers through the appropriate analyses when you need to request further information from them?

This section might seem discouraging, but I do not intend it to be. Using unique effect sizes in your meta-analysis can provide exciting opportunities to answer unique research questions. At the same time, it is important that you are realistic about your ability to use these unique effect sizes, and proceed with caution (but do proceed).

7.6 SUMMARY

In this chapter, I have described how you can compute several unique effect sizes (i.e., those beyond the basic *r, g,* and *o* described in Chapter 5) and their standard errors. These include single-variable information, namely, means, proportions, and standard deviations; unstandardized mean differences, which are useful when studies use a common metric for the variable of interest; independent associations, such as those obtained through multiple regression; and two miscellaneous effect sizes (internal consistency and longitudinal change) in lesser detail. Although I see great opportunity in using these and other unique effect sizes in meta-analysis, there are also some challenges to doing so, and I have tried to offer practical advice to help you decide whether their use is appropriate for your particular meta-analysis.

7.7 RECOMMENDED READINGS

Becker, B. J. (2003). Introduction to the special section on metric in meta-analysis. *Psychological Methods, 8,* 403–405.—This special section, consisting of this introduction and four papers, provides a useful discussion of the opportunities and challenges of capturing meaningful information of the scale in meta-analysis.

Borenstein, M. (2009). Effect sizes for continuous data. In H. Cooper, L. V. Hedges, & J. C. Valentine (Eds.), *The handbook of research synthesis and meta-analysis* (2nd ed., pp. 221–235). New York: Russell Sage Foundation.—This chapter represents an updated and thorough description of computing effect sizes, including coverage of unstandardized and longitudinal effect sizes.

Rodriguez, M. C., & Maeda, Y. (2006). Meta-analysis of coefficient alpha. *Psychological Methods, 11,* 306–322.—My choice of this article as a recommended reading might seem arbitrary, in that it is about one of several effect sizes I considered in this chapter.

However, I think it is worth reading for two reasons. First, meta-analysis of Cronbach's alpha is valuable and represents a fairly small addition to your coding and analyses. Second, this article demonstrates a typical approach to how quantitative researchers describe and evaluate the meta-analysis of a unique effect size.

NOTES

1. This requirement of identical scales can be violated when the different scales are due to the primary study authors scoring comparable measures in different ways. For example, if two primary studies both use a 6-item scale with items having values from 1 to 5, one study may form a composite by averaging the items, whereas the other forms a composite by summing the items. In this case, it would be possible to transform one of the two means to the same scale of the other (i.e., multiplying the average by 6 to obtain the sum, or dividing the sum by 6 to obtain the average; see Equation 7.1), and the means of the two studies could then be combined and compared. More generally, it might even be possible to transform studies using different scales into a common metric (from the example I provided of one study using a 0–4 scale and the other using a 1–100 scale).

2. In other situations, you may be interested in meta-analytically combining or comparing proportions of individuals falling into one of multiple categories (e.g., children who can be classified as victimized, aggressive, or both aggressive and victimized). In these cases, I recommend coding multiple dichotomous proportions, akin to dummy variables coded for analysis of three or more groups in multiple regression (see e.g., Cohen et al., 2003). In the current example, you would code the proportion of children who are victimized only, the proportion who are aggressive only, and the proportion who are both aggressive and victimized. You would then perform three separate meta-analyses of these three effect sizes (i.e., proportions).

3. According to Lipsey and Wilson (2001, p. 39), using the proportion as an effect size becomes problematic with proportions less than 0.20 or greater than 0.80. In these cases, meta-analysis of proportions underestimates the confidence intervals of mean proportions (i.e., meta-analytically combined across studies) and overestimates the heterogeneity of these proportions across studies.

4. If necessary, you could alternatively calculate standard deviations and variances from other reported information. For instance, you could determine the total variance from an ANOVA table by summing the model and error variances.

5. If it is plausible that both floor and ceiling effects occur within a set of studies, also examine the quadratic association.

6. Specifically, Bond and colleagues (2003) suggest two major alterations. First, they suggest that the usual formula for the standard error of the mean effects size,

$$SE = \sqrt{\frac{1}{\sum w}}$$

be replaced with

$$SE = \sqrt{\frac{1}{\sum_{j=1}^{k} w_j}\left(1 + \frac{4}{\left(\sum_{j=1}^{k} w_j\right)^2}\sum_{L=1}^{k}\left(\frac{(k-1)w_L\left(\sum_{j \neq L}^{k} wj\right)}{(k-1)df_L - 4(k-2)}\right)\right)}$$

over the k studies. Second, they suggest that the test of heterogeneity across studies be modified from a χ^2 test to an F-test where

$$F = \frac{\sum_{j=1}^{k} w_j\left(UM_j - \overline{UM}\right)^2}{\left(k^2 - 1 + 2(k-2)\sum_{j=1}^{k}\frac{1}{df_j}\left(1 - \frac{w_j}{\sum_{L=1}^{k} w_L}\right)^2\right)/(k+1)}$$

$$df_{\text{numerator}} = k - 1$$

and

$$df_{\text{denominator}} = \frac{k^2 - 1}{3\sum_{j=1}^{k}\frac{1}{df_j}\left(1 - \frac{w_j}{\sum_{L=1}^{k} w_L}\right)^2}$$

7. Computationally, the standardized regression coefficient is found by multiplying the unstandardized coefficient by the ratio of the standard deviation of the predictor (X) to the standard deviation of the dependent variable (Y): $\beta_X = B_X\,(sd_X/sd_Y)$ (Cohen et al., 2003, p. 82).

8. Meta-analysis of other forms of reliability, such as test–retest or parallel forms reliabilities, can be performed using the correlation coefficient (r) that indexes these reliabilities. You should include only one type of reliability (e.g., internal consistency, parallel forms, or test–retest) in a meta-analysis; separate meta-analyses for each type of reliability would provide a comprehensive view of the reliability of an item.

9. With the rising use of growth curve modeling, this is not necessarily the case. In these models, time can be analyzed continuously, yielding a standardized

association between time and the variable of interest. However, I do not believe that procedures for meta-analytically combining and comparing growth curve results across studies have yet been developed.

10. We could also compute g_{change} in an unbiased manner in the presence of attrition if the attrition is completely at random (i.e., MCAR; see Little et al., 2000; Schafer & Graham, 2002). However, this is not a testable assumption. Furthermore, the presence of attrition would create difficulty in computing the standard error of g_{change} because this standard error is dependent on a common (nonattriting) sample size.

Part III

Putting the Pieces Together

Combining and Comparing Effect Sizes

8

Basic Computations

Computing Mean Effect Size and Heterogeneity around This Mean

Now that—after months of hard work—you have a collection of effect sizes from the studies included in your meta-analytic review, you can begin the process of combining these effect sizes across studies in order to draw conclusions about the typical effect size in this area of research. Specifically, you can answer two fundamental questions about this research. First, what is the typical effect size (e.g., correlation between *X* and *Y*, difference between two groups) found in the empirical literature? Second, is the diversity of effect sizes found in these studies greater than you would expect from sampling fluctuation alone? The answer to this second question will be important in qualifying your answer to the first question, and will likely guide decisions about whether you explore moderators, or explanations of diversity in effect sizes across studies (see Chapter 9), and the type of model you use to describe the typical effect size (see Chapter 10).

In this chapter, I first describe the logic of differentially weighting results of studies based on the precision of their effect size estimate (Section 8.1). I then discuss ways that you can summarize the typical effect size from a collection of studies, focusing especially on the weighted mean effect size (Section 8.2). Next, I describe how you can make inferences about this mean effect size, specifically in terms of statistical significance testing and confidence intervals around this mean (Section 8.3). The second half of the chapter turns to the analysis of variability in effect sizes across studies (Section 8.4), including statistically testing heterogeneity and an index for representing the amount of heterogeneity (Section 8.5). In the "practical matters" section of this chapter, I consider an important preliminary step before drawing inferences about mean effect size or heterogeneity, the preparation of a set of independent effect sizes (Section 8.6).

8.1   THE LOGIC OF WEIGHTING

Although the democratic process of giving equal weight to each study has some appeal, the reality is that some studies provide better effect size estimates than others, and therefore should be given more weight than others in aggregating results across studies. In this section, I describe the logic of using different weights based on the precision of the effect size estimates.

The idea of the precision of an effect size estimate is related to the standard errors that you computed when calculating effect sizes (see Chapters 5–7). Consider two hypothetical studies: the first study relied on a sample of 10 individuals, finding a correlation between X and Y of .20 (or a Fisher's transformation, Z_r, of . 203); and the second study relied on a sample of 10,000 individuals, finding a correlation between X and Y of .30 (Z_r = .310). Before you take a simple average of these two studies to find the typical correlation between X and Y,[1] it is important to consider the precision of these two estimates of effect size. The first study consisted of only 10 participants, and from the equation for the standard error of Z_r ($SE = 1/\sqrt{(N-3)}$; see Chapter 5), I find that the expectable deviation in Z_r from studies of this size is .378. The second study consisted of many more participants (10,000), so the parallel standard error is 0.010. In other words, a small sample gives us a point estimate of effect size (i.e., the best estimate of the population effect size that can be made from that sample), but it is possible that the actual effect size is much higher or lower than what was found. In contrast, a study with a large sample size is likely to be much more precise in estimating the population effect size. More formally, the standard error of an effect size, which is inversely related to sample size,[2] quantifies the amount of imprecision in a particular study's estimate of the population effect size.

Figure 8.1 further illustrates this concept of precision of effect sizes. In this figure, I have represented five studies of varying sample size, and therefore varying precision in their estimates of the population effect sizes. In this figure, I am in the fortunate—if unrealistic—position of knowing the true population effect size, represented as a vertical line in the middle of the figure. Study 1 yielded a point estimate of the effect size (represented as the

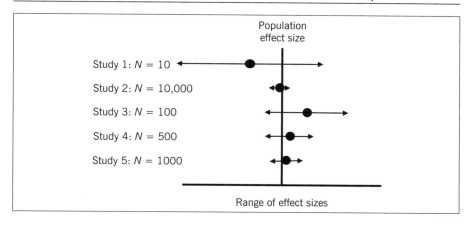

FIGURE 8.1. Conceptual representation of imprecision of effect size estimates.

circle to the right of this study) that was considerably lower than the true effect size, but this study also had a large standard error, and the resulting confidence interval of that study was large (represented as the horizontal arrow around this effect size). If I only had this study to consider, then my best estimate of the population would be too low, and the range of potential effect sizes (i.e., the horizontal range of the confidence interval arrow) would be very large. Note that the confidence interval of this study does include the true population effect size, but this study by itself is of little value in determining where this unknown value lies.

The second study of Figure 8.1 includes a large sample. You can see that the point estimate of the effect size (i.e., the circle to the right of this study) is very close to the true population effect size. You also see that the confidence interval of this study is very narrow; this study has a small standard error and therefore high precision in estimating the population effect size. Clearly, the results of this study offer a great deal of information in determining where the true population effect size lies, and I therefore would want to give more weight to these results than to those from Study 1 when trying to determine this population effect size.

The remaining three studies in Figure 8.1 contain sample sizes between those of Studies 1 and 2. Two observations should be noted regarding these studies. First, although none of these studies perfectly estimates the population effect size (i.e., none of the circles fall perfectly on the vertical line), the larger studies tend to come closer. Second, and related, the confidence intervals all[3] contain the true population effect size.

The crucial difference between the hypothetical situation depicted in Figure 8.1 and reality is that you do not know the true population effect size when you are conducting a meta-analysis. In fact, one of the primary purposes of conducting a meta-analysis is to obtain a best estimate of this population effect size. In other words, you want to decide where to draw the vertical line in Figure 8.1. As I hope is clear at this point, it would make sense to draw this line so that it is closer to the effect size estimates from studies with narrow confidence intervals (i.e., small standard errors), and give less emphasis to ensuring that the line is close to those from studies with wide confidence intervals (i.e., large standard errors). In other words, you want to give more weight to some studies (those with small standard errors) than to others (those with large standard errors).

How do you quantify this differential weighting? Although the choices are virtually limitless,[4] the statistically defensible choice is to weight effect sizes by the inverse of their variances in point estimates (i.e., standard errors squared). In other words, you should determine the weight of a particular study i (w_i) from the standard error of the effect size estimate from that study (SE_i) using the following equation:

Equation 8.1: Weight for study i

$$w_i = \frac{1}{SE_i^2}$$

- SE_i is the standard error of the effect size estimate for study i.

In all analyses I describe in this chapter, you will use this weight. I suggest that you make a variable in your meta-analytic database representing this weight for each study in your meta-analysis. In the running example of this chapter, shown in Table 8.1, I consider 22 studies providing correlations between relational aggression and peer rejection. In addition to listing the study, I have columns showing the sample size, corrected effect sizes in original r and transformed Z_r metrics, and the standard errors (SE_{Z_r}) of these estimates. Note that these effect sizes have been corrected for two artifacts (see Chapter 6)—unreliability and artificial dichotomization (when relevant)—so the standard errors are also adjusted and not directly computable from sample size (for details, see Chapter 6). This table also shows the weight (w) for each study, computed from the standard errors using Equation 8.1.

TABLE 8.1. Example Meta-Analysis of (Artifact-Corrected) Correlations between Relational Aggression and Peer Rejection

Study	Sample size (N)	Effect size (r)	Transformed ES (Z_r)	Standard error (SE)	Weight (w)	wES (w * Z_r)	wES² (w * Z_r²)
Blachman (2003)	228	.525	.583	.0693	208.12	121.27	70.66
Crick & Grotpeter (1995)	491	.198	.201	.0579	297.81	59.74	11.98
Crick et al. (1997)	65	.311	.322	.1325	56.95	18.34	5.90
Geiger (2003)	458	.554	.624	.0484	427.07	266.55	166.37
Hawley et al. (2007)	929	.161	.162	.0346	835.96	135.72	22.03
Henington (1996)	904	.336	.349	.0347	831.95	290.69	101.57
Johnson (2003)	74	.396	.419	.1223	66.89	28.02	11.73
Leff (1995)	151	.617	.721	.0855	136.66	98.48	70.97
Miller (2001)	150	.557	.628	.0845	139.90	87.90	55.23
Murray-Close & Crick (2006)	590	.575	.655	.0426	550.97	361.12	236.69
Nelson et al. (2005)	180	.039	.039	.0831	144.75	5.70	0.22
Ostrov (under review)[a]	139	.358	.375	.0892	125.71	47.14	17.68
Ostrov & Crick (2007)	132	.049	.049	.0922	117.70	5.81	0.29
Ostrov et al. (2004)[b]	60	.000	.000	.1386	52.05	0.00	0.00
Pakaslahti & Keltikangas-Järvinen (1998)	839	.326	.339	.0381	689.52	233.68	79.19
Phillipsen et al. (1999)	262	-.048	-.048	.0642	242.93	-11.73	0.57
Rys & Bear (1997)	266	.454	.489	.0636	246.94	120.85	59.15
Salmivalli et al. (2000)	209	.253	.258	.0715	195.52	50.54	13.06
Tomada & Schneider (1997)	314	.160	.162	.0589	288.73	46.71	7.56
Werner (2000)	881	.477	.519	.0351	810.71	420.41	218.01
Werner & Crick (2004)	517	.469	.509	.0455	482.45	245.37	124.79
Zalecki & Hinshaw (2004)	228	.572	.651	.0702	202.92	132.06	85.94
Sum (Σ)					7,152.21	2,764.36	1,359.60

Note. Hand calculations of these values may not produce exact replications due to rounding errors.
[a]Article was under review during the preparation of this meta-analytic review. It has subsequently been published as Ostrov (2008).
[b]Effect size is lower-bound estimate based on authors' report of only nonsignificant associations.

179

8.2 MEASURES OF CENTRAL TENDENCY IN EFFECT SIZES

8.2.1 Choices of Indices of Central Tendency

Turning momentarily away from the topic of weighting, I now consider the ways in which you can represent the central tendency of effect sizes from a series of studies in your meta-analysis. As with representing central tendency within a primary data analysis, you can consider the mode, median, and mean as possible indices.

The mode (the most commonly occurring value) is not a good choice for representing typical effect sizes in a meta-analysis. The problem is that effect sizes computed from multiple studies are likely to fall along such a fine-grained continuum that identifying the most commonly occurring value is meaningless. Although grouping effect sizes into categories might alleviate the problem, such categorizations are arbitrary and likely lead to a loss of information. In short, I view the mode as a poor choice for describing typical effect sizes in a meta-analytic review.

The median (the middle value of a rank-ordered list of values, or the 50th percentile) is a better choice for representing typical effect sizes in a meta-analysis. This value is easy to determine (e.g., in the example data of Table 8.1, the median effect size is $r = .35$) and is a valuable supplement in many situations because it is less influenced by skew in effect sizes than is the mean. At the same time, the disadvantage of the median, as typically computed, is that it does not differentially weight studies by the precision of their point estimates of effect sizes (see previous section). For this reason, I view the median as at best being a supplement to the mean.

The mean effect size is generally the most important index of central tendency in your meta-analyses. It is widely used in primary research, and therefore well understood by readers. Importantly, it is also possible to differentially weight effect sizes, and therefore give more weight to some studies than to others, by computing a weighted mean effect size. This weighted mean effect size (or the random-effects variant I describe in Chapter 10) represents critical information that will be reported in your meta-analytic reviews.

8.2.2 Computing the Weighted Mean Effect Size

The weighted mean effect size across studies is computed from the weights (w_i) and effect sizes (ES_i) from each of the studies i using the following equation:

Equation 8.2: Weighted mean effect size ($\overline{ES}$)

$$\overline{ES} = \frac{\sum (w_i ES_i)}{\sum w_i}$$

- w_i is the weight for study i.
- ES_i is the effect size estimate from study i.

In other words, the mean effect size is calculated by computing the product of each study's effect size by its weight (creating a separate variable representing this product in your database), summing these products across studies, and dividing this value by the sum of weights across studies. The logic of this equation is more obvious if you consider using $w = 1$ for all studies, or giving equal weight to all studies. Here, the mean is simply the sum of effect sizes divided by the number of effect sizes, the traditional formula for the (unweighted) mean.

Equation 8.2 is generic in that it can be used with any of the effect sizes I have described in this book. With those effect sizes that are typically transformed (e.g., r is typically transformed to Z_r), this formula is applied to the transformed effect size from each study, and the average effect size is then back-transformed to the more interpretable effect size for reporting.

To illustrate the calculation of this weighted mean effect size, consider again the data in Table 8.1. In this table (just to the right of w), I have added a column showing the product of w and the effect size (here, Z_r) for each study. I then summed these values across the 22 studies (easily done within any spreadsheet or basic statistical software package) to obtain the value 2764.36, which is the numerator of Equation 8.2. Also shown at the bottom of Table 8.1 is the sum of weights (w) across the 22 studies, 7152.21, which comprises the denominator of Equation 8.2. I then compute the weighted mean effect size as $\overline{Z_r} = 2764.36/7152.21 = .387$. For reporting, I would transform this mean Z_r into mean r using Equation 5.3, yielding $\overline{r} = .368$.

This average effect size is a crucially important result of your meta-analytic review (and it wasn't nearly as difficult to compute as you might have thought!). After you compute this average effect size, you have valuable information to describe the typical effect sizes in the area of your meta-analysis. However, it is also important to consider the effect size in terms of its statistical significance and confidence intervals, the topic to which I turn next.

8.3 INFERENTIAL TESTING AND CONFIDENCE INTERVALS OF AVERAGE EFFECT SIZES

The key to making inferences regarding statistical significance about, or computing confidence intervals around, this (weighted) mean effect size is to compute a standard error of estimate. Here, I am referring to the standard error of estimating the overall, average effect size, as opposed to the standard error of effect size estimates from each individual study. The standard error of this estimate of average effect size is computed from the following equation:

Equation 8.3: Standard error of the mean effect size ($SE_{\overline{ES}}$)

$$SE_{\overline{ES}} = \sqrt{\frac{1}{\sum w_i}}$$

- w_i is the weight for study i.

The logic of this equation is that you want to cumulate the amount of precision across studies to estimate the precision of your estimate of mean effect size. This logic is clear if you consider Z_r effect size (without artifact corrections), in which the standard error for each study is $1 / \sqrt{(N - 3)}$ and the weight for each study is therefore $N - 3$. If there are many studies with large sample sizes, then the sum of ws (i.e., the denominator in Equation 8.3) will be large, and the standard error of estimate of the mean effect size will be small (i.e., the estimate will be precise). In contrast, if a meta-analysis includes just a few studies with small sample sizes, then the sum of ws is small and the standard error of the estimate of mean effect size will be relatively large. Although the equations for standard errors of other effect sizes are not as straightforward (in that they are not as simply related to sample size), they all follow this logic.

After computing this standard error of the mean effect size, you can use this value to make statistical inferences and to compute confidence intervals. To evaluate statistical significance, one can perform a Wald test, which simply involves dividing a parameter estimate (i.e., the mean effect size) by its standard error:

Equation 8.4: Statistical significance test of the mean effect size

$$Z = \frac{\overline{ES}}{SE_{\overline{ES}}}$$

- $\overline{ES}$ is the mean effect size across studies.
- $SE_{\overline{ES}}$ is the standard error of the mean effect size.

This test is evaluated according to the standard normal distribution, sometimes called the Z test (note that this is different from Fisher's Z_r transformation). The statistical significance of this test can be obtained by looking up the value of Z in any table of standard normal deviates (where e.g., $|Z| > 1.96$ denotes $p < .05$). This test can also be modified from a test of an effect size of zero in order to test the difference from any other null hypothesis value, ES_0, by changing the numerator to $\overline{ES} - ES_0$.

The standard error of the mean effect size can also be used to compute confidence intervals. Specifically, you can compute the lower (ES_{LB}) and upper (ES_{UB}) bounds for the effect size using the following equation:

Equation 8.5: Lower- and upper-bound effect sizes for confidence intervals

$$ES_{LB} = \overline{ES} - Z_{1-\alpha}SE_{\overline{ES}}$$

$$ES_{UB} = \overline{ES} + Z_{1-\alpha}SE_{\overline{ES}}$$

- $\overline{ES}$ is the mean effect size across studies.
- $Z_{1-\alpha}$ is the two-tailed standard normal deviate for a given level of significance.
- $SE_{\overline{ES}}$ is the standard error of the mean effect size.

This equation can be used to compute any level of confidence interval desired, though 95% confidence intervals (i.e., two-tailed $\alpha = .05$, so $Z = 1.96$) are typical. If the effect size you are using is one that is transformed (e.g., Z_r, $\ln(o)$), you should calculate the mean, lower-bound, and upper-bound effect sizes using these transformed values, and then back-translate each into interpretable effect size metrics (e.g., r, o).

To illustrate these computations using the running example, I refer again to Table 8.1. I have already summed the weights (w) across the 22 studies, so I can apply Equation 8.3 to obtain the standard error of the mean effect size,

$SE_{\bar{z}_r} = \sqrt{1/\sum w} = \sqrt{1/7152.21} = .0118$. I can use this standard error to evaluate the statistical significance of the average effect size (Z_r) using the Wald test of Equation 8.4, $Z = .387/.0118 = 32.70$, $p < .001$. I would therefore conclude that this average effect size is significantly greater than zero (i.e., there is a positive association between relational aggression and peer rejection). To create 95% confidence intervals, I would compute the lower-bound value of the effect size using Equation 8.5 as $Z_{rLB} = \bar{Z}_r - Z_{1-\alpha}SE_{\overline{ES}} = .387 - 1.96*.0118 = .363$, which would then be transformed (using Equation 5.3) for reporting to a lower-bound $r = .348$. Similarly, I would compute the upper-bound value $Z_{rUB} = \bar{Z}_r + Z_{1-\alpha}SE_{\overline{ES}} = .387 + 1.96 * .0118 = .410$, which is converted to upper bound $r = .388$ for reporting. To summarize, the mean correlation of this example meta-analysis is .368, which is significantly greater than zero ($p < .001$), and the 95% confidence interval of this correlation ranges from .348 to .388.

8.4   EVALUATING HETEROGENEITY AMONG EFFECT SIZES

In Figure 8.1, all of the studies had confidence intervals that contained the vertical line representing the overall population effect size. This situation is called homogeneity—most of the studies capture a common population effect size, and the differences that do exist among their point estimates of effect sizes (i.e., the circles in Figure 8.1) are no more than expected by random-sampling fluctuations. Although not every study's confidence interval needs to overlap with a common effect size in order to conclude homogeneity (these are, after all, only probabilistic confidence intervals), most should. More formally, there is an expectable amount of deviation among study effect size estimates, based on their standard errors of estimate, and you can compare whether the actual observed deviation among your study effect sizes exceeds this expected value.

If the deviation among studies does exceed the amount of expectable deviation, you conclude (with some qualifications I describe below) that the effect sizes are heterogeneous. In other words, the single vertical line in Figure 8.1 representing a single common effect size is not adequate. In the situation of heterogeneous effect sizes, you have three options: (1) ignore the heterogeneity and analyze the data as if it is homogeneous (as you might expect, the least justifiable choice); (2) conduct moderator analyses (see Chapter 9), which attempt to predict between-study differences in effect size using the characteristics of studies coded (e.g., methodological features, characteristics of the sample); or (3) fit an alternative model to that of Figure 8.1, in which the population effect size is modeled as a distribution rather than a vertical line (a random-effects model; see Chapter 10).

8.4.1 Significance Test of Heterogeneity

The heterogeneity (vs. homogeneity) of effect sizes is frequently evaluated by calculating a statistic Q. This test is called either a homogeneity test or, less commonly, a heterogeneity test; other terms used include simply a Q test or Hedges's test for homogeneity (or Hedges's Q test). I prefer the term "heterogeneity test" given that the alternate hypothesis is of heterogeneity, and therefore a statistically significant result implies heterogeneity. This test involves computing a value (Q) that represents the amount of heterogeneity in effect sizes among studies in your meta-analysis using the following equation (Cochran, 1954; Hedges & Olkin, 1985, p. 123; Lipsey & Wilson, 2001, p. 116):

Equation 8.6: Significance test for heterogeneity (Q)

$$Q = \sum \left(w_i \left(ES_i - \overline{ES} \right)^2 \right) = \sum \left(w_i ES_i^2 \right) - \frac{\left(\sum \left(w_i ES_i \right) \right)^2}{\sum w_i}$$

$dr = \kappa - 1$

- w_i is the weight of study i.
- ES_i is the effect size estimate from study i.
- $\overline{ES}$ is the mean effect size across studies.
- k is the number of studies.[5]

The left portion of this equation is the definitional formula for Q and is relatively straightforward to understand. One portion of this equation simply computes the (squared) deviation between the effect size from each study and the mean effect size across studies, which is your best estimate of the population effect size, or vertical line of Figure 8.1. This squared deviation is multiplied by the study weight, which you recall (Equation 8.1) is the inverse of the squared standard error of that study. In other words, the equation is essentially the ratio of the (squared) deviations between the effect sizes to the (squared) expected deviation. Therefore, when studies are homogeneous, you expect this ratio to be close to 1.0 for each study, and so the sum of this ratio across all studies is going to be approximately equal to the number of studies (k) minus 1 (the minus 1 is due to the fact that the population effect size is

estimated by your mean effect size from your sample of studies). When studies are heterogeneous, you expect the (squared) deviations between studies
and mean effect sizes to be larger than the (squared) expected deviations, or
standard errors. Therefore, the ratio will be greater than 1.0 for most studies, and the resulting sum of this ratio across studies will be higher than the
number of studies minus 1.

Exactly how high should Q be before you conclude heterogeneity? Under
the null hypothesis of homogeneity, the Q statistic is distributed as χ^2 with
$df = k - 1$. Therefore, you can look up the value of the Q with a particular df
in any chi-square table, such as that of Table 8.2,[6] to determine whether the
effect sizes are more heterogeneous than expected by sampling variability
alone.

The equation in the right portion of Equation 8.5 provides the same
value of Q as the definitional formula on the left (it is simply an algebraic
rearrangement). However, this computational equation is easier to compute
from your meta-analytic database. Specifically, you need three variables (or
columns in a spreadsheet): the w_i and $w_i ES_i$ that you already calculated to
compute the mean effect size, and $w_i ES_i^2$ that can be easily calculated. To
illustrate, the rightmost column of Table 8.1 displays this $w_i ES_i^2$ for each of
the 22 studies in the running example, with the sum $(\Sigma w_i ES_i^2)$ found to be
1359.60 (bottom of table). Given the previously computed (when calculating
the mean effect size) sums, $\Sigma w_i = 7152.21$ and $\Sigma w_i ES_i = 2764.36$, you can compute the heterogeneity statistic in this example using Equation 8.6,

$$Q = \sum \left(w_i ES_i^2 \right) - \frac{\left(\sum \left(w_i ES_i \right) \right)^2}{\sum w_i} = 1359.60 - \frac{(2764.36)^2}{7152.21} = 291.17$$

You can evaluate this Q value using $df = k - 1 = 22 - 1 = 21$. From Table 8.2,
you see that this value is statistically significant ($p < .001$). As I describe in
the next section, this statistically significant Q leads us to reject the null
hypothesis of homogeneity and conclude the alternate hypothesis of heterogeneity.

8.4.2   Interpreting the Test of Heterogeneity

The Q statistic is used to evaluate the null hypothesis of homogeneity versus the alternate hypothesis of heterogeneity. If the Q exceeds the critical
χ^2 value given the df and level of statistical significance chosen (see Table
8.2), then you conclude that the effect sizes are heterogeneous. That is, you
would conclude that the effect sizes are not all estimates of a single popula-

TABLE 8.2. Critical Values of χ^2 by df and Level of Significance (p)

df	$p = .1$	$p = .05$	$p = .01$	$p = .005$	$p = .001$
1	2.706	3.841	6.635	7.879	10.828
2	4.605	5.991	9.210	10.597	13.816
3	6.251	7.815	11.345	12.838	16.266
4	7.779	9.488	13.277	14.860	18.467
5	9.236	11.070	15.086	16.750	20.515
6	10.645	12.592	16.812	18.548	22.458
7	12.017	14.067	18.475	20.278	24.322
8	13.362	15.507	20.090	21.955	26.124
9	14.684	16.919	21.666	23.589	27.877
10	15.987	18.307	23.209	25.188	29.588
11	17.275	19.675	24.725	26.757	31.264
12	18.549	21.026	26.217	28.300	32.909
13	19.812	22.362	27.688	29.819	34.528
14	21.064	23.685	29.141	31.319	36.123
15	22.307	24.996	30.578	32.801	37.697
16	23.542	26.296	32.000	34.267	39.252
17	24.769	27.587	33.409	35.718	40.790
18	25.989	28.869	34.805	37.156	42.312
19	27.204	30.144	36.191	38.582	43.820
20	28.412	31.410	37.566	39.997	45.315
21	29.615	32.671	38.932	41.401	46.797
22	30.813	33.924	40.289	42.796	48.268
23	32.007	35.172	41.638	44.181	49.728
24	33.196	36.415	42.980	45.559	51.179
25	34.382	37.652	44.314	46.928	52.620
26	35.563	38.885	45.642	48.290	54.052
27	36.741	40.113	46.963	49.645	55.476
28	37.916	41.337	48.278	50.993	56.892
29	39.087	42.557	49.588	52.336	58.301
30	40.256	43.773	50.892	53.672	59.703
35	46.059	49.802	57.342	60.275	66.619
40	51.805	55.758	63.691	66.766	73.402

df	$p = .1$	$p = .05$	$p = .01$	$p = .005$	$p = .001$
45	57.505	61.656	69.957	73.166	80.077
50	63.167	67.505	76.154	79.490	86.661
55	68.796	73.311	82.292	85.749	93.168
60	74.397	79.082	88.379	91.952	99.607
65	79.973	84.821	94.422	98.105	105.988
70	85.527	90.531	100.425	104.215	112.317
75	91.061	96.217	106.393	110.286	118.599
80	96.578	101.879	112.329	116.321	124.839
85	102.079	107.522	118.236	122.325	131.041
90	107.565	113.145	124.116	128.299	137.208
95	113.038	118.752	129.973	134.247	143.344
100	118.498	124.342	135.807	140.169	149.449
110	129.385	135.480	147.414	151.948	161.581
120	140.233	146.567	158.950	163.648	173.617
130	151.045	157.610	170.423	175.278	185.571
140	161.827	168.613	181.840	186.847	197.451
150	172.581	179.581	193.208	198.360	209.265
160	183.311	190.516	204.530	209.824	221.019
170	194.017	201.423	215.812	221.242	232.719
180	204.704	212.304	227.056	232.620	244.370
190	215.371	223.160	238.266	243.959	255.976
200	226.021	233.994	249.445	255.264	267.541
210	236.655	244.808	260.595	266.537	279.066
220	247.274	255.602	271.717	277.779	290.556
230	257.879	266.378	282.814	288.994	302.012
240	268.471	277.138	293.888	300.182	313.437
250	279.050	287.882	304.940	311.346	324.832
300	331.789	341.395	359.906	366.844	381.425
350	384.306	394.626	414.474	421.900	437.488
400	436.649	447.632	468.724	476.606	493.132
450	488.849	500.456	522.717	531.026	548.432
500	540.930	553.127	576.493	585.207	603.446

tion value, but rather, multiple population values. If Q does not exceed this value, then you fail to reject the null hypothesis of homogeneity.

This description makes clear that evaluation of Q (i.e., of heterogeneity vs. homogeneity) is a statistical hypothesis test. This observation implies two cautions in interpreting findings regarding Q. First, you need to be aware that this test of heterogeneity provides us information about the likelihood of results being homogeneous versus heterogeneous, but does not tell us the *magnitude* of heterogeneity if it exists (a consideration you should be particularly sensitive to, given your attention to effect sizes as a meta-analyst). I describe an alternative way to quantify the magnitude of heterogeneity in the next Section (8.4.3). Second, you need to consider the statistical power of this heterogeneity test—if you have inadequate power, then you should be very cautious in interpreting a nonsignificant result as evidence of homogeneity (the null hypothesis). I describe the statistical power of this test in Section 8.4.4.

8.4.3   An Alternative Representation of Heterogeneity

Whereas the Q statistic and associated significance test for heterogeneity can be useful in drawing conclusions about *whether* a set of effect sizes in your meta-analysis are heterogeneous versus homogeneous, they do not indicate *how* heterogeneous the effect sizes are (with heterogeneity of zero representing homogeneity). One useful index of heterogeneity in your meta-analysis is the I^2 index. This index is interpreted as the percentage of variability among effect sizes that exists between studies relative to the total variability among effect sizes (Higgins & Thompson, 2002; Huedo-Medina, Sánchez-Meca, Marín-Martínez, & Botella, 2006). The I^2 index is computed using the following equation (Higgins & Thompson, 2002; Huedo-Medina et al., 2006):

Equation 8.7: Computing I^2 to index magnitude of heterogeneity

$$I^2 = \frac{\hat{\tau}^2}{\hat{\tau}^2 + \sigma^2} = \begin{cases} \dfrac{Q - (k-1)}{Q} \times 100\% & \text{when } Q > (k-1) \\ 0 & \text{when } Q \le (k-1) \end{cases}$$

- $\hat{\tau}^2$ is the estimated between-study variability (see Chapter 10).
- σ^2 is the within-study variability (see Chapter 10).
- Q is the statistic computed for significance tests of heterogeneity (see Equation 8.6).
- k is the number of studies.

The left portion of this equation uses terms that I will not describe until Chapter 10, so I defer discussion of this portion for now. The right portion of the equation uses the previously computed test statistic for heterogeneity (Q) and the number of studies in the meta-analysis (k). The right portion of the equation actually contains a logical statement, whereby I^2 is bounded at zero when Q is less than expected under the null hypothesis of homogeneity (lower possibility), but the more common situation is the upper possibility. Here, the denominator consists of Q, which can roughly be considered the total heterogeneity among effect sizes, whereas the numerator consists of what can roughly be considered the total heterogeneity minus the expected heterogeneity given only sampling fluctuations. In other words, the ratio is roughly the between-study variability (total minus within-study sampling variability) relative to total variability, put onto a percentage (i.e., 0 to 100%) scale.

I^2 is therefore a readily interpretable index of the magnitude of heterogeneity among studies in your meta-analysis, and it is also useful in comparing heterogeneity across different meta-analyses. Unfortunately, because it is rather new, it has not been frequently used in meta-analyses, and it is therefore difficult to offer suggestions about what constitutes small, medium, or large amounts of heterogeneity.[7] In the absence of better guidelines, I offer the following suggestions of Huedo-Medina and colleagues (2006) that $I^2 \approx 25\%$ is a small amount of heterogeneity, $I^2 \approx 50\%$ is a medium amount of heterogeneity, and $I^2 \approx 75\%$ is a large amount of heterogeneity (as mentioned, $I^2 \approx 0\%$ represents homogeneity). In the example meta-analysis of relational aggression with peer rejection I described earlier, $I^2 = 92.8\%$.

8.4.4   Statistical Power in Testing Heterogeneity

Although the Q test of heterogeneity is a statistical significance test, many meta-analysts make conclusions of homogeneity when they fail to reject the null hypothesis. This practice is counter to the well-known caution in primary data analysis that you cannot *accept* the null hypothesis (rather, you simply fail to reject it). On the other hand, if there is adequate statistical power to detect heterogeneity and the results of the Q statistic are not significant, then perhaps conclusions of homogeneity—or at least the absence of substantial heterogeneity—can be reasonably made. The extent to which this argument is tenable depends on the statistical power of your heterogeneity test.

Computing the statistical power of a heterogeneity test is extremely complex, as it is determined by the number of studies, the standard errors of effect size estimates for these studies (which is largely determined by sample size), the magnitude of heterogeneity, the theoretical distribution of effect sizes around a population mean (e.g., the extent to which an effect size index is normally [e.g., Z_r is approximately normally distributed] vs. non-normally [e.g., r is skewed, especially at values far from zero] distributed), and the extent to which assumptions of the effect size estimates from each study are violated (e.g., assuming equal variance between two groups when this is not true) (see, e.g., Alexander, Scozzaro, & Borodkin, 1989; Harwell, 1997). In this regard, computing the statistical power of the heterogeneity test for your particular meta-analysis is very difficult, and likely precisely possible only with complex computer simulations.

Given this complexity, I propose a less precise but much simpler approach to evaluating whether your meta-analysis has adequate statistical power to detect heterogeneity. First, you should determine a value of I^2 (see previous subsection) that represents the minimum magnitude of heterogeneity that you believe is important (or, conversely, the maximum amount of heterogeneity that you consider inconsequential enough to ignore). Then, consult Figure 8.2 to determine whether the number of studies in your meta-analysis can conclude that your specified amount of heterogeneity (I^2) will be detected. This figure displays the minimum level of I^2 that will result in a statistically significant value of Q for a given number of studies, based on $p = .05$. If the figure indicates that the number of studies in your meta-analysis could detect a smaller level of I^2 than what you specified, it is reasonable to conclude that the test of heterogeneity in your meta-analysis is adequate. I stress that this is only a rough guide, which I offer only as a simpler alternative to more complex power analyses; however, I feel that it is likely adequate for most meta-analyses.[8] Accepting Figure 8.2 as a rough method of determining whether tests of heterogeneity have adequate statistical power, it becomes clear that this test is generally quite powerful. Based on the suggestions of $I^2 \approx 25\%$, 50%, and 75% representing small, medium, and large amounts of heterogeneity, respectively, you see that meta-analyses consisting of 56 studies can detect small heterogeneity, those with as few as 9 studies can detect medium heterogeneity, and all meta-analyses (i.e., combination of two or more studies) can detect large heterogeneity.

Before concluding that the test of heterogeneity is typically high in statistical power, you should consider that the I^2 index is the percentage ratio of between-study variance to total variance, with total variance made up of both between- and within-study variance. Given the same dispersion of effect sizes from a collection of studies with large standard errors (small samples) rather than small standard errors (large samples), the within-study variance

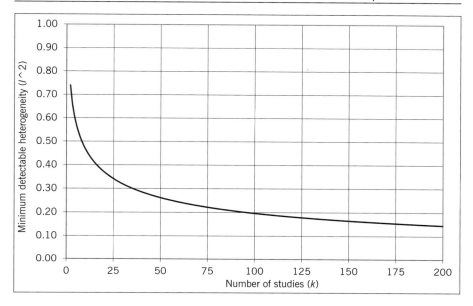

FIGURE 8.2. Number of studies needed to detect heterogeneity among effect sizes.

will be larger and the I^2 will therefore be smaller (because this larger within-study variance goes into the numerator or Equation 8.7). Given these situations of large standard errors (small sample sizes) among studies, the test of heterogeneity can actually have low power because the I^2 is smaller than expected (see Harwell, 1997, for a demonstration of situations in which the test has low statistical power). For this reason, it is important to carefully consider what values of I^2 are meaningful given the situation of your own meta-analysis and those in similar situations, more so than relying too heavily on guidelines such as those I have provided.

8.5 PRACTICAL MATTERS: **NONINDEPENDENCE AMONG EFFECT SIZES**

An important qualifier to the analyses I have described in this chapter (and those I will describe in subsequent chapters) is that they should be performed with a set of independent effect sizes. In primary data analysis, it is well known that a critical assumption is of independent observations; that each case (e.g., person) is a random sample from the population independent of the likelihood of another participant being selected. In meta-analysis, this assumption is that each effect size in your analysis is independent from others; this assumption is usually considered satisfied if each study of a particular sample of individuals provides one effect size to your meta-analysis.

As you will quickly learn when coding effect sizes, this assumption is often violated—single studies often provide multiple effect sizes. This multitude of effect sizes from single studies creates nonindependence in meta-analytic datasets in that effect sizes from the same study (i.e., the same sample of individuals) cannot be considered independent.

These multiple effect sizes arise for various reasons, and the reason impacts how you handle these situations. The end goal of handling each type of nonindependence is to obtain one single effect size from each study for any particular analysis.

8.5.1   Multiple Effect Sizes from Multiple Measures

One potential source of multiple effect sizes from a single study is that the authors report multiple effect sizes based on different measures. For example, the study by Rys and Bear (1997) in the example meta-analysis of Table 8.1 provided effect sizes of the association between relational aggression and peer rejection based on a peer-report (corrected r = .556) and teacher-report (corrected r = .338) measures of relational aggression. Or a single study might examine an association at two distinct time points. For example, Werner and Crick (2004) studied children in second through fourth grades and then re-administered measures to these same children approximately one year later, finding concurrent correlations between relational aggression and rejection of r = .479 and .458 at the first and second occasions, respectively.

In these situations, you have two options for obtaining a single effect size. The first option is to determine if one effect size is more central to your interests and to use only that effect size. This decision should be made in consultation with your study inclusion/exclusion criteria (see Chapter 3), and you should only reach this decision if it is clear that one effect size should be included whereas the other should not. Using the two example studies mentioned, I might choose one of the two measurement approaches of Rys and Bear (1997) if I had a priori decided that peer reports of relational aggression were more important than teacher reports (or vice versa). Or I might decide to use only the first measurement occasion of the study by Werner and Crick (2004) if something occurred after this first data collection so as to make the subsequent results less relevant for my meta-analysis (e.g., if they had implemented an intervention and I was only interested in the association between relational aggression and rejection in normative situations). These decisions should *not* be based on which effect size estimate best fits your hypotheses (i.e., do not simply choose the largest effect size); it is best if you can make this decision without looking at the value of the effect size.

The second, and likely more common, option is to average these multiple effect sizes. Here, you should compute the average effect size (see Equation 8.2) among these multiple effect sizes and use this average as your single effect size estimate for the study (if the effect size is one that is typically transformed, such as Z_r or $\ln(o)$, then you should average the transformed effect sizes).[9] To illustrate, I combined the two effect sizes from Rys and Bear (1997) by converting both correlations (.556 and .338 for peer and teacher reports) to Z_r (.627 and .352) and then averaged these values to yield the $Z_r = .489$ shown in Table 8.1; I back-transformed this value to $r = .454$ for summary in this table. Similarly, I converted the correlations at times 1 and 2 from Werner and Crick (2004), $r = .479$ and .458 to $Z_r = .522$ and .495, and computed the average of these two, which is shown in Table 8.1 as $Z_r = .509$ (and the parallel $r = .469$). If Rys and Bear (1997) had more than two measurement approaches, or if Werner and Crick (2004) had more than two measurement occasions, I could compute the average of these three or more effect sizes in the same way to yield a single effect size per study.

8.5.2 Multiple Effect Sizes from Subsets of Participants

A second potential source of multiple effect sizes from a single study is that the effect sizes are separately reported for subgroups of the sample. For example, effect sizes might be reported separately by gender, ethnicity, or multiple treatment groups. If each of these groups should be included in your meta-analysis given your inclusion/exclusion criteria, then your goal is to compute an average effect size for these multiple groups.[10] Two considerations distinguish this situation from that of the previous subsection, however. First, if you average effect sizes across multiple subgroups, your effective sample size for the study (used in computing the standard error for the study) is now the sum of the multiple combined groups. Second, the average in this situation should be a weighted average so that larger subgroups have greater contribution to the average than smaller subgroups.

To illustrate, a study by Hawley et al. (2007) used data from 407 boys and 522 girls, reporting information to compute effect sizes for boys (corrected $r = .210$ and $Z_r = .214$) and girls (corrected $r = .122$ and $Z_r = .122$), but not for the overall sample. To obtain one common effect size for this sample, I computed the weighted average effect size using Equation 8.2 to obtain the value $Z_r = .162$ (and $r = .161$) shown in Table 8.1. The standard error of this effect size is based on the total sample size, combining the sizes of the multiple subgroups (here, $407 + 522 = 929$). It is important to note that this computed effect size is different from what would have been obtained if you could simply compute the effect size from the raw data. Specifically, this effect size from combined subgroups represents the association between the variables of interest *controlling for the variable on which subgroups were created* (in this example, gender). If you expect that this covariate control will—or even could—change the effect sizes (typically reduce them), then it would be useful to create a dichotomous variable for studies in which this method of combining subgroups was used for evaluation as a potential moderator (see Chapter 9).

It is also possible that some studies will report multiple effect sizes for multiple subgroups. In fact, the Rys and Bear (1997) study I described earlier actually reported effect sizes separately by measure of aggression and gender, so that the coded data consisted of correlations of peer-reported relational aggression with rejection for 132 boys (corrected $r = .590$, $Z_r = .678$) and 134 girls (corrected $r = .520$, $Z_r = .577$) and correlations of teacher-reported relational aggression with rejection for these boys (corrected $r = .270$, $Z_r = .277$) and girls (corrected $r = .402$, $Z_r = .427$). In this type of situation, I suggest a two-step process in which you average effect sizes first within groups and then across groups (summing the sample size in the second round of averaging). For this example of the Rys and Bear (1997) study, I would first average the effect sizes from peer and teacher reports within the 132 boys (yielding $Z_r = .478$), and then compute this same average within the 134 girls (yielding $Z_r = .502$). I would then compute the weighted average of these effect sizes across boys and girls, which produces the $Z_r = .489$ (and transformation to $r = .454$) shown in Table 8.1. You could also reverse the steps of this two-step process—in this example, first computing a weighted average effect size across gender for each of the two measures, and then averaging across the two measures (the order I took to produce the effect sizes described earlier)—to obtain the same results.

8.5.3 Effect Sizes from Multiple Reports of the Same Study

A third potential source of nonindependence is when data from the same study are disseminated in multiple reports (e.g., multiple publications, a dissertation that is later published). It is important to keep in mind that when I refer to a single effect size per study, I mean one effect size per sample of participants. Therefore, the multiple reports that might arise from a single primary dataset should be treated as a single study. If the two reports provide different effect size estimates (presumably due to analysis of different measures, rather than a miscalculation in one or the other report), then you should average these as I described earlier. If the two reports provide some overlapping effect size estimates (e.g., the two reports both provide the correlation between relational aggression and rejection; both reports provide a Time 1 correlation but the second report also contains the Time 2 correlation), these repetitive values should be omitted.

Unfortunately, the uncertainty that arises from this sort of multiple reporting is greater than I have described here. Often, it is unclear if authors of separate reports are using the same dataset. In this situation, I recommend comparing the descriptions of methods carefully and contacting the authors if you are still uncertain. Similarly, authors might report results that seem to come from the full sample in one report and only a subset in another. Here, I suggest selecting values from the full sample when effect sizes are identical. Having made these suggestions, I recognize that every meta-analyst is likely to come across unique situations. As with much of my previous advice on these difficult issues, I strongly suggest contacting the authors of the reports to obtain further information.

8.6 SUMMARY

In this chapter, I have described initial efforts of combining effect sizes across studies. Specifically, I described the logic of weighting studies according to the precision of their effect size estimates, methods of computing a weighted average effect size and drawing inferences about this mean, and a way of evaluating the heterogeneity—or between-study variability—of effect sizes across studies. This last topic will guide my foci for the next two chapters: systematically predicting between-study differences through moderator analysis (Chapter 9) and modeling the heterogeneity of effect sizes through random-effects models (Chapter 10).

8.7 RECOMMENDED READINGS

Huedo-Medina, T. B., Sánchez-Meca, J., Marín-Martínez, F., & Botella, J. (2006). Assessing heterogeneity in meta-analysis: Q statistic or I^2 index? *Psychological Methods, 11*, 193–206.—This chapter provides a thoughtful overview of the relative strengths of using statistical tests of heterogeneity versus the heterogeneity effect size I described in this chapter.

Shadish, W. R., & Haddock, C. K. (1994). Combining estimates of effect size. In H. Cooper & L. V. Hedges (Eds.), *The handbook of research synthesis* (pp. 261–281). New York: Russell Sage Foundation.—This chapter offers an overview of the entire process of combining effect sizes within a concise 21 pages. The chapter also contains an appendix with basic SAS code to aid in these analyses.

NOTES

1. Actually, you would not simply average the correlation coefficients, r. Instead, you would average the Fisher's transformed correlation, Z_r, to obtain the average Z_r, and then back-transform this Z_r to r for reporting (see Chapter 5).

2. The standard error is always inversely related to sample size, but in some instances it is related to other factors. For some effect sizes (e.g., g, see Chapter 5), the standard error is related to the effect size itself. Adjusting effect sizes for artifacts also affects the standard error (see Chapter 6). Nevertheless, you can always conceptually think of standard error as an index of imprecision.

3. In real meta-analyses with more studies, you should *not* expect all studies to have confidence intervals that overlap with a true population effect size. Because confidence intervals are probabilistic, only an expectable percentage of studies should have confidence intervals containing the population effect size. For example, 95% confidence intervals imply that 95% of studies will contain the population effect size, but 5% will not. If your meta-analysis contains 40 studies, you should expect that 2 (on average) should not contain this effect size within their 95% confidence interval. If many more than this 5% do not contain a single population effect size, however, heterogeneity may exist, as I describe later in this chapter.

4. Some meta-analysts also give weight to the quality of the study; however, I recommend against this practice. A problem with this practice is that any choice of weighting based on study quality is arbitrary. If you believe that study quality influences the effect sizes in your meta-analysis, I suggest that you instead code study quality (or better yet, specific features of the methodology that you believe constitute the quality of studies) and evaluate these as potential moderators of effect sizes.

5. Here and throughout the book, I refer to k as the number of studies. It is more accurate to think of k as the number of effect sizes, though this is identical to the number of studies when each study provides one (and only one) effect size to your meta-analysis. For further consideration of this issue, see Section 8.5.

6. This table was made in MS Excel using the "chiinv" function. You can use this function to determine the exact p for any values of Q and df.

7. Though it is possible to calculate this value from prior meta-analyses in your area of interest. To do so, you would just identify the reported Q and number of studies, and then calculate I^2 from this information.

8. As I will stress in later chapters, I do not believe that the significance test for heterogeneity is especially critical in guiding your choice to examine moderators (Chapter 9) or in deciding between fixed- versus random-effects models (Chapter 10).

9. Strictly speaking, this practice is problematic because the weight you use for this study does not account for the number of effect sizes nor the extent to which the effect sizes are very similar versus different (similar effect sizes would suggest smaller standard errors and larger weights than different effect sizes). Despite the limits of this approach, this approach of averaging multiple effect sizes within a study is the most common practice in published meta-analyses.

10. An alternative practice sometimes used is to simply treat the subgroups as separate samples—and therefore separate cases—within your meta-analysis. The advantage of this practice is that you are better able to test the subgroup features (e.g., sex) as a moderator. I have some reservations about this practice, however, in that it is likely that the two "cases" are partially interdependent because of the methodological (e.g., recruitment practices, measures) features of the study. If most of the studies report results separately for the same subgroups, then it seems that a better approach would be to compute an effect size representing the difference in effect sizes between the subgroups within each study (i.e., the differential index for independent correlations described in Chapter 7) and meta-analytically combine this index across studies. However, if many studies do not report results separately by the same subgroups, and it is valuable to your goals to separate subgroup results for moderator analyses, then you might consider the following: Initially treat the subgroup results as separate cases within your meta-analysis. However, compute the intraclass correlation coefficient (ICC), indexing the similarity of effect sizes within studies. If this value is low—I suggest ICC < .05 as a reasonable criterion—then you are likely safe in treating effect sizes from multiple subgroups in some studies as if they were independent. However, if the ICC > .05, then the assumption of independence is violated and I recommend averaging subgroup effect sizes within studies. I should emphasize that my recommendations have not been empirically evaluated.

9

Explaining Heterogeneity among Effect Sizes
Moderator Analyses

When meta-analyses contain substantial heterogeneity in effect sizes across studies (see Chapter 8), it is usually informative to investigate the sources of this heterogeneity through moderator analyses. In fact, these moderator analyses are often of more interest than the average effect sizes, depending on the research questions you wish to answer (see Chapter 2).

Before describing these analyses, it is useful to take a step back to consider the general approach of these analyses. These analyses attempt to explain the heterogeneity of effect sizes across studies using coded study characteristics as predictors. In other words, the goal of conducting these moderator analyses is to identify characteristics of the studies that are associated with studies finding higher or lower effect sizes. The reason that these analyses are called "moderator analyses" becomes clear if you recall that the most commonly used effect sizes are of associations of two variables, X and Y (see Chapter 5). Given that moderation is defined as an association between two variables varying at different levels of the moderator (e.g., Baron & Kenny, 1986; Little, Card, Bovaird, Preacher, & Crandall, 2007), you can think of moderator analyses in meta-analysis as investigating whether the association between X and Y (i.e., the effect size) varies consistently based on the level of the moderator (i.e., study characteristics).

The potential moderators evaluated in meta-analysis can be either categorical (e.g., studies using one type of measure versus another) or continuous (e.g., average age of participants), and it is possible—and often useful—to investigate multiple predictors simultaneously. I discuss these three situations in the next three sections (Sections 9.1 to 9.3, respectively). I then describe an alternative way of performing these analyses within a structural equation modeling (SEM) framework (Section 9.4). Finally, I discuss the practical matter of considering the limits to interpreting results of meta-analytic moderator analyses (Section 9.5).

9.1 CATEGORICAL MODERATORS

9.1.1 Evaluating the Significance of a Categorical Moderator

The logic of evaluating categorical moderators in meta-analysis parallels the use of ANOVA in primary data analysis. Whereas ANOVA partitions variability in scores across individuals (or other units of analysis) into variability existing between and within groups, categorical moderator analysis in meta-analysis partitions between-study heterogeneity into that between and within groups of studies (Hedges, 1982; Lipsey & Wilson, 2001, pp. 120–121). In other words, testing categorical moderators in meta-analysis involves comparing groups of studies classified by their status on some categorical moderator.

Given this logic of partitioning heterogeneity, it makes sense to start with the heterogeneity equation (Equation 8.6) from Chapter 8, reproduced here for convenience:

Equation 9.1: Q statistic for heterogeneity

$$Q_{total} = \sum \left(w_i \left(ES_i - \overline{ES} \right)^2 \right) = \sum \left(w_i ES_i^2 \right) - \frac{\left(\sum \left(w_i ES_i \right) \right)^2}{\sum w_i}$$

$$df_{total} = k - 1$$

- w_i is the weight of study i.
- ES_i is the effect size estimate from study i.
- $\overline{ES}$ is the mean effect size across studies.
- k is the number of studies.

You might have noticed that I have changed the notation of this equation slightly, now giving the subscript "total" to this Q statistic. The reason for this subscript is to make it explicit that this is the total, overall heterogeneity among all effect sizes. The logic of testing categorical moderators is based on the ability to separate this total heterogeneity (Q_{total}) into two components, the between-group heterogeneity ($Q_{between}$) and the within-group heterogeneity (Q_{within}), such that:

> **Equation 9.2: Partitioning of total heterogeneity into between- and within-group components**
>
> $$Q_{total} = Q_{between} + Q_{within}$$
>
> - Q_{total} is the heterogeneity among all study effect sizes.
> - $Q_{between}$ is the heterogeneity accounted for by between-group differences.
> - Q_{within} is the heterogeneity within the groups.

The key question when evaluating categorical moderators is whether there is greater-than-expectable between-group heterogeneity. If there is, then this implies that the groups based on the categorical study characteristic differ and that the categorical moderator is therefore reliably related to effect sizes found in the studies. If the groups do not differ, then this implies that the categorical moderator is not related to effect sizes (or, in the language of null hypothesis significance testing, that you have failed to find evidence for this moderation).

The most straightforward way to compute the between-group heterogeneity ($Q_{between}$) is to rearrange Equation 9.2, so that $Q_{between} = Q_{total} - Q_{within}$. Because you have already computed the total heterogeneity (Q_{total}; Equation 9.1), you only need to compute and subtract the within-group heterogeneity (Q_{within}) to obtain the desired $Q_{between}$. To compute the heterogeneity within *each group*, you apply a formula similar to that for total heterogeneity to just the studies in that group:

> **Equation 9.3: Heterogeneity within group g (Q_g)**
>
> $$Q_g = \sum \left(w_i \left(ES_i - \overline{ES}_g \right)^2 \right) = \sum \left(w_i ES_i^2 \right) - \frac{\left(\sum \left(w_i ES_i \right) \right)^2}{\sum w_i}$$
>
> $$df_g = k_g - 1$$
>
> - w_i is the weight of study i.
> - ES_i is the effect size estimate from study i.
> - $\overline{ES}_g$ is the mean effect size across studies within group g.
> - k_g is the number of studies in group g.

That is, you compute the heterogeneity within each group (g) using the same equation as for computing total heterogeneity, restricting the included studies to *only those studies within group g*. After computing the within-group heterogeneity (Q_g) for each of the groups, you compute the within-group heterogeneity (Q_{within}) simply by summing the heterogeneities (Q_gs) from all groups. More formally:

Equation 9.4: Within-group heterogeneity (Q_{within})

$$Q_{within} = \sum_{g=1}^{G} Q_g$$

$$df_{within} = \sum_{g=1}^{G} df_g = k - G$$

- G is the number of groups.
- Q_g is the heterogeneity within group g.
- df_{within} is the within-groups degrees of freedom.
- df_g is the degrees of freedom within group g ($df_g = k_g - 1$, where k_g is the number of studies in group g).
- k is the total number of studies (across all groups).
- G is the number of groups.

As mentioned, after computing the total heterogeneity (Q_{total}) and the within-group heterogeneity (Q_{within}), you compute the between-group heterogeneity by subtracting the within-group heterogeneity from the total heterogeneity (i.e., $Q_{between} = Q_{total} - Q_{within}$; see Equation 9.2). The statistical significance of this between-group heterogeneity is evaluated by considering the value of $Q_{between}$ relative to $df_{between}$, with $df_{between} = G - 1$. Under the null hypothesis, $Q_{between}$ is distributed as χ^2 with $df_{between}$, so you can consult a chi-square table (such as Table 8.2; or use functions such as Microsoft Excel's "chiinv" as described in footnote 6 of Chapter 8) to evaluate the statistical significance to make inferences about moderation.

To illustrate this test of categorical moderators, consider again the example meta-analysis of 22 studies reporting associations between children and adolescents' relational aggression and rejection by peers. As shown in Chapter 8, these studies yield a mean effect size $\bar{Z}_r = .387$ ($\bar{r} = .368$), but there was significant heterogeneity among these studies around this mean effect size, $Q_{(21)} = 291.17$, $p < .001$. This heterogeneity might suggest the importance of explaining this heterogeneity through moderator analysis, and I hypothesized that one source of this heterogeneity might be due to the use of different reporters to assess relational aggression. As shown in Table 9.1, these studies variously used observations, parent reports, peer reports, and teacher reports to assess relational aggression, and this test of moderation evaluates whether associations between relational aggression and rejection systematically differ across these four methods of assessing aggression.

I have arranged these 27 effect sizes (note that these come from 22 independent studies; I am using effect sizes involving different methods from the same study as separate effect sizes[1]) into four groups based on the method of assessing aggression. To compute Q_{total}, I use the three sums across all 27 studies (shown at the bottom of Table 9.1) within Equation 9.1:

$$Q_{total} = \sum \left(w_i \, ES_i^2\right) - \frac{\left(\sum \left(w_i \, ES_i\right)\right)^2}{\sum w_i} = 1413.09 - \frac{(2889.26)^2}{7857.64} = 350.71$$

I then compute the heterogeneity within each of the groups using the sums from each group within Equation 9.3. For the three observational studies, this within-group heterogeneity is

$$Q_{within\,observations} = 4.45 - \frac{(28.53)^2}{293.94} = 1.68$$

Using the same equation, I also compute within-group heterogeneities of $Q_{within\_parent} = 0.00$ (there is no heterogeneity in a group of one study), $Q_{within\_peer} = 243.16$, and $Q_{within\_teacher} = 40.73$. Summing these values yields $Q_{within} = 1.68 + 0.00 + 243.16 + 40.73 = 285.57$. Given that $Q_{between} = Q_{total} - Q_{within}$, the between-group heterogeneity is $Q_{between} = 350.71 - 285.57 = 65.14$. This $Q_{between}$ is distributed as chi-square with $df = G - 1 = 4 - 1 = 3$ under the null hypothesis of no moderation (i.e., no larger-than-expected between group differences). The value of $Q_{between}$ in this example is large enough ($p < .001$; see Table 8.2 or any chi-square table) that I can reject this null hypothesis and accept the alternate hypothesis that the groups differ in their effect sizes. In other words, moderator analysis of the effect sizes in Table 9.1 indicates that method of assessing aggression moderates the association between relational aggression and peer rejection.

9.1.2   Follow-Up Analyses to a Categorical Moderator

If you are evaluating a categorical moderator consisting of two levels—in other words, a dichotomous moderator variable—then interpretation is simple. Here, you just conclude whether the between-group heterogeneity is significant, then inspect the within-group mean effect sizes (i.e., weighted means computed using studies from each group separately). The decision and interpretation is then straightforward as to which group of studies yields stronger effect sizes.

The situation is more complex when the categorical moderator has three or more levels—that is, when the moderator test is an omnibus comparison. Here, the significant between-group heterogeneity indicates that at least some groups differ from others, but exactly where those differences lie is unclear. This situation is akin to follow-up analyses conducted with a three or more level ANOVA, and decisions of how to handle these situations in meta-analysis are as thorny as they are for ANOVAs used in primary studies. However, the variety of possibilities that exist for ANOVA follow-up analyses have not been translated into a meta-analytic framework. Therefore, the two choices are between an overly liberal and an overly conservative approach.

9.1.2.a   The Liberal Approach

This approach is liberal in that one makes no attempt to control cumulative (a.k.a. family-wise) type I errors when following up a finding of significant between-group heterogeneity. Instead, you just perform a series of all possible two-group comparisons to identify which groups differ in the magnitudes of their effect sizes. To perform these comparisons, you would use the same logic described in the previous subsection for testing between-group heterogeneity, but would (1) restrict the calculation of total heterogeneity (Q_{total}) to studies from the two groups, (2) sum the within-group heterogeneity (Q_{within}) only from these two groups, and (3) evaluate the resultant between-group heterogeneity ($Q_{between}$) as a 1 df χ^2 test (because $G = 2$ in this comparison, so $df_{between} = 2 - 1$). You would then repeat this two-group comparison for all possible combinations among the groups of the categorical moderator (the total number of comparisons is $G(G-1)/2$).

This approach parallels Fisher's Least Significant Difference test in ANOVA (see e.g., Keppel, 1991, p. 171). Like this test in ANOVA, the obvious problem with using this approach in categorical moderator analyses in ANOVA is that it allows for higher-than-desired rates of type I error in the follow-up comparisons (i.e., not controlling for cumulative, or family-wise, type I error). A second problem with this approach occurs when different groups have different effective sample sizes (i.e., many studies with large samples vs. few studies with small samples) or amounts of within-group heterogeneity. In these situations, this approach can yield surprising results, in which groups that appear to have quite different average effect sizes are not found to differ (because the groups have small effective sample sizes or large

TABLE 9.1. Example Categorical Moderator Analysis of Method of Measuring Aggression Predicting Associations between Relational Aggression and Peer Rejection

Method/study	Sample size (N)	Effect size (r)	Transformed ES (Z_r)	Standard error (SE)	Weight (w)	wES (w * Z_r)	wES² (w * Z_r^2)
Observation (k = 3)							
Ostrov (under review)[a]	139	.181	.183	.0897	124.18	22.72	4.16
Ostrov & Crick (2007)	132	.049	.049	.0922	117.70	5.81	0.29
Ostrov et al. (2004)[b]	60	.000	.000	.1386	52.05	0.00	0.00
Within-group sums (Σ)					293.94	28.53	4.45
Parent report (k = 1)							
Blachman (2003)	228	.525	0.583	.0693	208.12	121.27	70.66
Within-group sums (Σ)					208.12	121.27	70.66
Peer report (k = 17)							
Crick & Grotpeter (1995)	491	.198	.201	.0579	297.81	59.74	11.98
Crick et al. (1997)	65	.443	.476	.1347	55.15	26.24	12.48
Geiger (2003)	458	.554	.624	.0484	427.07	266.55	166.37
Hawley et al. (2007)	929	.161	.162	.0346	835.96	135.72	22.03
Hemington (1996)	904	.336	.349	.0347	831.95	290.69	101.57
Johnson (2003)	74	.531	.591	.1222	66.92	39.55	23.37
Leff (1995)	151	.617	.721	.0855	136.66	98.48	70.97
Miller (2001)	150	.557	.628	.0845	139.90	87.90	55.23

Study	N						
Murray-Close & Crick (2006)	590	.575	.655	.0426	550.97	361.12	236.69
Nelson et al. (2005)	180	.090	.090	.0831	144.75	13.04	1.17
Pakaslahti & Keltikangas-Järvinen (1998)	839	.326	.339	.0381	689.52	233.68	79.19
Phillipsen et al. (1999)	262	−.048	−.048	.0642	242.93	−11.73	0.57
Rys & Bear (1997)	266	.556	.627	.0642	242.84	152.16	95.34
Salmivalli et al. (2000)	209	.253	.258	.0715	195.52	50.54	13.06
Tomada & Schneider (1997)	314	.313	.324	.0580	296.76	96.01	31.06
Werner (2000)	881	.477	.519	.0351	810.71	420.41	218.01
Werner & Crick (2004)	517	.469	.509	.0455	482.45	245.37	124.79
Within-group sums (Σ)					6447.89	2565.46	1263.90
Teacher (k = 6)							
Crick et al. (1997)	65	.167	.168	.1305	58.68	9.88	1.66
Johnson (2003)	74	.074	.075	.1223	66.83	4.98	0.37
Nelson et al. (2005)	180	−.011	−.011	.0900	123.53	−1.39	0.02
Ostrov (under review)[a]	139	.513	.567	.0887	127.22	72.13	40.90
Rys & Bear (1997)	266	.338	.352	.0631	250.96	88.40	31.14
Tomada & Schneider (1997)[b]	314	.000	.000	.0597	280.47	0.00	0.00
Within-group sums (Σ)					907.70	174.00	74.09
Total sums (Σ)					7857.64	2889.26	1413.09

Note. Hand calculations of these values may not produce exact replications due to rounding errors.
[a]Article was under review during the preparation of this meta-analytic review. It has subsequently been published as Ostrov (2008).
[b]Effect size is lower-bound estimate based on author's reporting only nonsignficant associations.

heterogeneity), whereas groups that seem to have more similar average effect sizes are found to differ (because the groups have large effective sample sizes or small heterogeneity).

9.1.2.b   The Conservative Approach

A conservative approach to multiple follow-up comparisons of a significant omnibus moderator result parallels the approach in ANOVA commonly called Bonferroni correction (a.k.a. Dunn test; see Keppel, 1991, p. 167). Using this approach, you make the same series of comparisons between all possible two-group combinations as in the liberal approach, but the resultant $Q_{between}$s are evaluated using an adjusted level of statistical significance (i.e., some value smaller than the chosen type I error rate, e.g., $\alpha = .05$). Specifically, you divide the desired type I error rate (e.g., $\alpha = .05$) by the number of comparisons[2] made (i.e., by $G(G - 1)/2$). This Bonferroni-adjusted level of significance (α_B) is then used as the basis for making inferences about whether the between-group heterogeneity statistics ($Q_{between}$) provide evidence to reject the null hypotheses (i.e., concluding that groups differ).

There are two limitations to this approach. First, like this approach used in ANOVAs in primary studies, it is overly conservative and leads to diminished statistical power (i.e., higher type II error rates). The extent to which this limitation is problematic will depend on the sample sizes and numbers of studies in the groups you wish to compare. If all groups of the categorical moderator contain a large number of studies with large sample sizes (i.e., there is high statistical power), then the cost of this overly conservative approach might be minimal. However, if even some of the groups have a small number of studies or small sample sizes, then the loss of statistical power is problematic. The second limitation of this conservative approach is similar to that of the liberal approach—that seemingly larger differences in group mean effect sizes might not be significantly different, whereas seemingly small differences are found to be different.

9.1.2.c   Conclusions Regarding Follow-Up Analyses

The choice between an overly liberal and an overly conservative approach is not an easy one to make. In weighing between these approaches, I suggest that you consider (1) the relative cost of type I (erroneously concluding differences) versus type II (failing to detect differences) errors, and (2) the expectable power of your meta-analysis (meta-analyses with many studies with large sample sizes tend to have high power). Alternatively, you might avoid this problem by specifying meaningful planned contrasts that can be evaluated within a regression framework (see below).

9.2 CONTINUOUS MODERATORS

Continuous moderators in meta-analysis are coded study variables that can be considered to vary along a continuum of possible values. For example, mean characteristics of the sample (age, SES, percentage of ethnic minorities, percentage male or percentage female) or methodology (e.g., dose of a drug, number of therapy sessions in intervention) might be evaluated as continuous moderators. Just as the evaluation of categorical moderators relied on an adaptation of ANOVA, the evaluation of continuous moderators relies on an adaptation of regression. Specifically, test of continuous moderation involves (weighted) regression of the effect sizes (dependent variable) onto the continuous moderator (independent variable, or predictor). Significant prediction indicates that the effect sizes vary in a linear manner with the continuous moderator; in other words, this moderator systematically relates to the association between X and Y.

The adaptation of standard regression of effect sizes onto a continuous predictor that is key to meta-analytic moderator analysis is the "weighted" I parenthetically stated. Here, the regression analysis is weighted by the inverse variance weight, w (see Chapter 8). This weighting has three implications. First, as is desirable (see Chapter 8), studies with more precise effect size estimates will be given more weight in the analysis than those with less precise estimates. Second, the mean squares of the regression (standard output, often in an ANOVA table, of all standard statistical packages such as SPSS or SAS) represents the heterogeneity among the effect sizes that is accounted for by the linear prediction of the continuous moderator. You use this value to evaluate the statistical significance of the regression model. Third, this weighting impacts the standard errors of the regression coefficients. Although the regression coefficients themselves are accurate and directly interpretable (e.g., are effect sizes larger or smaller when values of the moderator are greater?), the standard errors of the regression coefficients are not correct and need to be hand calculated (which, fortunately, is simple).

Because this weighted regression approach to testing continuous moderators is most clearly illustrated through example, let me return to the sample meta-analysis of associations between relational aggression and peer rejection. As shown in Table 9.2, I coded the mean age (in years) of the samples for these 22 studies, and I want to evaluate whether age moderates the asso-

TABLE 9.2. Example Meta-Analysis of (Artifact Corrected) Correlations between Relational Aggression and Peer Rejection Predicted by the Continuous Moderator, Age

Study	Sample size (N)	Effect size (r)	Transformed ES (Z_r)	Standard error (SE)	Weight (w)	Age (years)
Blachman (2003)	228	.525	.583	.0693	208.12	9.2
Crick & Grotpeter (1995)	491	.198	.201	.0579	297.81	9.4
Crick et al. (1997)	65	.311	.322	.1325	56.95	4.5
Geiger (2003)	458	.554	.624	.0484	427.07	8.0
Hawley et al. (2007)	929	.161	.162	.0346	835.96	14.7
Henington (1996)	904	.336	.349	.0347	831.95	7.5
Johnson (2003)	74	.396	.419	.1223	66.89	6.0
Leff (1995)	151	.617	.721	.0855	136.66	9.5
Miller (2001)	150	.557	.628	.0845	139.90	16.0
Murray-Close & Crick (2006)	590	.575	.655	.0426	550.97	9.0
Nelson et al. (2005)	180	.039	.039	.0831	144.75	4.8
Ostrov (under review)[a]	139	.358	.375	.0892	125.71	3.6
Ostrov & Crick (2007)	132	.049	.049	.0922	117.70	4.1
Ostrov et al. (2004)[b]	60	.000	.000	.1386	52.05	4.6
Pakaslahti & Keltikangas-Järvinen (1998)	839	.326	.339	.0381	689.52	14.5
Phillipsen et al. (1999)	262	−.048	−.048	.0642	242.93	8.7
Rys & Bear (1997)	266	.454	.489	.0636	246.94	9.5
Salmivalli et al. (2000)	209	.253	.258	.0715	195.52	15.5
Tomada & Schneider (1997)	314	.160	.162	.0589	288.73	9.0
Werner (2000)	881	.477	.519	.0351	810.71	8.0
Werner & Crick (2004)	517	.469	.509	.0455	482.45	8.0
Zalecki & Hinshaw (2004)	228	.572	.651	.0702	202.92	9.0

[a]Article was under review during the preparation of this meta-analytic review. It has subsequently been published as Ostrov (2008).
[b]Effect size is lower-bound estimate based on author's reporting only nonsignificant associations.

ciations between relational aggression and rejection. To do so, I regress the effect sizes (Fisher's transformation of the correlation between relational aggression and rejection, Z_r) onto the hypothesized continuous moderator age, using the familiar regression equation. $Z_r = B_0 + B_1(Age) + e$, with w as a weight. To do this, I use a standard statistical software package such as SPSS or SAS. In SPSS, I would specify Z_r as the dependent variable, age as the independent variable, and w as the WLS (weighted least squares) weight.

The results give six pieces of information of interest: from an ANOVA table, (1) the sum of square of the regression model ($SS_{regression}$ or SS_{model}) = 9.312; (2) the residual sum of squares[3] ($SS_{residual}$ or SS_{error}) = 281.983; and (3) the residual mean squares ($MS_{residual}$ or MS_{error}) = 14.099; and from a table of coefficients, (4) the unstandardized regression coefficient (B_1) = −.0112 with (5) an associated standard error = .0138; and (6) the intercept (B_0) = .496. The $SS_{regression}$ is the heterogeneity accounted for by the linear regression model; it is often reported in published meta-analyses as $Q_{regression}$ and is evaluated for statistical significance by comparing the value to a χ^2 distribution (Table 8.2 or using calculators such as Excel's "chiinv" function) with df = number of predictors (here, df = 1). In this example, the value of 9.312 is considered statistically significant by standard criteria (p = .0023), so I conclude that there is moderation of the association between relational aggression and rejection by age.

Because this analysis included only one predictor, the statistical significance of the model informs the statistical significance of the single predictor. However, when including multiple predictors (see next section), it is useful to also evaluate statistical significance by examining the regression coefficients and their standard errors. In this example, the unstandardized regression coefficient was −.0112, and its standard error, as computed by the statistical analysis program, was .0138. However, this standard error is inaccurate, and must be adjusted. This adjustment is to divide the standard error from the output by the square root of the residual mean square:

$$SE_{adjusted} = \frac{SE_{output}}{\sqrt{MS_{residual}}} = \frac{.0138}{\sqrt{14.099}} = .00368$$

I then evaluate the statistical significance of this predictor by dividing the regression coefficient (B_1) by this adjusted standard error, $Z = −.0112/.00368 = −3.05$, considering this Z value according to the standard normal deviate (i.e., Z) distribution to yield a two-tailed p (here, p = .0023). Note that in this example with a single predictor, the statistical significance of the regression model and of the single regression coefficient are identical, given that $Z^2 = \chi^2_{(df=1)}$ (i.e., $−3.05^2 = 9.31$).

To interpret this moderation, it is useful to compute implied effect sizes at different levels of the continuous moderator. Given the intercept ($B_0 = .096$) and regression coefficient of age ($B_1 = -.0112$), I can compute the predicted effect sizes at various ages using the equation $\hat{Z}_r = B_0 + B_1 (Age) = .496 - .0112 (Age)$. For illustration of this moderation, I would choose representative values of the moderator (age) that fall within the range observed among these studies and make some conceptual sense; in this example, I might choose the ages of 5, 10, and 15 years. I then successively insert these values for age into the prediction equation, yielding implied Z_rs = .440, .384, and .328, respectively. I then back-transform these implied Z_rs (or any other transformed effect sizes) into their meaningful metric for reporting: implied rs = .41, .37, and .32, respectively.

9.3   A GENERAL MULTIPLE REGRESSION FRAMEWORK FOR MODERATION

After considering the regression approach to analyzing continuous moderators (previous section), you are probably wondering whether this approach allows for evaluation of multiple moderators—it does. However, before considering inclusion of multiple moderators, I think it is useful to take a step back to consider how a regression approach can serve as a general approach to evaluating moderators in meta-analysis (in this context, the analyses are sometimes referred to as meta-regression). In this section, I describe how an empty (intercept-only) model accomplishes basic tests of mean effect size and heterogeneity (9.3.1), how you can evaluate categorical moderators in this framework through the use of dummy codes (9.3.2), and how this flexible approach can be used to consider unique moderation of a wide range of coded study characteristics (9.3.3). I will then draw general conclusions about this framework and suggest some more complex possibilities. I write this section with the assumption that you have a solid grounding in multiple regression; if not, you can read this section trying to obtain the "gist" of the ideas (for a thorough instruction of multiple regression, see Cohen et al., 2003).

9.3.1   The Empty Model for Computing Average Effect Size and Heterogeneity

An empty model in regression is one in which the dependent variable is regressed against no predictors, but only a constant (i.e., the value of 1 for all cases). This is represented in the following equation, which includes only an intercept (constant) as a predictor:

> ### Equation 9.5: Empty model used to estimate mean effect size and heterogeneity
>
> $ES_i = B_0(1) + e_i$
>
> - ES_i is the effect size (e.g., Z_r) for study i.
> - B_0 is the model intercept (interpreted as the mean in this empty model).
> - e_i is the deviation of the effect size of study i from the mean effect size (with the variance interpreted as the heterogeneity).

Performing a weighted regression of effect sizes predicted only by a constant will yield information about the weighted mean effect size and the heterogeneity, and therefore might serve as a useful initial analysis that is less tedious than the hand-spreadsheet-calculations I described in Chapter 8. Considering the example of 22 studies of relational aggression and peer rejection summarized in Table 9.2, I perform the following steps: First, I place the effect sizes (Z_rs) and inverse variance weights (w) into a statistical software package (e.g., SPSS or SAS). I then create a variable in which every study had the value 1 (the constant). Finally, I regress effect sizes onto this constant, weighted by w, specifying no intercept (i.e., having the program not automatically include the constant in the model, as I am using the constant as a predictor). The unstandardized regression coefficient is .387, which represents the mean effect size (as Z_r). The standard error of this regression coefficient from the program is adjusted as described above,

$$SE_{adjusted} = \frac{SE_{output}}{\sqrt{MS_{residual}}} = \frac{.0440}{\sqrt{113.865}} = .0118$$

to yield the standard error of this mean effect size for use in significance testing or estimating confidence intervals. Finally, the residual sum of squares ($SS_{residual}$ or SS_{error}) = 291.17 is the heterogeneity (Q) statistic, evaluated as χ^2 with 21 (number studies – 1) degrees of freedom. These results are identical to those reported in Chapter 8 and illustrate how the empty model can be used to compute the mean effect size, make inferences about this mean, and evaluate the heterogeneity of effect sizes across studies.

9.3.2 Evaluating Categorical Moderators

In primary data analysis, it has long been recognized that ANOVA is simply a special case of multiple regression (e.g., Cohen, 1968). The same comparability applies to meta-analytic evaluation of categorical moderators. As with translation of ANOVA into multiple regression in primary analysis, the "trick" is to create a series of dichotomous variables that fully capture the different groups. The most common approach is through the use of dummy variables.

To illustrate the use of dummy variables in analyzing continuous moderators, consider the data from Table 9.3, which consists of 27 effect sizes (from 22 studies, as in Table 9.2) using four methods of measuring relational aggression (previously summarized in Table 9.1). As with the ANOVA approach, I want to evaluate whether the method of assessing aggression moderates the associations between relational aggression and rejection. To perform this same evaluation in a regression framework, I need to compute three dummy codes (number of groups minus 1) to represent group membership. If I selected observational methods as my reference group, then I would assign the value 0 for all three dummy codes for studies using observational methods. I could make the first dummy code represent parent report (vs. observation) and assign values of 1 to this variable for all studies using this method and values of 0 for all studies that do not. Similarly, I could make dummy variable 2 represent peer report and dummy variable 3 represent teacher report. These dummy codes are displayed in Table 9.3 as DV1, DV2, and DV3 (for now, ignore the column labeled "Age" and everything to the right of it; I will use these data below).

To evaluate moderation by reporter within a multiple regression framework, I regress effect sizes onto the dummy variables representing group membership (in this case, three dummy variables), weighted by the inverse variance weight, w. This is expressed in the following equation:

Equation 9.6: Using dummy variables to evaluate categorical moderators

$ES_i = B_0 + B_1(DV1) + B_2(DV2) + B_3(DV3) + e_i$

- ES_i is the effect size (e.g., Z_r) for study i.
- B_0 is the model intercept.
- B_1, B_2, and B_3 are the regression coefficients for the dummy variables.
- DV1, DV2, and DV3 are the dummy variables created to indicate group membership (with number of dummy variables = number of groups − 1).
- e_i is the residual deviation of the effect size of study i from the group effect size (with the variance interpreted as the residual, or within-group, heterogeneity).

Using a statistical software package (e.g., SPSS or SAS), I regress the effect sizes (Z_rs) onto the three dummy variables (DV1, DV2, and DV3), weighted by the inverse variance weight (w) (here, I am requesting that the program include the constant in the model because I have not used the constant as a predictor). The output from the ANOVA table of this regression parallels the results from the ANOVA I described in Section 9.1: The total sum of squares (SS_{total}) provides the total heterogeneity (Q_{total}) = 350.71; the residual or error sum of squares ($SS_{residual}$ or SS_{error}) provides the within-group heterogeneity (Q_{within}) = 285.57; and the regression or model sum of squares ($SS_{regression}$ or SS_{model}) provides the between-group heterogeneity ($Q_{between}$) = 65.14. This last value is compared to a χ^2 distribution (e.g., Table 8.2) to evaluate whether the categorical moderator is significant. This regression analysis also yields coefficients and their (incorrect) standard errors. If I adjust these standard errors, I can evaluate the statistical significance of the regression coefficients as indicative of whether each group differs from the reference group. To illustrate: In this example, in which I coded observational methods as the reference group, I could consider the regression coefficient of DV2 (denoting use of peer reports) = .301 by dividing it by the corrected standard error

$$(SE_{adjusted} = \frac{SE_{output}}{\sqrt{MS_{residual}}} = \frac{.2102}{\sqrt{12.416}} = .0597)$$

to yield Z = .301 / .0597 = 5.05. I would thus conclude that studies using peer-report methods yield larger effect sizes than studies using observational methods. More generally, I could compute the implied values of each of the four methods via the prediction equation comprised of the intercept and regression coefficients for the dummy variables:

$$\hat{Z}_r = B_0 + B_1(DV1) + B_2(DV2) + B_3(DV3) = .097 + .486(DV1) + .301(DV2) + .095(DV3)$$

Because I used observational methods as my reference group, the implied mean effect size for this group is Z_r = .097. For studies using parent reports (the first dummy variable), the implied effect size is Z_r = .583 (.097 + .486); for studies using peer reports (the second dummy variable), the implied effect size is Z_r = .398 (.097 + .301); and so on. When using transformed effect sizes such as Z_r, you should transform these implied values back to the more intuitive metric (e.g., r) for reporting.

As in primary analysis (see Cohen & Cohen, 1983), dummy variables represent just one of several options for coding group membership in meta-analytic tests of categorical moderators. Dummy variables have the advan-

TABLE 9.3. Example Moderator Analyses within General Regression Framework

Study	Method	Sample size (N)	Effect size (r)	Transformed ES (Z_r)	Weight (w)	DV1	DV2	DV3	Age (years)	EC1	EC2	EC3	C_Age
Blachman (2003)	Parent	228	.525	.583	208.12	1	0	0	9.2	.97	-.82	-.12	-0.33
Crick & Grotpeter (1995)	Peer	491	.198	.201	297.81	0	1	0	9.4	-.03	.18	-.12	-0.13
Crick et al. (1997)	Peer	65	.443	.476	55.15	0	1	0	4.5	-.03	.18	-.12	-5.03
	Teacher	65	.167	.168	58.68	0	0	1	4.5	-.03	-.82	.88	-5.03
Geiger (2003)	Peer	458	.554	.624	427.07	0	1	0	8.0	-.03	.18	-.12	-1.53
Hawley et al. (2007)	Peer	929	.161	.162	835.96	0	1	0	14.7	-.03	.18	-.12	5.17
Henington (1996)	Peer	904	.336	.349	831.95	0	1	0	7.5	-.03	.18	-.12	-2.03
Johnson (2003)	Peer	74	.531	.591	66.92	0	1	0	6.0	-.03	.18	-.12	-3.53
	Teacher	74	.074	.075	66.83	0	0	1	6.0	-.03	-.82	.88	-3.53
Leff (1995)	Peer	151	.617	.721	136.66	0	1	0	9.5	-.03	.18	-.12	-0.03
Miller (2001)	Peer	150	.557	.628	139.90	0	1	0	16.0	-.03	.18	-.12	6.47
Murray–Close & Crick (2006)	Peer	590	.575	.655	550.97	0	1	0	9.0	-.03	.18	-.12	-0.53

Study	Source	N											
Nelson et al. (2005)	Peer	180	.090	.090	144.75	0	1	0	4.8	-.03	.18	-.12	-4.73
	Teacher	180	-.011	-.011	123.53	0	0	1	4.8	-.03	-.82	.88	-4.73
Ostrov (under review)[a]	Obs.	139	.181	.183	124.18	0	0	0	3.6	-.03	-.82	-.12	-4.73
	Teacher	139	.513	.567	127.22	0	0	1	3.6	-.03	-.82	.88	-5.93
Ostrov & Crick (2007)	Obs.	132	.049	.049	117.70	0	0	0	4.1	-.03	-.82	-.12	-5.43
Ostrov et al. (2004)[b]	Obs.	60	.000	.000	52.05	0	0	0	4.6	-.03	-.82	-.12	-4.93
Pakaslahti & Keltikangas-Järvinen (1998)	Peer	839	.326	.339	689.52	0	1	0	14.5	-.03	.18	-.12	4.97
Phillipsen et al. (1999)	Peer	262	-.048	-.048	242.93	0	1	0	8.7	-.03	.18	-.12	-0.83
Rys & Bear (1997)	Peer	266	.556	.627	242.84	0	1	0	9.5	-.03	.18	-.12	-0.03
	Teacher	266	.338	.352	250.96	0	0	1	9.5	-.03	-.82	.88	-0.03
Salmivalli et al. (2000)	Peer	209	.253	.258	195.52	0	1	0	15.5	-.03	.18	-.12	5.97
Tomada & Schneider (1997)	Peer	314	.313	.324	296.76	0	1	0	9.0	-.03	.18	-.12	-0.53
	Teacher[b]	314	.000	.000	280.47	0	0	1	9.0	-.03	-.82	.88	-0.53
Werner (2000)	Peer	881	.477	.519	810.71	0	1	0	8.0	-.03	.18	-.12	-1.53
Werner & Crick (2004)	Peer	517	.469	.509	482.45	0	1	0	8.0	-.03	.18	-.12	-1.53

[a]Article was under review during the preparation of this meta-analytic review. It has subsequently been published as Ostrov (2008).
[b]Effect size is lower-bound estimate based on author's reporting only nonsignficant associations.

tages of explicitly comparing all groups to a reference group, which might be of central interest in some analyses. However, dummy variables have the disadvantages of not allowing for easy comparisons between groups that are not the reference group (e.g., between peer and teacher reports in the example just presented) and that are not centered around 0 (a consideration I describe below). Effects coding (see Cohen & Cohen, 1983, p. 198) still relies on a reference group, but centers on the independent variables. For example, effects for four groups would use three effects codes, which might be $-\frac{1}{2}$, $-\frac{1}{2}$, and $-\frac{1}{2}$ for the reference group; $\frac{1}{2}$, 0, and 0 for the second group; 0, $\frac{1}{2}$, and 0 for the third group; and 0, 0, and $\frac{1}{2}$ for the fourth group.[4] Another alternative is contrast coding (Cohen & Cohen, 1983, p. 204), which allows for flexibility in creating specific planned comparisons among subsets of groups.

9.3.3   Evaluating Multiple Moderators

Having considered the regression framework for analyzing mean effect sizes, categorical moderators, and a single continuous moderator, you have likely inferred that this multiple regression approach can be used to evaluate multiple moderators. Doing so is no more complex than entering multiple categorical (represented with one or more dummy variables, effects codes, or contrast codes) or continuous predictors in this meta-analytic multiple regression.

However, one important consideration is that of centering (i.e., subtracting the mean value of a predictor from the values of this predictor). Although the statistical significance of either the overall model or individual predictors will not be influenced by whether or not you center, centering does offer two advantages. First, it permits more intuitive interpretation of the intercept as the mean effect size across studies. Second, it removes nonessential colinearity when evaluating interaction or power polynomial terms. To appropriately center predictors for this type of regression, you perform two steps. First, you compute the weighted (by inverse variance weights, w) average value of each predictor. Second, you compute a centered predictor variable by subtracting this weighted mean from scores on the original (uncentered) variable for each study. This process works for either continuous variables or dichotomous variables (this method of centering dummy variables converts them to effects codes).

To illustrate centering and evaluation of multiple moderators, I turn again to the example meta-analysis of the associations between relational aggression and rejection. In this illustration, I want to evaluate moderation both by method of measuring aggression and by age. Specifically, I want to evaluate whether either *uniquely* moderates these effect sizes (controlling for any overlap between method and age that may exist among these studies; see Section 9.4). Table 9.3 displays these 27 effect sizes (from 22 studies), as well as values for the two predictors: three dummy variables denoting the four categorical levels of method, and the continuous variable age. To create the centered variables, I first computed the weighted mean for each of the three dummy variables and age; these values were .0265, .8206, .1155, and 9.533, respectively.[5] I then subtracted these values from scores on each of these four variables, resulting in the four centered variables shown on the right side of Table 9.3. I have labeled the three centered dummy codes as effects codes (EC1, EC2, and EC3), and the centered age variable "C_Age."

When I then regress the effect size (Z_r) onto these four predictors (EC1, EC2, EC3, and C_Age), weighted by w, I obtain $SS_{regression}$ = 93.46. Evaluating this amount of heterogeneity explained by the model ($Q_{regression}$) as a 4 df (df = number of predictors), I conclude that this model explains a significant amount of heterogeneity in these effect sizes. Further, each of the four regression coefficients is statistically significant: EC1 = .581 (adjusted SE = .092, Z = 6.29, $p < .001$), EC2 = .415 (adjusted SE = .063, Z = 6.54, $p < .001$), EC3 = .152 (adjusted SE = .068, Z = 2.23, $p < .05$), and centered Age[6] = −.020 (adjusted SE = .004, Z = −5.32, $p < .001$). Inspection of the regression coefficient (with corrected standard errors) allows me to evaluate whether age is a significant unique moderator (i.e., above and beyond moderation by method), but I cannot directly evaluate the unique moderation of method beyond age because this categorical variable is represented with three effects codes (though in this example the answer is obvious, given that each effects code is statistically significant). To evaluate the unique prediction by this categorical variable (or any other multiple variable block), I can perform a hierarchical (weighted) multiple regression in which centered age is entered at step 1 and the three effects codes are entered at step 2. Running this analysis yields $SS_{regression}$ = 3.56 at step 1 and $SS_{regression}$ = 93.46 at step 2. I conclude that the unique heterogeneity predicted by the set of effects codes representing the categorical method moderator is significant ($Q_{(df=2)}$ = 93.64 − 3.56 = 90.08, $p < .001$). I could similarly re-analyze these data with the three effects codes at step 1 and centered age at step 2 to evaluate the unique prediction by age. This is equivalent to inspecting the regression weight relative to its corrected standard error in the final model (as is the case for the unique moderation of any single variable predictor).[7]

Two additional findings from this weighted multiple regression analysis merit attention. First, the intercept estimate (B_0) is .368, with a corrected standard error of .0113; these values are identical to those obtained by fitting an empty model to these 27 effect sizes. This means that I can still interpret the mean effect size and its statistical significance and confidence intervals within the moderator analysis, demonstrating the value of centering these predictors. Second, the residual sum of squares should be noted (SS_{residual} or $SS_{\text{error}} = 257.24$), as this represents the heterogeneity among effect sizes left unexplained by this model (Q_{residual}; which can be evaluated for statistical significance according to a chi-square distribution with $df = k -$ no. of predictors $- 1$). As I elaborate below, the size of this residual, or unexplained, heterogeneity is one consideration in evaluating the adequacy of the moderation model.

9.3.4   Conclusions and Extensions of Multiple Regression Models

As I hope is clear, this weighted multiple regression framework for analyzing moderators in meta-analysis is a flexible approach. Extending from an empty model in which mean effect sizes and heterogeneity are estimated, this framework can accommodate any combination of multiple categorical or continuous moderator variables as predictors. This general approach also allows for the evaluation of more complex moderation hypotheses. For example, one can test interactive combinations of moderators by creating product terms. Similarly, one can evaluate nonlinear moderation by the creation of power polynomial terms. These possibilities represent just a sample of many that are conceivable—if conceptually warranted—within this regression framework.

9.4   AN ALTERNATIVE SEM APPROACH

Cheung (2008) described an approach to meta-analysis within an SEM framework that can be used for moderator analyses as described in this chapter, as well as estimating fixed-effects means as described in Chapter 8 and more complex models (random- and mixed-effects models) described in Chapter 10. You should be aware that this is not SEM in the sense of multivariate, latent variable analyses (such as described in Chapter 12), but instead uses the flexibility of the SEM approach and software (e.g., ability to place model constraints) to fit meta-analytic models of a single effect size and coded study characteristics as predictors. In the context of moderator analyses, this approach is also advantageous over the regression approach I have described earlier in that it can use the advanced methods of missing data management in SEM when some studies do not report values for the characteristics you wish to evaluate as moderators.[8]

Although this alternative SEM approach is flexible, it does require an understanding of SEM as well as the use of specialized software.[9] Given this restriction, I will write this section with the assumption that you are familiar with SEM (if you are not, I recommend Kline, 2010, as an accessible introduction). Next, I describe the data transformation central to this approach, how this model can be used to estimate (fixed-effects) mean effect sizes (Chapter 8), and how this model can be used for moderator analyses. I consider this model again in Chapter 10 when I describe how it can be used for random- and mixed-effects models.

9.4.1 Transformations to Produce Equal Errors across Studies

As you recall, different studies in a meta-analysis are believed to have different sampling variances (i.e., squared standard errors) that provided the basis for differentially weighting the studies (see Chapter 8). The initial "key" to this SEM approach to meta-analysis is to rescale effect sizes and their predictors for each study so that the studies have equal sampling errors. This allows you to treat each study as an equally weighted case in the analyses because the weighting is accounted for by a transformation of study effect sizes and their predictors (i.e., study characteristics). This transformation factor is the square root of the weight you would normally use for a fixed-effects analysis (i.e., $w_i = 1 / SE_i^2$). You apply this transformation factor by multiplying it by the effect sizes and predictors (including the intercept) (Cheung, 2008, p. 186):

Equation 9.7: Transformations of effect sizes and predictors to produce equal errors across studies

$$ES_i^* = ES_i \sqrt{W_i}$$

$$X_i^* = X_i \sqrt{W_i}$$

- ES_i^* is the transformed effect size for study i.
- ES_i is the original (untransformed) effect size for study i.
- W_i is the weight, equal to $1 / (SE_i^2)$, for study i.
- X_i^* is the transformed value of the predictor (including intercept) for study i.
- X_i is the original (untransformed) value of the predictor (including intercept, 1) for study i.

Once these transformed effect sizes and predictors are created, the analyses within an SEM context do not require additional weighting, so each study is treated as an equally weighted case (to be clear, studies are still differentially weighted, but this occurs in the transformation rather than in the analyses). Next, I describe and illustrate how this approach can be used to estimate (fixed-effects) mean effect sizes and to evaluate moderators. This presentation follows closely that of Cheung (2008), but I use the example meta-analysis of relational aggression and peer rejection to illustrate these analyses.

9.4.2 Estimating Mean Effect Sizes

Although you already know how to estimate mean effect sizes (Chapter 8), it is useful to revisit these issues within this SEM approach. To evaluate a mean effect size, a model is fit in which the transformed effect size (ES^*) is regressed onto the transformed intercept (X_0^*). The intercept is just a constant 1.0 (literally, a variable with the value of 1 for each study) that is then transformed using Equation 9.7. Although the model is simple and could otherwise be performed using traditional software for regression, there are two important constraints you need to place on this model that require SEM software: (1) you fix the variance of ES^* to 1.0, and (2) you fix the indicator intercept of ES^* to 0. Given these constraints, the mean effect size is represented as the regression coefficient from the transformed intercept.

I demonstrate this SEM representation by estimating the mean of the relational aggression with rejection association among the 22 studies shown in Table 9.2. To illustrate the computations of Equation 9.7, consider the first study (Blachman, 2003), which had an effect size $Z_r = .583$ and weight (W) = 208.12. Using Equation 9.7, I find that the transformed effect size, Z_r^*, is equal to $.583\sqrt{208.12} = 8.411$. The predictor in this model is a transformed intercept 1.0, computed using Equation 9.7 to be $1\sqrt{208.12} = 14.426$. I also apply these transformations of effect sizes and intercept to the other 21 studies in Table 9.2.

The path diagram representing this analysis, as well as Mplus syntax,[10] is shown in Figure 9.1. From this figure, you see that the transformed effect size (Fisher's Z_r, subjected to the transformation of Equation 9.7 to obtain Z_r^*) is regressed onto the transformed intercept (the constant 1.0 transformed with Equation 9.7 to obtain X^*). The regression coefficient (b_0) in this example is estimated to be .386, which is identical (within rounding error) to the mean Z_r from these studies using the methods I described in Chapter 8. The standard error of this estimate is .012, which is also identical to the standard

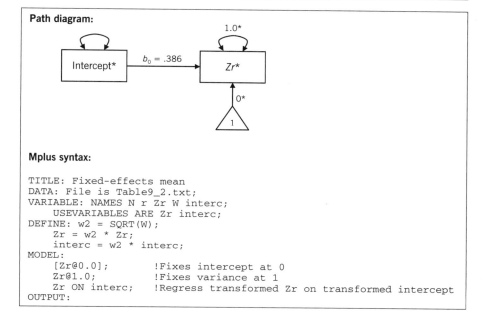

Path diagram:

Mplus syntax:

```
TITLE: Fixed-effects mean
DATA: File is Table9_2.txt;
VARIABLE: NAMES N r Zr W interc;
    USEVARIABLES ARE Zr interc;
DEFINE: w2 = SQRT(W);
    Zr = w2 * Zr;
    interc = w2 * interc;
MODEL:
    [Zr@0.0];        !Fixes intercept at 0
    Zr@1.0;          !Fixes variance at 1
    Zr ON interc;    !Regress transformed Zr on transformed intercept
OUTPUT:
```

FIGURE 9.1. Path diagram and Mplus syntax to estimate (fixed-effects) mean effect size.

error of the mean effect size computed in Chapter 8. Therefore, the statistical significance ($Z = .386/.012 = 32.68$, $p < .001$) is also identical (within rounding) to the previously obtained results. In short, this approach yields identical values to those if you used the methods described in Chapter 8.

9.4.3 Evaluating Moderators

From here, it is straightforward to add predictors to evaluate (categorical or continuous) moderators of this effect size. You simply make the same transformation described in Equation 9.7 (i.e., multiplying by the square root of the weight) to these predictors, and then add them to the predictive model.

I illustrate this analysis using the meta-analysis summarized in Table 9.3, in which I want to evaluate age (a continuous variable) and method of measuring aggression (three dummy coded variables) as potential moderators of the relational aggression with peer rejection association. As I did earlier using the multiple regression approach, I center these variables to assist interpretation.

Considering the first study, the effect size and intercept are transformed as already described. For this study, the centered values of the moderators (i.e., the values of Table 9.3 minus their means) are C_Age = −0.33 (= 9.2 − 9.53), EC1 = 0.97 (= 1 − .03), EC2 = −0.82, and EC3 = −0.12. When these four predictors are transformed (Equation 9.7) by multiplying by the square root of the study weight, the transformed values are C_Age* = −4.76, EC1* = 13.99, EC2* = −11.83, and EC3* = −1.73.

Figure 9.2 shows the path diagram and Mplus script for adding centered age and the three effects codes representing measurement type, to evaluate these coded study characteristics as moderators of the association between relational aggression and rejection. You evaluate moderator effects by inspecting the regression coefficients of the transformed moderators predicting transformed effect size. In this example, as when performed within a regression context, each of the three effects codes (EC1: b_1 = 0.582, SE = .092, Z = 6.30, p < .001; EC2: b_2 = 0.415, SE = .063, Z = 6.55, p < .001; EC3: b_3 = 0.152, SE = .068, Z = 2.24, p < .05) as well as centered age (b_4 = −0.020, SE = .004, Z = 5.33, p < .001) were significant moderators. Further, the intercept was significant and represents the overall mean Z_r (b_0 = 0.370, SE = .011, Z = 32.78, p < .001). All of these values are identical (within rounding error) to those found through regression analyses. However, the key advantage of this SEM approach is that it could have accommodated all studies even if some had missing values for the study characteristics age or method of assessing aggression.

9.5 PRACTICAL MATTERS: THE LIMITS OF INTERPRETING MODERATORS IN META-ANALYSIS

Notwithstanding the considerable flexibility of a regression framework and the SEM approach for moderator analysis in meta-analysis, you should consider three potential limits when drawing conclusions from moderator analyses.

9.5.1 Empirically Confounded Moderators

Just as you want to avoid highly correlated predictors in a multiple regression analysis of primary data, it is important to ensure that the moderator variables (i.e., predictors) are not too highly correlated in meta-analysis. If they are, then two problems can emerge. First, it might be difficult to detect the

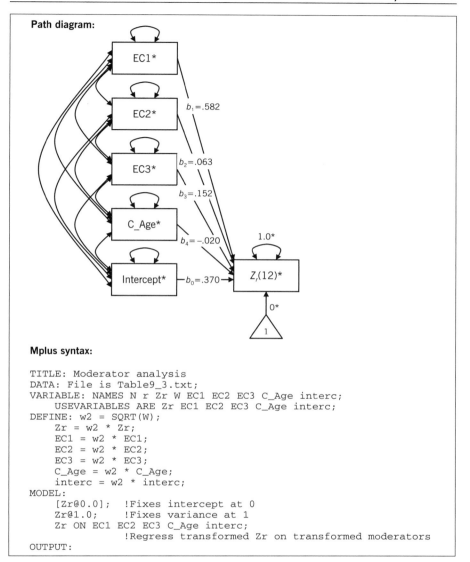

Path diagram:

Mplus syntax:

```
TITLE: Moderator analysis
DATA: File is Table9_3.txt;
VARIABLE: NAMES N r Zr W EC1 EC2 EC3 C_Age interc;
    USEVARIABLES ARE Zr EC1 EC2 EC3 C_Age interc;
DEFINE: w2 = SQRT(W);
    Zr = w2 * Zr;
    EC1 = w2 * EC1;
    EC2 = w2 * EC2;
    EC3 = w2 * EC3;
    C_Age = w2 * C_Age;
    interc = w2 * interc;
MODEL:
    [Zr@0.0];   !Fixes intercept at 0
    Zr@1.0;     !Fixes variance at 1
    Zr ON EC1 EC2 EC3 C_Age interc;
            !Regress transformed Zr on transformed moderators
OUTPUT:
```

FIGURE 9.2. Path diagram and Mplus syntax to evaluate moderation.

unique association of a moderator above and beyond the other highly correlated moderators. Second, if they are extremely highly correlated, you can get
inaccurate regression estimates that have large standard errors (the so-called
bouncing beta problem).

Fortunately, it is easy—though somewhat time-consuming—to evaluate
multicolinearity in meta-analytic moderator analyses. To do so, you regress
each moderator (predictor) onto the set of all other moderators, weighted by
the same weights (i.e., inverse variances of effect size estimates) as you have
used in the moderator analyses. To illustrate using the example data shown
in Table 9.3, I would regress age onto the three dummy variables representing
the four categorical methods of assessing aggression. Here, R^2 = .41, far less
than the .90 that is often considered too high (e.g., Cohen et al., 2003, p. 424).
I would then repeat the process for other moderator variables, successively
regressing (weighted by w) them on the other moderator variables.

9.5.2 Conceptually Confounded (Proxy) Moderators

A more difficult situation is that of uncoded confounded moderators. These
include a large range of other study characteristics that might be correlated
across studies with the variables you have coded. For example, studying
a particular type of sample (e.g., adolescents vs. young children) might be
associated with particular methodological features (e.g., using self-reports
vs. observations; if I had failed to code this methodology, then this feature
would potentially be an uncoded confounded moderator). Here, results indicating moderation by the sample characteristics might actually be due to
moderation by methodology. Put differently, the moderator in my analysis is
only a proxy for the true moderator. Moreover, because the actual moderator
(type of measure) is conceptually very different from the moderator I actually tested (age), my conclusion would be seriously compromised if I failed to
consider this possibility.

There is no way to entirely avoid this problem of conceptually confounded, or proxy, moderators. But you can reduce the threat it presents by
coding as many alternative moderator variables as possible (see Chapter 5).
If you find evidence of moderation after controlling for a plausible alternative
moderator, then you have greater confidence that you have found the true
moderator (whereas if you did not code the alternative moderator, you could
not empirically evaluate this possibility). At the same time, a large number of
alternative possibilities might be argued to be the true moderator, of which
the predictor you have considered is just a proxy, and it is impossible to

anticipate and code all of these possibilities. For this reason, some argue that findings of moderation in meta-analysis are merely suggestive of moderation, but require replication in primary studies where confounding variables could arguably be better controlled. I do not think there is a universal answer for how informative moderator results from meta-analysis are; I think it depends on the conceptual arguments that can be made for the analyzed moderator versus other, unanalyzed moderators, as well as the diversity of the existing studies in using the analyzed moderator across a range of samples, methodologies, and measures. Despite the ambiguities inherent in meta-analytic moderator effects, assessing conceptually reasonable moderators is a worthwhile goal in most meta-analyses in which effect sizes are heterogeneous (see Chapter 8).

9.5.3 Ensuring Adequate Coverage in Moderator Analyses

When examining and interpreting moderators, an important consideration is the coverage, or the extent to which numerous studies represent the range of potential moderator values considered. The literature on meta-analysis has not provided clear guidance on what constitutes adequate coverage, so this evaluation is more subjective than might be desired. Nevertheless, I try to offer my advice and suggestions based on my own experience.

As a first step, I suggest creating simple tables or plots showing the number of studies at various levels of the moderator variables. If you are testing only the main effects of the moderators, it is adequate to look at just the univariate distributions.[11] For example, in the meta-analysis of Table 9.3, I might create frequency tables or bar charts of the methods of assessing aggression, and similar charts of the continuous variable age categorized into some meaningful units (e.g., early childhood, middle childhood, early adolescence, and middle adolescence; or simply into, e.g., 2-year bins). Whether or not you report these tables or charts in a manuscript, they are extremely useful in helping you to evaluate the extent of coverage. Considering the method of assessing aggression, I see that these data contained a reasonable number of effect sizes from peer- ($k = 17$) and teacher- ($k = 6$) report methods, but fewer from observations ($k = 3$) and only one using parent reports. Similarly, examining the distribution of age among these effect sizes suggests a gap in the early adolescence range (i.e., no studies between 9.5 and 14.5 years).

What constitutes adequate coverage? Unfortunately, there are no clear answers to this question, as it depends on the overall size of your meta-analysis, the correlations among moderators, the similarity of your included studies on characteristics not coded, and the conceptual certainty that the moderator considered is the true moderator rather than a proxy. At an extreme, one study representing a level of a moderator (e.g., the single study using parent report in this example) or one study in a broad area of a continuous moderator (e.g., if there was only one study during early childhood) is not adequate coverage, as it is impossible to know what other features of that study are also different from those of the rest of the studies. Conversely, five studies covering an area of a moderator probably constitute adequate coverage for most purposes (again, I base this recommendation on my own experience; I do not think that any studies have more formally evaluated this claim). Beyond these general points of reference, the best advice I can provide is to carefully consider these studies: Do they all provide similar effect sizes? Do they vary among one another in other characteristics (which might point to the generalizability of these studies for this region of the moderator)? Are the studies comparable to the studies at other levels of the moderator (if not, then it becomes impossible to determine whether the presumed moderator is a true or proxy moderator)?

9.6 SUMMARY

In a meta-analysis, moderator variables are coded study characteristics that are evaluated as predictors of effect sizes. It is possible to evaluate categorical moderators in an approach similar to ANOVA, continuous moderators in an approach similar to regression, and to evaluate flexible combinations of these in either a general multiple regression or SEM framework. In this chapter, I have described each of these approaches as well as some limitation in interpreting moderator effects in meta-analysis.

9.7 RECOMMENDED READINGS

Lipsey, M. W. (2003). Those confounded moderators in meta-analysis: Good, bad, and ugly. The Annals, 587, 69–81.—This article provides an accessible and thoughtful conceptual consideration for interpreting moderator effects from meta-analysis.

Lipsey, M. W., & Wilson, D. B. (2001). Practical meta-analysis. Thousand Oaks, CA: Sage.—This book provides a clear and concise description of the ANOVA and regression approaches to moderator analyses that I have described in this chapter (see especially pp. 120–124 and 135–140).

NOTES

1. Although using multiple effect sizes from the same study violates the assumption of independence, I believe that this practice is acceptable when analyzing categorical moderators and the interdependent effect sizes are placed in different groups. Because it is reasonable to expect multiple effect sizes from the same study to be more similar (i.e., positively correlated) than independent effect sizes, the impact of this interdependence will be to attenuate between-group differences. Therefore, violation of the independence assumption in this case is likely to impose a conservative bias (i.e., increase in type II error rates). I believe that this negative consequence is outweighed by the advantage of being able to include all relevant effect sizes in this example.

2. The formula I have provided for the number of comparisons differs from that sometimes provided in textbooks on ANOVA (e.g., Keppel, 1991, p. 167). My formula assumes that you are only interested in comparing two groups with each other (i.e., pairwise mean comparisons in ANOVA terminology), so the number of possible comparisons is $G(G-1)/2$ (e.g., for 4 groups, the number of comparisons is $4(4-1)/2 = 6$). I assume that you will not compare different combinations of groups (e.g., whether the mean effect sizes of Groups 1 and 2 combined differ from the mean effect sizes of Groups 3 and 4 combined). If these multigroup comparisons are of interest, then the total number of comparisons that can be made using G groups is $1 + (3^G - 1)/2 - 2^G$. Using this correction will result in very conservative comparisons, and I strongly recommend considering planned comparisons rather than this approach if you are interested in these combined group comparisons.

3. I do not use the residual sum of squares in this section, but it is useful to record. This value represents the residual heterogeneity ($Q_{residual}$), or heterogeneity effect sizes not accounted for by the regression model.

4. These effects codes would assume that all groups have equal sizes (here, equal numbers of studies). Effects codes derived from centering (described below) can accommodate different group sizes.

5. Because not all programs readily provide this weighted average, it is useful to keep in mind that you can compute this weighted average of the predictor by regressing the predictor variable onto a constant, weighted by the inverse variance weights (w).

6. There is an interesting suppressor effect among these 27 effect sizes: By itself, age is only a marginally significant predictor ($Q_{regression(1)} = 3.56$, $p = .059$). However, when controlling for these effects for method, the effect of age is statistically significant.

7. In the hierarchical multiple regression, ($Q_{regression(1)} = 28.33$, $p < .001$). In the simultaneous regression, the regression coefficient was statistically significant according to a Z-test: $Z = -.0203 / .00382 = -5.32$. Note that $(-5.32)^2 = 28.33$.

8. Namely, this approach allows you to use FIML techniques of missing data management (see, e.g., Arbuckle, 1996). This approach is superior to the practice of removing studies that have missing study characteristics in that FIML will provide less biased and more statistically powerful results. This approach is especially valuable when simultaneously evaluating multiple moderators, for which many studies might otherwise be removed for missing values on one of the several coded study characteristics (moderators).

9. For reasons I describe in the next chapter on random- and mixed-effects models, I recommend using Mplus or Mx SEM packages.

10. Note that the Mplus syntax in this figure calculates the transformations of Equation 9.7 directly from the raw effect size (Z_r) and intercept (1.0).

11. If you are interested in evaluating interactions among moderators, it would be valuable to consider multivariate distributions. For example, if I were interested in the interaction of age and method of assessing aggression in the example meta-analysis, I would create a two-dimensional plot with method on one axis and age on the other, then plot the studies within this space. Here, I would look for any areas of this space where there are few or no studies.

10

Fixed-, Random-, and Mixed-Effects Models

In Chapter 8, I presented an approach to computing mean effect sizes and drawing inferences or computing confidence intervals about these means. In Chapter 9, I described methods of evaluating moderators in the presence of initial heterogeneity. Both of these analyses assumed homogeneity at some level; in Chapter 8, this assumption was that the effect sizes were homogeneous (i.e., no more variability than expected due to random-sampling fluctuations), and in Chapter 9, this assumption was that the effect sizes were homogeneous after accounting for differences by moderator variables (i.e., conditional homogeneity). These models assuming homogeneity (or conditional homogeneity) are termed fixed-effects models.

In this chapter, I present an alternative approach, known as random-effects models (e.g., Hedges, 1983; Hedges & Vevea, 1998; Overton, 1998; Raudenbush, 1994), in which you model this unexplained heterogeneity. In Section 10.1 I compare the fixed-effects models discussed in Chapter 8 with these random-effects models, and in Section 10.2 I describe how you compute the mean effect size (and draw inferences and compute confidence intervals) within these random-effects models. In Section 10.3 I describe how to analyze moderators while also modeling unexplained heterogeneity (mixed-effects, or conditionally random, models). I then continue from the introduction of the SEM representation of meta-analysis from Chapter 9 to discuss how this approach can be used to estimate random- and mixed-effects models (Section 10.4). Finally, I consider some practical matters in choosing among these models, presenting both conceptual and statistical power considerations (Section 10.5).

10.1   DIFFERENCES AMONG MODELS

It is easiest to begin with the simple case in which you are interested only in the mean effect size among a set of studies, both in identifying the mean effect size and in computing its standard errors for inferential testing or for computing of confidence intervals. Even in this simple case, there are a number of conceptual, analytic, and interpretive differences between fixed- and random-effects meta-analytic models (see also Hedges & Vevea, 1998; Kisamore & Brannick, 2008).

10.1.1   Conceptual Differences

The conceptual differences between fixed- and random-effects models can be illustrated through Figure 8.1, which I have reproduced in the top of Figure 10.1. As you recall, the top of Figure 10.1 displays effect sizes from five studies, all (or at least most) of which have confidence intervals that overlap with a single population effect size, now denoted with θ using traditional symbol conventions (e.g., Hedges & Vevea, 1998). This overlap with a single population effect size, with deviations of study effect sizes due to only sampling fluctuations (i.e., study-specific confidence intervals), represents the fixed-effects model of meta-analysis.

The bottom portion of Figure 10.1 displays the random-effects model. Here, the confidence intervals of the individual study effect sizes do not necessarily overlap with a single population effect size. Instead, they overlap with a *distribution* of population effect sizes. In other words, random-effects models conceptualize a population distribution of effect sizes, rather than a single effect size as in the fixed-effects model. In a random-effects model, you estimate not only a single population mean effect size (θ), but rather a distribution of population effect sizes represented by a central tendency (μ) and standard deviation (τ).

10.1.2   Analytic Differences

These conceptual differences in fixed- versus random-effects models can also be expressed in equation form. These equations help us understand the computational differences between these two models, described in Section 10.2.

Equation 10.1 expresses this fixed-effects model of study effect sizes being a function of a population effect size and sampling error:

Equation 10.1: Equation for effect sizes for studies in fixed-effects model

$$ES_i = \theta + \varepsilon i$$

- ES_i is the (observed) effect size for study i.
- θ is the (single) population effect size.
- ε_i is the deviation of study i from the population effect size.

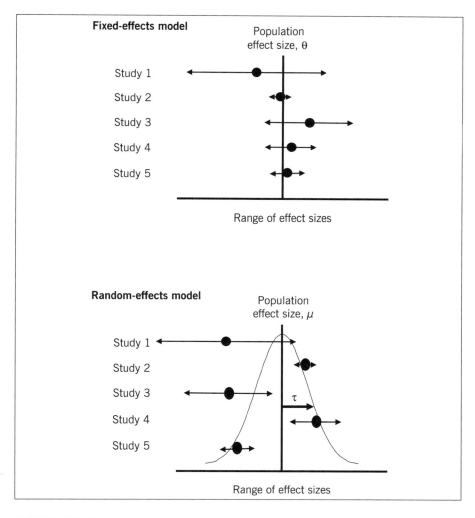

FIGURE 10.1. Conceptual representation of fixed- versus random-effects models.

In this fixed-effects model, the effect sizes for each study (ES_i) are assumed to be a function of two components: a single population effect size (θ) and the deviation of this study from this population effect size (ε_i). The population effect size is unknown but is estimated as the weighted average of effect sizes across studies (this is often one of the key values you want to obtain in your meta-analysis). The deviation of any one study's effect size from this population effect size (ε_i) is unknown and unknowable, but the distribution of these deviations across studies can be inferred from the standard errors of the studies. The test of heterogeneity (Chapter 8) is a test of the null hypothesis that this variability in deviations is no more than what you expect given sampling fluctuations alone (i.e., homogeneity), whereas the alternative hypothesis is that these deviations are more than would be expected by sampling fluctuations alone (i.e., heterogeneity).

I indicated in Chapter 9 that the presence of significant heterogeneity might prompt us to evaluate moderators to systematically explain this heterogeneity. An alternative approach would be to model this heterogeneity within a random-effects model. Conceptually, this approach involves estimating not only a mean population effect size, but also the variability in study effect sizes due to the population variability in effect sizes. These two estimates are shown in the bottom of Figure 10.1 as μ (mean population effect size) and τ (population variability in effect sizes). In equation form, this means that you would conceptualize each study effect size arising from three sources:

Equation 10.2: Equation for effect sizes for studies in random-effects model

$ES_i = \mu + \xi + \varepsilon_i$

- ES_i is the (observed) effect size for study i.
- μ is the mean of the distribution of population effect sizes.
- ξ_i is the reliable (not due to sampling deviation) deviation of study i from the mean of the distribution of population effect sizes.
- ε_i is the conditional deviation (sampling deviation) of study i from the distribution of population effect sizes.

As shown by comparing the equations for fixed- versus random-effects models (Equation 10.1 vs. Equation 10.2, respectively), the critical difference is that the single parameter of the fixed-effects model, the single population effect size (θ), is decomposed into two parameters (the central tendency and study deviation, μ and ξ_i) in the random-effects model. As I describe in more detail in Section 10.2, the central tendency of this distribution of population effect sizes is best estimated by the weighted mean of effect sizes from the studies (though with a different weight than used in a fixed-effects model). The challenge of the random-effects model is to determine how much of the variability in each study's deviation from this mean is due to the distribution of population effect sizes (ξ_is, sometimes called the random-effects variance; e.g., Raudenbush, 1994) versus sampling fluctuations (ε_is, sometimes called the estimation variance). Although this cannot be determined for any single study, random-effects models allow you to partition this variability across the collection of studies in your meta-analysis. I describe these computations in Section 10.2.

10.1.3 Interpretive Differences

Before turning to these analyses, however, it is useful to think of the different interpretations that are justified when using fixed- versus random-effect models. Meta-analysts using fixed-effects models are only justified in drawing conclusions about the specific set of studies included in their meta-analysis (what are sometimes termed conditional inferences; e.g., Hedges & Vevea, 1998). In other words, if you use a fixed-effects model, you should limit your conclusions to statements of the "these studies find … " type.

The use of random-effects models justifies inferences that generalize beyond the particular set of studies included in the meta-analysis to a population of potential studies of which those included are representative (what are sometimes termed unconditional inferences; Hedges & Vevea, 1998). In other words, random-effects models allow for more generalized statements of the "the literature finds … " or even "there is this magnitude of association between X and Y" type (note the absence of any "these studies" qualifier).[1] Although meta-analysts generally strive to be comprehensive in their inclusion of relevant studies in their meta-analyses (see Chapter 3), the truth is that there will almost always be excluded studies about which you still might wish to draw conclusions. These excluded studies include not only those that exist that you were not able to locate, but also similar studies that might be conducted in the future or even studies that contain unique permutations of methodology, sample, and measures that are similar to your sampled studies but simply have not been conducted.

I believe that most meta-analysts wish to make the latter, generalized statements (unconditional inferences) most of the time, so random-effects models are more appropriate. In fact, I often read meta-analyses in which the authors try to make these conclusions even when they used fixed-effects models; such conclusions are inappropriate. I recommend that you frame your conclusions carefully in ways that are appropriate given your statistical model (i.e., fixed- vs. random-effects), and consider the conclusions you wish to make when deciding between these models. I return to this and other considerations in selecting between fixed- and random-effects models in Section 10.5.

10.2   ANALYSES OF RANDOM-EFFECTS MODELS

A random-effects model in meta-analysis can be estimated in four general steps: (1) estimating the heterogeneity among effect sizes, (2) estimating population variability in effect sizes, (3) using this estimate of population variability to provide random-effects weights of study effect sizes, and (4) using these random-effects weights to estimate a random-effects mean effect size and standard errors of this estimate (for significance testing and confidence intervals). I illustrate each of these steps using the example meta-analysis dataset of 22 studies providing associations between relational aggression and peer rejection. These studies, together with the variables computed to estimate the random-effects model, are summarized in Table 10.1.

10.2.1   Estimating Heterogeneity

The first step is to estimate the heterogeneity, indexed by Q, in the same way as described in Chapter 8. As you recall, the heterogeneity (Q) is computed using Equation 8.6, reproduced here:

Equation 10.3: Estimating heterogeneity (Q)

$$Q = \sum \left(w_i \left(ES_i - \overline{ES} \right)^2 \right) = \sum \left(w_i ES_i^2 \right) - \frac{\left(\sum \left(w_i ES_i \right) \right)^2}{\sum w_i}$$

$$df = k - 1$$

- w_i is the weight of study i.
- ES_i is the effect size estimate from study i.
- $\overline{ES}_i$ is the mean effect size across studies.
- k is the number of studies.

TABLE 10.1. Example Random-Effects Model of (Artifact-Corrected) Correlations between Relational Aggression and Peer Rejection

Study	Sample size (N)	Age (years)	Effect size (Z_r)	Standard error (SE)	Weight (w)	wES	wES²	w²	w*	w*ES
Blachman (2003)	228	9.2	.583	0.0693	208.12	121.27	70.66	43315.0	21.94	11.51
Crick & Grotpeter (1995)	491	9.4	.201	0.0579	297.81	59.74	11.98	88693.4	22.66	4.49
Crick et al. (1997)	65	4.5	.322	0.1325	56.95	18.34	5.90	3242.9	17.14	5.34
Geiger (2003)	458	8.0	.624	0.0484	427.07	266.55	166.37	182388.9	23.20	12.85
Hawley et al. (2007)	929	14.7	.162	0.0346	835.96	135.72	22.03	698829.8	23.83	3.84
Henington (1996)	904	7.5	.349	0.0347	831.95	290.69	101.57	692141.3	23.83	8.00
Johnson (2003)	74	6.0	.419	0.1223	66.89	28.02	11.73	4474.6	17.95	7.11
Leff (1995)	151	9.5	.721	0.0855	136.66	98.48	70.97	18675.3	20.80	12.84
Miller (2001)	150	16.0	.628	0.0845	139.90	87.90	55.23	19570.9	20.87	11.62
Murray-Close & Crick (2006)	590	9.0	.655	0.0426	550.97	361.12	236.69	303565.1	23.48	13.51
Nelson et al. (2005)	180	4.8	.039	0.0831	144.75	5.70	0.22	20953.4	20.98	0.83
Ostrov (under review)[a]	139	3.6	.375	0.0892	125.71	47.14	17.68	15802.7	20.52	7.35
Ostrov & Crick (2007)	132	4.1	.049	0.0922	117.70	5.81	0.29	13853.1	20.30	1.00
Ostrov et al. (2004)[b]	60	4.6	.000	0.1386	52.05	0.00	0.00	2709.6	16.67	0.00
Pakaslahti & Keltikangas-Järvinen (1998)	839	14.5	.339	0.0381	689.52	233.68	79.19	475442.6	23.69	7.73
Phillipsen et al. (1999)	262	8.7	-.048	0.0642	242.93	-11.73	0.57	59016.0	22.28	-1.07
Rys & Bear (1997)	266	9.5	.489	0.0636	246.94	120.85	59.15	60977.2	22.31	10.12
Salmivalli et al. (2000)	209	15.5	.258	0.0715	195.52	50.54	13.06	38226.3	21.79	5.51
Tomada & Schneider (1997)	314	9.0	.162	0.0589	288.73	46.71	7.56	83367.0	22.61	3.63
Werner (2000)	881	8.0	.519	0.0351	810.71	420.41	218.01	657255.5	23.81	11.35
Werner & Crick (2004)	517	8.0	.509	0.0455	482.45	245.37	124.79	232756.5	23.34	10.94
Zalecki & Hinshaw (2004)	228	9.0	.651	0.0702	202.92	132.06	85.94	41174.7	21.88	12.52
Sum (Σ)					7152.21	2764.36	1359.60	3756432	475.89	161.02

Note. Hand calculations of these values may not produce exact replications due to rounding errors.
[a]Article was under review during the preparation of this meta-analytic review. It has subsequently been published as Ostrov (2008).
[b]Effect size is lower-bound estimate based on author's reporting only nonsignificant associations.

235

As in Chapter 8, I estimate Q in the example meta-analysis by creating three columns (variables)—w, wES, and wES^2—shown in Table 10.1. This yields $Q = 291.17$, which is high enough (relative to a χ^2 distribution with 21 df) to reject the null hypothesis of homogeneity and accept the alternate hypothesis of heterogeneity. Put another way, I conclude that the observed variability in effect sizes across these 22 studies is greater than expectable due to sampling fluctuation alone. This conclusion, along with other considerations described in Section 10.5, might lead me to use a random-effects model in which I estimate a distribution, rather than single point, of population effect sizes.

10.2.2 Estimating Population Variability

To estimate population variability, you partition the observed heterogeneity into that expectable due to sampling fluctuations and that representing true deviations in population effect sizes. Although you can never know the extent to which one particular study's deviation from the central tendency is due to sampling fluctuation versus its place in the distribution of population effect sizes, you can make an estimate of the magnitude of population variability based on the observed heterogeneity (total variability) and that which is expectable given the study standard errors. Specifically, you estimate population variability in effect sizes (τ^2) using the following equation:

Equation 10.4: Estimating population variability in effect sizes (τ^2)

$$\tau^2 = \frac{Q - (k - 1)}{\left(\sum w_i\right) - \dfrac{\left(\sum w_i^2\right)}{\left(\sum w_i\right)}}$$

Note: Equation is used if $Q \geq k - 1$. If $Q < k - 1$, $\tau^2 = 0$.

- Q is the heterogeneity statistic (see Equation 10.3).
- k is the number of studies.
- w_i is the weight of study i.

Although the denominator of this equation is not intuitive, you can understand this equation well enough by considering the numerator. Because the expected value of Q under the null hypothesis of homogeneity is equal to the degrees of freedom $(k - 1)$, a homogeneous set of studies will result in a numerator equal to zero, and therefore the population variance in effect sizes is estimated to be zero.[2] In contrast, when there is considerable heterogeneity, then Q is larger than the degrees of freedom $(k - 1)$, and this heterogeneity beyond that expected by sampling fluctuation results in a large estimate of the population variance, τ^2 (recalling that Q is a significance test based on the number of studies and total sample size in the meta-analysis, the denominator adjusts for the sums of weights in a way that makes the estimate of population variance similar for small and large meta-analyses).

To estimate the population variance in the example meta-analysis shown in Table 10.1, I compute a new variable (column) w^2. I then apply Equation 10.4 to obtain

$$\tau^2 = \frac{Q - (k - 1)}{\left(\sum w_i\right) - \dfrac{\left(\sum w_i^2\right)}{\left(\sum w_i\right)}} = \frac{291.17 - (22 - 1)}{7152.21 - \dfrac{3756432}{7152.21}} = \frac{270.17}{6627} = .0408$$

10.2.3 Computing Random-Effects Weights

Having estimated the population variability in effect sizes, the next step is to compute new, random-effects weights for each study. Before describing this computation, it is useful to consider the logic of these random-effects weights. As shown in Chapter 8, the reason for weighting effect sizes in a meta-analysis is to account for the imprecision of effect sizes, so as to give more weight to studies providing more precise effect size estimates than to those providing less precise estimates. In the fixed-effects model described in Chapter 8, imprecision in study effect sizes was assumed to be due only to the standard error of that particular effect size. This can be seen in Equation 10.1, which shows that each study's effect size is conceptualized as a function of the single population effect size and sampling deviation from that value. As seen in Equation 10.2, random-effects models consider two sources of a deviation of effect sizes around a mean: population variance (ξ_i, which has an estimated variance of τ^2) and sampling fluctuation (ε_i). In other words, random-effects models consider two sources of imprecision in effect size estimates: population variability and sampling fluctuation.

To account for these two sources of imprecision, random-effects weights are comprised of both an overall estimated population variance (τ^2) and a study-specific standard error (SE_i) for sampling fluctuation. Specifically, random-effects weights (w_i^*) are computed using the following equation:

Equation 10.5: Computing random-effects weights (w_i^*)

$$w_i^* = \frac{1}{\tau^2 + SE_i^2}$$

- τ^2 is the estimated population variance of effect sizes.
- SE_i is the standard error (i.e., sampling fluctuation) of the effect size of study i.

To illustrate this computation, consider the first study in Table 10.1 (Blachman, 2003). This study had a weight of 208.12 in the fixed-effects model (based on $w = 1/(.0693^2)$, allowing for rounding error). In the random-effects model, I compute a new weight as a function of the estimated population variance ($\tau^2 = .0408$) and the study-specific standard error ($SE = .0693$, to yield a study-specific sampling variance $SE^2 = .0048$):

$$w_i^* = \frac{1}{\tau^2 + SE_i^2} = \frac{1}{.0408 + .0693^2} = 21.94$$

The random-effects weights of all 22 studies are shown in Table 10.1 (second column from right). You should make two observations from these weights. First, these random-effects weights are smaller (much smaller in this example) than the fixed-effects weights. The implication of these smaller weights is that the sum of weights across studies will be smaller, and the standard error of the average mean will therefore be larger, in the random- relative to fixed-effects model. Second, although the studies still have the same relative ranking of weights using random- or fixed-effects models (i.e., studies with the largest weights for one had the largest weights for the other), the discrepancies in weights across studies is less for random- than for fixed-effects models. This fact impacts the relative influence of studies that are extremely large (outliers in sample size). I further discuss these and other differences between fixed- and random-effects models in Section 10.5.

10.2.4 Estimating and Drawing Inferences about Random-Effects Means

The final step of the random-effects analysis is to estimate the mean effect size and to make inferences about it (through significance testing or computing confidence intervals). These computations parallel those for fixed-effects models described in Chapter 8, except that the ws of the fixed-effects models are replaced with the random-effects weights, $w*$. To illustrate using this example of 22 studies (see the rightmost columns of Table 10.1), I compute the random-effects mean effect size (see Equation 8.2).

$$\bar{Z}_r = \frac{\sum (w * Z_r)}{\sum (w *)} = \frac{161.02}{475.89} = .338$$

(which I would transform to report as the random-effects mean correlation, $\bar{r} = .326$). Note that the random-effects mean is not identical to that of the fixed-effects mean computed in Chapter 8 ($\bar{Z}_r = .387$, $\bar{r} = .367$), though in this example they are reasonably close.

The standard error of this mean effect size is computed as (see Equation 8.3):

$$SE_{\bar{Z}_r} = \sqrt{\frac{1}{\sum (w *)}} = \sqrt{\frac{1}{475.89}} = .0458$$

This standard error can then be used for significance testing ($Z = .338 / .0458 = 7.38$, $p < .001$) of computing confidence intervals (95% confidence interval of Z_r is .249 to .428, translating to a confidence interval for r of .244 to .404). Note that the standard error from the random-effects model is considerably larger than that computed in Chapter 8 under the fixed-effects model (.0118), resulting in lower Z values of the significance test (7.38 vs. 32.70 for the fixed-effects model) and wider confidence intervals (vs. 95% confidence interval for r of .348 to .388).

10.3 MIXED-EFFECTS MODELS

Mixed-effects models, sometimes called conditionally random models, combine the (fixed-effects) moderator analyses of Chapter 9 with the estimation of variance in population effect sizes (random-effects) described earlier in this chapter. These models are useful when you want to evaluate moderators in meta-analysis, and you (1) either want the generalizability provided by random-effects models, or (2) fixed-effects moderator analyses (as described in Chapter 9) indicate significant residual heterogeneity (i.e., Q_{within} in ANOVA framework or $Q_{residual}$ in regression framework).

Mixed-effects models follow the logic of moderator analyses within a general regression framework (see Chapter 9.3). However, these models include additional terms representing population variability in effect sizes, above and beyond systematic variability accounted for by moderators as well as sampling fluctuations. The general equation for mixed-effects models can be represented by the following equation:

Equation 10.6: General equation for mixed-effects models

$$ES_i = B_0 + B_1(X_1) + B_2(X_2) + \ldots + \xi_i + \varepsilon_i$$

- ES_i is the effect size (e.g., Z_r) for study i.
- B_0 is the model intercept (interpretable as mean if moderators are centered.
- B_1, B_2, ... are the regression coefficients for the moderator variables.
- X_1, X_2, ... are the moderator variables.
- ξ_i is the reliable (not due to sampling deviation) deviation of study i from the predicted value (given the values of the moderators).
- ε_i is the sampling deviation of study i.

Unfortunately, estimating mixed-effects models requires intensive, fairly complex methods. Specifically, estimating mixed-effects models requires iterative matrix algebra (or analysis within an SEM framework, which I present in the next section). I describe and illustrate this estimation using the example meta-analysis (Table 10.1) of 22 studies next, evaluating sample age as a moderator in the context of between-study heterogeneity. However, I forewarn you that the material presented in the remainder of this section is complex.

Before describing the estimation of mixed-effects models, however, it is useful to begin by describing the analysis of a moderator variable within a fixed-effects framework using matrix algebra. After describing this fixed-effects framework, I will describe and illustrate the estimation of mixed-effects models through an iterative matrix algebra.

10.3.1 Matrix Algebra of Fixed-Effects Moderator Analysis

The general regression framework of analyzing moderators within the fixed-effects context (Section 9.3) can be solved using matrix algebra given the following equation (from Overton, 1998):

Equation 10.7: Matrix equation for general regression framework of fixed-effects moderator analysis

$$B = (X' V^{-1} X)^{-1} X' V^{-1} Y$$

- **B** is an $m \times 1$ vector (where m is the number of predictors + 1) containing the unstandardized regression coefficients of the intercept (first row) and predictors.
- **X** is a $k \times m$ matrix (where k is the number of studies and m is the number of predictors + 1) consisting of 1s in the first column (intercept) and values of the moderators in the other cells.
- **V** is a $k \times k$ matrix with squared standard errors for the k studies on the diagonal and zeros on the off-diagonal elements.
- **Y** is a $k \times 1$ vector of effect sizes from k studies.

To illustrate this computation with the example meta-analysis of 22 studies summarized in Table 9.4, in which I am interested in whether age moderates the association between relational aggression and peer rejection the following matrices are created:

$$X_{(22 \times 2)} = \begin{vmatrix} 1 & 9.2 \\ 1 & 9.4 \\ \dots & \dots \\ 1 & 9.0 \end{vmatrix}$$

$$V_{(22 \times 22)} = \begin{bmatrix} .0048 & 0 & \dots & 0 \\ 0 & .0034 & \dots & 0 \\ \dots & \dots & \dots & 0 \\ 0 & 0 & 0 & .0049 \end{bmatrix}$$

$$Y_{(22 \times 1)} = \begin{bmatrix} .583 \\ .201 \\ \dots \\ .651 \end{bmatrix}$$

Working through the matrix algebra to solve Equation 10.7 (using any basic matrix algebra calculator) yields the following matrix:

$$\mathbf{B}_{(2 \times 1)} = \begin{bmatrix} .4957 \\ -.0112 \end{bmatrix}$$

The value in the first row (.4957) represents the intercept, and the value in the second row (–.0112) represents the regression coefficient of the first predictor, age (additional rows would contain additional regression coefficients if I had included additional predictors).

Variances of these estimates of the regression coefficients are obtained via the diagonal of the $m \times m$ matrix, $\xi = (\mathbf{X}' \mathbf{V}^{-1} \mathbf{X})^{-1}$. In this example,

$$\xi_{(2 \times 2)} = \begin{bmatrix} .00143 & -.00013 \\ -.00013 & .000013 \end{bmatrix}$$

Standard errors of these estimates can be computed as the square roots of these values. In this example, the standard error of the estimate of the intercept is .0378 ($\sqrt{.00143}$), and the standard error of the regression coefficient (i.e., moderation by age) is .0037 ($\sqrt{.000013}$). Note that these values are identical to those reported in Chapter 9.

10.3.2 Estimation of Mixed-Effects Models

Mixed-effects models are estimated iteratively (see simulation by Overton, 1998)—that is, through a series of estimations of $\mathbf{B}$ using $\mathbf{V}$, recomputing the weights in this new solution to yield a new set of values for $\mathbf{V}$, and then using these new values of $\mathbf{V}$ to reestimate $\mathbf{B}$, with the process repeating itself until a certain standard of convergence is reached (see Overton, 1998).

10.3.2.a Iteration 1

The fixed-effects estimation of $\mathbf{B}$ serves as the first iteration. Here, the matrix of weights ($\mathbf{V}$) assumes that $\tau^2 = 0$. From this solution, you compute the model predicted values of the effect size for each study using the following matrix equation (Overton, 1998):

Equation 10.8: Matrix equation for predicted effect sizes given model

$$\hat{Y} = X\,B = X\,(X'\,V^{-1}\,X)^{-1}\,X'\,V^{-1}\,Y$$

- **Y** is a $k \times 1$ vector (where k is the number of studies) of predicted effect sizes for each of k studies.
- **X** is a $k \times m$ matrix (where k is the number of studies and m is the number of predictors + 1) consisting of 1s in the first column (intercept) and values of the moderators in the other cells.
- **B** is a $m \times 1$ vector (where m is the number of predictors + 1) containing the unstandardized regression coefficients of the intercept (first row) and predictors.
- **V** is a $k \times k$ matrix with squared standard errors for the k studies on the diagonal and zeros on the off-diagonal elements.
- **Y** is a $k \times 1$ vector of effect sizes from k studies.

To illustrate using the example meta-analysis of 22 studies:

$$\hat{Y}_{(22 \times 1)} = \begin{bmatrix} .393 \\ .391 \\ ... \\ .395 \end{bmatrix}$$

You then consider the discrepancies between the actual (observed) effect sizes of the studies and these predicted (by the intercept and any moderators) values. Specifically, you compute a matrix, **D**, representing k squared deviations that serve as estimates of the population conditional variance (τ^2):

Equation 10.9: Matrix equation for computing deviation matrix (D)

$$D = (Y - \hat{Y})^2 - (V\,U)$$

- **Y** is a $k \times 1$ vector of observed effect sizes from k studies.
- **$\hat{Y}$** is a $k \times 1$ vector of predicted effect sizes for each of k studies.
- **V** is a $k \times k$ matrix with squared standard errors for the k studies on the diagonal and zeros on the off-diagonal elements.
- **U** is a $k \times 1$ vector constant (all cells = 1).

To illustrate with the example meta-analysis, the **D** from the first iteration (i.e., fixed-effects model) is:

$$\mathbf{D}_{(22 \times 1)} = \begin{bmatrix} .0312 \\ .0328 \\ ... \\ .0604 \end{bmatrix}$$

You then take the weighted average of these k estimates (22 in this example) in **D** to provide a single estimate of the population conditional variance (τ^2) using the following equation:

Equation 10.10: Estimation of τ^2 as weighted average of elements of D

$\tau^2 = \mathbf{U}' \, \mathbf{V}^{-2} \, \mathbf{D} \, (\mathbf{U}' \, \mathbf{V}^{-2} \, \mathbf{U})^{-1}$

- **U** is a $k \times 1$ vector constant (all cells = 1).
- **V** is a $k \times k$ matrix with squared standard errors for the k studies on the diagonal and zeros on the off-diagonal elements.
- **D** is a $k \times 1$ vector containing estimates of τ^2.

Applying this equation to the example data of 22 studies yields an estimated $\tau^2 = .0240$.

10.3.2.b Subsequent Iterations

This estimated τ^2 is now added to the standard errors of each study (sampling fluctuations), such that $v_i^* = \tau^2 + SE_i^2$. For example, the first study in the example dataset would receive the value that $v_1^* = .0240 + (.0693)^2 = .0288$. These k v_i^*s would be entered in the diagonal of the new matrix **V*** for iteration 2. Equation 10.7 is then recomputed using **V*** to yield a new set of estimated regression coefficients. In the example data, these values at the second iteration are $B_0 = .2700$ and $B_1 = .0112$.

These regression coefficients are used to compute new predicted scores using Equation 10.8, new discrepancy scores are estimated, and a new **D** is computed using Equation 10.9 (note that at this step, the original **V** is used because you want to subtract out only the sampling variance). The τ^2 is then reestimated using Equation 10.10 (using $\mathbf{V}^*$). This process continues until the estimated τ^2 changes minimally between successive iterations. Although the convergence criteria have not been well studied, Overton (1998, citing Erez et al., 1996) suggested that $\Delta \tau^2$ less than 10^{-10} is adequate and usually achieved by the seventh iteration. Using the example meta-analysis of 22 studies, I achieved this level of convergence in six iterations.

Overton (1998) has shown that a small correction for τ^2 following the final iteration improves the estimation of mixed-effects models. This correction multiplies the obtained τ^2 by $k/(k - m)$, where k = the number of studies and m = number of predictors (including constant). Applying this correction within the example meta-analysis yields the final estimates of $\tau^2 = .0499$, with regression weights estimated as $B_0 = .2548$ (intercept) and $B_1 = .0128$ (moderating effect of age).

10.4 A STRUCTURAL EQUATION MODELING APPROACH TO RANDOM- AND MIXED-EFFECTS MODELS

In Chapter 9, I introduced an alternative approach to meta-analysis based on Cheung's (2008) description of meta-analysis within the context of structural equation modeling. Here, I extend the logic of this approach to describe how it can be used to estimate random- and mixed-effects models (following closely the presentation by Cheung, 2008). As when I introduced this approach in Chapter 9, I should caution you that this material requires a fairly in-depth understanding of SEM, and you might consider skipping this section if you do not have this background. If you do have a solid background in SEM, however, this perspective may be advantageous in two ways. First, if you are familiar with SEM programs that can estimate random slopes (e.g., Mplus, MX; I elaborate on this requirement below), then you might find it easier to use this approach than the matrix algebra required for the mixed-effects model that I described earlier. Second, as I mentioned in Chapter 9, this approach uses the FIML method of missing data management of SEM, which allows you to retain studies that have missing values of study characteristics that you wish to evaluate as moderators.

Next, I describe how this SEM representation of meta-analysis can be used to estimate random- and mixed-effects models. To illustrate these approaches, I consider the 22 studies reporting correlations between relational aggression with rejection shown in Table 10.1.

10.4.1 Estimating Random-Effects Models

The SEM representation of random-effects meta-analysis (Cheung, 2008) parallels the fixed-effects model I described in Chapter 9 (see Figure 9.2) but models the effect size predicted by intercept path as a random slope (see, e.g., Bauer, 2003; Curran, 2003; Mehta & Neale, 2005; Muthén, 1994). In other words, this path varies across studies, which captures the between-study variance of a random-effects meta-analysis. Importantly, this SEM representation can only estimate these models using software that perform random slope analyses.[3]

One[4] path diagram convention for denoting randomly varying slopes is shown in Figure 10.2. This path diagram contains the same representation of regressing the transformed effect size onto the transformed intercept as

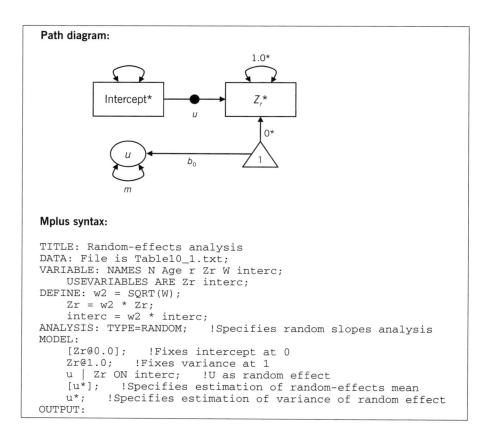

Path diagram:

Mplus syntax:

```
TITLE: Random-effects analysis
DATA: File is Table10_1.txt;
VARIABLE: NAMES N Age r Zr W interc;
    USEVARIABLES ARE Zr interc;
DEFINE: w2 = SQRT(W);
    Zr = w2 * Zr;
    interc = w2 * interc;
ANALYSIS: TYPE=RANDOM;    !Specifies random slopes analysis
MODEL:
    [Zr@0.0];    !Fixes intercept at 0
    Zr@1.0;    !Fixes variance at 1
    u | Zr ON interc;    !U as random effect
    [u*];    !Specifies estimation of random-effects mean
    u*;    !Specifies estimation of variance of random effect
OUTPUT:
```

FIGURE 10.2. Path diagram and Mplus syntax to estimate random-effects model.

does the fixed-effects model of Chapter 9 (see Figure 9.1). However, there is a small circle on this path, which indicates that this path can vary randomly across cases (studies). The label u next to this circle denotes that the newly added piece to the path diagram—the latent construct labeled u—represents the random effect. The regression path (b_0) from the constant (i.e., the triangle with "1" in the middle) to this construct captures the random-effects mean. The variance of this construct (m, using Cheung's 2008 notation) is the estimated between-study variance of the effect size (what I had previously called τ^2).

To illustrate, I fit the data from 22 studies shown in Table 10.1 under an SEM representation of a random-effects model. As I described in Chapter 9, the effect sizes (Z_r) and intercepts (the constant 1) of each study are transformed by multiplying these values by the square root of the study's weight (Equation 9.7). This allows each study to be represented as an equally weighted case in the analysis, as the weighting is accomplished through these transformations.

The Mplus syntax shown in Figure 10.2 specifies that this is a random-slopes analysis by inserting the "TYPE=RANDOM" command, specifying that U represents the random effect with estimated mean and variance. The mean of U is the random-effects mean of this meta-analysis; here, the value was estimated to be 0.369 with a standard error of .049. This indicates that the random-effects mean Z_r is .369 (equivalent $r = .353$) and statistically significant ($Z = .369/.049 = 7.53$, $p < .01$; alternatively, I could compute confidence intervals). The between-study variance (τ^2) is estimated as the variance of U; here, the value is .047.

The random-effects mean and estimated between-study variance obtained using this SEM representation are similar to those I reported earlier (Section 10.2). However, they are not identical (and the differences are not due solely to rounding imprecision). The differences in these values are due to the difference in estimation methods used by these two approaches; the previously described version used least squares criteria, whereas the SEM representation used maximum likelihood (the most common estimation criterion for SEM). To my knowledge, there has been no comprehensive comparison of which estimation method is preferable for meta-analysis (or—more likely— under what conditions one estimator is preferable to the other). Although I encourage you to watch for future research on this topic, it seems reasonable to conclude for now that results should be similar, though not identical, for either approach.

10.4.2 Estimating Mixed-Effects Models

As you might anticipate, this SEM approach (if you have followed the material so far) can be rather easily extended to estimate mixed-effects models, in which fixed-effects moderators are evaluated in the context of random between-study heterogeneity. To evaluate mixed-effects models in an SEM framework, you simply build on the random-effects model (in which the transformed intercept predicting transformed effect size slope randomly varies across studies) by adding transformed study characteristics (moderators) as fixed predictors of the effect size.

I demonstrate this analysis using the 22 studies from Table 10.1, in which I evaluate moderation by sample age while also modeling between-study variance (paralleling analyses in Section 10.3). This model is graphically shown in Figure 10.3, with accompanying Mplus syntax. As a reminder, the effect size and all predictors (e.g., age and intercept) are transformed for each study by multiplying by the square root of the study weight (Equation 9.7). To evaluate the moderator, you evaluate the predictive path between the coded study characteristic (age) and the effect size. In this example, the value was estimated as $b_1 = .013$, with a standard error of .012, so it was not statistically significant ($Z = .013/.012 = 1.06$, $p = .29$). These results are similar to those obtained using the iterative matrix algebra approach I described in Section 10.3, though they will not necessarily be identical given different estimator criteria.

10.4.3 Conclusions Regarding SEM Representations

As with fixed-effects moderator analyses, the major advantage of estimating mixed-effects meta-analytic model in the SEM framework (Cheung, 2008) is the ability to retain studies with missing predictors (i.e., coded study characteristics in the analyses). If you are fluent with SEM, you may even find it easier to estimate models within this framework than using the other approaches.

You should, however, keep in mind several cautions that arise from the novelty of this approach. It is likely that few (if any) readers of your meta-analysis will be familiar with this approach, so the burden falls on you to describe it to the reader. Second, the novelty of this approach also means that some fundamental issues have yet to be evaluated in quantitative research. For instance, the relative advantages of maximum likelihood versus least squares criteria, as well as modifications that may be needed under certain condi-

Path diagram:

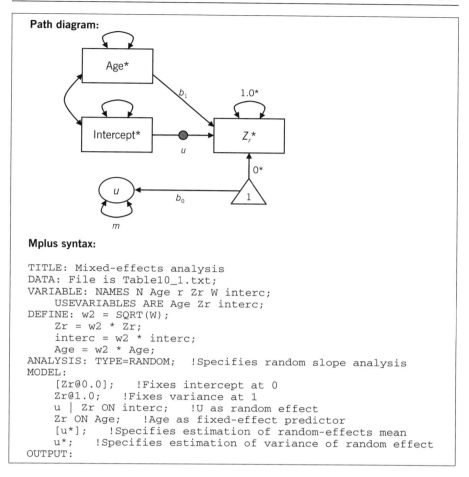

Mplus syntax:

```
TITLE: Mixed-effects analysis
DATA: File is Table10_1.txt;
VARIABLE: NAMES N Age r Zr W interc;
    USEVARIABLES ARE Age Zr interc;
DEFINE: w2 = SQRT(W);
    Zr = w2 * Zr;
    interc = w2 * interc;
    Age = w2 * Age;
ANALYSIS: TYPE=RANDOM;   !Specifies random slope analysis
MODEL:
    [Zr@0.0];    !Fixes intercept at 0
    Zr@1.0;   !Fixes variance at 1
    u | Zr ON interc;   !U as random effect
    Zr ON Age;   !Age as fixed-effect predictor
    [u*];   !Specifies estimation of random-effects mean
    u*;   !Specifies estimation of variance of random effect
OUTPUT:
```

FIGURE 10.3. Path diagram and Mplus syntax to estimate mixed-effects model.

tions (e.g., restricted maximum likelihood or other estimators with small numbers of studies) represent fundamental statistical underpinnings of this approach that have not been fully explored (see Cheung, 2008). Nevertheless, this representation of meta-analysis within SEM has the potential to merge to analytic approaches with long histories, and there are many opportunities to apply the extensive tools from the SEM field in your meta-analyses. For these reasons, I view the SEM representation as a valuable approach to consider, and I encourage you to watch the literature for further advances in this approach.

10.5　PRACTICAL MATTERS: **WHICH MODEL SHOULD I USE?**

In Sections 10.1 and 10.2, I have presented the random-effects model for estimating mean effect sizes, which can be contrasted with the fixed-effects model I described in Chapter 8. I have also described (Section 10.3) mixed-effects models, in which (fixed) moderators are evaluated in the context of conditional random heterogeneity; this section can be contrasted with the fixed-effects moderator analyses of Chapter 9. An important question to ask now is which of these models you should use in a particular meta-analysis. At least five considerations are relevant: the types of conclusions you wish to draw, the presence of unexplained heterogeneity among the effect sizes in your meta-analysis, statistical power, the presence of outliers, and the complexity of performing these analyses. I have arranged these in order from most to least important, and I elaborate on each consideration next. I conclude this section by describing the consequences of using an inappropriate model; these consequences serve as a further set of considerations in selecting a model.

Perhaps the most important consideration in deciding between a fixed- versus random-effects model, or between a fixed-effects model with moderators versus a mixed-effects model, is the types of conclusions you wish to draw. As I described earlier, conclusions from fixed-effects models are limited to only the sample of studies included in your meta-analysis (i.e., "these studies show …" type conclusions), whereas random- and mixed-effects models allow more generalizable conclusions (i.e., "the research shows … " or "there is..." type of conclusions). Given that the last-named type of conclusions are more satisfying (because they are more generalizable), this consideration typically favors the random- or mixed-effects models. Regardless of which type of model you select, however, it is important that you frame your conclusions in a way consistent with your model.

A second consideration is based on the empirical evidence of unexplained heterogeneity. By unexplained heterogeneity, I mean two things. First, in the absence of moderator analysis (i.e., if just estimating the mean effect size), finding a significant heterogeneity (Q) test (see Chapter 8) indicates that the heterogeneity among effect sizes cannot be explained by sampling fluctuation alone. Second, if you are conducting fixed-effects moderator analysis, you should examine the within-group heterogeneity (Q_{within}; for ANOVA analogue tests) or residual heterogeneity ($Q_{residual}$; for regression analog tests). If these are significant, you conclude that there exists heterogeneity among effect sizes *not* systematically explained by the moderators.[5] In both situations, you might use the absence versus presence of unexplained heterogeneity to inform your choice between fixed- versus random- or mixed-effects models (respectively). Many meta-analysts take this approach. However, I urge you to not make this your only consideration because the heterogeneity (i.e., Q) test is an inferential test that can vary in statistical power. In meta-analyses with many studies that have large sample sizes, you might find a significant residual heterogeneity that is trivial, whereas a meta-analysis with few studies having small sample sizes might fail to detect potentially meaningful heterogeneity. For this reason, I recommend against basing your model decision only on empirical findings of unexplained heterogeneity.

A third consideration is the relative statistical power of fixed- versus random-effects models (or fixed-effects with moderators versus mixed-effects models). The statistical power of a meta-analysis depends on many factors—number of studies, sample sizes of studies, degree to which effect sizes must be corrected for artifacts, magnitude of population variance in effect size, and of course true mean population effect size. Therefore, it is not a straightforward computation (see e.g., Cohn & Becker, 2003; Field, 2001; Hedges & Pigott, 2001, 2004). However, to illustrate this difference in power between fixed- and random-effects models, I have graphed some results of a simulation by Field (2001), shown in Figure 10.4. These plots make clear the greater statistical power of fixed-effects versus random-effects models. More generally, fixed-effects analyses will always provide as high (when $\tau^2 = 0$) or higher (when $\tau^2 > 0$) statistical power than random-effects models. This makes sense in light of my earlier observation that the random-effects weights are always smaller than the fixed-effects weights; therefore, the sum of weights is smaller and the standard error of the average effect size is larger for random- than for fixed-effects models. Similarly, analysis of moderators in fixed-effects models will provide as high or higher statistical power as mixed-effects models. For these reasons, it may seem that this consideration would always favor fixed-effects models. However, this conclusion must be tempered by the inappropriate precision associated with high statistical power when a fixed-effects model is used inappropriately in the presence of substantial variance in population effect sizes (see below). Nevertheless, statistical power is one important consideration in deciding among models: If you have questionable statistical power (small number of studies and/or small sample sizes) to detect the effects you are interested in, and you are comfortable with the other considerations, then you might choose a fixed-effects model.

The presence of studies that are outliers in terms of either their effect sizes or their standard errors (e.g., sample sizes) is better managed in ran-

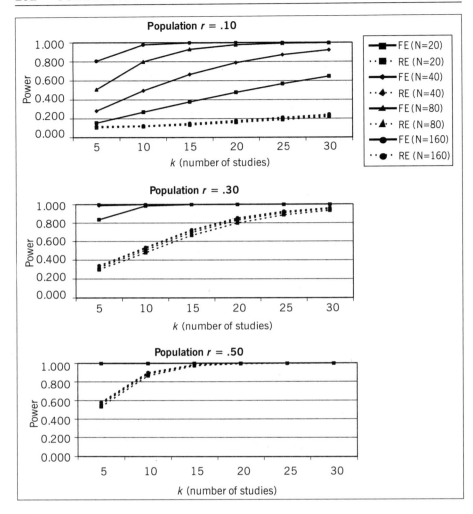

FIGURE 10.4. Examples of different statistical power of fixed- versus random-effects models. Values from simulation by Field (2001) showing power to detect mean effect, by number of studies (k) of various sample sizes (N), at population $r = .10, .30,$ and $.50$ for fixed-effects (solid lines; homogeneous population effect size) and random-effects (dashed lines; heterogeneous population effect size) models.

dom- than fixed-effects models. Outliers consisting of studies that have extreme effect sizes have more influence on the estimated mean effect size in fixed-effects analysis because the analyses—to anthropomorphize—must "move the mean" substantially to fall within the confidence interval of the extreme effect size (see top of Figure 10.1). In contrast, studies with extreme effect sizes impact the population variance (τ^2) more so than the estimated mean effect size in random-effects models. Considering the bottom of Figure 10.1, you can imagine that an extreme effect size can be accommodated by widening the spread of the population effect size distribution (i.e., increasing the estimate of τ) in a random-effects model.

A second type of outlier consists of studies that are extreme in their sample sizes, especially those with much larger sample sizes than other studies. Because sample size is strongly connected to the standard error of the study's effect size, and these standard errors in turn form the weight in fixed-effects models (see Chapter 8), you can imagine that a study with an extremely large sample could be weighted much more heavily than other studies. For example, in the 22 study meta-analyses I have presented (see Table 10.1), four studies with large samples (Hawley et al., 2007; Henington, 1996; Pakaslahti and Keltikangas-Järvinen, 1998; Werner, 2000) comprise 44% of the total weight in the fixed-effects analysis (despite being only 18% of the studies) and are given 13 to 16 times the weight of the smallest study (Ostrov, Woods, Jansen, Casas, & Crick, 2004). Although I justified the use of weights in Chapter 8, this degree of weighting some studies far more than others might be too undemocratic (and I have seen meta-analyses with even more extreme weighting, with single studies having more weight than all other studies combined). As I have mentioned, random-effects models reduce these discrepancies in weighting. Specifically, because a common estimate of τ^2 is added to the squared standard error for each study, the weights become more equal across studies as τ^2 becomes larger. This can be seen by inspecting the random-effects weights (w^*) in Table 10.1: Here the largest study is only weighted 1.4 times the smallest study. In sum, random-effects models, to the extent that τ^2 is large, use weights that are less extreme, and therefore random- (or mixed-) effects models might be favored in the presence of sample size outliers.

Perhaps the least convincing consideration is the complexity of the models (the argument is so unconvincing that I would not even raise it if it was not so commonly put forward). The argument is that fixed-effects models, whether for only computing mean effect sizes (Chapter 8) or for evaluating moderators (Chapter 9) are far simpler than random- and mixed-effects models. Although simplicity is not a compelling rationale for a model (and a rationale that will not go far in the publication process), I acknowledge that you should be realistic in considering how complex of a model you can use and report. I suspect that most readers will be able to perform computations for random-effect models, so if you are not analyzing moderators and the other considerations point you toward this model, I encourage you to use it. Mixed-effects models, in contrast, are more complex and might not be tractable for many readers. Because less-than-optimal answers are better than no answers at all, I do think it is reasonable to analyze moderators within a fixed-effects model if this is all that you feel you can do—with the caveat that you should recognize the limitations of this model. Even better, however, is for you to enlist the assistance of an experienced meta-analyst who can help you with more complex—and more appropriate—models.

At this point, you might see some advantages and disadvantages to each type of model, and you might still feel uncertain about which model to choose. I think this decision can be aided by considering the consequences of choosing the "wrong" model. By "wrong" model, I mean that you choose (1) a random- or mixed-effects model when there is no population variability among effect sizes, or (2) a fixed-effects model when there really exists substantial population variability among effect sizes. In the first situation, using random-effects models in the absence of population variability, there is little negative consequence other than a little extra work. Random- and mixed-effects models will yield similar results as fixed-effects models when there is little population variability in effect sizes (e.g., because estimated τ^2 is close to zero, Equation 10.2 functionally reduces to Equation 10.1). If you decide on a random- (or mixed-) effects model only to find little population variability in effect sizes, you still have the advantage of being able to make generalizable conclusions (see the first consideration above). In contrast, the second type of inappropriate decision (using a fixed-effects model in the presence of unexplained population variability) is problematic. Here, the failure to model this population variability leads to conclusions that are inappropriately precise—in other words, artificially high significance tests and overly narrow confidence intervals.

In conclusion, random-effects models offer more advantages than fixed-effects models, and there are no disadvantages to using random-effects models in the absence of population variability in effect sizes. For this reason, I generally recommend random-effects models when the primary goal is estimated and drawing conclusions about mean effect sizes. When the focus of your meta-analysis is on evaluating moderators, then my recommendations are more ambivalent. Here, mixed-effects models provide optimal results, but the complexity of estimating them might not always be worth the effort unless you are able to enlist help from an experienced meta-analyst. For moderator analyses, I do view fixed-effects models as acceptable, provided you examine unexplained (residual) heterogeneity and are able to show that it is either not significant or small in magnitude.[6]

10.6 SUMMARY

Random-effects models conceptualize the population of effect sizes as falling along a distribution with both a mean and variance, above and beyond variance due to sampling fluctuations of individual studies. These random effects can be contrasted with the fixed-effects models described in Chapter 8, which conceptualize a single population effect size with any variability among effect sizes in studies due to sampling fluctuations. In this chapter, I have highlighted the differences between these models, and I have described how to estimate random-effects models for meta-analysis. I then described mixed-effects models, which are the random-effects extensions of the (fixed-effects) moderator analyses of Chapter 9. I also showed how both random- and mixed-effects models can be represented as structural equation models with random slopes. To assist in selecting between fixed- versus random- or mixed-effects models, I have encouraged you to consider several factors.

10.7 RECOMMENDED READINGS

Cheung, M. W.-L. (2008). A model for integrating fixed-, random-, and mixed-effects meta-analyses in structural equation modeling. *Psychological Methods, 13*, 182–202.—This article presents the approach to modeling meta-analysis within an SEM framework that I describe in this chapter.

Hedges, L. V., & Vevea, J. L. (1998). Fixed- and random-effects models in meta-analysis. *Psychological Methods, 3*, 486–504.—This article is one of the seminal early articles describing fixed- versus random-effects models. Although somewhat challenging, the paper is worth reading given that it provides the foundation for much subsequent work on this topic.

Overton, R. C. (1998). A comparison of fixed-effects and mixed (random-effects) models for meta-analysis tests of moderator variable effects. *Psychological Methods, 3*, 354–379.—This is a challenging article to read; however, it is one of the best sources of information for conducting mixed-effects analyses.

Raudenbush, S. W. (1994). Random effects models. In H. Cooper & L. V. Hedges (Eds.), *The handbook of research synthesis* (pp. 301–321). New York: Russell Sage Foundation.—

This chapter is the most comprehensive summary of the topic, including a nice mixture of accessible and challenging information.

NOTES

1. This does not mean that you extend conclusions beyond the general types of studies in your meta-analysis, but that you expand beyond the specific studies. For instance, I might perform a meta-analysis of three studies using samples that are 10, 12, and 14 years old. Under a fixed-effects model, I can only make conclusions about studies of 10-, 12-, and 14-year-olds; I should not make conclusions about results involving 11- or 13-year-olds. Under a random-effects model, I can make conclusions about the more generalized period of early adolescence from 10–14 years (including 11- and 13-year-olds). Neither model would allow me to safely extrapolate conclusions beyond these limits; so neither would inform my understanding of 4-year-old children or 40-year-old adults.

2. The note to Equation 10.4 fixes the variance at 0 for those occasions when Q is lower than this expected value, thus avoiding estimates of negative population variance.

3. At the time of this writing, I am aware of only two programs that can do this: Mplus and MX.

4. For alternate ways of representing random slopes in path diagrams, see Curran and Bauer (2007); Mehta and Neale (2005).

5. Some meta-analysts make it their explicit goal to continue to examine moderators until the residual heterogeneity is not significant. Although I see value in this approach—in attempting to systematically explore differences in the findings of studies until you can systematically explain all differences beyond sampling fluctuation—I do not think this must be the goal of every meta-analysis. If you have evaluated all moderators that you are interested in, and residual heterogeneity still exists, I see nothing wrong with simply acknowledging that there still remain differences among studies that you have not explained.

6. A reasonable—though untested—suggestion might be that the residual heterogeneity produces an I^2 of 25% or less (see Chapter 8).

11

Publication Bias

In Chapter 2, I described publication bias as a threat to both narrative and meta-analytic reviews. In Chapter 3, I emphasized the importance of thorough and systematic searching of the literature as one way of reducing the likely impact of this bias. Although search procedures are the most effective remedy to this file drawer problem, it is also possible to evaluate the presence of publication bias after studies have been collected and coded.

In this chapter, I first revisit the problem of publication bias in more depth than I did earlier in the book. I then review a range of analytic and graphical techniques that have been developed within the field of meta-analysis to detect the presence of publication. Finally, in the "practical matters" section, I provide what I view as a pragmatic perspective on the ever-present threat of publication bias.

11.1 THE PROBLEM OF PUBLICATION BIAS

Publication bias refers to the possibility that studies finding null (absence of statistically significant effect) or negative (statistically significant effect in opposite direction expected) results are less likely to be published than studies finding positive effects (statistically significant effects in expected direction).[1] This bias is likely due both to researchers being less motivated to submit null or negative results for publication and to journals (editors and reviewers) being less likely to accept manuscripts reporting these results (Cooper, DeNeve, & Charlton, 1997; Coursol & Wagner, 1986; Greenwald, 1975; Olson et al., 2002).

The impact of this publication bias is that the published literature might not be representative of the studies that have been conducted on a topic, in that the available results likely show a stronger overall effect size than if all studies were considered. This impact is illustrated in Figure 11.1, which is a reproduction of Figure 3.2. The top portion of this figure shows a distribution of effect sizes from a hypothetical population of studies. The effect sizes from these studies center around a hypothetical mean effect size (about 0.20), but have a certain distribution of effect sizes found due to random-sampling error and, potentially, population-level between-study variance (i.e., heterogeneity; see Chapters 8 and 9). Among those studies that happen to find small effect sizes, results are less likely to be statistically significant (in this hypothetical figure, I have denoted this area where studies find effect sizes less than ±0.10, with the exact range depending on the study sample sizes and effect size considered). Below this population of effect sizes of all studies conducted, I have drawn downward arrows of different thicknesses to

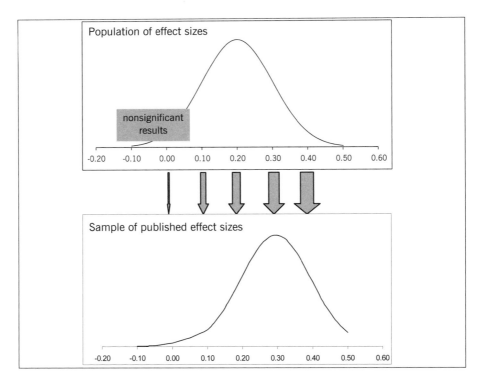

FIGURE 11.1. Illustration of publication bias in a hypothetical sample drawn from a population of studies.

represent the different likelihoods of the study being published, with thicker arrows denoting higher likelihood of publication. Consistent with the notion of publication bias, the hypothetical studies that fail to find significant effects are less likely to be published than those that do. This differential publication rate results in the distribution of published studies shown in the lower part of Figure 11.1. It can be seen that this distribution is shifted to the right, such that the mean effect size is now approximately 0.30. If the meta-analysis only includes this biased sample of published studies, then the estimate of the mean effect size is going to be considerably higher (around 0.30) than that in the true population of studies conducted. Clearly, this has serious implications for a meta-analysis that does not consider publication bias.

This publication bias is sometimes referred to by alternative names. Some have referred to it as the "file-drawer problem" (Rosenthal, 1979), conjuring images of researchers' file drawers containing manuscripts reporting null or negative (i.e., in the opposite direction expected) results that will never be seen by the meta-analyst (or anyone else in the research community). Another term proposed is "dissemination bias" (see Rothstein, Sutton, & Borenstein, 2005a). This latter term is more accurate in describing the broad scope of this problem, although the term "publication bias" is the more commonly used one (Rothstein et al., 2005a). Regardless of terminology used, the breadth of this bias is not limited just to significant results being published and non-significant results not being published (even in a probabilistic rather than absolute sense). One source of breadth of the bias is the existence of "gray literature," research that is between the file drawer and publication, such as in the format of conference presentations, technical reports, or obscure publication outlets (Conn, Valentine, Cooper, & Rantz, 2003; Hopewell, Clarke, & Mallett, 2005; also referred to as "fugitive literature" by, e.g., M. C. Rosenthal, 1994). There is evidence that null findings are more likely to be reported only in these more obscure outlets than are positive findings (see Dickersin, 2005; Hopewell et al., 2005) If the literature search is less exhaustive, these reports are less likely to be found and included in the meta-analysis than reports published in more prominent outlets.

Another source of breadth in publication bias may be in the underemphasis of null or negative results. For example, researchers are likely to make significant findings the centerpiece of an empirical report and only report nonsignificant findings in a table. Such publications, though containing the effect size of interest, might not be detected in key word searches or in browsing the titles of published works. Similarly, null or counterintuitive findings that are published may be less likely to be cited by others; thus, backward searches are less likely to find these studies.

Finally, an additional source of breadth in considering publication bias is due to the time lag of publication. There is evidence, at least in some fields, that significant results are published more quickly than null or negative results (see Dickersin, 2005). The impact on meta-analyses, especially those focusing on topics with a more recently created empirical basis, is that the currently published results are going to overrepresent significant positive findings, whereas null or negative results are more likely to be published after the meta-analysis is performed.

Recognizing the impact and breadth of publication bias is important but does not provide guidance in managing it. Ideally, the scientific process would change so that researchers are obligated to report the results of study findings.[2] In clinical research, the establishment of clinical trial registries (in which researchers must register a trial before beginning the study, with some journals motivating registration by only considering registered trials for publication) represents a step in helping to identify studies, although there are some concerns that registries are incomplete and that the researchers of registered trials may be unwilling to share unexpected results (Berlin & Ghersi, 2005). However, unless you are in the position to mandate research and reporting practices within your field, you must deal with publication bias without being able to prevent it or even fully know of its existence. Nevertheless, you do have several methods of evaluating the likely impact publication bias has on your meta-analytic results.

11.2 MANAGING PUBLICATION BIAS

In this section, I describe six approaches to managing publication bias within meta-analysis. I also illustrate some of these approaches through the example meta-analysis I have used throughout this book: a review of 22 studies reporting associations between relational aggression and peer rejection among children and adolescents. In Chapter 8, I presented results of a fixed-effects[3] analysis of these studies indicating a mean $r = .368$ ($SE = .0118$; $Z = 32.70$, $p < .001$; 95% confidence interval $= .348$ to $.388$). When using this example in this section, I evaluate the extent to which this conclusion about the mean association is threatened by potential publication bias.

Table 11.1 displays these 22 studies. The first five columns of this table are the citation, sample size, untransformed effect size (r), transformed effect size (Z_r), and standard error of the transformed effect size (SE). The remaining columns contain information that I explain when using these data to illustrate methods of evaluating publication bias.

TABLE 11.1. Example Meta-Analysis Used to Illustrate Analyses for Publication Bias

Study	Sample size (N)	Effect size (r)	Transformed ES (Z_r)	Standard error (SE)	Published (1 = yes)	v^*	ES*	z	1/SE
Blachman (2003)	228	.525	.583	.525	0	.005	2.87	7.57	14.43
Crick & Grotpeter (1995)	491	.198	.201	.198	1	.003	-3.28	3.42	17.26
Crick et al. (1997)	65	.311	.322	.311	1	.017	-0.49	2.35	7.55
Geiger (2003)	458	.554	.624	.554	0	.002	5.06	11.45	20.67
Hawley et al. (2007)	929	.161	.162	.161	1	.001	-6.90	4.65	28.91
Henington (1996)	904	.336	.349	.336	1	.001	-1.14	9.69	28.84
Johnson (2003)	74	.396	.419	.396	0	.015	0.27	3.24	8.18
Leff (1995)	151	.617	.721	.617	0	.007	3.94	7.22	11.69
Miller (2001)	150	.557	.628	.557	0	.007	2.89	6.59	11.83
Murray–Close & Crick (2006)	590	.575	.655	.575	1	.002	6.57	13.50	23.47
Nelson et al. (2005)	180	.039	.039	.039	1	.007	-4.22	0.47	12.03
Ostrov (under review)[a]	139	.358	.375	.358	0	.008	-0.13	4.02	11.21
Ostrov & Crick (2007)	132	.049	.049	.049	1	.008	-3.69	0.54	10.85
Ostrov et al. (2004)[b]	60	.000	.000	.000	1	.019	-2.80	0.00	7.21
Pakaslahti & Keltikangas-Järvinen (1998)	839	.326	.339	.326	1	.001	-1.32	8.57	26.26
Phillipsen et al. (1999)	262	-.048	-.048	-.048	1	.004	-6.89	-0.75	15.59
Rys & Bear (1997)	266	.454	.489	.454	1	.004	1.65	7.13	15.71
Salmivalli et al. (2000)	209	.253	.258	.253	1	.005	-1.82	3.54	13.98
Tomada & Schneider (1997)	314	.160	.162	.160	1	.003	-3.90	2.73	16.99
Werner (2000)	881	.477	.519	.477	0	.001	3.99	13.57	28.47
Werner & Crick (2004)	517	.469	.509	.469	1	.002	2.78	10.30	21.96
Zalecki & Hinshaw (2004)	228	.572	.651	.572	1	.005	3.82	8.15	14.24

[a]Article was under review during the preparation of this meta-analytic review. It has subsequently been published as Ostrov (2008).
[b]Effect size is lower-bound estimate based on authors' report of only nonsignificant associations.

11.2.1   Moderator Analyses

One of the best methods to evaluate the potential impact of publication bias is to include unpublished studies in the meta-analysis and empirically evaluate whether these studies yield smaller effect sizes than published studies. In the simplest case, this involves evaluating the moderation of effect sizes (Chapter 10) by the dichotomous variable, published versus unpublished study. Two caveats to this approach merit consideration. First, it is necessary to make sure that the meta-analysis includes a sufficient number of unpublished studies to draw reliable conclusions about potential differences. Second, it is important to consider other features on which published versus unpublished studies might differ, such as the quality of the methodology (e.g., internal validity of an experimental design) and measures (e.g., use of reliable vs. unreliable scales). You should control for such differences when comparing published and unpublished studies.

A more elaborate variant of this sort of moderator analysis is to code more detailed variables regarding publication status. For instance, you might code a more continuous publication quality variable (e.g., distinguishing unpublished data, dissertations, conference presentations, low-tier journal articles, and top-tier journal articles, if this captures a meaningful continuum within your field). You might also code whether the effect size of interest is a central versus peripheral result in the study; for instance, Card et al. (2008) considered whether terms such as "gender" or "sex" appeared in titles of works reporting gender differences in childhood aggression.

Regardless of which variables you code, the key question is whether these variables are related to the effect sizes found in the studies (i.e., whether these act as moderators). If you find no differences between published and unpublished studies (or absence of moderating effects of other variables such as publication quality and centrality), and there is adequate power to detect such moderation, then it is safe to conclude that there is no evidence of publication bias within this area. If differences do exist, you have the choice of either (1) interpreting results of published and unpublished studies separately, or (2) performing corrections for publication bias described below (Section 11.3).

To illustrate this approach to evaluating publication bias, I consider one approach I have described: moderation by the categorical moderator "published." This categorical variable is shown in the sixth column of Table 11.1 and is coded as 1 for studies that were published ($k = 15$) and 0 for unpublished studies ($k = 7$). Notice that this comparison is possible only because I included unpublished studies in this meta-analysis and the search was thorough enough to obtain a sufficient number of unpublished studies for comparison. Moderator analyses (Chapter 9) indicated a significant difference between published and unpublished studies ($Q_{between(1df)}$ = 77.47, p < .001). In the absence of publication bias, I would *not* expect this moderator effect, so its presence is worrisome. When I inspect the mean effects sizes within each group, I find that the unpublished studies yield higher associations ($\bar{r}$ = .51) than the published studies ($\bar{r}$ = .31). This runs counter to the possibility that nonsignificant/low effect size studies are less likely to be published; if there is a bias, it appears that studies finding *large* effect sizes are less likely to be published and therefore any publication bias might serve to *diminish* the effect size I find in this meta-analysis. However, based on my knowledge of the field (and conversations with other experts about this finding), I see no apparent reason why there would be a bias against publishing studies finding strong positive correlations. I consider this finding further in light of my other findings regarding potential publication bias below.

11.2.2   Funnel Plots

Funnel plots represent a graphical way to evaluate publication bias (Light & Pillemer, 1984; see Sterne, Becker, & Egger, 2005). The funnel plots are simply a scatterplot of the effect sizes found in studies relative to their sample size (with some variants on this general pattern). In other words, you would simply plot points for each study denoting their effect size relative to their sample size. Figure 11.2 shows a hypothetical outline of a funnel plot, with the effect size Z_r on the y-axis and sample size (N) on the x-axis.[4] Specifically, the solid lines within this figure represent the 95% confidence interval of effect sizes centered around r = .30 (Z_r = .31; see below) at various sample sizes[5]; if you plot study effect sizes and sample sizes from a sample with this mean effect size, then most (95%) of the points should fall within the area between these solid lines. On the left, you can see that there is considerably larger expectable variability in effect sizes with small sample sizes; conceptually, you expect that studies with small samples will yield a wider range of effect sizes due to random-sampling variability. In contrast, as sample sizes increase, the expectable variability in effect sizes becomes smaller (i.e., the standard errors become smaller), and so the funnel plot shows a narrower distribution of effect sizes at the right of Figure 11.2. Evaluation of publication bias using funnel plots involves visually inspecting these plots to ensure symmetry and this general triangular shape.

Let's now consider how publication bias would affect the shape of this funnel plot. Note the dashed line passing through the funnel plot. This line represents the magnitude of effect size needed to achieve statistical signifi-

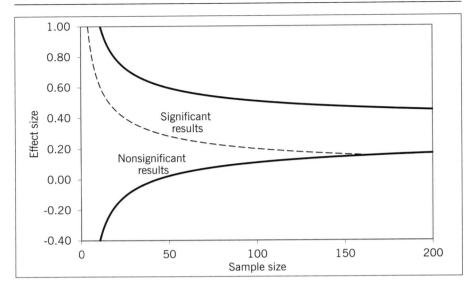

FIGURE 11.2. Hypothetical funnel plot.

cance ($p < .05$) at various sample sizes. The area above and to the right of this dashed line would denote studies finding significant effects, whereas the area below and to the left of it would contain studies that do not yield significant effects. If publication bias exists, then you would see few points (i.e., few studies in your meta-analysis) that fall within this nonsignificant region. This would cause your funnel plot to look asymmetric, with small sample studies finding large effects present but small studies finding small effects absent.

Publication bias is not the only possible cause of asymmetric funnel plots. If studies with smaller samples are expected to yield stronger effect sizes (e.g., studies of intervention effectiveness might be able to devote more resources to a smaller number of participants), then this asymmetry may not be due to publication bias. In these situations, you would ideally code the presumed difference between small and large sample studies (e.g., amount of time or resources devoted to participants) and control for this[6] before creating the funnel plot.

Several variants of the axes used for funnel plots exist. You might consider alternative choices of scale on the effect size axis. I recommend relying on effect sizes that are roughly normally distributed around a population effect size, such as Fisher's transformation of the correlation (Z_r), Hedges's g, or the natural log of the odds ratio (see Chapter 5). Using normally distributed effect sizes, as opposed to non-normal effect sizes (e.g., *r* or *o*) allows for better examination of the symmetry of funnel plots. Similarly, you have choices of how to scale the sample size axis. Here, you might consider using the natural log of sample size, which aids interpretation if some studies use extremely large samples that compress the rest of the studies into a narrow range of the funnel plot. Other choices include choosing standard errors, their inverse (precision), or weights ($1 / SE^2$) on this axis; this option is recommended when you are analyzing log odds ratios (Sterne et al., 2005) and might also be useful when the standard error is not perfectly related to sample size (e.g., when you correct for artifacts). I see no problem with examining multiple funnel plots when evaluating publication bias. Given that the examination of funnel plots is somewhat subjective, I believe that examining these plots from several perspectives (i.e., several different choices of axis scaling) is valuable in obtaining a complete picture about the possibility of publication bias.

To illustrate the use of funnel plots—as well as the major challenges in their use—I have plotted the 22 studies from Table 11.1 in Figure 11.3.

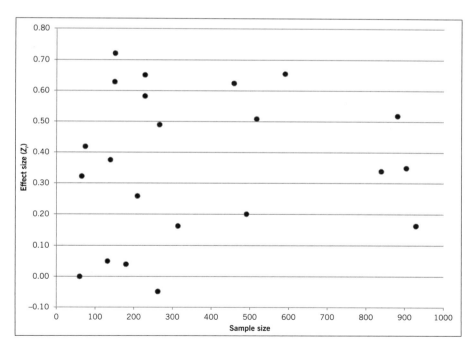

FIGURE 11.3. Funnel plot of 22 studies in example meta-analysis.

I created this plot simply by constructing a scatterplot with transformed effect size (fourth column in Table 11.1) on the vertical axis and sample size (second column in Table 11.1) on the horizontal axis. My inspection of this plot leads me to conclude that there is no noticeable asymmetry or sparse representation of studies in the low effect size—low sample size area (i.e., where results would be nonsignificant). I also perceive that the effect sizes tend to become less discrepant with larger sample sizes—that is, that the plot becomes more vertically narrow from the left to the right. However, you might not agree with these conclusions. This raises the challenge of using funnel plots—that the interpretations you take from these plots are necessarily subjective. This subjectivity is especially prominent when the number of studies in your meta-analysis is small; in my example with just 22 studies, it is extremely difficult to draw indisputable conclusions.

11.2.3 Regression Analysis

Extending the logic of funnel plots, you can more formally test for asymmetry by regressing effect sizes onto sample sizes. The presence of an association between effect sizes and sample sizes is similar to an asymmetric funnel plot in suggesting publication bias. In the case of a positive mean effect size, publication bias will be evident when studies with small sample sizes yield larger effect size estimates than studies with larger samples; this situation would produce a negative association between sample size and effect size. In contrast, when the mean effect size is negative, then publication bias will be indicated by a positive association (because studies with small samples yield stronger negative effect size estimates than studies with larger samples). The absence of an association, given adequate statistical power to detect one, parallels the symmetry of the funnel plot in suggesting an absence of publication bias.

Despite the conceptual simplicity of this approach, recommended practices (see Sterne & Egger, 2005) build on this conceptual approach but make it somewhat more complex. Specifically, two variants of this regression approach are commonly employed. The first involves considering an adjusted rank correlation between studies' effect sizes and standard errors (for details, see Begg, 1994; Sterne & Egger, 2005). To perform this analysis, you use the following two equations to compute, for each study i, the variance of the study's effect size from the mean effect size (v_i^*) and the standardized effect size for study (ES_i^*):

Equations 11.1 and 11.2: Equations used in adjusted rank correlation approach

11.1: adjusted variance of estimate: $v_i^* = SE_i^2 - \dfrac{1}{\sum \dfrac{1}{SE^2}}$

11.2: adjusted effect size: $ES_i^* = \dfrac{ES_i - M_{ES}}{\sqrt{v_i^*}}$

- M_{ES} is the mean effect size.
- SE_i is the standard error for study i.
- $\sum \dfrac{1}{SE^2}$ is the summation of inverse variances across all studies (or the sum of weights calculated in previous meta-analytic equations; see Chapter 8).

After computing these variables, you then estimate Kendall's rank correlation between v_i^* and ES_i^*. A significant correlation indicates funnel plot asymmetry, which may suggest publication bias. An absence of correlation contraindicates publication bias, if power is adequate.

A comparable approach is Egger's linear regression, in which you regress the standard normal deviate of the effect size of each study from zero (i.e., for study i, $z_i = ES_i / SE_i$) onto the precision (the inverse of the SE, or $1/ SE_i$): $z_i = B_0 + B_1 \text{precision}_i + e_i$. Somewhat counterintuitively, the slope (B_1) represents the average effect size (because both the DV and predictor have SE in their denominator, this is similar to regressing the ES onto a constant, which yields the mean ES). The intercept (B_0, which is similar to regressing the ES onto the SE) is expected to be zero, and a nonzero intercept (the significance of which can be evaluated using common statistical software) indicates asymmetry in the funnel plot, or the possibility of publication bias.

These regression approaches to evaluating funnel plot asymmetry (which can be indicative of publication bias) are advantageous over visual inspection of funnel plots in that they reduce subjectivity by providing results that can be evaluated in terms of statistical significance. However, these regression approaches depend on the *absence* of statistically significant results to conclude an absence of publication bias (which is typically what you hope to demonstrate). Therefore, their utility depends on adequate statistical power to detect asymmetry. Although the number of simulation studies are limited (for a review, see Sterne & Egger, 2005), preliminary guidelines for the number of studies needed to ensure adequate power can be provided. When publication bias is severe (and targeting 80% power), at least 17 studies are needed with Egger's linear regression approach, and you should have at least 40 studies for the rank correlation method (note that this is an extrapolation from previous simulations and should be interpreted with caution). When publication bias is moderate, you should have at least 50 to 60 studies for Egger's linear regressions and at least 150 studies for the rank correlation approaches. However, I emphasize again that these numbers are extrapolated well beyond previous studies and should be viewed with extreme caution until further studies investigate the statistical power of these approaches.

Considering again the 22 studies of my example meta-analysis, I evaluated the association between effect size and sample size using both the adjusted rank correlation approach and Egger's linear regression approach. Columns seven and eight in Table 11.1 show the two transformed variables for the former approach, and computation of Kendall's rank correlation yielded a nonsignificant value of $-.07$ ($p = .67$). Similarly, Egger's regression of the values in the ninth column onto those in the tenth was nonsignificant ($p = .62$). I would interpret both results as failing to indicate evidence of publication bias. However, I should be aware that my use of just 22 studies means that I only have adequate power to detect severe publication bias using Egger's linear regression approach, and I do not have adequate power with the rank correlation method.

11.2.4   Failsafe *N*

11.2.4.a   Definition and Computation

Failsafe numbers (failsafe *N*) help us evaluate the robustness of a meta-analytic finding to the existence of excluded studies. Specifically, the failsafe number is the number of excluded studies, all averaging an effect size of zero, that would have to exist for their inclusion in the meta-analysis to lower the average effect size to a nonsignificant level.[7] This number, introduced by Rosenthal (1979) as an approach to dealing with the "file drawer problem," also can be thought of as the number of excluded studies (all with average effect sizes equal to zero) that would have to be filed away before you would conclude that no effect actually exists (if the meta-analyst had been able to analyze results from all studies conducted). If this number is large enough, you conclude that it is unlikely that you could have missed so many studies (that researchers' file drawers are unlikely to be filled with so many null results), and therefore that this conclusion of the meta-analysis is robust to this threat.

The computation of a failsafe number begins with the logic of an older method of combining research results, known as Stouffer's or the sum-of-Zs method (for an overview of these earlier methods of combining results, see Rosenthal, 1978). This method involves computing the significance level of the effect from each study (the one-tailed p value), converting this to a standard normal deviate (Z_i, with positive values denoting effects in expected direction), and then combining these Zs across the k studies to obtain an overall combined significance (given by standardized normal deviate, Z_c):

Equation 11.3: Stouffer's method of combining levels of significance

$$Z_c = \frac{\sum Z_i}{\sqrt{k}}$$

- Z_i is the standard normal deviate of significance from study i.
- Z_c is the combined standard normal deviate of significance across studies.
- k is the number of studies.

Failsafe N extends this approach by asking the question, How many studies could be added to those in the meta-analysis (going from k to $k + N$ in the denominator term of Equation 11.4), all with zero effect sizes (Zs = 0, so the numerator term does not change), before the significance level drops to some threshold value (e.g., $Z_c = Z_\alpha = 1.645$ for one-tailed $p = .05$)? The equation can be rearranged to yield the computation formula for failsafe N:

Equation 11.4: Computing failsafe N

$$N = k\left(\frac{Z_c}{Z_\alpha}\right)^2 - k$$

- k is the number of studies.
- Z_c is the combined standard normal deviate of significance across studies.
- Z_α is the threshold value of significance (e.g., 1.645 for one-tailed $p = .05$).

Examination of these equations makes clear the two factors that impact the failsafe N. The first is the level of statistical significance (Z_c) yielded from the included results (which is a function of effect size and sample size of the study); the larger this value, the larger the failsafe N. The second factor is the number of included studies, k. Increasing numbers of included studies results in increasing failsafe Ns (because the first occurrence of k in Equation 11.5 is multiplied by a ratio greater than 1 [when results are significant], this offsets the subtraction by k). This makes intuitive sense: Meta-analyses finding a low p value (e.g., far below .05) from results from a large number of studies need more excluded, null results to threaten the findings, whereas meta-analyses with results closer to what can be consider a "critical" p value (e.g., just below .05) from a small number of studies could be threatened by a small number of excluded studies.

How large should failsafe N be before you conclude that results are robust to the file drawer problem? Despite the widespread use of this approach over about 30 years, no one has provided a statistically well-founded answer. Rosenthal's (1979) initial suggestion was for a tolerance level (i.e., adequately high failsafe N) equal to $5k + 10$, and this initial suggestion seems to have been the standard most commonly applied since. Rosenthal (1979) noted what is a plausible number of studies filed away likely depends on the area of research, but no one has further investigated this speculation. At the moment, the $5k + 10$ is a reasonable standard, though I hope that future work will improve on (or at least provide more justification for) this value.

11.2.4.b   Criticisms

Despite their widespread use, failsafe numbers have been criticized in several ways (see Becker, 2005). Although these criticisms are valuable in pointing out the limits of using failsafe N exclusively, I do not believe that they imply that you should not use this approach. Next, I briefly outline the major criticisms against failsafe N and suggest considerations that temper these critiques.

One criticism is of the premise of computing the number of studies with *null* results. The critics argue that other possibilities could be considered, such as studies in the opposite direction as those found in the meta-analysis. It is true that any alternative effect size could be chosen; but it seems that selection of null results (i.e., those with effect sizes close to 0), which are the studies expected to be suppressed under most conceptualizations of publication bias, represents the most appropriate single value to consider.

A second criticism of the failsafe number is that it does not consider the sample sizes of the excluded studies. Sample sizes of included studies are indirectly considered in that larger samples sizes yield larger Z_is than smaller studies, given the same effect size. In contrast, excluded studies are assumed to have effect sizes of zero and therefore Zs equal to zero regardless of sample size. So, the failsafe number would not differentiate between excluded studies with sample sizes equal to 10 versus 10,000. I believe this is a fair critique of failsafe N, though the impact depends on excluded studies with zero effect sizes (on average) having larger sample sizes than included studies. This seems unlikely given the previous consideration of publication bias and funnel plots. If there is a bias, I would expect that excluded studies are primarily those with small (e.g., near zero) effect sizes and *small* sample sizes (however, I acknowledge that I am unaware of empirical support for this expectation).

A third criticism involves the failure of failsafe N to model heterogeneity among obtained results. In other words, the Stouffer method of obtaining the overall significance (Z_c) among included studies, which is then used in the computation of failsafe N, makes no allowance for whether these studies are homogeneous (centered around a mean effect size with no more deviation than expected by sampling error) or heterogeneous (deviation around mean effect size is greater than expected by sampling error alone; see Chapter 10). This is a valid criticism that should be kept in mind when interpreting failsafe N. I especially recommend against using failsafe N when heterogeneity necessitates the use of random-effects models (Chapter 9).

A final criticism of Rosenthal's (1979) failsafe N is the focus on statistical significance. As I have discussed throughout this book, one advantage of meta-analysis is a focus on effect sizes; a number that indicates the number of excluded studies that would reduce your results to nonsignificance does not tell you how these might affect your results in terms of effect size. For this, an alternative failsafe number can be considered, which I describe next.

11.2.4.c   An Effect Size Failsafe N

An alternative approach that focuses on effect sizes was proposed by Orwin (1983; see also Becker, 2005). Using this approach, you select an effect size[8] (smaller than that obtained in the meta-analysis of sampled studies) that represents the smallest meaningful effect size (either from guidelines such as r = ±.10 for a small effect size, or preferably an effect size that is meaningful in the context of the research). This value is denoted as ES_{min}.[9] You then compute a failsafe number (N_{ES}) from the meta-analytically combined average effect size (ES_M) from the k included studies using:

Equation 11.5: Effect size failsafe N

$$N_{ES} = \frac{k(M_{ES} - ES_{min})}{ES_{min} - ES_{excluded}}$$

- k is the number of studies.
- M_{ES} is the average effect size from the meta-analysis.
- ES_{min} is the smallest meaningful effect size.
- $ES_{excluded}$ is the average effect size of excluded studies.

The denominator of this equation introduces an additional term that I have not yet described, $ES_{excluded}$. This represents the expected (i.e., specified by the meta-analyst) average effect size of excluded studies. A reasonable choice, paralleling the assumption of Rosenthal's (1979) approach, might be zero. In this case, the failsafe number (N_{ES}) would tell us how many excluded studies with an average effect size of zero would have to exist before the true effect size would be reduced to the smallest meaningful effect size (ES_{min}). Although this is likely a good choice for many situations, the flexibility to specify alternative effect sizes of excluded studies addresses the first criticism of traditional approaches described above.

Although this approach to failsafe N based on minimum effect size alleviates two critiques of Rosenthal's original approach, it is still subject to the other two criticisms. First, this approach still assumes that the excluded studies have the same average sample size as included studies. I believe that this results in a conservative bias in most situations; if the excluded studies tend to have smaller samples than the included studies, then the failsafe N is smaller than necessary. Second, this approach also does not model heterogeneity, and therefore is not informative when you find significant heterogeneity and rely on random-effects models. A third limitation, unique to this approach, is that there do not exist solid guidelines for determining how large the failsafe number should be before you conclude that results are robust to the file drawer problem. I suspect that this number is smaller than Rosenthal's (1979) $5k + 10$ rule, but more precise numbers have not been developed.

To illustrate computation of these failsafe numbers, I again consider the example meta-analysis of Table 11.1. Summing the Zs (not the Z_rs) across the 22 studies yields 127.93, from which I compute Z_c = 127.93 / $\sqrt{22}$ = 27.27. To compute Rosenthal's (1979) failsafe number of studies with effect sizes of zero needed to reduce the relational aggression with rejection association to nonsignificance, I apply Equation 11.4:

$$N = k\left(\frac{Z_c}{Z_\alpha}\right)^2 - k = 22\left(\frac{27.27}{1.645}\right)^2 - 22 = 6026$$

This means that there could exist up to 6,026 studies, with an average correlation of 0, before my conclusion of a significant association is threatened. This is greater than the value recommended by Rosenthal (1979) (i.e., $5k + 10$ = 5*22 + 10 = 120), so I would conclude that my conclusion of an association between relational aggression and rejection is robust to the file drawer problem. However, it is more satisfying to discuss the robustness of the *magnitude*, rather than just the significance of this association, so I also use Orwin's (1983) approach of Equation 11.5. Under the assumption that excluded studies have effect sizes of 0 (i.e., in Equation 11.5, $ES_{excluded}$ = 0), I find that 5 excluded studies could reduce the average correlation to .30, 19 could reduce it to .20, and 59 would be needed to reduce it to .10. Although there are no established guidelines for Orwin's failsafe numbers, it seems reasonable to conclude that it is plausible that the effect size could be less than a medium correlation (i.e., less than the standard of r = ±.30) but perhaps implausible that the effect size could be less than a small correlation (i.e., less than the standard of r = ±.10).

11.2.5   Trim and Fill

The trim and fill method is a method of correcting for publication bias (see Duval, 2005) that involves a two-step iterative procedure. The conceptual rationale for this method is illustrated by considering the implications of publication bias on funnel plots (recall that the corner of the funnel denoting studies with small sample sizes and small effect sizes is underrepresented), which causes bias in estimating both the mean effect size and the heterogeneity around this effect size. The trim and fill approach uses a two-step correction that attempts to provide more accurate estimates of both mean and spread in effect sizes.

The first step of this approach is to temporarily "trim" studies contributing to funnel plot asymmetry. Considering Figure 11.2 (in which the funnel plot is expected to be asymmetric in having more studies in the upper left section than the lower left section when there is publication bias), this trimming involves temporarily removing studies until you obtain a symmetric funnel plot (often shaped like a bar in the vertical middle of this plot). You then estimate an unbiased mean effect size from the remaining studies for use in the second step.

The second step involves reinstating the previously trimmed studies (resulting in the original asymmetric funnel plot) and then imputing studies in the underrepresented section (lower left of Figure 11.2) until you obtain a symmetric funnel plot. This symmetric funnel plot allows for accurate estimation of both the mean and heterogeneity (or between-study variance) of effect sizes. This two-step process is repeated several times until you reach a convergence criterion (in which trimming and filling produce little change to estimates).

As you might expect, this is not an approach performed by hand, and the exact statistical details of trimming and filling are more complex than I have presented here (for details, see Duval, 2005). Fortunately, this approach is included in some software packages for meta-analysis (this represents an exception to my general statement that meta-analysis can be conducted by hand or with a simple spreadsheet program, though you could likely program this approach into traditional software packages). There also exist variations depending on modeling of between-study variability beyond sampling fluctuation (random- versus fixed-effects) and choice of estimation method. These methods have not yet been fully resolved.

Despite the need for specialized software and some unresolved statistical issues, the trim and fill method represents a useful way to correct for potential publication bias. Importantly, this method is *not* to be used as the primary reporting of results of a meta-analysis. In other words, you should not impute study values, analyze the resulting dataset including these values, and report the results as if this was what was "found" in the meta-analysis. Instead, you should compute results using the trim and fill method for comparison to those found from the studies actually obtained. If the estimates are comparable, then you conclude that the original results are robust to publication bias, whereas discrepancies suggest that the obtained studies produced biased results.

11.2.6   Weighted Selection Approaches

An additional method of managing publication bias is through selection method approaches (Hedges & Vevea, 2005), also called weighted distribution theory corrections (Begg, 1994). These methods are complex, and I do not attempt to fully describe them fully here (see Hedges & Vevea, 2005). The central concept of these approaches is to construct a distribution of inclusion likelihood (i.e., a selection model) that is used for weighting the results obtained. Specifically, studies with characteristics that are related to lower likelihood of inclusion are given more weight than studies with characteristics related to higher likelihood of inclusion.

This distribution of inclusion likelihood is based on characteristics of studies that are believed to be related to inclusion in the meta-analysis. For example, you might expect the likelihood to be related to the level of statistical significance, such that studies finding significant results are more likely to be included than those that do not. Because it is usually difficult to empirically derive values for this likelihood distribution, the most common practice is to base these on a priori models. A variety of models have been suggested (see Begg, 1994; Hedges & Vevea, 2005), including models that propose equal likelihood for studies with $p < .05$ and then a gradually declining likelihood, as well as models that consist of steps corresponding to diminished likelihood at ps that are psychologically salient (e.g., $ps = .01, .05, .10$). Other models focus more on effect sizes, sometimes in combination with standard errors. Your choice of one of these models should be guided by the underlying selection process that you believe is operating, though this decision can be difficult to make in the absence of field-specific information. It is also necessary for these approaches to be applied within a meta-analysis with a large number of studies. In sum, this weighted selection approach appears promising, but some important practical issues need to be resolved before they can be widely used.

11.3   PRACTICAL MATTERS: WHAT IMPACT DO SAMPLING BIASES HAVE ON META-ANALYTIC CONCLUSIONS?

The short answer to the question, "What impact do sampling biases have on the conclusions of a meta-analysis?" is "I don't know." As a meta-analyst you do not know, your readers do not know, and it is not possible to know unless you could obtain every study that has ever been conducted on the topic of the meta-analysis. Because obtaining every study is almost never possible (and if you did, there is by definition no bias because you have obtained *the population* of studies), this question is impossible to answer.

The magnitude of sampling bias likely varies considerably from field to field and even from one meta-analysis to another. So, it is appropriate to always be concerned about the extent to which publication bias impacts the findings of a meta-analysis. Does this mean every meta-analysis should be viewed as untrustworthy and uninformative? Absolutely not. You should remember that the available literature is all that we as scientists have, so if you dismiss this literature as not valuable, then we have nothing on which to base our empirical sciences. Moreover, it is important to remember that a meta-analytic review is no more subject to sampling bias than other literature reviews. In fact, meta-analysis offers two advantages over traditional approaches to literature review that allow us to face the challenge of sampling bias. First, meta-analysts typically are more exhaustive in searching the literature than those performing narrative reviews, and the search procedures are made transparent in the reporting of meta-analyses. Second, only meta-analysis allows you to evaluate and potentially correct for publication/sampling bias. Although there is no guarantee that these methods will perfectly fix the problem, they are far better than simply ignoring it.

11.4 SUMMARY

Publication bias poses a threat to the conclusions drawn in a meta-analysis. Fortunately, there exist several methods for detecting potential bias, as well as various methods of correction (though none are universally agreed upon). I recommend considering multiple approaches to identifying these threats (especially for publication bias, for which there are numerous approaches). The value of considering multiple approaches was illustrated through an ongoing example meta-analysis, in which some approaches suggested potential bias whereas others did not. The more evidence you can bring to bear on these potential problems, the more likely you are to come to satisfying conclusions. I also recommend keeping updated with the literature on these topics, as these represent some of the most active areas of quantitative research on meta-analysis.

11.5 RECOMMENDED READINGS

Begg, C. B. (1994). Publication bias. In H. Cooper & L. V. Hedges (Eds.), *The handbook of research synthesis* (pp. 399–409). New York: Russell Sage Foundation.—This chapter is a reasonably comprehensive, yet concise, overview of the issues involved in considering and evaluating publication bias in meta-analysis.

Rothstein, H. R., Sutton, A. J., & Borenstein, M. (Eds.). (2005b). *Publication bias in meta-analysis: Prevention, assessment and adjustments.* Hoboken, NJ: Wiley.—This is the book to read if you want to learn as much as possible about publication bias. This edited book contains 16 chapters, each considering in depth different methodological and statistical approaches to avoiding, detecting, or correcting publication bias.

NOTES

1. Although this statement is accurate for most types of publication bias, others could exist. For example, if a particular therapy has a potential adverse side effect, it is plausible that studies demonstrating this effect are more likely to be suppressed. In this case, publication bias might be in the direction of overrepresentation of null (absence of adverse effects of the therapy) or negative (lower rates of adverse effects with the therapy) results.

2. Some (Antes & Chalmers, 2003; Chalmers, 1990) have argued that a researcher conducting a study but not fully reporting the results is unethical. This point is easy to see when you consider clinical work in which side effects (unexpected findings) are not reported or when studies failing to support a treatment are suppressed. The same argument applies, however, to basic research. Not reporting or selectively reporting results poses costly (in terms of time and effort) obstacles to the progression of basic science, even if the immediate impact on individuals is not as evident as in applied research. Moreover, studies are often conducted using external funding (public or private) and involve the time of the individuals participating in the study; relegating the findings from these investments to the file drawer represents a waste of the limited resources available to science.

3. To evaluate publication bias for the random-effects model I presented in Chapter 10, the test of moderation by publication status would rely on a mixed-effects model. Examination of funnel plots and the effect size with sample size association do not differ whether you use a fixed- or random-effects model. Computation of failsafe numbers assumes a fixed-effects model and has not yet been extended to the random-effects framework.

4. It is also common to denote the effect sizes on the x-axis and the sample sizes on the y-axis. Either choice is acceptable, as they allow the same examination. My choice of plotting effect sizes on the y-axis and sample size on the x-axis is simply because this is more consistent with the regression-based methods (in which you examine whether effect sizes are predicted by sample size) described in the next subsection.

5. This particular plot assumes homogeneity, or the absence of between-study variability beyond expectable sampling fluctuations (i.e., the standard errors of effect sizes). In the presence of heterogeneity, you expect greater dispersion of effect sizes (i.e., a wider vertical span between the two solid lines), but the funnel plot should retain this symmetric shape.

6. A method of "controlling for" this variable would be to regress effect sizes onto this variable and then plot residuals (instead of effect sizes) in relation to sample

size. Although this funnel plot would not display the mean effect size, you could still evaluate the symmetry for presence of publication bias. This same method can be useful if there exist moderators of effect sizes that make visual inspection of effect size funnel plots difficult.

7. This number is only meaningful when you have found a significant result. If the obtained result is nonsignificant, then it is not meaningful to ask how many more null results would be needed to reduce it to nonsignificance (it is already there). In fact, using nonsignificant results in the equations for failsafe N will yield negative numbers.

8. I recommend conducting these analyses with the same scale of effect size used in the meta-analysis. For instance, if Fisher's Z_r transformation of the correlation, or the natural logarithm of the odds ratio, were used in the meta-analysis, these should also be used in this computation.

9. I use different terminology here than that of Orwin (1983) and others (e.g., Becker, 2005). My rationale for this terminology is to ensure consistency with terminology used in my earlier presentation of Rosenthal's (1979) approach. It is also worth noting here that I do not believe that you are limited to only selecting one minimum meaningful value. I see value in reporting multiple failsafe Ns, such as the number needed to reduce an effect size to a medium magnitude and to a small magnitude.

12

Multivariate Meta-Analytic Models

In Chapter 7 (Section 7.3), I described the difficulties of using multivariate statistics (e.g., regression coefficients) as effect sizes in meta-analyses. However, this does not mean that we cannot answer multivariate questions through meta-analysis. Rather than inserting multivariate statistics into our meta-analysis, we can use meta-analysis to obtain bivariate statistics (e.g., correlations) that are then used in multivariate analyses. This approach avoids the problems of using multivariate statistics as effect sizes (e.g., the necessity that all studies use the same variables in multivariate analyses), but itself contains some difficulties of analytic complexity and requires that studies have collectively examined all bivariate relations informing the multivariate analysis.

In this chapter, I introduce the cutting-edge practice of using meta-analysis to obtain sufficient statistics for multivariate analysis. I first describe the general logic of this practice and then provide an overview of two statistical approaches to fitting these multivariate meta-analytic models. Finally, I turn to the practical matter of connecting meta-analytic findings to theories, a connection especially relevant to multivariate models that better evaluate theoretical propositions than simpler models.

Before beginning this chapter, I want to make you aware of three important cautions. First, I should warn you that the material presented in this chapter is more technically challenging than most of the rest of this book. The techniques I describe here rely on familiarity with matrix representations of multivariate analyses, which I recognize many readers do not consider in their day-to-day analyses. Second, I have not attempted to fully explain some nuances of these approaches, as they quickly become even more technically challenging than the material I do present. Third, because the techniques I describe here are relatively new, many unresolved issues remain. Although I attempt to provide an up-to-date, nontechnical overview of what we currently know and make speculations about what I think are answers to unresolved issues (making clear what is established vs. speculation), you should bear in mind that the state of the art in this area is rapidly changing, so if you use these techniques you should consult the most recent research.

12.1   META-ANALYSIS TO OBTAIN SUFFICIENT STATISTICS

12.1.1   Sufficient Statistics for Multivariate Analyses

As you may recall (fondly or not) from your multivariate statistics courses, nearly all multivariate analyses do not require the raw data. Instead, you can perform these analyses using sufficient statistics—summary information from your data that can be inserted into matrix equations to provide estimates of multivariate parameters. Typically, the sufficient statistics are the variances and covariances among the variables in your multivariate analysis, along with some index of sample size for computing standard errors of these parameter estimates. For some analyses, you can instead use correlation to obtain standardized multivariate parameter estimates. Although the analysis of correlation matrices, rather than variance/covariance matrices, is often less than optimal, a focus on correlation matrices is advantageous in the context of multivariate meta-analysis for the same reason that correlations are generally preferable to covariances in meta-analysis (see Chapter 5). I next briefly summarize how correlation matrices can be used in multivariate analyses, focusing on multiple regression, exploratory factor analysis, and confirmatory factor analysis. Although these represent only a small sampling of possible multivariate analyses, this focus should highlight the wide range of possibilities of using multivariate meta-analysis.

12.1.1.a   Multiple Regression

Multiple regression models fit linear equations between a set of predictors (independent variables) and a dependent variable. Of interest are both the unique prediction each independent variable has to the dependent variable above and beyond the other predictors in the model (i.e., the regression coefficient, B) and the overall prediction of the set (i.e., the variance in the dependent variable explained, R^2). Both the standardized regression coefficients of each predictor and overall variance explained (i.e., squared multiple correlation, R^2) can be estimated from (1) the correlations among the independent variables (a square matrix, $\mathbf{R}_{ii}$, with the number of rows and columns equal to the number of predictors), and (2) the correlations of each independent variable with the dependent variable (a column vector, $\mathbf{R}_{iy}$, with the number of rows equal to the number of predictors, using the following equations[1] (Tabachnick & Fidell, 1996, p. 142):

Equation 12.1: Matrix equations for multiple regression

$$\mathbf{B}_i = \mathbf{R}_{ii}^{-1}\mathbf{R}_{iy}$$

$$R^2 = \mathbf{R}'_{iy}\mathbf{B}_i$$

- $\mathbf{B}_i$ is a $k \times 1$ vector of standardized regression coefficients.
- $\mathbf{R}_{ii}$ is a $k \times k$ matrix of correlations among independent variables.
- $\mathbf{R}_{iy}$ is a $k \times 1$ vector of correlations of independent variables with the dependent variable.
- R^2 is the proportion of variance in the dependent variable predicted by the set of independent variables.
- k is the number of predictors.

12.1.1.b   Exploratory Factor Analysis

Exploratory factor analysis (EFA) is used to extract a parsimonious set of factors that explain associations among a larger set of variables. This approach is commonly used to determine (1) how many factors account for the associations among variables, (2) the strengths of associations of each variable on a factor (i.e., the factor loadings), and (3) the associations among the factors (assuming oblique rotation). For each of these goals, exploratory factor analysis is preferred to principal components analysis (PCA; see, e.g., Widaman, 1993, 2007), so I describe EFA only. I should note that my description here is brief and does not delve into the many complexities of EFA; I am being brief because I seek only to remind you of the basic steps of EFA without providing a complete overview (for more complete coverage, see Cudeck & MacCallum, 2007).

Although the matrix algebra of EFA can be a little daunting, all that is initially required is the correlation matrix ($\mathbf{R}$) among the variables, which is a square matrix of p rows and columns (where p is the number of variables). From this correlation matrix, it is possible to compute a matrix of eigenvectors, $\mathbf{V}$, which has p rows and m columns (where m is the number of factors).[2]

To determine the number of factors that can be extracted, you extract the maximum number of factors[3] and then examine the resulting eigenvalues contained in the diagonal matrix $(m \times m)$ **L**:

Equation 12.2: Matrix equations for computing eigenvalues from EFA factor extraction

L = V′RV

- **L** is a $m \times m$ diagonal matrix of eigenvalues.
- **V** is a $p \times m$ matrix of eigenvectors.
- **R** is a $p \times p$ matrix of correlations among variables.
- p is the number of variables.
- m is the number of factors.

You decide on the number of factors to retain based on the magnitudes of the eigenvalues contained in **L**. A minimum (i.e., necessary but not sufficient) threshold is known as Kaiser's (1970) criterion, which states that the eigenvalue is greater than 1.0. Beyond this criterion, it is common to rely on a scree plot, sometimes with parallel analysis, as well as considering the interpretability of rival solutions, to reach a final determination of the number of factors to retain.

The analysis then proceeds with a specified number of factors (i.e., some fixed value of m that is less than p). Here, the correlation matrix (**R**) is expressed in terms of a matrix of unrotated factor loadings (**A**), which are themselves calculated from the matrices of eigenvectors (**V**) and eigenvalues (**L**):

Equation 12.3: Matrix equations for computing unrotated factor loadings in EFA

R = AA′
$$A = V\sqrt{L}$$

- **R** is a $p \times p$ matrix of correlations among variables.
- **V** is a $p \times m$ matrix of eigenvectors.
- **L** is a $m \times m$ diagonal matrix of eigenvalues.
- p is the number of variables.
- m is the number of factors.

In order to improve the interpretability of factor loadings (contained in the matrix **A**), you typically apply a rotation of some sort. Numerous rotations exist, with the major distinction being between orthogonal rotations, in which the correlations among factors are constrained to be zero, versus oblique rotations, in which nonzero correlations among factors are estimated. Oblique rotations are generally preferable, given that it is rare in social sciences for factors to be truly orthogonal. However, oblique rotations are also more computationally intensive (though this is rarely problematic with modern computers) and can yield various solutions using different criteria, given that you are attempting to estimate both factor loadings and factor intercorrelations simultaneously. I avoid the extensive consideration of alternative estimation procedures by simply stating that the goal of each approach is to produce a reproduced (i.e., model implied) correlation matrix that closely corresponds (by some criterion) to the actual correlation matrix (**R**). This reproduced matrix is a function of (1) the pattern matrix (**A**), which here (with oblique rotation) represents the unique relations of variable with factors (controlling for associations among factors), and (2) the factor correlation matrix (**Φ**), which represents the correlations among the factors[4]:

Equation 12.4: Matrix equation for reproduced correlation matrix in EFA

$$\hat{R} = A\Phi A'$$

- $\hat{R}$ is a $p \times p$ matrix of model-implied correlations among variables.
- **A** is a $p \times m$ matrix of unique associations between variables and factors (controlling for associations among factors).
- **Φ** is a $m \times m$ matrix of correlations among factors.
- p is the number of variables.
- m is the number of factors.

When the reproduced correlation matrix ($\hat{R}$) adequately reproduces the observed correlation matrix (**R**), the analysis is completed. You then interpret the values within the pattern matrix (**A**) and matrix of factor correlations (**Φ**) to address the second and third goals of EFA described above.

12.1.1.c   Confirmatory Factor Analysis

In many cases, it may be more appropriate to rely on a confirmatory, rather than an exploratory, factor analysis. A confirmatory factor analysis (CFA) is estimated by fitting the data to a specified model in which some factor loadings (or other parameters, such as residual covariances among variables) are specified as fixed to zero versus freely estimated. Such a model is often a more realistic representation of your expected factor structure than is the EFA.[5]

Like the EFA, the CFA estimates associations among factors (typically called "constructs" or "latent variables" in CFA) as well as strengths of associations between variables (often called "indicators" or "manifest variables" in CFA) and constructs. These parameters are estimated as part of the general CFA matrix equation[6]:

Equation 12.5: Matrix equation for CFA

$$\Sigma = \Lambda \Psi \Lambda' + \Theta$$

- Σ is a $p \times p$ matrix of model-implied variances and covariances among manifest variables.
- Λ is a $p \times m$ matrix of factor loadings of manifest variables regressed onto constructs.
- Ψ is a $m \times m$ matrix of variances and covariances among constructs (latent variables).
- Θ is a $p \times p$ matrix of residual variances and covariances among manifest variables.
- p is the number of manifest variables.
- m is the number of constructs (latent variables).

To estimate a CFA, you place certain constraints on the model to set the scale of latent constructs (see Little, Slegers, & Card, 2006) and ensure identification (see Kline, 2010, Ch. 6). For example, you might specify that there is no factor loading of a particular indicator on a particular construct (vs. an EFA, in which this would be estimated even if you expected the value to be small). Using Equation 12.5, a software program (e.g., Lisrel, EQS, Mplus) is used to compute values of factor loadings (values within the Λ matrix), latent variances and covariances (values within the Ψ matrix), and residual variances (and sometimes residual covariances; values within the Θ matrix) that yield a model implied variance/covariance matrix, Σ. The values are selected so that this model-implied matrix closely matches the observed (i.e., from the data) variances and covariance matrix (**S**) according to some criterion (most commonly, the maximum likelihood criterion minimizing a fit function). For CFA of primary data, the sufficient statistics are therefore the variances and covariances comprising **S**; however, it is also possible to use correlation coefficients such as would be available from meta-analysis to fit CFAs (see Kline, 2010, Ch. 7).[7]

12.1.2   The Logic of Meta-Analytically Deriving Sufficient Statistics

The purpose of the previous section was not to fully describe the matrix equations of multiple regression, EFA, and CFA. Instead, I simply wish to illustrate that a range of multivariate analyses can be performed using only correlations. Other multivariate analyses are possible, including canonical correlations, multivariate analysis of variance or covariance, and structural equation modeling. In short, any analysis that can be performed using a correlation matrix as sufficient information can be used as a multivariate model for meta-analysis.

The "key" of multivariate meta-analysis then is to use the techniques of meta-analysis described throughout this book to obtain average correlations from multiple studies. Your goal is to compute a meta-analytic mean correlation for each of the correlations in a matrix of p variables. Therefore, your task in a multivariate meta-analysis is not simply to perform one meta-analysis to obtain one correlation, but to perform multiple meta-analyses to obtain all possible correlations among a set of variables. Specifically, the number of correlations in a matrix of p variables is equal to $p(p-1)/2$. This correlation matrix (**R**) of these mean correlations is then used in one of the multivariate analyses described above.

12.1.3   The Challenges of Using Meta-Analytically Deriving Sufficient Statistics

Although the logic of this approach is straightforward, several complications arise (see Cheung & Chan, 2005a). The first is that it is unlikely that every study that provides information on *one* correlation will provide information on *all* correlations in the matrix. Consider a simple situation in which you wish to perform some multivariate analysis of variables X, Y, and Z. Study 1 might provide all three correlations (r_{XY}, r_{XZ}, and r_{YZ}). However, Study 2 did not measure Z, so it only provides one correlation (r_{XY}); Study 3 failed to measure Y and so also provides only one correlation (r_{XZ}); and so on. In other words, multivariate meta-analysis will almost always derive different average correlations from different subsets of studies.

This situation poses two problems. First, it is possible that different correlations from very different sets of studies could yield a correlation matrix that is nonpositive definite. For example, imagine that three studies reporting r_{XY} yield an average value of .80 and four studies reporting r_{XZ} yield an average value of .70. However, the correlation between Y and Z is reported in three different studies, and the meta-analytic average is −.50. It is not logically possible for there to exist, within the population, a strong positive correlation between X and Y, a strong positive correlation between X and Z, but a strong negative correlation between Y and Z.[8] Most multivariate analyses cannot use such nonpositive definite matrices. Therefore, the possibility that such nonpositive definite matrices can occur if different subsets of studies inform different correlations within the matrix represents a challenge to multivariate meta-analysis.

Another challenge that arises from the meta-analytic combination of different studies for different correlations within the matrix has to do with uncertainty about the effective sample size. Although many multivariate analyses can provide parameter estimates from correlations alone, the standard errors of these estimates (for significance testing or constructing confidence intervals) require knowledge of the sample size. When the correlations are meta-analytically combined from different subsets of studies, it is unclear what sample size should be used (e.g., the smallest sum of participants among studies for one of the correlations; the largest sum; or some average?).

A final challenge of multivariate meta-analysis is how we manage heterogeneity among studies. By computing a matrix of average correlations, we are implicitly assuming that one value adequately represents the populations of effect sizes. However, as I discussed earlier, it is more appropriate to test this homogeneity (vs. heterogeneity; see Chapter 8) and to model this population heterogeneity in a random-effects model if it exists (see Chapter 9). Only one of the two approaches I describe next can model between-study variances in a random-effects model.

12.2   TWO APPROACHES TO MULTIVARIATE META-ANALYSIS

Given the challenges I described in the previous section, multivariate meta-analysis is considerably more complex than simply synthesizing several correlations to serve as input for a multivariate analysis. The development of models that can manage these challenges is an active area of research, and the field has currently not resolved which approach is best. In this section, I describe two approaches that have received the most attention: the meta-analytic structural equation modeling (MASEM) approach describe by Cheung and Chan (2005a) and the generalized least squares (GLS) approach by Becker (e.g., 2009). I describe both for two reasons. First, you might read meta-analyses using either approach, so it is useful to be familiar with both. Second, given that research on both approaches is active, it is difficult for me to predict which approach might emerge as superior (or, more likely, superior in certain situations). However, as the state of the field currently stands, the GLS approach is more flexible in that it can estimate either fixed- or random-effects mean correlations (whereas the MASEM approach is limited to fixed-effects models[9]). For this reason, I provide considerably greater coverage of the GLS approach.

To illustrate these approaches, I expand on the example described earlier in the book. Table 12.1 summarizes 38 studies that provide correlations among relational aggression (e.g., gossiping), overt aggression (e.g., hitting), and peer rejection.[10] Here, 16 studies provide all three correlations among these variables, 6 provide correlations of both relational and overt aggression to peer rejection, and 16 provide the correlation between overt and relational aggression. This particular example is somewhat artificial, in that (1) a selection criterion for studies in this review was that results be reported for both relational and overt forms of aggression (otherwise, there would not be perfect overlap in the correlations of these two forms with peer rejection), and (2) for simplicity of presentation, I selected only the first 16 studies, out of 82 studies in the full meta-analysis, that provided only the overt with relational aggression correlation. Nevertheless, the example is realistic in that the three correlations come from different subsets of studies, and contain different numbers of studies and participants (for $r_{relational\text{-}overt}$, $k = 32$, $N = 11,642$; for $r_{relational\text{-}rejection}$ and $r_{overt\text{-}rejection}$, $k = 22$, $N = 8,081$). I next use this example to illustrate how each approach would be used to fit a multiple regression of both forms of aggression predicting peer rejection.

12.2.1 The MASEM Approach

One broad approach to multivariate meta-analysis is the MASEM approach described by Cheung and Chan (2005a). This approach relies on SEM methodology, so you must be familiar with this technique to use this approach. Given this restriction, I write this section with the assumption that you are at least somewhat familiar with SEM (if you are not, I highly recommend Kline, 2010, as an accessible introduction).

TABLE 12.1. Example Multivariate Meta-Analysis of Correlations among Relational Aggression, Overt Aggression, and Peer Rejection

Study	Sample size (N)	Relational–overt r	Relational–rejection r	Overt–rejection r
Andreou (2006)	403	.472		
Arnold (1998)	110	.707		
Berdugo-Arstark (2002)	128	.549		
Blachman (2003)	228	.440	.483	.592
Brendgen et al. (2005)	468	.420		
Butovskaya et al. (2007)	212	.576		
Campbell (1999)	139	.641		
Carpenter (2002)	75	.260		
Carpenter & Nangle (2006)	82	.270		
Cillessen & Mayeux (2004)	607	.561		
Cillessen et al. (2005)	224	.652		
Côté et al. (2007)	1183	.345		
Coyne & Archer (2005)	347	.540		
Crain (2002)	134	.870		
Crick (1995)	252	.656		
Crick (1996)	245	.770		
Crick (1997)	1166	.630		
Crick & Grotpeter (1995)	491	.540	.121	.228
Crick et al. (1997)	65	.607	.280	.367
Geiger (2003)	458	.650	.520	.480
Hawley et al. (2007)	929	.669	.146	.089
Henington (1996)	904	.561	.310	.295
Johnson (2003)	74	.735	.368	.527
Leff (1995)	151	.790	.570	.570
Miller (2001)	150	.530	.530	.420
Murray-Close & Crick (2006)	590	.700	.540	.510
Nelson et al. (2005)	180	.584	.030	.304
Ostrov (under review)[a]	139	.403	.332	.402
Ostrov & Crick (2007)	132	.030	.045	.155
Ostrov et al. (2004)	60		.000[b]	.100
Pakaslahti & Keltikangas-Järvinen (1998)	839	.580	.269	.250
Phillipsen et al. (1999)	262		−.045	.013
Rys & Bear (1997)	266		.423	.378
Salmivalli et al. (2000)	209	.681	.240	.385
Tomada & Schneider (1997)	314	.666	.153	.240
Werner (2000)	881		.440	.430
Werner & Crick (2004)	517		.440	.430
Zalecki & Hinshaw (2004)	228	.440	.516	.562

[a]Article was under review during the preparation of this meta-analytic review. It has subsequently been published as Ostrov (2008).
[b]Effect size is lower-bound estimate based on author's reporting only nonsignficant associations.

In this approach, you treat the correlation matrix from each study as sufficient statistics for a group in a multigroup SEM. In other words, each study is treated as a group, and the correlations obtained from each study are entered as the data for that group. Although the multigroup approach is relatively straightforward if all studies provided all correlations, this is typically not the case. The MASEM approach accounts for situations in which some studies do not include some variables, by not estimating the parameters involving those variables for that "group." However, the parameter estimates are constrained equal across groups, so identification is ensured (assuming that the overall model is identified). Note that this approach considers the completeness of studies in terms of variables rather than correlations (in contrast to the GLS approach described in Section 12.2.2). In other words, this approach assumes that if a variable is present in a study, the correlations of that variable with all other variables in the study are present. To illustrate using the example, if a study measured relation aggression, overt aggression, and peer rejection, then this approach requires that you obtain all three correlations among these variables. If a study measured all three variables, but failed to report the correlation between overt aggression and rejection (and you could not obtain this correlation), then you would be forced to treat the study as if it failed to measure either overt aggression or rejection (i.e., you would ignore either the relational-overt or the relational-rejection correlation).

The major challenge to this approach comes from the equality constraints on all parameters across groups. These constraints necessarily imply that the studies are homogeneous. For this reason, Cheung and Chan (2005a) recommended that the initial step in this approach be to evaluate the homogeneity versus heterogeneity of the correlation matrices. They propose a method in which you evaluate heterogeneity through nested-model comparison of an unrestricted model in which the correlations are freely estimated across studies (groups) versus a restricted model in which they are constrained equal.[11] If the change is nonsignificant (i.e., the null hypothesis of homogeneity is retained), then you use the correlations (which are constrained equal across studies) and their asymptotic covariance matrix as sufficient statistics for your multivariate model (e.g., multiple regression in my example or, as described by Cheung & Chan, 2005a, within an SEM). However, if the change is significant (i.e., the alternate hypothesis of heterogeneity), then it is not appropriate to leave the equality constraints in place. In this situation of heterogeneity, this original MASEM approach cannot be used to evaluate models for the entire set of studies (but see footnote 9). Cheung and Chan (2005a) offer two recommendations to overcome this problem. First, you might divide studies based on coded study characteristics until you achieve within-group homogeneity. If you take this approach, then you must focus on moderator analyses rather than make overall conclusions. Second, if the coded study characteristics do not fully account for the heterogeneity, you can perform the equivalent of a cluster analysis that will empirically classify studies into more homogeneous subgroups (Cheung & Chan, 2005b). However, the model results from these multiple empirically identified groups might be difficult to interpret.

Given the requirement of homogeneity of correlations, this approach might be limited if your goal is to evaluate an overall model across studies. In the illustrative example, I found significant heterogeneity (i.e., increase in model misfit when equality constraints across studies were imposed). I suspect that this heterogeneity is likely more common than homogeneity. Furthermore, I was not able to remove this heterogeneity through coded study characteristics. To use this approach, I would have needed to empirically classify studies into more homogeneous subgroups (Cheung & Chan, 2005b); however, I was dissatisfied with this approach because it would have provided multiple sets of results without a clear conceptual explanation. Although this MASEM approach might be modified in the future to accommodate heterogeneity (look especially for work by Mike Cheung), it currently did not fit my needs within this illustrative meta-analysis of relational aggression, overt aggression, and peer rejection. As I show next, the GLS approach was more tractable in this example, which illustrates its greater flexibility.

12.2.2 The GLS Approach

Becker (1992; see 2009 for a comprehensive overview) has described a GLS approach to multivariate meta-analysis. This approach can be explained in seven steps; I next summarize these steps as described in Becker (2009) and provide results for the illustration of relational and overt aggression predicting peer rejection.

12.2.2.a Data Management

The first step is to arrange the data in a way that information from each study is summarized in two matrices. The first matrix is a column vector of the Fisher's transformed correlations (Z_r) from each study i, denoted as z_i. The number of rows of this matrix for each study will be equal to the number of correlations provided; for example, from the data in Table 12.1, this matrix will have one row for the Andreou (2006) study, three rows for the Blachman (2003) study, and two rows for the Ostrov et al. (2004) study. The second matrix for each study is an indicator matrix ($\mathbf{X}_i$) that denotes which correlations are represented in each study. The number of columns in this matrix will be constant across studies (the total number of correlations in the meta-analysis), but the number of rows will be equal to the number of correlations in the particular study. To illustrate these matrices, consider the 33rd study in Table 12.1, that by Rys and Bear (1997); the matrices (note that the $\mathbf{z}$ matrix contains Fisher's transformations of rs shown in the table) for this study are:

$$z_{33} = \begin{bmatrix} .451 \\ .398 \end{bmatrix}, \mathbf{X}_{33} = \begin{bmatrix} 0 & 1 & 0 \\ 0 & 0 & 1 \end{bmatrix}$$

Note that this study, which provides two of the three correlations, is represented with matrices of two rows. The indicator matrix ($\mathbf{X}_{33}$) specifies that these two correlations are the second and third correlations under consideration (the order is arbitrary, but needs to be consistent across studies; here, I have followed the order shown in Table 12.1).

12.2.2.b   Estimating Variances and Covariances of Study Effect Size Estimates

Just as it was necessary to compute the standard errors of study effect size estimates in all meta-analyses (see Chapters 5 and 8), we must do so in this approach to multivariate meta-analysis. Here, I describe the variances of estimates of effect sizes, which is simply the standard error squared: $Var(Z_r) = SE_{Zr}^2$. So the variances of each Z_r effect size are simply $1 / (N_i - 3)$. However, for a multivariate meta-analysis, in which multiple effect sizes are considered, you must consider not only the variance of estimate of each effect size, but also the *covariances* among these estimates (i.e., the uncertainty of estimation of one effect size is associated with the uncertainty of estimation of another effect size within the same study). The covariance of the estimate of the Fisher's transformed correlation between variables s and t with the estimate of the transformed correlation between variables u and v (where u or v could equal s or t) from Study i is computed from the following equation (Becker, 1992, p. 343; Beretvas & Furlow, 2006, p. 161)[12]:

Equation 12.6: Covariance of estimate of Fisher's transformed correlation between variables *s* and *t* with the estimate of the transformed correlation between variables *u* and *v* in Study *i*

$$Cov(Z_{ist}, Z_{iuv}) = \frac{\left[\begin{array}{c} 0.5\rho_{ist}\,\rho_{iuv}\left(\rho_{isu}^2 + \rho_{isv}^2 + \rho_{itu}^2 + \rho_{itv}^2\right) + \rho_{isu}\,\rho_{itv} + \rho_{isv}\,\rho_{itu} \\ -\left(\rho_{ist}\,\rho_{isu}\,\rho_{isv} + \rho_{its}\,\rho_{itu}\,\rho_{itv} + \rho_{ius}\,\rho_{iut}\,\rho_{iuv} + \rho_{ivs}\,\rho_{ivt}\,\rho_{ivu}\right) \end{array}\right]}{N_i\left[\left(1 - \rho_{ist}^2\right)\left(1 - \rho_{iuv}^2\right)\right]}$$

- Z_{ist} is the Fisher's transformed estimate of the correlation between variables *s* and *t* from Study *i*.
- Z_{iuv} is the Fisher's transformed estimate of the correlation between variables *u* and *v* from Study *i*.
- ρ_{ist} is the population correlation between variables *s* and *t* for Study *i* (see text).
- ρ_{iuv} is the population correlation between variables *u* and *v* for Study *i* (see text).
- ρ_{isu} is the population correlation between variables *s* and *u* for Study *i* (see text).
- ρ_{isv} is the population correlation between variables *s* and *v* for Study *i* (see text).
- ρ_{itu} is the population correlation between variables *t* and *u* for Study *i* (see text).
- ρ_{itv} is the population correlation between variables *t* and *v* for Study *i* (see text).
- N_i is the sample size of Study *i*.

In this equation, the covariances of estimates are based on two types of information: (1) the sample size, contained in the denominator, is known for each study; and (2) the population correlations, are unknown. Although this population correlation is study-specific (in the sense of assuming a population distribution of effect sizes consistent with a random effects model; see Chapter 10), simulation studies (Furlow & Beretvas, 2005) have shown that the mean correlation across the studies of your meta-analysis is a reasonable estimate of the population correlations for use in this equation. Becker (2009) demonstrates the use of simple sample-size-weighted mean correlations as estimates of these population correlations; that is,

$$\bar{r} = \sum(N_i r_i) \Big/ \sum(N_i)$$

From the ongoing example of data shown in Table 12.1, I find sample-size-weighted mean correlations of .565, .318, and .330 for the relational-overt, relational-rejection, and overt-rejection associations, respectively. Inserting these mean correlations into Equation 12.6, I can then compute the variances and covariances of estimates for each study based on the study's effect size. For instance, the fourth study (Blachman, 2003), which had a sample size (N_4) of 228, has the following matrix of variances and covariances of estimates:

$$Cov\left(z_4\right)=\begin{bmatrix} .0020 & .0007 & .0006 \\ .0007 & .0035 & .0019 \\ .0006 & .0019 & .0035 \end{bmatrix}$$

Studies that do not report all three correlations will have matrices that are smaller; specifically, their matrices will have numbers of columns and rows equal to the number of reported effect sizes.

12.2.2.c   Estimating a Fixed-Effects Mean Correlation Matrix

After computing effect size (z_i), indicator (X_i), and estimation variance/covariance ($Cov(z_i)$) matrices for each study (i), you then create three large matrices that combine these matrices across the individual studies. The first of these is z, which is a column vector of all of the individual effect sizes vectors from the studies (z_is) stacked. In the example from Table 12.1, this vector would be:

$$z = \begin{bmatrix} .512 \\ .881 \\ .617 \\ .472 \\ .527 \\ .681 \\ .448 \\ \vdots \\ .571 \\ .635 \end{bmatrix}$$

The first three values of this vector (.512, .881, and .617) are the Z_rs from the single effect sizes provided by the first three studies (Andreou, 2006;

Arnold, 1998; and Berdugo-Arstark, 2002 from Table 12.1). The next three values (.472, .527, and .681) are the three Z_rs from the fourth study (Blachman, 2003), which provided three effect sizes. The next value (.448) is the single Z_r from the fifth study (Brendgen et al., 2005). I have omitted the values of this matrix until the last (38th) study (Zalecki & Hinshaw, 2004), which provided two effect sizes (Z_rs = .571 and .635). In total, this z vector has 76 rows (i.e., a 76 × 1 matrix) that contain the 76 effect sizes from these 38 studies.

The second large matrix is **X**, which is a stacked matrix of the indicator matrices of the individual studies (**X**$_i$). Because all of the study indicator matrices had three columns, this matrix also has three columns. However, each study provides a number of rows to this matrix equal to the number of effect sizes; therefore there will be 76 rows in the **X** matrix in the example. Specifically, this matrix will look as follows:

$$\mathbf{X} = \begin{bmatrix} 1 & 0 & 0 \\ 1 & 0 & 0 \\ 1 & 0 & 0 \\ 1 & 0 & 0 \\ 0 & 1 & 0 \\ 0 & 0 & 1 \\ 1 & 0 & 0 \\ \vdots & \vdots & \vdots \\ 0 & 1 & 0 \\ 0 & 0 & 1 \end{bmatrix}$$

The first three rows indicate that the first three studies provide effect sizes for the relational-overt association (the first column, as in Table 12.1). Rows four to six are from the fourth study (Blachman, 2003), indicating that the three effect sizes (corresponding to values in the z vector) are Fisher's transformations of the relational-overt, relational-rejection, and overt-rejection correlations, respectively. Row seven indicates that the fifth study (Brendgen et al., 2005) contributed an effect size of the relational-overt (i.e., first) association. Again, I have omitted further values of this matrix until the last (38th) study (Zalecki & Hinshaw, 2004), which has two rows in this matrix indicating that it provided effect sizes for the second (relational-rejection) and third (overt-rejection) associations. In total, this **X** matrix has a number of rows equal to the total number of effect sizes (76 in this example) and a number of columns equal to the number of correlations you are considering (3 in this example).

The final combined matrix is $\hat{\Psi}$, which contains the variances/covariances of estimates from the individual studies. Specifically, this matrix is a blockwise diagonal matrix in which the estimate variance/covariance matrix from each study i is placed near the diagonal, and all other values are 0. This is probably most easily understood by considering this matrix in the context of my ongoing example:

$$
\hat{\Psi} =
\begin{bmatrix}
.0011 & 0 & 0 & 0 & 0 & 0 & 0 & \cdots & 0 & 0 \\
0 & .0042 & 0 & 0 & 0 & 0 & 0 & \cdots & 0 & 0 \\
0 & 0 & .0036 & 0 & 0 & 0 & 0 & \cdots & 0 & 0 \\
0 & 0 & 0 & .0020 & .0007 & .0006 & 0 & \cdots & 0 & 0 \\
0 & 0 & 0 & .0007 & .0035 & .0019 & 0 & \cdots & 0 & 0 \\
0 & 0 & 0 & .0006 & .0019 & .0035 & 0 & \cdots & 0 & 0 \\
0 & 0 & 0 & 0 & 0 & 0 & .0010 & \cdots & 0 & 0 \\
\vdots & \vdots & \vdots & \vdots & \vdots & \vdots & \vdots & \ddots & 0 & 0 \\
0 & 0 & 0 & 0 & 0 & 0 & 0 & 0 & .0035 & .0019 \\
0 & 0 & 0 & 0 & 0 & 0 & 0 & 0 & .0019 & .0035
\end{bmatrix}
$$

Here, the first three elements along the diagonal represent the variances of the estimates of the single effect sizes provided by these three studies. The next study is represented in the square starting in cell 4, 4 (fourth row, fourth column) to cell 6, 6. These values represent the variances and covariances among estimates of the three effect sizes from this study, which were shown above as $Cov(z_4)$. The variance of the single effect size of study 5 is shown next along the diagonal. I have again omitted the remaining values until the last (38th) study (Zalecki & Hinshaw, 2004). This study provided two effect sizes, and the variances (both .0035) and covariance (.0019) of these estimates are shown as a square matrix around the diagonal. Note that all other values in this matrix are 0. In total, this $\hat{\Psi}$ matrix is a square, symmetric matrix with 76 (total number of effect sizes in this example) rows and columns.

These three matrices, z, $\mathbf{X}$, and, $\hat{\Psi}$ are then used to estimate (via generalized least squares methods) fixed-effects mean effect sizes, which are contained in the column vector ζ. The equation to do so is somewhat daunting looking, but is a relatively simple matter of matrix algebra (Becker, 2009, p. 389):

Equation 12.7: Generalized least squares estimation of fixed-effects mean effect sizes

$$\zeta = (\mathbf{X}'\hat{\Psi}^{-1}\mathbf{X})^{-1}\mathbf{X}'\hat{\Psi}^{-1}\mathbf{z}$$

- ζ is a column vector of fixed-effects estimated mean effect sizes, with dimensions of number of effect sizes of interest $\times$ 1.
- $\mathbf{X}$ is the indicator matrix, with dimensions of number of effect sizes reported across all studies $\times$ number of effect sizes of interest.
- $\hat{\Psi}$ is the blockwise diagonal matrix of variances/covariances of estimates of effects sizes in the studies, which is a square matrix with numbers of rows and columns equal to the number of effect sizes reported across all studies.
- $\mathbf{z}$ is the column vector of effect sizes reported in the studies, with dimensions of number of effect sizes reported across all studies $\times$ 1.

In the ongoing example, working through the matrix algebra yields the following:

$$\hat{\zeta} = \begin{bmatrix} .664 \\ .330 \\ .343 \end{bmatrix}$$

These findings indicate that the fixed-effects mean Z_rs are .66, .33, and .34 for the relational-overt, relational-rejection, and overt-rejection associations, respectively. Back-transforming these values to the more interpretable r yields .58, .32, and .33. If these fixed-effects values are of interest (see Section 12.2.2.d on evaluating heterogeneity), then you are likely interested in drawing inference about these mean effect sizes. Variances of the estimates of the mean Z_rs (i.e., the squared standard errors) are found on the diagonal of the matrix obtained using the following equation (Becker, 2009, p. 389):

Equation 12.8: Variances of estimates of fixed-effects mean effect sizes

$$\text{Var}(\hat{\zeta}) = (\mathbf{X}'\hat{\Psi}^{-1}\mathbf{X})^{-1}$$

- ζ is a column vector of fixed-effects estimated mean effect sizes.
- $\mathbf{X}$ is the indicator matrix.
- $\hat{\Psi}$ is the blockwise diagonal matrix of variances/covariances of estimates of effects sizes in the studies.

12.2.2.d   Evaluating Heterogeneity of Effect Sizes

Just as when you are analyzing a single effect size, the appropriateness of a fixed-effects model depends on whether effect sizes are homogeneous versus heterogeneous. If they are heterogeneous, then you should use a random-effects model (see Chapter 10), which precludes the MASEM approach (Cheung & Chan, 2005a). The test of heterogeneity in the multivariate case is an omnibus test of whether *any* of the effect sizes significantly vary across studies (more than expected by sampling fluctuation alone; see Chapter 8). Becker (2009) described a significance test that relies on a Q value as in the univariate case, but here this value must be obtained through matrix algebra using the following equation (Becker, 2009, p. 389):

Equation 12.9: Omnibus test of heterogeneity (Q) of a set of effect sizes

$$Q = \mathbf{z}'(\hat{\Psi}^{-1} - \hat{\Psi}^{-1}\mathbf{X}(\mathbf{X}'\hat{\Psi}^{-1}\mathbf{X})^{-1}\mathbf{X}'\hat{\Psi}^{-1})\mathbf{z}$$

- **z** is the column vector of effect sizes reported in the studies, with dimensions of number of effect sizes reported across all studies × 1.
- $\hat{\Psi}$ is the blockwise diagonal matrix of variances/covariances of estimates of effect sizes in the studies, which is a square matrix with numbers of rows and columns equal to the number of effect sizes reported across all studies.
- **X** is the indicator matrix, with dimensions of number of effect sizes reported across all studies × number of effect sizes of interest.

This Q value is evaluated as a χ^2 distribution, with *df* equal to the number of effect sizes reported across all studies minus the number of effect sizes of interest.

In the example meta-analysis of studies in Table 12.1, $Q = 1450.90$. Evaluated as a χ^2 value with 73 *df* (i.e., 76 reported effect sizes minus 3 effect sizes of interest), this value is statistically significant ($p < .001$). This significant heterogeneity indicates (1) the need to rely on a random effects model to obtain mean effect sizes, or (2) the potential to identify moderators of the heterogeneity in effect sizes.

12.2.2.e   Estimating a Random-Effects Mean Correlation Matrix

As you recall from Chapter 10, one method of dealing with between-study heterogeneity of a single effect size is to estimate the between-study variance (τ^2), and then account for this variance as uncertainty in the weights applied to studies when computing the (random-effects) mean effect size. The same logic applies here, except now you must estimate and account for several between-study variances—one for each effect size in your multivariate model.

The first step, then, is to estimate between-study variances. Although there likely also exists population-level (i.e., beyond sampling fluctuation) covariation in effect sizes across studies, Becker (2009) stated that in practice these covariances are intractable to estimate and that accounting only for between-study variance appears adequate.[13] Therefore, you simply estimate the between-study variance (τ^2) for each effect size of interest (as described in Chapter 10). In the ongoing example, the estimated between-study variances are .0372, .0357, and .0296 for the relational-overt, relational-rejection, and overt-rejection effect sizes.

As you recall from Chapter 10, the estimated between-study variance for a single effect size (τ^2) is added to the study-specific sampling variance (SE_i^2) to represent the total uncertainty of the study's point estimate to the effect size, and the random-effects weight is the inverse of this uncertainty: $w_i* = 1/(\tau^2 + SE_i^2)$. In this GLS approach, we modify the previously described matrix of variances/covariances of estimates of studies ($\hat{\Psi}$) by adding the appropriate between-study variance estimate to the variances (i.e., diagonal elements) to produce a random-effects matrix, $\hat{\Psi}^{RE}$. To illustrate using the ongoing example:

$$\hat{\Psi}^{RE} = \begin{bmatrix} .0384 & 0 & 0 & 0 & 0 & 0 & 0 & \cdots & 0 & 0 \\ 0 & .0414 & 0 & 0 & 0 & 0 & 0 & \cdots & 0 & 0 \\ 0 & 0 & .0408 & 0 & 0 & 0 & 0 & \cdots & 0 & 0 \\ 0 & 0 & 0 & .0393 & .0007 & .0006 & 0 & \cdots & 0 & 0 \\ 0 & 0 & 0 & .0007 & .0392 & .0019 & 0 & \cdots & 0 & 0 \\ 0 & 0 & 0 & .0006 & .0019 & .0331 & 0 & \cdots & 0 & 0 \\ 0 & 0 & 0 & 0 & 0 & 0 & .0382 & \cdots & 0 & 0 \\ \vdots & \vdots & \vdots & \vdots & \vdots & \vdots & \vdots & \ddots & 0 & 0 \\ 0 & 0 & 0 & 0 & 0 & 0 & 0 & 0 & .0392 & .0019 \\ 0 & 0 & 0 & 0 & 0 & 0 & 0 & 0 & .0019 & .0331 \end{bmatrix}$$

Comparison of the values in this matrix relative to those in the fixed-effects $\hat{\Psi}$ is useful. Here we see that the first value on the diagonal (for the first study, Andreou, 2006) is .0384, which is the sum of τ^2 (.0372) for the effect size indexed by this value (relational-overt) and the study-specific variance of this estimate from the fixed-effects matrix (.0011) (note that rounding error might produce small discrepancies). Similarly, the second value on the diagonal is for the second study, which also provided an effect size of the relational-overt association, and this value (.0414) is the sum of the same τ^2 (.0372) as Study 1 (because they both report relational-overt effect sizes) plus that study's sample-size specific variance of sampling error from the fixed-effects matrix (.0042). Consider next the fourth through sixth values on the diagonal, which are for the three effect sizes from Study 4 (Blachman, 2003). The first value (.0393) is for the relational-overt effect size estimate, which is the sum of the τ^2 for that effect size (.0372) plus the sampling variance for this study and this effect size (.0020). The second value for this study is .0392, which is the sum of the τ^2 for the relational-rejection effect size (.0357) and the sampling variance for this study and this effect size found in the parallel cell of the fixed-effects matrix (Ψ), .0035. The third value for this study (.0331) is similarly the sum of the τ^2 for the overt-rejection effect size (.0296) and sampling variance (.0035). Note that the off-diagonal elements (covariances of effect size estimates) do not change in this approach because we have assumed no between-study covariance of population effect sizes.

After computing this matrix of random-effects variances and covariances of estimates ($\hat{\Psi}^{RE}$), it is relatively straightforward to estimate a matrix of random-effects mean effect sizes. You simply use Equation 12.7, but insert $\hat{\Psi}^{RE}$ rather than $\hat{\Psi}$. Standard errors of these random-effects mean effect sizes can be estimated using Equation 12.8. In the ongoing illustration, the random-effects mean correlations (back-transformed from Z_rs) are .59 (95% confidence interval = .54 to .63) for relational-overt, .32 (95% confidence interval = .24 to .39) for relational-rejection, and .36 (95% confidence interval = .29 to .43) for overt-rejection.

12.2.2.f   Fitting a Multivariate Model to the Matrix of Average Correlations

After obtaining the meta-analytically derived matrix of average correlations, it is now possible to fit a variety of multivariate models. Considering the ongoing example, I am interested in fitting a multiple regression model in which relational and overt aggression are predictors of rejection. Recalling that multiple regression analyses partition the correlation matrix into dependent and independent variables (see Equation 12.1), it is useful to display the results of the random-effects mean correlations (which I express more precisely here) as follows:

$$\overline{\mathbf{R}} = \begin{bmatrix} 1 & .3197 & .3623 \\ .3197 & 1 & .5877 \\ .3623 & .5877 & 1 \end{bmatrix}$$

This overall correlation matrix is then partitioned into matrices of (1) the correlations of the dependent variable (rejection) with the predictors (relational and overt aggression), $\mathbf{R}_{iy}$; and (2) the correlations among the predictors, $\mathbf{R}_{ii}$:

$$\mathbf{R}_{iy} = \begin{bmatrix} .3197 \\ .3623 \end{bmatrix}$$

$$\mathbf{R}_{ii} = \begin{bmatrix} 1 & .5877 \\ .5877 & 1 \end{bmatrix}$$

Applying these matrices within Equation 12.1 yields regression coefficients of .16 for relational aggression and .27 for overt aggression. These two predictors explained 14.9% of the variance in the dependent variable in this model (i.e., $R^2 = .149$).

12.3 PRACTICAL MATTERS: THE INTERPLAY BETWEEN META-ANALYTIC MODELS AND THEORY

As with any data-analytic approach, meta-analytic techniques are most valuable when applied in the service of theories relevant to the content of your review. I place this discussion on the interplay between meta-analysis and theory in this chapter on multivariate meta-analysis because many of our theories are multivariate and therefore benefit from multivariate analyses. However, consideration of theory is important for any meta-analysis—univariate or multivariate—just as it is for any form of data analysis in primary research.

A full philosophical consideration of what constitutes a "theory" lies far beyond the scope of this book. Instead, I next frame my discussion of the interplay between theories and meta-analytic results in terms of the metaphor of a "nomological net" (called a "nomological network" by Cronbach & Meehl, 1955). In this metaphor, the knots of the net represent constructs, and the webbing among the knots represent associations among the constructs. The coverage of the net represents the scope of the theory in terms of the phenomena the theory attempts to explain. Theory specifies expectations for this net in terms of what the knots are (i.e., what constructs are relevant); the webbing among the knots (i.e., what directions and magnitudes of associations among the constructs are expected); and the coverage of the net (i.e., what, when, and for whom the theory is applicable). Different theories may specify nets that differ in terms of their knots, webbing, and coverage; in fact, potentially infinite nets (theories) could be specified.[14] Thus, theory informs your meta-analysis in the very fundamental ways of specifying the constructs you consider (i.e., your definition of constructs of interest), the associations you investigate (i.e., the effect sizes you meta-analyze), and the scope (i.e., breadth of samples and designs included) you include in your meta-analysis (i.e., the inclusion criteria; see Chapter 3).[15]

Having described how theory guides your meta-analysis, I next turn to how your meta-analysis can evaluate theories. I organize this consideration around the three pieces of the nomological net metaphor: constructs (knots), associations (webbing), and scope (coverage). Following this consideration of how meta-analysis can evaluate theories, I then turn to the topic of model evaluation and building with multivariate meta-analysis.

12.3.1 Evaluating Variables and Constructs to Inform Concepts

It is useful to consider the indirect way by which theories inform measurement in science (for more in-depth treatments, see, e.g., Britt, 1997; Jaccard & Jaccoby, 2010). When theories describe things, the things that they describe are concepts. *Concepts* are the most abstract representation of something—the ideas we hold in our minds that a thing exists. For example, any layperson will have a concept of what aggression is. Well-articulated theories go further than abstract concepts to articulate *constructs*, which are more specifically defined instances of the concept. For example, an aggression scholar might define the construct of aggression "as behavior that is aimed at harming or injuring another person or persons" (Parke & Slaby, 1983, p. 550). Such a definition of a construct is explicit in terms of what lies within and outside of the boundaries (e.g., an accident that injures someone is not aggression because that was not the "aim"). Constructs might be hierarchically organized; for instance, the construct of "aggression" might encompass more specific constructs such as "relational aggression" and "overt aggression" such as I consider in the illustrative example of this chapter. Theories may differ in terms of whether they focus on separable lower-order constructs (within the nomological net metaphor: multiple knots) or singular higher-order constructs (a single, larger knot in the net).

Despite their specificity, constructs cannot be directly studied. Instead, a primary research study must use *variables*, which are rules for assigning numbers that we think reasonably capture the level of the construct. These variables might be single items (e.g., frequency of punching) or the aggregation of multiple items (frequency of punching, calling names, and spreading rumors). They may have either meaningful (e.g., number of times observed in a week) or arbitrary (e.g., a 5-point Likert-type scale) metrics. They may have different levels of measurement, ranging from continuous (e.g., number of times a child is observed enacting aggression), to ordinal (e.g., a child's average score among multiple Likert-type items), to dichotomous (e.g., the presence versus absence of a field note recording a child's aggression). Regardless, variables are the researcher's rule-bound system of assigning values to represent constructs. However, there are an infinite number of variables (i.e., ways of assigning values) that could represent a construct, and every primary study will need to select a limited subset of these variables.

Meta-analysis is a powerful tool to evaluate variables and constructs to inform theoretical concepts. As mentioned, any single primary study must select a limited subset of variables; however, the collection of studies likely contains a wider range of variables. Meta-analytic combination of these multiple studies—each containing a subset of variables representing the construct—will provide a more comprehensive statement of the construct itself. This is especially true if (1) the individual studies use a small subset of variables, but the collection of studies contains many subsets with low overlap so as to provide coverage of many ways to measure the construct; and (2) you correct for artifacts so as to eliminate less interesting heterogeneity across methods of measurement (e.g., correcting for unreliability). Tests of moderation across approaches to measuring variables can also inform whether some approaches are better representations of the construct than others.

Furthermore, meta-analysis can clarify the hierarchical relations among constructs by informing the magnitude of association among constructs that might be theoretically separable (or not). For example, I provided the example of a hierarchical organization of the construct of aggression, which might be separated into relational and overt forms (i.e., two lower-order constructs) on theoretical grounds. Meta-analysis can inform whether the constructs are indeed separate by combining correlations from studies containing variables representing these constructs. If the correlation is not different from 1.0 (or −1.0 for constructs that might be conceptualized as opposite ends of a single continuum), then differentiation of the constructs is not supported; however, if the confidence intervals of the correlation do not include ±1.0, then this is evidence supporting their differentiation.[16] For instance, in the full, artifact-corrected meta-analysis of 98 studies reporting associations between relational and overt aggression (this differs from the limited illustrative example above; see Card et al., 2008), we found an average correlation of .76 with a 95% confidence interval ranging from .72 to .79, supporting the separate nature of these two constructs.

12.3.2 Evaluating Associations

As I mentioned in Chapter 5, the most common effect sizes used in meta-analyses are two variable associations, which can be considered between two continuous variables (e.g., r), between a dichotomous grouping variable and a continuous variable (e.g., g), or between two dichotomous variables (o). These associations represent the webbing of the nomological net.

If well-articulated, theories should offer hypotheses about the presence, direction, and strength of various associations among constructs. These hypotheses can directly be tested in a meta-analysis by combining all available empirical evidence. Meta-analytic synthesis provides an authoritative (in that it includes all available empirical evidence) and usually precise (if a large number of studies or studies with large samples are included) estimate of the presence, direction, and magnitude of these associations, and thus play a key role in evaluating hypothesized associations derived from a theory. If you correct for artifacts (see Chapter 6), then it is possible to summarize and evaluate associations among *constructs*, which are more closely linked to theoretically derived hypotheses than potentially imperfectly measured *variables*, as I described earlier.

A focus on associations can also help inform the structure of constructs specified by theories. I described in the previous section how meta-analysis can be used to evaluate whether lower-order constructs *can be* separated (i.e., the correlation between them is smaller than ±1.0). Meta-analysis can also tell us if it is *useful* to separate constructs by evaluating whether they differentially relate to other constructs. If there is no evidence supporting differential relations to relevant constructs,[17] then the separation is not useful even if it is possible (i.e., even if the correlation between the constructs is not ±1.0), whereas differential associations would indicate that the separation of the constructs is both possible and useful. In the meta-analysis of relational and overt aggression, my colleagues and I evaluated associations with six constructs, finding differential relations for each and thus supporting the usefulness of separating these constructs.

Most meta-analyses will only evaluate one or a small number of these hypotheses. Because most useful theories will specify numerous associations (typically more than could be evaluated in a single meta-analysis), a single meta-analysis is unlikely to definitively confirm or refute a theory. Through many separate meta-analyses evaluating different sections of the webbing of the net, however, meta-analysis provides a cumulative approach to gathering evidence for or against a theory.

12.3.3 Evaluating Scope

In the metaphor of the nomological net, the coverage (size and location) of the net represents the scope of phenomena the theory attempts to explain. As I mentioned in Section 12.3.2, a series of meta-analyses can inform empirical support for a theory across this scope, thus showing which sections of the net are sound versus in need of repair.

Meta-analysis can also inform the scope of a theory through moderator analyses. As you recall from Chapter 9, moderator analyses tell us whether the strength, presence, or even direction of associations differs across different types of samples and methodologies used by studies. Theories predicting universal associations would lead to expectations that associations (i.e., the webbing in the net) are consistent across a wide sampling or methodological scope, and therefore moderation is not expected.[18] If moderation is found through meta-analysis, then the theory might need to be limited or modified to account for this nuance in scope. In contrast, some theories explicitly predict changes in associations.[19] Evaluating moderation within a meta-analysis, in which studies may vary more in their sample or methodological features than is often possible in a single study, provides a powerful evaluation of the scope of theories. However, you should still be aware of the samples and methodologies represented among the studies of your meta-analysis in order to accurately describe the scope that you can evaluate versus that which is still uncertain.

12.3.4 Model Building and Evaluation

Perhaps the most powerful approach to comparing competing theories is to evaluate multivariate models predicted by these theories. *Models* are portrayals of how multiple constructs relate to one another in often complex ways. Within the metaphor of the nomological net, associations can be said to be small pieces consisting of a piece of webbing between two knots, whereas models are larger pieces of the net (though usually still just a piece of the net) consisting of several knots and the webbing among them. Because virtually all contemporary theorists have knowledge of a similar body of existing empirical research, different theories will often agree on the presence, direction, and approximate magnitude of a single association.[20] However, theories often disagree as to the relative importance or proximity of causation among the constructs.

These disagreements can often be explicated as competing models, which can then be empirically tested. After specifying these competing models, you then use the methods of multivariate meta-analysis to synthesize the available evidence as sufficient data to fit these competing models (as described earlier in this chapter). Within these models, it is possible to compare relative strengths of association to evaluate which constructs are stronger predictors of others and to pit competing meditational models to evaluate which constructs are more proximal predictors than others. Such model comparisons can empirically evaluate the predictions of competing theories, thus providing relative support for one or another. However, you should also keep in mind that your goal might be less about supporting one theory over the other than about reconciling discrepancies. Toward this goal, meta-analytic moderator analyses can be used to evaluate under what conditions (of samples, methodology, or time) the models derived from each theory are supported. Such conclusions would serve the function of integrating the competing theories into a broader, more encompassing theory.

In the structural equation modeling literature, it is well known that a large number of equivalent models can fit the data equally well (e.g., Mac-Callum, Wegener, Uchino, & Fabrigar, 1993). In other words, you can evaluate the extent to which a particular model explains the meta-analytically derived associations, and even compare multiple models in this regard, but you cannot conclude that this is the only model that explains the associations. Because multivariate meta-analytic synthesis provides a rich set of associations among multiple constructs—perhaps a set not available in any one of the primary studies—these data can be a valuable tool in evaluating alternate models. Although I discourage entirely exploratory data mining, it is useful to explore alternate models that are plausible even if not theoretically derived (as long as you are transparent about the exploratory nature of this endeavor). Such efforts have the potential to yield unexpected models that might suggest new theories. In this regard, meta-analysis is not limited to only evaluating existing theories, but can serve as the beginning of an inductive theory to be evaluated in future research.

12.4 SUMMARY

In this chapter, I have described how you can use meta-analysis to evaluate multivariate models. I first reminded you that most multivariate models can be estimated using correlation matrices, and then I described the general logic and challenges of using meta-analysis to derive these correlation matrices. Next I presented two cutting-edge approaches to performing multivariate meta-analysis, focusing especially on the GLS approach (e.g., Becker, 2009) given its greater current flexibility. I then described the interplay between theory and meta-analysis—a topic relevant to all meta-analyses but especially applicable to multivariate meta-analysis. Specifically, I considered how meta-analyses are informed by, and can be used to evaluate, three pieces of the nomological net metaphor of theories: constructs (knots), associations (webbing), and scope (coverage). Finally, I described the possibilities of evaluating competing theoretically derived models using multivariate meta-analysis.

12.5 RECOMMENDED READINGS

Becker, B. J. (2009). Model-based meta-analysis. In H. Cooper, L. V. Hedges, & J. C. Valentine (Eds.), *The handbook of research synthesis and meta-analysis* (2nd ed., pp. 377–395). New York: Russell Sage Foundation.—This chapter represents a complete overview of the GLS approach to multivariate meta-analysis. Although the approach is technically challenging, this chapter is relatively accessible to readers without extensive statistical training.

Cheung, M. W.-L., & Chan, W. (2005a). Meta-analytic structural equation modeling: A two-stage approach. *Psychological Methods, 10,* 40–64.—This article is the seminal introduction to the MASEM approach. Although I have not emphasized this approach as much as the GLS approach in this chapter, it is worth becoming familiar with this approach, given that advances that address the shortcomings (i.e., necessity of homogeneity; see footnote 9) may be developed in the near future.

Miller, N., & Pollock, V. E. (1994). Meta-analytic synthesis for theory development. In H. Cooper & L. V. Hedges (Eds.), *The handbook of research synthesis* (pp. 457–483). New York: Russell Sage Foundation.—This chapter is one of very few writings devoted entirely to the interplay between theory and meta-analysis. Although my own presentation did not follow that of this chapter closely, this work is a valuable reading for further consideration of this interplay.

NOTES

1. In this section, I do not describe matrix equations for standard error estimates of these parameters in order both to conserve space and to avoid technical complexity. Equations for these standard errors can be found in any intermediate to advanced textbook on multivariate statistics.

2. Description of the computation of eigenvectors is beyond the scope of this book. The computation is covered in most multivariate statistics books (e.g., Appendix A.7 of Tabachnick & Fidell, 1996) and is nearly always performed using a matrix calculator.

3. This number varies by the method of factor analysis. Maximum likelihood factor analysis can extract a maximum number of factors such that the number of parameter estimates (factor loadings, residual variances, factor intercorrelations) is less than or equal to the number of variances and covariances in the input matrix. Principal factors analysis can extract a number of factors one less than the number of variables. Principal components analysis can extract a number of components equal to the number of variables (because the residual variance is assumed to be 0).

4. Keep in mind that EFA (vs. PCA) also models residual variances of the variables. The matrix of residual variances is not shown in this equation for predicted correlations because the expected values of residuals are 0 and traditional EFA does not model correlated residuals.

5. Strictly speaking, an EFA is appropriate when you have no expectations about either the number of factors or which variables are likely to substantially load on ehich factors. I believe that this absence of expectations is rarely the situation. Instead, researchers typically have expectations (perhaps multiple alternative expectations that can be compared) about the number of factors and pattern of strong versus weak loadings. In the latter situation, a confirmatory model such as CFA is more appropriate.

6. This equation is for general CFA in which Σ is a predicted variance/covariance matrix. In meta-analytic CFA, Σ will usually be a predicted correlation matrix (but see Beretvas & Furlow, 2006 for an alternative).

7. Beretvas and Furlow (2006) described an alternative approach, in which you would also meta-analytically combine standard deviations to produce a variance/covariance matrix for analysis. Cheung and Chan (2009) have also described an approach to synthesizing covariance matrices.

8. The following equation (from Kline, 2010) provides the possible values of the correlation between Y and Z (r_{YZ}) given the correlations between X and Y (r_{XY}) and between X and Z (r_{XY}):

$$\left(r_{XY}\, r_{XZ}\right) \pm \sqrt{\left(1 - r_{XY}^2\right)\left(1 - r_{XZ}^2\right)}$$

From the example in the text, where r_{XY} = .80 and r_{XZ} = .70, the range of possible values of r_{YZ} is from .13 to .99.

9. As this book was being finalized, I learned that Mike Cheung is extending his approach to random-effects models. I encourage readers to search for his recent work and his website for updated details.

10. Note that the values for the relational-rejection association do not perfectly agree with previous presentations of these data (e.g., Table 8.1) because the values presented here are *not* corrected for artifacts.

11. An alternative criterion for comparison would be to rely on the practical fit indices provided in CFA. For instance, you might decide that if the restricted (correlations constrained equal) model has acceptable fit (e.g., RMSEA < .08; CFI > .90), then the homogeneity restriction is tenable. You should be aware, however, that this approach to evaluating homogeneity versus heterogeneity differs from the approach I have described elsewhere in the book (Chapter 8) and has not been evaluated.

12. If you read Becker (2009) for further description of this approach, please be aware that there is an error in the printing of this equation (p. 387, Equation 20.2) in which the third through sixth ρ s are not squared).

13. Others have argued that these covariances can and often should be estimated. The solutions proposed are rather technically complex, but interested readers can consult Kalaian and Raudenbush (1996), look for ongoing work by Adam Hafdahl (following Hafdahl, 2009, 2010), or consider adapting a Bayesian approach (Prevost et al., 2007).

14. The possibility of an infinite number of nets is analogous to Popper's (1959) portrayal of theories as being provisional approximations of the world until they are falsified and replaced by theories that better account for observations. For further consideration see Chapter 1 of Cook and Campbell (1979).

15. Of course, existing theories also guide these decisions in the body of primary research. The implication of this fact is that it might not be possible to evaluate a theory through meta-analysis if there do not exist primary studies guided by this theoretical perspective.

16. Here, it would be critical to correct for artifacts so that a 1.0 population correlation does not appear smaller due to attenuation of the effect sizes in the studies.

17. With relevance defined by theoretical propositions of concepts—and in turn constructs—that should have differential relations to the presumably separate constructs.

18. The evaluation of the universality of a theory is valuable only if there is adequate representation of a wide range of samples and methodologies in the literature.

19. For example, some theories of human development describe the concept of *differentiation*, that phenomena become more separate with development, which would predict moderation of the correlation between constructs with age (see e.g., Lerner, 2002, p. 118).

20. Exceptions can exist, however. When theories disagree, it is likely that (1) the theories were put forth before empirical literature existed, (2) the theorists have incomplete knowledge of the available empirical literature, (3) the theorists disagree in the conclusion they reach in synthesizing the literature, or (4) there is imperfect correspondence between the variables used in primary studies and the

constructs specified by either or both theories. Given the advantages of meta-analysis as a method of drawing authoritative conclusions from the existing empirical research (see Chapter 2), meta-analysis is highly valuable in resolving disagreements about a single association arising from the first three sources. With regard to the fourth source, you can carefully code the correspondence between the theoretical construct and the variables used in primary studies and then evaluate meta-analytic moderator analyses to potentially reconcile these conflicting views.

Part IV

The Final Product

Reporting Meta-Analytic Results

13

Writing Meta-Analytic Results

After many long—yet hopefully enjoyable—months of planning your meta-analysis, searching for and retrieving relevant research reports, coding study characteristics and effect sizes from these reports, and then meta-analytically combining and comparing these effect sizes comes what is arguably the most important step: presenting the results to the world. This chapter provides strategies for successfully making this presentation. Specifically, in this chapter I describe the nuts and bolts of writing (or otherwise presenting) your meta-analysis, such as what to report in each section of your report, using figures and tables, and avoiding common problems in writing your results. Before turning to these details, however, it is useful to take a step back and revisit some dimensions along which literature reviews vary.

13.1 DIMENSIONS OF LITERATURE REVIEWS, REVISITED

Before I turn to specific recommendations for writing the results of your meta-analysis, it is important for you to recognize that there is no single "right" way to write these results. As I described in Chapter 1 (see also Cooper, 1988), literature reviews vary along several dimensions. Before you begin to write the results of your meta-analysis, you should have a clear understanding of the goals, organization, and audience for this report.

13.1.1   Goals of Meta-Analysis

You began the meta-analysis with some goal in mind, and it is important that you keep this goal in mind as you write your report. As I described in Chapter 2 (see also Cooper, 1988), the goal of conducting a meta-analytic review (indeed, most literature reviews) is usually that of integration. However, this general goal of integration entails at least two subgoals (see Cooper, 1988).

One aspect of integration is generalization from specific instances. For example, the example meta-analysis I have described throughout this book (involving the association between relational aggression and peer rejection) relied on a number of studies, each specific in terms of age of the sample, method of measuring relational aggression, and a number of other features. By combining results (Chapters 8 and 10) across these specific instances (studies), it is possible to make statements that are more generalized, albeit within the bounds of the population defined by the studies represented in the meta-analysis. This generalization is not made uncritically, however. Through the comparison of studies (i.e., moderator analyses; Chapter 9) that differ on conceptually relevant characteristics, it is possible to empirically evaluate where findings can (absence of moderation) and cannot (presence of moderation) be generalized.

A second aspect of integration involves the resolution of conflicting findings or conclusions. Often, conflicting conclusions come from only seemingly conflicting findings from the Null Hypothesis Significance Testing (NHST) Framework, as I illustrated in Chapter 5. In these cases, meta-analysis, which focuses on effect sizes across studies rather than conclusions regarding statistical significance, typically provides considerable clarity. In other cases, conflicting findings (and resulting conflicting conclusions) might not really be conflicting, but simply due to sampling fluctuations. Here, formal tests of heterogeneity of effect sizes (Chapter 8) will provide clearer conclusions about whether findings are truly conflicting. Finally, results might truly be conflicting (effect sizes are heterogeneous); here, meta-analytic results still have much to offer. One approach would be to accept this conflicting evidence (i.e., heterogeneous effect sizes), yet still offer the best generalizable answer through random-effects models (Chapter 8). Alternatively, you might use meta-analytic approaches to go beyond the *existence* of conflicting findings (i.e., reporting the random-effects mean) to evaluate the *sources* of conflicting findings through moderator analyses (Chapter 9).[1]

Although the goal of your meta-analysis likely involves one or both of these aspects of integration, this does not have to be your only goal in writing the results of your review. Other goals of literature reviews include (1) critiquing the body of research that you have reviewed and (2) identifying key directions for future conceptual, methodological, and empirical work (see Chapter 2 and Cooper, 1988). Although neither of these goals is directly met by the techniques of meta-analysis, they are certainly goals that you, the author (and the person who has just carefully studied the available literature), can certainly address in your writing.

13.1.2   Organization of the Meta-Analysis

The results of simple meta-analyses (i.e., those reporting only mean effect sizes and a limited number of moderators analyses from a single sample of studies) have less flexibility as to how they can be organized. However, more complex meta-analytic reviews (i.e., those with many moderator analyses or those comprised of several discrete meta-analyses of different samples of empirical literature) can be organized in various ways. Cooper (1988) stated that literature reviews are commonly organized in three ways: historically (i.e., studies reviewing the progress of a field of study across time), conceptually (i.e., studies addressing a common idea or question are organized together), or methodologically (i.e., studies with similar methodological or measurement approaches are organized together). Although each of these organizational approaches is an option, you are most likely to organize the results of your meta-analytic review either conceptually or methodologically. To illustrate a conceptual organization, the manuscript containing the example meta-analytic review I have used throughout this book (Card et al., 2008) reported results of eight separate meta-analyses: one meta-analysis investigating gender differences in relational aggression, a second meta-analysis investigating the association of relational aggression with overt forms of aggression, and six smaller meta-analysis investigating associations of relational aggression with six distinct adjustment correlates. To illustrate a methodological organization, a meta-analysis might separately report results of concurrent naturalistic, longitudinal naturalistic, and experimental studies of a particular effect.

13.1.3   Audience for the Meta-Analysis

Given that I have characterized the writing of your meta-analysis as "presenting the results to the world," it makes sense that you would want to have in mind who is in that world—in other words, your intended audience. The potential audience for meta-analyses varies in terms of both their knowledge of the topic you have focused on and their familiarity with meta-analytic techniques. Scientists specializing in the area of your review are likely familiar with the terminology and theoretical perspectives, so they typically need less introduction and guidance in these areas (though you should not neglect this entirely). However, they may be unfamiliar with meta-analytic techniques, depending on the prevalence of meta-analyses in your particular field. Scientists outside of your specialized area will need more introduction to the topic area and may or may not be familiar with meta-analytic techniques. Practitioners, policymakers, and educated laypeople will almost universally need more didactic explanation of your topic and meta-analytic techniques.

Complicating matters even further, it is likely that your presentation will reach multiple audiences. If you decide that the only readers you care to inform are specialists in your field who are familiar with meta-analysis—and you write your report only for this audience—you should realize that you are probably targeting a very small audience, and the likelihood that your report will be published in a widely read outlet is small. Even if you decide to target a broader range of scientists within your field, you should recognize that others (e.g., educators, practitioners, policymakers) may read your report. Therefore, you are diminishing the potential impact of your review if it is not accessible to a broader audience of readers.

Conversely, you should be aware that some of the details that can be confusing and intimidating to readers unfamiliar with meta-analysis would be the very details that some readers (those very familiar with meta-analysis) will expect to see. The challenge, then, is to effect a balance between (1) providing enough technical details for content experts familiar with meta-analysis to evaluate your work, versus (2) not overwhelming other readers with *too much* technical detail. Although this can be a difficult line to walk, and it is likely that you cannot make 100% of readers 100% happy, I do think the following principles can help achieve this balance.

First, ask yourself what you find more discouraging when you read a report: (1) when you simply cannot understand what the authors have done, or (2) the authors provide what seems to be excessive detail of what they have done. My own reaction, and I suspect the reaction of many of you, is that it is better to be bored by too much detail than confused by too little. Following this principle, my suggestion is that it is better to report a potentially important piece of information than to omit it.

My recommendation that you err on the side of reporting too much rather than too little comes with a corollary: You do not have to report everything in the narrative text of your manuscript. Depending on the editorial style of your publication outlet, it may be preferable to place some details in tables, footnotes, appendices, or supplemental online documents. Doing so allows interested readers to evaluate these details, but does not distract attention for other readers. If space restrictions at your publication outlet preclude these options, then noting that full results are available upon request (and then providing them upon request) is an option.

My third recommendation is to write at multiple levels. What I mean by writing at multiple levels is that your text has pieces that make it understandable to audiences with a broad range of background in your topic and in meta-analysis. How you accomplish this is to provide a clear, jargon-free statement that is understandable to a broad audience in tandem with more technical details. For example, technical details can be placed in parentheses, as in the following: "Associations between relational aggression and peer rejection are stronger among studies using peer reports of relational aggression than those using observations (mean rs = .34 versus .09, $\chi^2_{(df=1)}$ = 21.05, p < .001)." Similarly, you might ensure that each paragraph containing technical information consists of (1) a clear first sentence of what you evaluated, (2) one or more sentences reporting the detailed (technical) results, and (3) a clear final sentence or two stating what you found in jargon-free terms. I do not intend these to be absolute rules; rather they are my own suggestions for accomplishing the difficult task of writing at multiple levels.

13.2   WHAT TO REPORT AND WHERE TO REPORT IT

In this section, I discuss the basic structural sections of a manuscript and special considerations in reporting meta-analytic results within these sections. Two caveats are in order here. First, I expect that you are aware of the ways that manuscripts (whether primary studies or meta-analyses) are structured within your field, in terms of what the goals of each section are, expectations about typical length, and writing conventions (e.g., as described in the American Psychological Association, 2009, *Publication Manual*). Second, I want to point out that in many ways, reports of meta-analyses are *not* different from reports of primary research. Your goal is still to provide an empirically grounded exposition that adds meaningful knowledge to your field, and the manuscript reporting your meta-analysis should make this exposition in a similar way as you would when reporting results of a primary research study.

I next outline sections of a manuscript following a structure commonly found in social science research reports: the title, introduction, method, results, discussion, references, and appendices sections. Even if your field typically uses a different structure for reporting empirical findings, I believe that these suggestions will still be useful to consider and adapt to the reporting practices in your field.

13.2.1 Title

As with any manuscript, the title of your meta-analysis should be an accurate and concise statement of your research goals, questions, or findings. Your title should therefore reflect the substantive focus of your review, which is reflected by the constructs comprising the effect sizes included in your meta-analysis. I think it is also preferable to indicate that your manuscript is a meta-analysis (or similar terms such as "meta-analytic review," "quantitative review," or "quantitative research synthesis"; see Chapter 1). Clearly denoting this is likely to draw the reader's attention.

13.2.2 Introduction

The introduction section of a report of a meta-analysis tries to accomplish the same goals as the introduction of any empirical paper: to provide a background in theory, methods, prior findings, or unresolved questions that orients readers to the goals, research questions, or hypotheses of your meta-analytic review. In presenting this case for a meta-analytic review, it is important to provide support for all aspects of your study selection and analyses. In terms of study selection, your introduction should make a clear case for why the population of studies—in terms of sample, measurement, design, and source characteristics—that you defined in your meta-analysis are important for study. Similarly, your introduction should provide a rationale for all of the analyses you report in the results section. For instance, providing evidence for a range of research findings could be useful in building the case for the uncertainty of typical findings and the need to combine these results in a meta-analysis to obtain a clearer understanding of these typical findings. If there is considerable variability in findings, as noted by previous scholars in your field and later in the findings of significant heterogeneity in your meta-analysis, then this is often motivation to perform moderator analyses (though see Chapters 8 and 9 for cautions). Of course, when you planned your meta-analysis, you made decisions about what study characteristics to code and eventually consider as moderators; you should describe the conceptual rationale for these potential moderators in your manuscript to ground and support the decisions to evaluate these moderators. In short, every decision you made in terms of defining a population of studies and analyses should be previously supported with a rationale in the introduction section of your manuscript.

13.2.3 Method

The method section of your manuscript is where reporting practices become somewhat unique for meta-analyses versus primary research. Nevertheless, the same goals apply: to explain your research process in explicit enough detail that a reader fully understands what you have done to the point where he or she could, in principle, perfectly replicate your study (meta-analysis) based solely on what you have written. Next, I describe four general aspects of your methodology that you should report.

13.2.3.a Literature Search Procedures

As I described in Chapter 3, the quality of a meta-analysis is substantially impacted by the extent to which the included studies adequately represent the population about which you wish to draw conclusions. The adequacy of this representation is in turn determined by the quality of your literature search. For this reason, it is important to explicitly describe your literature search procedures. For example, if you used electronic databases as one search strategy (and virtually every modern meta-analysis will), then it is important to detail the databases searched, the key words used (including wildcard characters), any logical operations (e.g., "and," "or"), and the date of your last searches of these databases. You should provide similarly detailed descriptions of other search strategies (e.g., journals or conference programs searched and time span considered). Of course, it is preferable to provide brief rationales for these searches (e.g., "In order to identify unpublished studies ... ") rather than merely list your search strategies.

13.2.3.b Study Inclusion and Exclusion Criteria

I mentioned in the previous subsection that the quality of a meta-analysis is impacted by whether the studies represent a population. This statement implies that the reader needs to have a clear idea of what the population is, which is defined by the inclusion and exclusion criteria you have specified. Therefore, it is critical that you clearly state your inclusion criteria that define the population of interest, as well as exclusion criteria that delineate the outer boundaries of what your population does not include. In Chapter 3, I suggested that, before searching the literature, you specify a set of inclusion and exclusion criteria. I also indicated that these criteria may need to be modified as you search the literature and begin coding studies as unexpected situations arise. In the method section of your report, you should fully detail these inclusion and exclusion criteria, specifying which criteria you specified a priori (before searching and coding) and which you specified post hoc (while searching and coding). I note here that these inclusion and exclusion criteria explicate the *intended* sampling frame of your meta-analysis (see Chapter 3); it will also be important to address how well the studies *actually covered* this sampling frame in the results section (see Section 13.2.4.a).

13.2.3.c   Coding of Study Characteristics and Effect Sizes

As you know by this point in your efforts, many decisions must be made while coding the studies that comprise your meta-analysis. It is important that you fully describe this coding process for readers. Three general aspects of the coding process that you should describe are the coding of study characteristics, the coding of effect sizes, and evidence of the reliability of your coding decisions.

As I described in Chapter 4, you could potentially code for a wide range of study characteristics in your meta-analysis. Whereas you have (or should have) provided a rationale for these study characteristics in the introduction section, here in the method section your task is to explicitly operationalize the characteristics you have coded. At a minimum, you should list the characteristics you coded, defining each term as necessary given the background of your audience and defining each of the possible values for each characteristic. For some characteristics (usually the "low-inference codes"; Chapter 4, Cooper, 2009a), this description can be very brief. For example, in describing "age" in the example meta-analysis I have described throughout this book, I might write "Age was coded as the mean age in years of the sample." For other characteristics (especially "high-inference codes"; Chapter 4, Cooper, 2009a), the description may need to be considerably more extensive. For example, in describing the study characteristic "source of information" in this meta-analysis, it might (depending on the audience's familiarity with these measurement practices) be necessary for me to write a sentence or two for each of the possible codes (e.g., "Self-reports were defined as any scale in which the child provided information about his or her own frequency of relational aggression, including paper-and-pencil questionnaires, responses to online surveys, and individual interviews"). Coding of even higher inference characteristics, such as "study quality" (see Chapter 4) might require multiple paragraphs. With many coded study characteristics, especially those requiring extensive descriptions, full description of all of these characteristics could take considerable space. Depending on the audience's knowledge of your field and the space available in your publication outlet, it may be useful to present some of these details in a table or an appendix, or make them available upon request. However, the suggestion I offered earlier might be useful: When in doubt, err on the side of reporting too much rather than too little.

You should also describe your coding of effect sizes (Chapter 5) and any artifact corrections you perform (Chapter 6). In terms of describing your coding of effect sizes, you should be sure to answer three key questions. First, how do the signs of the effect size represent directions of results? For instance, in a meta-analysis of gender differences, it is important to specify whether positive effect sizes denote females or males scoring higher. Second, what effect size did you use and why? If you used a standard effect size (i.e., r, g or d, o), then it is usually sufficient to just state this (though you should keep the audience in mind). However, if you use an advanced or unique effect size (Chapter 7), you will usually need to further justify and describe this effect size. The third question you should be sure to answer is: How did you manage the various methods of reporting effects in the literature to obtain a common effect size? If you are writing to an audience that is somewhat familiar with meta-analysis, you can likely refer them to an external source (such as this book) for details of most computations. However, you should be especially clear about how you handled situations in which studies provided inadequate information. For example, did you assume the lower-bound effect size for studies reporting only that an effect was significant, and did you assume effect sizes of zero (or 1 for odds ratios) for studies reporting that an effect was nonsignificant? In these latter cases, it may be useful to report the percentage of effect sizes for which you made lower-bound estimates to give the reader a sense of the potential biasing effects.

Finally, you should provide evidence of the reliability of your coding, following the guidelines I offered in Chapter 4. Specifically, report how you determined reliability (intercoder and/or intracoder; number of studies doubly coded), and the results of these reliability evaluations. If reliabilities of coding decisions were very consistent across codes (i.e., various study characteristics and effect sizes), then it is acceptable to report a range; however, if there was variability, you should report reliabilities for each of your codes separately. If initial reliability estimates were poor and led to modification of your coding protocol, you should transparently report this fact. Finally, you should offer some evaluation of whether or not you believe the reliability of coding was adequate (if it was not, then it will be useful to address this limitation in the discussion section of your report).

13.2.3.d Data-Analytic Strategy

Because meta-analytic techniques are unfamiliar to many readers in many fields, and because there are differences in analytic practices among different meta-analysts, it is important that you clearly state your data-analytic strategies. If extensive description is needed, I prefer to describe these strategies as a distinct subsection of the manuscript, usually at the end of the method section, but sometimes at the beginning of the results section (you should read some articles in your field that use meta-analytic techniques, or other advanced techniques that require description, to see where this material is typically placed). Alternatively, if you can adequately describe your techniques concisely, and many readers in your field are at least somewhat familiar with meta-analysis, then you might decide to omit this section and instead provide these details throughout the results section before you present the results of each analysis.

There are at least five key elements of your data-analytic strategy that you should specify. First, you should describe how you managed multiple effect sizes from studies (see Chapter 8). Second, you should specify which weights you used for studies in your meta-analysis (e.g., inverse squared standard errors; Chapter 8). If your audience is entirely unfamiliar with meta-analysis, you might also provide justification for these weights (see Chapter 8). Third, you should describe the process of analyzing the central tendencies of effect sizes. For instance, did you base your decision to use a fixed- versus random-effects model on the results of an initial heterogeneity test, or did you make an a priori decision to use one or the other (see Chapter 10)? Fourth, you should describe your process and method of moderator analyses. Specifically, you should describe (1) whether your decision to pursue moderator analyses was guided by initial findings of heterogeneity; (2) the order in which you evaluated multiple moderators (e.g., one at a time, all at once, or some conceptually-based sequence); (3) if you followed a sequence of moderator analyses, whether you used residual heterogeneity tests along the way to decide to continue or to stop; and (4) what approach to moderator analysis you used (e.g., ANOVA- or regression-based?). Finally, you should make clear how you evaluated potential publication bias (see Chapter 11).

13.2.4 Results

As you might expect, the results section of the report contains some information unique from that in the results section of a primary study. At the same time, the underlying goal is the same in both: to accurately and clearly report the findings of your analyses to provide illumination of the research questions/hypotheses that motivated the study/meta-analysis. In this section, I describe four pieces of information that will generally be present in your results. I do not necessarily intend to suggest how you should organize your results section; for a single, relatively simple meta-analysis, this organization might be useful, but for a more complex meta-analysis or a review with several meta-analyses, you will likely follow a more conceptual or methodological organization as I described earlier.

13.2.4.a Descriptive Information

An important set of results, yet one that is often overlooked, is simply the description of the sample of studies that comprised your meta-analytic review. This information can often be summarized in a table, but the importance of this information merits at least a paragraph, if not an entire subsection, near the beginning of your results section. If your report includes multiple meta-analyses, it might be useful to report this descriptive information for both the overall collection of studies (i.e., all studies included in any of your meta-analyses) and the subsets of studies that comprised each meta-analysis.

Necessary descriptive information to report includes the number of studies (usually denoted by k), as well as the total number of participants in these studies (N, which is the sum of the Ns across the studies). I also strongly advise that you report the number of studies at different levels of coded study characteristics used in moderator analyses. For categorical characteristics, this is simply the number of studies with each value, whereas for continuous characteristics, you might report the means, standard deviations, and ranges. If your initial coding protocol included study characteristics that you ultimately did not use as moderators because of a lack of variability in values across studies, I suggest also reporting this information.

In addition to reporting this descriptive information, it is worth writing some comments about these data, as they describe both the sample for your meta-analysis and the state of the empirical literature in your field. For instance, it is useful to note if some values of your moderators are underrepresented in the existing literature (e.g., few studies have sampled certain types of individuals, few studies have used a particular methodology), or if certain combinations of moderators (e.g., particular methodologies with certain types of individuals) are underrepresented. It is also useful to comment on study characteristics that did not vary, and potentially to discuss the implications of this homogeneity in the discussion. In short, it is useful to describe the nature of the sample of studies (and by implication, the field of your meta-analysis), and to point out the sampling, measurement, and methodological strengths and shortcomings of this body of research.

13.2.4.b Central Tendencies and Heterogeneity

Turning to the analytic results, most reports describe the results of central tendency and heterogeneity tests before the results of moderator analyses. Regarding central tendency, or (usually) mean effect sizes, you should clearly state whether the mean was obtained through fixed- or random-effects models, the standard error of this mean effect size, and the (typically 95%) confidence interval of this mean. Although the confidence interval generally suffices for significance testing, you might also choose to report the statistical significance of this effect size. In reporting these results, be sure to provide "words" that help readers make sense of the "numbers." Put differently, avoid simply listing means, confidence intervals, and the like, but rather provide narrative descriptions of them. For instance, it might be useful to some readers to have the direction of association described (e.g., to interpret a positive mean correlation: "Higher levels of relational aggression are associated with higher peer rejection"), and it is usually useful to characterize the magnitude of effect sizes according to standards in your field or else commonly applied guidelines (e.g., Cohen, 1969, characterization of $rs \approx \pm.10$, .30, and .50 as small, medium, and large, respectively).

In addition to the mean effect size, it is important to describe the heterogeneity of effect size to give readers a sense of the consistency versus variability as well as range of findings. Although you will almost certainly report the results of the heterogeneity test, the Q statistic described in Chapter 8 (Section 8.4), you should bear in mind the limits of this statistic given that it is a statistical significance test (i.e., it can have very high or low statistical power). For this reason, it may be useful to supplement reporting of the Q statistic with a description of the magnitude of heterogeneity. One possibility might be to describe quantitatively the magnitude of this heterogeneity by reporting the I^2 index. Another possibility might be to visually display the heterogeneity using one of the figures I describe in Section 13.3. With either approach, it is important to describe (again, using words) this homogeneity or heterogeneity, and how this information was used in decisions regarding other analyses (e.g., to use random-effects models, to perform moderator analyses).

13.2.4.c   Moderator Analyses

If moderator analyses are conducted in your meta-analysis (and most meta-analyses will involve some moderator analyses), then it is important to fully report these results. Specifically, you should report the Q statistic, degrees of freedom, and significance level for each moderator analysis you perform (whether performed within an ANOVA or a regression framework; see Chapter 9). It is also common to report the within-group or residual heterogeneity (Q) remaining after accounting for this moderator or set of moderators. For categorical moderators with more than two levels, it is also necessary to report results of follow-up comparisons (see Chapter 9).

You should not stop at reporting only the significance tests of your moderator analyses; it is also important to report the numbers of studies and the typical effect sizes at various levels of the moderators. For a single categorical moderator this is straightforward: You simply report the numbers of studies and mean effect sizes within each of the levels of the moderator. For multiple categorical moderators, you should report the numbers of studies and mean effect sizes within the various combinations across the multiple moderator variables. For continuous moderators, it is *not* advisable to artificially categorize the continuous moderator variable and then report information (numbers of studies and mean effect sizes) within these artificial groups, though this practice is sometimes followed. Instead, I suggest using the intercept and regression coefficient(s) of your regression-based moderator analysis to compute predicted effect sizes at different levels of the moderator, and then report these predicted effect sizes across a range of the moderator variable values well-covered by the studies in your meta-analysis. In Chapter 9 (Section 9.2), I presented an example in which effect sizes of the association between relational aggression and peer rejection were predicted by (i.e., moderated by) the mean ages of the samples, and I computed the expected effect sizes for the ages 5, 10, and 15 years (intuitive values that represented the span of most studies in the meta-analysis).

Before concluding my suggestions for reporting moderator analysis results, I want to remind you of a key threat to moderator analysis in meta-analytic reviews: that the variable you have identified as the moderator is not the "true" moderator in that it is only associated with or serves as a proxy for the true moderator. If alternate potential moderators are study characteristics that you have coded, then it is important to report results either (1) ruling out these alternative explanations, or (2) showing that the variable you believe is the true moderator is predictive of effect sizes after controlling for the alternative moderator variables (see Section 9.4). You should report these findings in the results section. However, it is also worth considering that you can never definitively determine whether the moderator variable you have identified is the true moderator, or whether it simply serves as a proxy for another, uncoded study characteristic that is the true moderator. This is a limitation that should be considered in the discussion section of your report.

13.2.4.d Diagnostic Analyses

Earlier (Chapters 2, 11) I described the widely known threat to meta-analyses (and all other literature reviews) posed by publication bias. Given that this threat is both widely known and potentially severely biasing to results of a meta-analysis, it is important to report evidence evaluating this threat. Specifically, you should report your efforts (1) to evaluate the presence of this threat, such as moderator analyses, funnel plots, or regression analyses; (2) show how plausible it is that there could exist enough missed literature with zero results so as to invalidate your conclusions (i.e., various failsafe numbers); and (3) and detail the approaches you used to correct for this potential bias (e.g., trim and fill, weighted selection) (see Chapter 11). After providing all available evidence regarding potential publication bias, you should offer the reader a clear statement of how likely publication bias may have impacted your findings.

13.2.5 Discussion

The discussion section of your report should place the findings of your meta-analytic review in the context of your field. Whereas it is tempting to let the numbers speak for themselves, do not assume that they speak to the reader. Although the discussion section likely allows the most liberty in terms of writing (you can think of it as your opportunity to add the "qualitative finesse" that some critics have charged is absent from meta-analyses; see Chapter 2), you should consider including at least four components of this section. I discuss each of these components next in an order in which they commonly (though not necessarily) appear in discussion sections of meta-analytic reports.

13.2.5.a Review of Findings

Although you should be careful to avoid extensive repetition of results in the discussion section, it is sometimes useful to provide a brief overview of key findings, especially if the results section was long, technical, or complex. It is useful to highlight the findings that you will most extensively discuss in this section, though you should certainly not omit findings that were unexpected or contradictory to your hypotheses (these are typically important to consider further).

13.2.5.b   Explanations and Implications of Findings

You should remember that the main purpose of your meta-analytic review was to answer some research questions, which presumably are important to your field in some way. The majority of your efforts in the discussion section should be directed to describing how your results provide these answers (when they do) and how these answers increase understanding within your field. For instance, do the findings of your review provide answers that support existing theory, support one theory over another, or suggest the need for refinement of existing theories in your field? Do the answers inform policy or practice in your field?

While providing answers to these questions is useful, you should also recognize the limits to the information provided by the existing research that comprised your review. This recognition can guide where more primary empirical research is needed, and it is important for your review to identify this need. For example, if you could not reach reasonably definitive conclusions to some of your research questions due to low statistical power (resulting from few studies or studies with small sample sizes), then you should state the need for further research to inform this question. Your descriptive summary of study characteristics also speaks to the types of studies that have not been performed (e.g., specific sample characteristics, measurement characteristics, etc., and combinations of these characteristics). Conversely, if you find that a large number of studies (or a number of studies with large samples) using very similar samples, measures, and the like, have been performed, and that the results are homogeneous and provide a very precise estimate of this effect size, then it is also valuable to state that more studies of this type are *not* needed (better that future research invest efforts toward providing new information). In short, I encourage you to remember that you have just spent months carefully studying and meta-analyzing nearly all of the work in the area of your meta-analysis, so you are in a very informed position to say where the field needs to go; it is a valuable contribution for you to make clear statements that guide these future efforts.

13.2.5.c   Limitations

As when you are reporting the results of any empirical study, it is important for you to acknowledge the limitations of your meta-analytic review.

Some of these limitations may be the shortcomings of the available empirical basis, and I have already encouraged you to make clear statements of what these limitations are. Other limitations are particular to literature reviews (including meta-analyses), such as the limitations of drawing conclusions about moderator variables and potential publication bias. You should also make clear limitations to what can be inferred from the types of studies and effect sizes you have included in your meta-analysis. For instance, you should describe the limitations to inferring causality from effect sizes from concurrent naturalistic studies (see Chapter 2). For every limitation you identify, I encourage you to provide a rationale for why this limitation is more or less threatening to your conclusions, and how future research might resolve these issues (this piece of advice is relevant for any research report, not just those using meta-analyses).

13.2.5.d Conclusions

Given the often high impact and broad readership of reports of meta-analyses, it is critical that your text conclude with a clear statement of how your meta-analytic review advances understanding, and why this advancement is important.

13.2.6 References

As with any other scholarly report, your meta-analytic review will include a list of references. Although typical practices vary across disciplines, I note two practices that are common in the field of Psychology (as described in the American Psychological Association, 2009, *Publication Manual*) and in many other areas social science. First, all of the studies included in your meta-analysis should be included in your reference list. Second, the first line of your reference section (after the "Reference" heading but before the first reference) should contain a statement such as "Studies preceded by an asterisk were included in the meta-analysis"; and then you should place an asterisk before the reference of the studies that were included in your meta-analytic review.

13.2.7 Appendices

Different journals have different standards and preferences for material being included in the main body of the text, in appendices printed at the end of the article, or (more recently) in appendices available through the journal's website. Depending on the practices of your targeted journal, however, it might be useful to consider using appendices for some of the lengthier information that is important to report yet not of interest to many readers. For instance, tables summarizing the coding of all studies included in your meta-analysis (see Section 13.3.2) are important because they allow readers to judge the completeness of your review and your coding practices; however, such tables are lengthy and often of peripheral interest to many readers. These tables might ideally be placed in an appendix rather than in the text proper.

13.3   USING TABLES AND FIGURES IN REPORTING META-ANALYSES

Tables and figures, if used effectively, can provide a large amount of data in an informative way, as well as reduce the burden of describing all of this information within the text (though you should not omit key findings from the text just because they are also displayed in tables or figures). In this section, I describe some approaches to presenting meta-analytic results in tables and in figures. I supplement description of each approach I describe by considering the relative frequencies of their use in a recent survey of meta-analyses published from 2000 to 2005 by Borman and Grigg (2009).[2]

13.3.1   Tables

There are two general types of tables used to summarize results of meta-analytic reviews: tables presenting summary information such as mean effect sizes, and tables summarizing coded aspects of the individual studies included in the meta-analysis. The use of both tables is common; in the survey by Borman and Grigg (2009), these tables were included in 74% and 89%, respectively, of published meta-analyses.

13.3.1.a   Summary Tables

Summary tables can be used to report aggregate information obtained from meta-analytic combination and comparison of multiple studies. This information can include information about the central tendency of effect sizes (e.g., mean, median), the distribution of these effect sizes (range, heterogeneity tests, indices of heterogeneity such as I^2), and results of moderator analyses. If your review contains a single meta-analysis (i.e., all studies included in a single meta-analysis), this table will likely be rather narrow, so you should consider if such a table is worth the space beyond summarizing such information in the text. However, if your review includes several meta-analyses (i.e., a series of meta-analyses of separate effect sizes), this table will be wider and contain a wealth of information more concisely summarized than can be done in text. Summary tables are especially useful in these latter situations.

Table 13.1 illustrates one of many ways (and not the only way) you might organize a summary table. Here, I summarize results for the ongoing example meta-analysis used throughout this book involving associations between relational aggression and peer rejection. The first two rows display results of the heterogeneity test and its significance (denoted by asterisks) and the I^2 index to quantify the magnitude of heterogeneity. The next two rows display the random-effects mean effect size (with significance level) and confidence intervals around these means. The remaining rows display the results of two moderator analyses: the categorical moderator "reporter" and the continuous moderator age. After reporting the omnibus test ($Q_{between}$) of the categorical moderator, I report the mean associations within each group (type of reporter),[3] denoting significant differences between groups with alphabetic subscripts. For the continuous moderator variable (age), I report its signifi-

TABLE 13.1. Summary Table of Meta-Analyses of Associations of Relational and Overt Aggression with Peer Rejection

	Relational aggression with peer rejection
Heterogeneity (Q; $df = 21$)	291.17***
I^2	92.8%
Random-effects mean r	.33***
95% confidence interval	.24 to .40
Moderator effects	
Reporter ($Q_{b(3)}$)	65.14***
Observation ($k = 3$)	.10$_a$
Parent ($k = 1$)	.52***$_c$
Peer ($k = 3$)	.38***$_b$
Self ($k = 0$)	—
Teacher ($k = 6$)	.19***$_a$
Age ($Q_{regression(1)}$)	9.31**
β_{Zr}	−.011
$\hat{r}$ at 5, 10, and 15 years	.41, .37, .22

Note. Significant differences among reporters from follow-up comparisons are denoted by different alphabetic subscripts.
*$p < .05$; **$p < .01$; ***$p < .001$.

cance ($Q_{regression}$), followed by the unstandardized regression coefficient and predicted correlations at various meaningful values of the moderator. This table could be expanded in various ways, such as by including additional rows to report the results of more moderator analyses (including comparisons of published vs. unpublished studies to evaluate publication bias), or by adding additional columns to report the results of other meta-analyses (e.g., Card et al., 2008, also reported results involving associations of overt forms of aggression with peer rejection, as well as associations of relational aggression with various other aspects of adjustment).

13.3.1.b Tables of Individual Studies

It is very useful—and arguably even necessary—to provide a detailed listing of the values you coded for each of the studies included in your meta-analytic review. This sort of table should report, for each of the studies included in your meta-analytic review, basic citation information for the study (e.g., authors, year), sample size, your coding for all of the study characteristics used in your review (for either descriptive purposes or in moderator analyses), and effect sizes. If you performed any artifact adjustments (see Chapter 6), the artifact information (e.g., reliability estimates, dichotomizations) should also be reported.

The most common order of studies within this type of table is to list studies either alphabetically by author names or else chronologically by year of publication. Although such ordering is useful for readers to find a particular study or to see if any studies were excluded, it is not necessarily the most informative approach (Borman & Grigg, 2009). A preferable way to organize these tables is likely according to some important characteristics of studies, such as by moderator variables found to be important in your meta-analyses.

To illustrate this sort of table, Table 13.2 presents coded details of the studies used in the meta-analysis on relational aggression and peer rejection. Here, I have organized studies first by reporter (one of the moderator variables) and then by age (another moderator variable). You can see that this table contains a row for each study,[4] columns for each study characteristic coded, and the coded effect size.

13.3.2 Figures

The statement "a picture is worth a thousand words" is a cliché but nevertheless, it is true: Thoughtful use of figures to present meta-analytic results is

TABLE 13.2. Example Table Reporting Coding of Individual Studies

Study	Sample size (N)	Method	Age (years)	Effect size (r)
Ostrov (under review)[a]	139	Obs.	3.6	.181
Ostrov & Crick (2007)	132	Obs.	4.1	.049
Ostrov et al. (2004)[b]	60	Obs.	4.6	.000
Blachman (2003)	228	Parent	9.2	.525
Crick et al. (1997)	65	Peer	4.5	.443
Nelson et al. (2005)	180	Peer	4.8	.090
Johnson (2003)	74	Peer	6.0	.531
Henington (1996)	904	Peer	7.5	.336
Geiger (2003)	458	Peer	8.0	.554
Werner (2000)	881	Peer	8.0	.477
Werner & Crick (2004)	517	Peer	8.0	.469
Phillipsen et al. (1999)	262	Peer	8.7	−.048
Murray-Close & Crick (2006)	590	Peer	9.0	.575
Tomada & Schneider (1997)	314	Peer	9.0	.313
Crick & Grotpeter (1995)	491	Peer	9.4	.198
Leff (1995)	151	Peer	9.5	.617
Rys & Bear (1997)	266	Peer	9.5	.556
Pakaslahti & Keltikangas-Järvinen (1998)	839	Peer	14.5	.326
Hawley et al. (2007)	929	Peer	14.7	.161
Salmivalli et al. (2000)	209	Peer	15.5	.253
Miller (2001)	150	Peer	16.0	.557
Ostrov (under review)[a]	139	Teacher	3.6	.513
Crick et al. (1997)	65	Teacher	4.5	.167
Nelson et al. (2005)	180	Teacher	4.8	−.011
Johnson (2003)	74	Teacher	6.0	.074
Tomada & Schneider (1997)	314	Teacher	9.0	.000[b]
Rys & Bear (1997)	266	Teacher	9.5	.338

[a]Article was under review during the preparation of this meta-analytic review. It has subsequently been published as Ostrov (2008).
[b]Effect size is lower-bound estimate based on author's reporting only nonsignficant associations.

an efficient way to present a large amount of information, including information about central tendency and variability in effect sizes, moderator effects, publication bias, and potential outlier studies. I next describe three types of figures that you can consider in presenting results of your meta-analysis, considering the type of information that is conveyed in each type of figure.

13.3.2.a   Forest Plots

These plots are rarely used in social sciences, though they are common in research syntheses of medical trials (Borman & Grigg, 2009). These plots, such as those illustrated in Figure 13.1, are formed by listing the studies included in the meta-analysis down the left side of the figure. The area to the right of each study displays information about the mean (filled circles) and 95% confidence intervals (horizontal lines) for each study in the meta-analysis. The thick vertical line represents the (weighted) mean of these effect sizes. Although it is not done in every instance, I have also included a vertical (dashed) line to indicate the null result of $r = .00$ to illustrate which studies yield significant effect sizes.

Forrest plots portray a range of information. First, they present information regarding both the point estimate and uncertainty of effect sizes from every study in your meta-analysis, serving a useful summary function similar to tables of individual studies. Second, the inclusion of the vertical line for the mean effect size makes this information apparent. Third, this plot provides visual information regarding the heterogeneity of studies. Observing that several (more than the approximately 1 in 20 expectable by chance) of the study confidence intervals do not contain the common mean effect size (vertical line) serves as visual evidence of significant heterogeneity, and the range of these study-specific effect sizes around this vertical provides some indication of the variability in these effect sizes. Although not apparent in Figure 13.1, this forest plot would also be useful for detecting studies with extreme effect sizes (far to the left or right of other studies with confidence intervals not approaching the rest of the studies).

The basic forest plot such as the one I have shown in Figure 13.1 can be extended in several ways (see Borman & Grigg, 2009). For instance, the studies could be ordered in some meaningful way rather than alphabetically, such as by a key study characteristic (i.e., moderator). If order is by a categorical moderator, then you might consider adding multiple vertical lines to denote different mean values within moderator groups. The sizes of the circles for study effect sizes could be larger or smaller to denote, for instance,

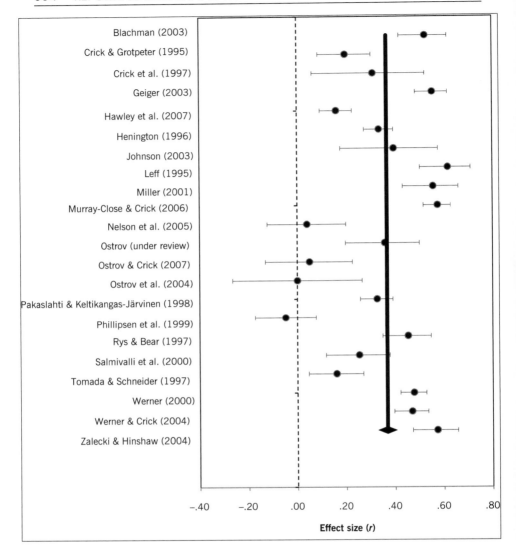

FIGURE 13.1. Example forest plot.

their relative weighting. It would also be possible to change the shapes or other characteristics (e.g., color, if presenting in color) of these study-specific effect sizes to indicate other features, such as values on a second moderator of interest. Finally, you might consider merging the information of a table of individual studies (e.g., sample sizes, coded scores on various moderators) and the forest plot by creating a hybrid table and figure. This would display a tremendous amount of information, though it might be rather large if you have a large (in terms of numbers of studies and coded study characteristics) meta-analysis.

13.3.2.b Stem-and-Leaf Plots

These plots are commonly used and convey considerable information, including information about central tendency, variability, and distributional form (e.g., skewness, modality) of a set of effect size, as well as pointing to potential outlier studies with extreme effect sizes. Stem-and-leaf plots consist of two parts. The "stem" is the vertical array of "bins" of possible effect sizes (e.g., correlations between .70 and .79, between .60 and .69, etc.), and each "leaf" is a single-digit number representing the effect size from a single study. These effect sizes can be either in the original metric (e.g., r, o) or in a transformed metric (e.g., Z_r, $\ln(o)$); the original metric is more intuitive for readers, but the transformed metric is more useful for assessing potential skew in the distribution of effect sizes.[5] Figure 13.2 presents a stem-and-leaf plot for the

```
 .7 |
 .6 | 2
 .5 | 35677
 .4 | 0578
 .3 | 1346
 .2 | 05
 .1 | 66
 .0 | 450
----------------------------------
-.0 | 5
-.1 |
```

FIGURE 13.2. Example stem-and-leaf plot. Values represent associations (r) between relational aggression and peer rejection for 22 studies in meta-analysis.

22 studies in the example meta-analysis. The numbers to the left of the vertical line comprise the stem, scaled in intervals of .1 with a range one value higher and one value lower than the most extreme effect sizes found among these 22 studies. To the right of the vertical line are the leaves, with each digit representing a single study. For example, the highest leaf is the value 2 connected to the stem at .6 to represent a study that found a correlation of .62 between relational aggression and peer rejection. The five digits (leaves) connected to the .5 stem denote five studies finding associations between .50 and .59 (specifically, .53, .55, .56, .57, and another .57; note that the leaves are arranged from lowest to highest values moving away from the stem).

Visual inspection of this figure provides a variety of information. First, the visual spacing of the leaves provides information about the number of studies finding effect sizes of approximate values (e.g., you can see that more studies find correlations in the .50 to .59 range than the .60 to .69 range; note that it is preferable to use a font that is uniform in width for all values so that the size of the rightward-extending bar represents the number of studies on that stem). Second, this sort of plot gives an approximate, though not precise, idea about central tendency. Recalling that the weighted mean $r = .37$ among these studies, you can see that this is near an approximate "balancing point" of the distribution of these effect sizes (though be aware that visual inspection of the funnel plot does not take into account differential weighting of studies). Third, stem-and-leaf plots visually display the heterogeneity of effect sizes across studies. In this example, there is considerable dispersion among the effect sizes, which is consistent with quantitative findings of significant heterogeneity and a large I^2. Fourth, stem-and-leaf plots provide visual information about the distribution of effect sizes. In this example, it appears that the effect sizes are somewhat skewed to have a longer tail toward the lower/negative values. Finally, it can be useful to study stem-and-leaf plots of studies with outlying effect sizes; in this example, no study dramatically departs from the others.

Stem-and-leaf plots are commonly used in reports of meta-analytic findings (about 30% of reports surveyed by Borman & Grigg, 2009). You can also extend the basic stem-and-leaf plot to provide more sophisticated information. For example, it is possible to provide multiple sets of leaves to represent studies with different study characteristics (i.e., different values of categorical moderators). By orienting these multiple sets of leaves side by side, scaled along a common vertical axis (i.e., stem), readers can gain an appreciation for the differences in central tendency, variability, distributional form, and possible outlier studies within each group of studies.

13.3.2.c   Funnel Plots

As seen in Chapter 11, funnel plots are a way of graphically evaluating potential publication bias (or other biases leading to censoring of nonsignificant
results). As you recall, these plots are scatterplots of the studies in your meta-
analysis, with one axis representing some function of sample sizes (or standard errors) and the other representing effect sizes. Because I described these
plots in Chapter 11, I will not discuss them here.

The main purpose of funnel plots is to identify potential publication
bias. However, these plots also display information about the mean effect size
(which can be shown as a line through the scatterplot) and about heterogeneity (i.e., the width of the funnel). According to the survey of published meta-
analyses by Borman and Grigg (2009), these plots are modestly frequently
used (12.5% of meta-analyses considered). My own impression is that the
value of funnel plots is primarily in terms of detecting publication bias. For
other information (e.g., mean effect sizes, heterogeneity), other figures are
more effective or as effective while using less space.

13.3.2.d   Other Figures

My consideration of forest plots, stem-and-leaf plots, and funnel plots only
touches on the many options available. These other options include schematic
plots (a.k.a. box-and-whisker plots, which provide clear information about
means, heterogeneity, and outliers); normal quantile plots (which are useful
in evaluating publication bias); and radial plots (which are fairly technical
plots of studies' mean effect sizes and precisions) described by Borman and
Grigg (2009). This variety of potential graphical displays is valuable in providing a wide range of tools for presenting the results of your meta-analysis.
When choosing a method of displaying your results, however, you should
always keep in mind what information is most important to convey.

13.4   PRACTICAL MATTERS: AVOIDING COMMON PROBLEMS IN REPORTING RESULTS OF META-ANALYSES

In this section, I identify 10 problems that I perceive to be common in reporting results of meta-analytic reviews. More importantly, I offer concrete suggestions for how you can avoid each. Although following these suggestions
will not guarantee that your meta-analytic report will be successful (whether

defined by publication in a top-outlet, high-impact, or any other criterion), doing so will help you avoid some of the most common obstacles.

1. *Disconnecting conceptual rationale and data analyses.* One of the more common problems with written reports of meta-analyses (and probably most empirical papers) is a disconnect between the conceptual rationale for the review in the introduction and the analyses and results actually presented. Every analysis performed should be performed for a reason, and this reason should be described in the Introduction of your paper. Even if some analyses were entirely exploratory, it is better to state as much rather than have readers guess why you performed a particular analysis. A good way to avoid this problem is simply to compile a list of analyses presented in your results section, and then identify the section in your introduction in which you justify this analysis.

2. *Providing insufficient details of methodology.* I have tried to emphasize the importance of describing your meta-analytic method in sufficient detail so that a reader could—at least in principle—replicate your review. This level of detail requires extensive description of your search strategies, inclusion and exclusion criteria, practices of coding both study characteristics and effect sizes, and the data-analytic strategy you performed. Because it is easier to know what you did than to describe it, I strongly recommend that you ask a colleague familiar with meta-analytic techniques to review a draft of your description to determine if he or she could replicate your methodology based only on what you wrote.

3. *Writing a phone book.* Phone books contain a lot of information, but you probably do not consider them terribly exciting to read. When presenting results of your meta-analysis, you have a tremendous amount of information to potentially present: results of many individual studies, a potentially vast array of summary statistics about central tendency and heterogeneity of effect sizes, likely a wide range of nuanced results of moderator analyses, analyses addressing publication bias, and so on. Although it is valuable to report most or all of these results (that is one of the main purposes of sharing your work with others), this reporting should not be an uninformative listing of numbers that fails to tell a coherent story. Instead, it is critical that the numbers are embedded within an understandable story. To test whether your report achieves this, try the following exercise: (1) Take what you believe is a near-complete draft of your results section, and delete every clause that contains a statistic from your meta-analysis or any variant of "statistical significance"; (2) read this text and see if what remains provides an understandable narrative that accurately (if not precisely) describes your results. If it does not,

then this should highlight to you places where you should better guide readers through your findings.

4. *Allowing technical complexity to detract from message.* Robert Rosenthal once wrote, "I have never seen a meta-analysis that was 'too simple'" (Rosenthal, 1995, p. 183). Given that Rosenthal was one of the originators of meta-analytic techniques (see Chapter 1) and has probably read far more meta-analytic reviews than you or I ever will, his insight is important. Although complex meta-analytic techniques can be useful to answer some complex research questions, you should keep in mind that many important questions can be answered using relatively simple techniques. I encourage you to use techniques that are as complex as needed to adequately answer your research questions, but no more complex than needed. With greater complexity of your techniques comes greater chances (1) of making mistakes that you may fail to detect, and (2) confusing your readers. Even if you feel confident in your ability to avoid mistakes, the costs of confusing readers is high in that they are less likely to understand and—in some cases—to trust your conclusions. The acronym KISS (Keep It Simple, Stupid) is worth bearing in mind. To test whether you have achieved adequate simplicity, I suggest that you (1) have a colleague (or multiple colleagues)—one who is unfamiliar with meta-analysis but is otherwise a regular reader of your targeted publication outlet—read your report; then (2) ask this colleague or colleagues to describe your findings to you. If there are any aspects that your colleague is unable to understand or that lead to inaccurate conclusions, then you should edit those sections to be understandable to readers not familiar with meta-analysis.

5. *Forgetting why you performed the meta-analysis.* Although I doubt that many meta-analysts really forget why they performed a meta-analysis, the written reports often seem to indicate that they have. This is most evident in the discussion section, where too many writers neglect to make clear statements about how the results of their meta-analysis answer the research questions posed and advance understanding in their field. Extending my earlier recommendation (problem 1 above) for ensuring connections between the rationale and the analyses performed, you should be sure that items on your list of analyses and conceptual rationales are addressed in the discussion section of your report. Specifically, be sure that you have clearly stated (1) the answers to your research questions, or why your findings did not provide answers, and (2) why these answers are important to understanding the phenomenon or guiding application (e.g., intervention, policy).

6. *Failing to consider the limits of your sample of studies.* Every meta-analysis, no matter how ambitious the literature search or how liberal the inclusion criteria, necessarily involves a finite—and therefore potentially

limited—sample of studies. It is important for you to state—or at least speculate—where these limits lie and how they qualify your conclusions. You should typically report at least some results evaluating publication bias (see Chapter 11), and comment on these in the discussion section. Evidence of publication bias does not constitute a fatal flaw of your meta-analysis if your literature search and retrieval strategies were as extensive as can be reasonably expected, but you should certainly be clear about the threat of publication bias. Similarly, you should clearly articulate the boundaries of your sample as determined by either inclusion/exclusion criteria (Chapter 3) or characteristics of the empirical literature performed (elucidated by your reporting of descriptive information about your sample of studies). Description of the boundaries of your sample should be followed with speculation regarding the limits of generalizability of your findings.

7. *Failing to provide (and consider) descriptive features of studies.* Problem 4 (allowing technical complexity to detract from your message) and problem 6 (failing to consider the limits of your sample) too often converge in the form of this problem: failing to provide basic descriptive information about the studies that comprise your meta-analysis. As mentioned, reporting this information is important for describing the sample from which you draw conclusions, as well as describing the state of the field and making recommendations for further avenues of research. The best way to ensure that you provide this information is to include a section (or at least a paragraph or two) at the beginning of your results section that provides this information.

8. *Using fixed-effects models in the presence of heterogeneity.* This is a rather specific problem but one that merits special attention. As you recall from Chapter 10, fixed-effects models assume a single population effect size (any variability among effect sizes across studies is due to sampling error), whereas random-effects models allow for a distribution of population effect sizes. If you use a fixed-effects model to calculate a mean effect size across studies in the presence of substantial heterogeneity, then the failure to model this heterogeneity provides standard errors (and resulting confidence intervals) that are smaller than is appropriate. To avoid this problem, you should always evaluate heterogeneity via the heterogeneity significance test (Q; see Chapter 8) as well as some index that is not impacted by the size of your sample (such as I^2; see Chapter 8). If there is evidence of statistically significant or substantial heterogeneity, then you are much more justified in using a random- rather than a fixed-effects model (see Chapter 10 for considerations). A related problem to avoid is making inappropriately generalized conclusions from fixed-effects models; you should be careful to frame your conclusions

according to the model you used to estimate mean effect sizes in your meta-analysis (see Chapter 10).

9. *Failing to consider the limits of meta-analytic moderator analyses.* I have mentioned that the results of moderator analyses are often the most important findings of a meta-analytic review. However, you should keep in mind that findings of moderation in meta-analyses are necessarily correlational—that certain study characteristics covary with larger or smaller effect sizes. This awareness should remind us that findings of moderation in meta-analyses (or any nonexperimental study) cannot definitively conclude that the presumed moderator is not just a proxy for another moderator (i.e., another study characteristic). You should certainly acknowledge this limitation in describing moderator results from your meta-analysis, and you should consider alternative explanations. Of course, the extent to which you can empirically rule out other moderators (through multiple regression moderator analyses controlling for them; see Chapter 10) diminishes the range of competing explanations, and you should note this as well. To ensure that you avoid the problem of overinterpreting moderator results, I encourage you to jot down (separate from your manuscript) at least three alternative explanations for each moderator result, and write about those that seem most plausible.

10. *Believing there is a "right way" to perform and report a meta-analysis.* Although this chapter (and other works; e.g., Clarke, 2009; Rosenthal, 1995) provides concrete recommendations for reporting your meta-analysis, you should remember that these are recommendations rather than absolute prescriptions. There are contexts when it is necessary to follow predetermined formats for reporting the results of a meta-analysis (e.g., when writing a commissioned review as part of the Campbell [*www.campbellcollaboration.org*] or Cochrane [*www.cochrane.org*] Collaborations), but these are typically exceptions to the typical latitude available in presenting the results of your review. This does not mean that you deceptively present your work, but rather that you should consider the myriad possibilities for presenting your results, keeping in mind the goals of your review, how you think the findings are best organized, the audience for your review, and the space limitations of your report. I believe that the suggestions I have made in this chapter—and throughout the book—are useful if you are just beginning to use meta-analytic techniques. But as you gain experience and consider how to best present your findings, you are likely to find instances where I have written "should" that are better replaced with "should usually, but ... ". I encourage this use of my (and others') recommendations as jumping points for your efforts in presenting your findings.

13.5 SUMMARY

In this chapter I have offered concrete suggestions for writing the results of your meta-analytic review. The first step is to consider the goals and potential audience for your report, as well as a meaningful organizational framework for presenting the findings. I then offered specific suggestions for each portion of a typical manuscript, and described how you can use tables and figures in conjunction with text to effectively convey information. I then highlighted 10 common problems in reports of meta-analytic findings and discussed how you can avoid these problems. I hope that these comments are useful to you in most effectively presenting the findings from your months of hard work on your meta-analytic review.

13.6 RECOMMENDED READINGS

Borman, G. D., & Grigg, J. A. (2009). Visual and narrative interpretation. In H. Cooper, L. V. Hedges, & J. C. Valentine (Eds.), *The handbook of research synthesis and meta-analysis* (2nd ed., pp. 497–519). New York: Russell Sage Foundation.—This chapter is a comprehensive overview of the wide variety of methods of presenting meta-analytic results in tables and figures. The chapter also includes some helpful advice on incorporating narrative description of your meta-analytic review.

Rosenthal, R., (1995). Writing meta-analytic reviews. *Psychological Bulletin, 118,* 183–192.—As the name implies, this article is an excellent overview of how you should write a meta-analysis. Although the article is now a bit dated, the advice given by this leader in the field of meta-analysis is invaluable.

NOTES

1. Or, you could do both through mixed-effects models, which estimate the variability in effect sizes both across and within study characteristics (see Chapter 10).

2. Specifically, Borman and Grigg (2009) surveyed 80 meta-analyses published in the journals *Psychological Bulletin* and *Review of Educational Research* during this period. Although their focus on these two particular journals might limit the generalizability of these findings, it is worth noting that these two journals are widely read within their respective disciplines and therefore provide a reasonably accurate portrayal of practices at least within these fields. Note that they present the results of their survey separately for these two journals, whereas I combine the results in the percentages I report here.

3. This example, containing only one study using parent reports as the categorical moderator, is perhaps not ideal (but might be realistic). Here, I would include a caveat in the text about interpreting this and other findings with small numbers of studies.

4. Note that this example contains a somewhat atypical situation in which some studies are listed twice if they provide results according to multiple reporters (see Chapter 9).

5. Because the skew of r is fairly small at small to moderate values, my preference is to use r rather than Z_r if most effect sizes are less than about ±.50. In contrast, the distribution of the odds ratio (o) is highly skewed, so I prefer to use $\ln(o)$ for this effect size in all cases.

References

Alexander, R. A., Carson, K. P., Alliger, G. M., & Carr, L. (1987). Correcting doubly truncated correlations: An improved approximation for correcting the bivariate normal correlation when truncation has occurred on both variables. *Educational and Psychological Measurement, 47*, 309–315.

Alexander, R. A., Scozzaro, M. J., & Borodkin, L. J. (1989). Statistical and empirical examination of the chi-square test for homogeneity of correlations in meta-analysis. *Psychological Bulletin, 106*, 329–331.

Algina, J., Keselman, H. J., & Penfield, R. D. (2005). An alternative to Cohen's standardized mean difference effect size: A robust parameter and confidence interval in the two independent groups case. *Psychological Methods, 10*, 317–328.

American Psychological Association. (2009). *Publication manual of the American Psychological Association* (6th ed.). Washington, DC: Author.

Andreou, E. (2006). Social preference, perceived popularity and social intelligence: Relations to overt and relational aggression. *School Psychology International, 27*, 339–351.

Antes, G., & Chalmers, I. (2003). Under-reporting of clinical trials is unethical. *Lancet, 361*, 978–979.

Arbuckle, J. L. (1996). Full information estimation in the presence of incomplete data. In G. A. Marcoulides & R. E. Schumacker (Eds.), *Advanced structural equation modeling: Issues and techniques* (pp. 243–277). Mahwah, NJ: Erlbaum.

Arnold, M. E. (1998). *Inflated sense of peer acceptance and hostile intent attributions in overtly and relationally aggressive children.* Unpublished dissertation, Texas A & M University.

Bailey, C. A., & Ostrov, J. M. (2008). Differentiating forms and functions of aggression in emerging adults: Associations with hostile attribution biases and normative beliefs. *Journal of Youth and Adolescence, 37*(6), 713–722.

Baron, R. M., & Kenny, D. A. (1986). The moderator–mediator variable distinction in social psychological research: Conceptual, strategic, and statistical considerations. *Journal of Personality and Social Psychology, 51*, 1173–1182.

Barr, D. R., & Sherrill, E. T. (1999). Mean and variance of truncated normal distributions. *The American Statistician, 53,* 357–361.

Bauer, D. J. (2003). Estimating multilevel linear models as structural equation models. *Journal of Educational and Behavioral Statistics, 28,* 135–167.

Baugh, F. (2002). Correcting effect sizes for score reliability: A reminder that measurement and substantive issues are linked inextricably. *Educational and Psychological Measurement, 62,* 254–263.

Bax, L., Yu, L.-M., Ikeda, N., & Moons, K. G. M. (2007). A systematic comparison of software dedicated to meta-analysis of causal studies. *BMC Medical Research Methodology, 7:40 (www.biomedcentral.com/1471-2288/7/40).*

Becker, B. J. (1992). Using results from replicated studies to estimate linear models. *Journal of Educational Statistics, 17,* 341–362.

Becker, B. J. (2003). Introduction to the special section on metric in meta-analysis. *Psychological Methods, 8,* 403–405.

Becker, B. J. (2005). Failsafe N or file-drawer number. In H. R. Rothstein, A. J. Sutton, & M. Borenstein (Eds.), *Publication bias in meta-analysis: Prevention, assessment and adjustments* (pp. 111–125). Hoboken, NJ: Wiley.

Becker, B. J. (2009). Model-based meta-analysis. In H. Cooper, L. V. Hedges, & J. C. Valentine (Eds.), *The handbook of research synthesis and meta-analysis* (2nd ed., pp. 377–395). New York: Russell Sage Foundation.

Begg, C. B. (1994). Publication bias. In H. Cooper & L. V. Hedges (Eds.), *The handbook of research synthesis* (pp. 399–409). New York: Russell Sage Foundation.

Berdugo-Arstark, H. (2002). *The relationship of negative emotionality, hostile attribution bias, and social orientation to overt and relational aggression.* Unpublished dissertation, Fordham University.

Beretvas, S. N., & Furlow, C. F. (2006). Evaluation of an approximate method of synthesizing covariance matrices for use in meta-analytic SEM. *Structural Equation Modeling, 13,* 153–185.

Berlin, J. A., & Ghersi, D. (2005). Preventing publication bias: Registries and prospective meta-analysis. In H. R. Rothstein, A. J. Sutton, & M. Borenstein (Eds.), *Publication bias in meta-analysis: Prevention, assessment and adjustments* (pp. 35–48). Hoboken, NJ: Wiley.

Blachman, D. R. (2003). *Predictors of peer rejection, acceptance, and victimization among girls with and without ADHD.* Unpublished dissertation, University of California, Berkeley.

Bond, C. F. Jr., Wiitala, W. L., & Richard, F. D. (2003). Meta-analysis of raw mean differences. *Psychological Methods, 8,* 406–418.

Bonett, D. A. (2007). Transforming odds ratios into correlations for meta-analytic research. *American Psychologist, 62,* 254–255.

Boorstin, D. J. (1983). *The discoverers.* New York: Random House.

Borenstein, M., Hedges, L. V., Higgins, J. P. T., & Rothstein, H. R. (2009). *Introduction to meta-analysis.* Hoboken, NJ: Wiley.

Borman, G. D., & Grigg, J. A. (2009). Visual and narrative interpretation. In H. Cooper, L. V. Hedges, & J. C. Valentine (Eds.), *The handbook of research synthesis and meta-analysis* (2nd ed., pp. 497–519). New York: Russell Sage Foundation.

Brendgen, M., Dionne, G., Girard, A., Boivin, M., Vitaro, F., & Pérusse, D. (2005). Examining genetic and environmental effects on social aggression: A study of 6-year-old twins. *Child Development, 76,* 903–946.

Britt, D. W. (1997). *A conceptual introduction to modeling: Qualitative and quantitative perspectives*. Mahwah, NJ: Erlbaum.

Brown, T. A. (2006). *Confirmatory factor analysis for applied research*. New York: Guilford Press.

Bushman, B. J., & Wang, M. C. (2009). Vote counting procedures in meta-analysis. In H. Cooper, L. V. Hedges, & J. C. Valentine (Eds.), *The handbook of research synthesis and meta-analysis* (2nd ed., pp. 207–220). New York: Russell Sage Foundation.

Butovskaya, M. L., Timentschik, V. M., & Burkova, V. N. (2007). Aggression, conflict resolution, popularity, and attitude to school in Russian adolescents. *Aggressive Behavior, 33*, 170–183.

Campbell, J. J. (1999). *Familial antecedents to children's relational and overt aggression*. Unpublished dissertation, University of North Carolina, Greensboro.

Card, N. A., & Little, T. D. (2007). Longitudinal modeling of developmental processes. *International Journal of Behavioral Development, 31*, 297–302.

Card, N. A., Stucky, B. D., Sawalani, G. M., & Little, T. D. (2008). Direct and indirect aggression during childhood and adolescence: A meta-analytic review of gender differences, intercorrelations, and relations to maladjustment. *Child Development, 79*, 1185–1229.

Carpenter, E. M. (2002). *A curriculum-based approach for social-cognitive skills training: An intervention targeting aggression in head start preschoolers*. Unpublished dissertation, University of Maine.

Carpenter, E. M., & Nangle, D. W. (2006). Caught between stages: Relational aggression emerging as a developmental advance in at-risk preschoolers. *Journal of Research in Childhood Education, 21*, 177–188.

Chalmers, I. (1990). Underreporting research is scientific misconduct. *Journal of the American Medical Association, 263*, 1405–1408.

Chalmers, I., Hedges, L. V., & Cooper, H. (2002). A brief history of research synthesis. *Evaluation and Health Professions, 25*, 12–37.

Cheung, M. W.-L. (2008). A model for integrating fixed-, random-, and mixed-effects meta-analyses in structural equation modeling. *Psychological Methods, 13*, 182–202.

Cheung, M. W.-L., & Chan, W. (2005a). Meta-analytic structural equation modeling: A two-stage approach. *Psychological Methods, 10*, 40–64.

Cheung, M. W.-L., & Chan, W. (2005b). Classifying correlation matrices into relatively homogeneous subgroups: A cluster analytic approach. *Educational and Psychological Measurement, 65*, 954–979.

Cheung, M. W.-L., & Chan, W. (2009). A two-stage approach to synthesizing covariance matrices in meta-analytic structural equation modeling. *Structural Equation Modeling, 16*, 28–53.

Cillessen, A. H. N., Jiang, X. L., West, T. V., & Laszkowski, D. K. (2005). Predictors of dyadic friendship quality in adolescence. *International Journal of Behavior Development, 29*, 165–172.

Cillessen, A. H. N., & Mayeux, L. (2004). From censure to reinforcement: Developmental changes in the association between aggression and social status. *Child Development, 75*, 147–163.

Clarke, M. (2009). Reporting format. In H. Cooper, L. V. Hedges, & J. C. Valentine (Eds.), *The handbook of research synthesis and meta-analysis* (2nd ed., pp. 521–534). New York: Russell Sage Foundation.

Cochran, W. G. (1954). The combination of estimates from different experiments. *Biometrics, 10,* 101–129.

Cohen, J. (1968). Multiple regression as a general data-analytic system. *Psychological Bulletin, 70,* 426–443.

Cohen, J. (1969). *Statistical power analysis for the behavioral sciences.* New York: Academic Press.

Cohen, J. (1994). The earth is round (*p* < .05). *American Psychologist, 49,* 997–1003.

Cohen, J., & Cohen, P. (1983). *Applied multiple regression/correlation analysis for the behavioral sciences* (2nd ed.). Mahwah, NJ: Erlbaum.

Cohen, J., Cohen, P., West, S. G., & Aiken, L. S. (2003). *Applied multiple regression/correlation analysis for the behavioral sciences* (3rd ed.). Mahwah, NJ: Erlbaum.

Cohn, L. D., & Becker, B. J. (2003). How meta-analysis increases statistical power. *Psychological Methods, 8,* 243–253.

Columbia World of Quotations. (1996). Searched online (July 22, 2008) at *www.bartleby.com.*

Conn, V. S., Valentine, J. C., Cooper, H. M., & Rantz, M. J. (2003). Grey literature in meta-analyses. *Nursing Research, 52,* 256–261.

Cook, T. D., & Campbell, D. T. (1979). *Quasi-experimentation: Design & analysis issues for field settings.* Boston: Houghton Mifflin.

Cooper, H. M. (1982). Scientific guidelines for conducting integrative research reviews. *Review of Educational Research, 52,* 291–302.

Cooper, H. M. (1984). *The integrative research review: A systematic approach.* Beverly Hills, CA: Sage.

Cooper, H. M. (1988). Organizing knowledge syntheses: A taxonomy of literature reviews. *Knowledge in Society, 1,* 104–126.

Cooper, H. M. (1998). *Synthesizing research: A guide for literature reviews.* Thousand Oaks, CA: Sage.

Cooper, H. M. (2003). Editorial. *Psychological Bulletin, 129,* 3–9.

Cooper, H. M. (2009a). *Research synthesis and meta-analysis: A step-by-step approach.* Thousand Oaks, CA: Sage.

Cooper, H. M. (2009b). Hypotheses and problems in research synthesis. In H. Cooper, L. V. Hedges, & J. C. Valentine (Eds.), *The handbook of research synthesis and meta-analysis* (2nd ed., pp. 19–35). New York: Russell Sage Foundation.

Cooper, H., DeNeve, K., & Charlton, K. (1997). Finding the missing science: The fate of studies submitted for review by a human subjects committee. *Psychological Methods, 2,* 447–452.

Cooper, H. M., & Rosenthal, R. (1980). Statistical versus traditional procedures for summarizing research findings. *Psychological Bulletin, 87,* 442–449.

Côté, S. M., Vaillancourt, T., Barker, E. D., Nagin, D., & Tremblay, R. E. (2007). The joint development of physical and indirect aggression: Predictors of continuity and change during childhood. *Development and Psychopathology, 19,* 37–55.

Coursol, A., & Wagner, E. E. (1986). Effect of positive findings on submission and acceptance rates: A note on meta-analysis bias. *Professional Psychology: Research and Practice, 17,* 136–137.

Coyne, S. M., & Archer, J. (2005). The relationship between indirect and physical aggression on television and real life. *Social Development, 14,* 324–338.

Crain, M. M. (2002). *The relationship of intent attributions, goals and outcome expectancies to relationally aggressive behavior in pre-adolescent girls.* Unpublished dissertation, Alliant International University.

Crick, N. R. (1995). Relational aggression: The role of intent attributions, feelings of distress, and provocation type. *Development and Psychopathology, 7,* 313–322.

Crick, N. R. (1996). The role of overt aggression, relational aggression, and prosocial behavior in the prediction of children's future social adjustment. *Child Development, 67,* 2317–2327.

Crick, N. R. (1997). Engagement in gender normative versus nonnormative forms of aggression: Links to social-psychological adjustment. *Developmental Psychology, 33,* 610–617.

Crick, N. R., Casas, J. F., & Mosher, M. (1997). Relational and overt aggression in preschool. *Developmental Psychology, 33,* 579–588.

Crick, N. R., & Grotpeter, J. K. (1995). Relational aggression, gender, and social-psychological adjustment. *Child Development, 66,* 710–722.

Cronbach, L. J. (1951). Coefficient alpha and the internal structure of tests. *Psychometrika, 16,* 297–334.

Cronbach, L. J., & Meehl, P. E. (1955). Construct validity in psychological tests. *Psychological Bulletin, 52,* 281–302.

Cudeck, R., & MacCallum, R. C. (Eds.) (2007). *Factor analysis at 100: Historic developments and future directions.* Mahwah, NJ: Erlbaum.

Curran, P. J. (2003). Have multilevel models been structural equation models all along? *Multivariate Behavioral Research, 38,* 529–569.

Curran, P. J., & Bauer, D. J. (2007). Building path diagrams for multilevel models. *Psychological Methods, 12,* 283–297.

DeVellis, R. F. (2003). *Scale development: Theory and applications* (2nd ed.). Thousand Oaks, CA: Sage.

Dickersin, K. (2005). Publication bias: Recognizing the problem, understanding its origins and scope, and preventing harm. In H. R. Rothstein, A. J. Sutton, & M. Borenstein (Eds.), *Publication bias in meta-analysis: Prevention, assessment and adjustments* (pp. 11–33). Hoboken, NJ: Wiley.

Duval, S. (2005). The trim and fill method. In H. R. Rothstein, A. J. Sutton, & M. Borenstein (Eds.), *Publication bias in meta-analysis: Prevention, assessment and adjustments* (pp. 127–144). Hoboken, NJ: Wiley.

Edwards, J. R., & Bagozzi, R. P. (2000). On the nature and direction of relationships between constructs and measures. *Psychological Methods, 5,* 155–174.

Eysenck, H. J. (1978). An exercise in mega-silliness. *American Psychologist, 33,* 517.

Fan, X. (2001). Statistical significance and effect size in education research: Two sides of a coin. *Journal of Educational Research, 94,* 275–282.

Field, A. P. (2001). Meta-analysis of correlation coefficients: A Monte Carlo comparison of fixed- and random-effects methods. *Psychological Methods, 6,* 161–180.

Fleiss, J. H. (1994). Measures of effect size for categorical data. In H. Cooper & L. V. Hedges (Eds.), *The handbook of research synthesis* (pp. 245–260). New York: Russell Sage Foundation.

Frick, R. W. (1996). The appropriate use of null hypothesis testing. *Psychological Methods, 1,* 379–390.

Furlow, C. F., & Beretvas, S. N. (2005). Meta-analytic methods of pooling correlation matrices for structural equation modeling under different patterns of missing data. *Psychological Methods, 10,* 227–254.

Geiger, T. C. (2003). *The influence of peer status, friendship, and children's social behavior on trajectories of children's peer victimization.* Unpublished dissertation, University of Minnesota.

Glass, G. V. (1976). Primary, secondary, and meta-analysis of research. *Educational Researcher, 5*, 3–8.

Glass, G. V., McGraw, B., & Smith, M. L. (1981). *Meta-analysis in social research.* Thousand Oaks, CA: Sage.

Graham, S. (1992). "Most of the subjects were White and middle class": Trends in published research on African Americans in selected APA journals, 1970–1989. *American Psychologist, 47*, 629–639.

Greenwald, A. G. (1975). Consequences of prejudice against the null hypothesis. *Psychological Bulletin, 82*, 1–20.

Gribbin, J. (2002). *Science: A history.* New York: BCA.

Grissom, R. J., & Kim, J. J. (2001). Review of assumptions and problems in the appropriate conceptualization of effect size. *Psychological Methods, 6*, 135–146.

Grissom, R. J., & Kim, J. J. (2005). *Effect sizes for research: A broad practical approach.* Mahwah, NJ: Erlbaum.

Haddock, C. K., Rindskopf, D., & Shadish, W. R. (1998). Using odds ratios as effect sizes for meta-analysis of dichotomous data: A primer on methods and issues. *Psychological Methods, 3*, 339–353.

Hafdahl, A. R. (2009). Improved Fisher z estimators for univariate random-effects meta-analysis of correlations. *British Journal of Mathematical and Statistical Psychology, 62*, 233–261.

Hafdahl, A. R. (2010). Random-effects meta-analysis of correlations: Monte Carlo evaluation of mean estimators. *British Journal of Mathematical and Statistical Psychology, 63*, 227–254.

Hall, S. M., & Brannick, M. T. (2002). Comparisons of two random-effects methods of meta-analysis. *Journal of Applied Psychology, 87*, 377–389.

Halpern, S. D., Karlawish, J. H. T., & Berlin, J. A. (2002). The continued unethical conduct of underpowered clinical trials. *Journal of the American Medical Association, 288*, 358–362.

Harlow, L. L., Mulaik, S. A., & Steiger, J. H. (Eds.). (1997). *What if there were no significance tests?* Mahwah, NJ: Erlbaum.

Harwell, M. (1997). An empirical study of Hedges' homogeneity test. *Psychological Methods, 2*, 219–231.

Hasselblad, V., & Hedges, L. V. (1995). Meta-analysis of screening and diagnostic tests. *Psychological Bulletin, 117*, 167–178.

Hawley, P. H., Little, T. D., & Card, N. A. (2007). The allure of a mean friend: Relationship quality and processes of aggressive adolescents with prosocial skills. *International Journal of Behavioral Development, 31*, 170–180.

Hedges, L. V. (1982). Fitting categorical models to effect sizes from a series of experiments. *Journal of Educational Statistics, 7*, 119–137.

Hedges, L. V. (1983). A random effects model for effect sizes. *Psychological Bulletin, 93*, 388–395.

Hedges, L. V. (1987). How hard is hard science, and how soft is soft science? The empirical cumulativeness of research. *American Psychologist, 42*, 443–455.

Hedges, L. V. (1992). Meta-analysis. *Journal of Educational Statistics, 17*, 279–296.

Hedges, L. V., & Olkin, I. (1985). *Statistical methods for meta-analysis.* San Diego, CA: Academic Press.

Hedges, L. V., & Pigott, T. D. (2001). The power of statistical tests in meta-analysis. *Psychological Methods, 6*, 203–217.

Hedges, L. V., & Pigott, T. D. (2004). The power of statistical tests for moderators in meta-analysis. *Psychological Methods, 9,* 426–445.

Hedges, L. V., & Vevea, J. L. (1998). Fixed- and random-effects models in meta-analysis. *Psychological Methods, 3,* 486–504.

Hedges, L. V., & Vevea, J. L. (2005). Selection method approaches. In H. R. Rothstein, A. J. Sutton, & M. Borenstein (Eds.), *Publication bias in meta-analysis: Prevention, assessment and adjustments* (pp. 145–174). Hoboken, NJ: Wiley.

Henington, C. D. (1996). *Social correlates of relational and overt aggression in boys and girls.* Unpublished dissertation, Texas A & M University.

Higgins, J. P. T., & Thompson, S. G. (2002). Quantifying heterogeneity in a meta-analysis. *Statistics in Medicine, 21,* 1539–1558.

Hopewell, S., Clarke, M., & Mallett, S. (2005). Grey literature and systematic reviews. In H. R. Rothstein, A. J. Sutton, & M. Borenstein (Eds.), *Publication bias in meta-analysis: Prevention, assessment and adjustments* (pp. 49–72). Hoboken, NJ: Wiley.

Howell, R. D., Breivik, E., & Wilcox, J. B. (2007). Reconsidering formative measurement. *Psychological Methods, 12,* 205–218.

Huedo-Medina, T. B., Sánchez-Meca, J., Marín-Martínez, F., & Botella, J. (2006). Assessing heterogeneity in meta-analysis: Q statistic or I^2 index? *Psychological Methods, 11,* 193–206.

Hunt, M. (1997). *How science takes stock: The story of meta-analysis.* New York: Russell Sage Foundation.

Hunter, J. E., & Schmidt, F. L. (1990). Dichotomization of continuous variables: The implications for meta-analysis. *Journal of Applied Psychology, 75,* 334–349.

Hunter, J. E., & Schmidt, F. L. (2004). *Methods of meta-analysis: Correcting error and bias in research findings* (2nd ed.). Thousand Oaks, CA: Sage.

Hunter, J. E., Schmidt, F. L., & Jackson, G. B. (1982). *Meta-analysis: Cumulating research findings across studies.* Beverly Hills, CA: Sage.

Hunter, J. E., Schmidt, F. L., & Le, H. (2006). Implications of direct and indirect range restriction for meta-analysis methods and findings. *Journal of Applied Psychology, 91,* 594–612.

Jaccard, J., & Jacoby, J. (2010). *Theory construction and model-building skills.* New York: Guilford Press.

James, L. R., Demaree, R. G., & Mulaik, S. A. (1986). A note on validity generalization procedures. *Journal of Applied Psychology, 62,* 440–450.

Johnson, D. R. (2003). *The relationship between relational aggression in preschool children and friendship stability, mutuality, and popularity.* Unpublished dissertation, Alliant International University.

Kalaian, H. A., & Raudenbush, S. W. (1996). A multivariate mixed linear model for meta-analysis. *Psychological Methods, 1,* 227–235.

Kenny, D. A., Kashy, D. A., & Cook, W. L. (2006). *Dyadic data analysis.* New York: Guilford Press.

Keppel, G. (1991). *Design and analysis: A researcher's handbook* (3rd ed.). Upper Saddle River, NJ: Prentice Hall.

Kerr, N. L. (1998). HARKing: Hypothesizing after the results are known. *Personality and Social Psychology Review, 2,* 196–217.

Kisamore, J. L., & Brannick, M. T. (2008). An illustration of the consequences of meta-analysis model choice. *Organizational Research Methods, 11,* 35–53.

Kline, R. B. (2005). *Principles and practice of structural equation modeling* (2nd ed.). New York: Guilford Press.

Kline, R. B. (2010). *Principles and practice of structural equation modeling* (3rd ed.). New York: Guilford Press.

Kovacs, M. (1992). *Children's depression inventory manual*. North Tonawanda, NY: Multi-Health Systems.

Kraemer, H. C., Gardner, C., Brooks, J. O., III, & Yesavage, J. A. (1998). Advantages of excluding underpowered studies in meta-analysis: Inclusionist versus exclusionist viewpoints. *Psychological Methods, 3,* 23–31.

Kraemer, H. C., & Thiemann, S. (1987). *How many subjects? Statistical power analysis in research*. Newbury Park, CA: Sage.

Le, H., & Schmidt, F. L. (2006). Correcting for indirect range restriction in meta-analysis: Testing a new meta-analytic procedure. *Psychological Methods, 11,* 416–438.

Leff, S. S. (1995). *Females' cognitions of their relationally aggressive peers as a function of sociometric and relationally aggressive status*. Unpublished dissertation, University of North Carolina, Chapel Hill.

Lerner, R. M. (2002). *Concepts and theories of human development* (3rd ed.). Mahwah, NJ: Erlbaum.

Light, R. J., & Pillemer, D. B. (1984). *Summing up: The science of reviewing research*. Cambridge, MA: Harvard University Press.

Lipsey, M. W. (2009). Identifying interesting variables and analysis opportunities. In H. Cooper, L. V. Hedges, & J. C. Valentine (Eds.), *The handbook of research synthesis and meta-analysis* (2nd ed., pp. 147–158). New York: Russell Sage Foundation.

Lipsey, M. W., & Wilson, D. B. (2001). *Practical meta-analysis*. Thousand Oaks, CA: Sage.

Little, T. D., Card, N. A., Bovaird, J. A., Preacher, K. J., & Crandall, C. S. (2007). Structural equation modeling of mediation and moderation with contextual factors. In T. D. Little, J. A. Bovaird, & N. A. Card (Eds.), *Modeling ecological and contextual effects in longitudinal studies* (pp. 207–230). Mahwah, NJ: Erlbaum.

Little, T. D., Card, N. A., Preacher, K. J., & McConnell, E. (2009). Modeling longitudinal data from research on adolescence. In R. M. Lerner & L. Steinberg (Eds.), *Handbook of adolescent psychology* (3rd ed., pp. 15–54). New York: Wiley.

Little, T. D., Lindenberger, U., & Nesselroade, J. R. (1999). On selecting indicators for multivariate measurement and modeling with latent variables: When "good" indicators are bad and "bad" indicators are good. *Psychological Methods, 4,* 192–211.

Little, T. D., Slegers, D. W., & Card, N. A. (2006). A non-arbitrary method of identifying and scaling latent variables in SEM and MACS models. *Structural Equation Modeling, 13,* 59–72.

MacCallum, R. C., & Browne, M. W. (1993). The use of causal indicators in covariance structure models: Some practical issues. *Psychological Bulletin, 114,* 533–541.

MacCallum, R. C., Zhang, S., Preacher, K. J., & Rucker, D. D. (2002). On the practice of dichotomization of quantitative variables. *Psychological Methods, 7,* 19–40.

Maruyama, G. M. (1998). *Basics of structural equation modeling*. Thousand Oaks, CA: Sage.

Maxwell, S. E. (2004). The persistence of underpowered studies in psychological research: Causes, consequences, and remedies. *Psychological Methods, 9*, 147–163.

McGrath, R. E., & Meyer, G. J. (2006). When effect sizes disagree: The case of *r* and *d. Psychological Methods, 11*, 386–401.

Meehl, P. E. (1978). Theoretical risk and tabular asterisks: Sir Karl, Sir Ronald, and the slow progress of soft psychology. *Journal of Consulting and Clinical Psychology, 46*, 806–834.

Mehta, P. D., & Neale, M. C. (2005). People are variables too: Multilevel structural equation modeling. *Psychological Methods, 10*, 259–284.

Miller, D. R. (2001). *Friendship and romantic relationship features among relationally aggressive adolescent girls.* Unpublished dissertation, California School of Professional Psychology.

Murphy, K. R., & Myors, B. (2004). *Statistical power analysis: A simple and general model for traditional and modern hypothesis tests.* Mahwah, NJ: Erlbaum.

Murray-Close, D., & Crick, N. R. (2006). Mutual antipathy involvement: Gender and associations with aggression and victimization. *School Psychology Review, 35*, 472–492.

Muthén, B. O. (1994). Multilevel covariance structure analysis. *Sociological Methods and Research, 22*, 376–398.

Nelson, D. A., Robinson, C. C., & Hart, C. H. (2005). Relational and physical aggression of preschool-age children: Peer status linkages across informants. *Early Education and Development, 16*, 115–139.

Olkin, I. (1990). History and goals. In K. W. Wachter & M. L. Straf (Eds.), *The future of meta-analysis* (pp. 3–10). New York: Russell Sage Foundation.

Olson, C. M., Rennie, D., Cook, D., Dickersin, K., Flanagin, A., Hogan, J., Zhu, Q., Reiling, J., & Pace, B. (2002). Publication bias in editorial decision making. *Journal of the American Medical Association, 28*, 2825–2828.

Orwin, R. G. (1983). A fail-safe *N* for effect size in meta-analysis. *Journal of Educational Statistics, 8*, 157–159.

Orwin, R. G., & Vevea, J. L. (2009). Evaluating coding decisions. In H. Cooper, L. V. Hedges, & J. C. Valentine (Eds.), *The handbook of research synthesis and meta-analysis* (2nd ed., pp. 177–203). New York: Russell Sage Foundation.

Ostrov, J. M. (2008). Forms of aggression and peer victimization during early childhood: A short-term longitudinal study. *Journal of Abnormal Child Psychology, 36*, 311–322.

Ostrov, J. M., & Crick, N. R. (2007). Forms and functions of aggression during early childhood: A short-term longitudinal study. *School Psychology Review, 36*, 22–43.

Ostrov, J. M., Woods, K. E., Jansen, E. A., Casas, J. F., & Crick, N. R. (2004). An observational study of delivered and received aggression, gender, and social-psychological adjustment in preschool: "This white crayon doesn't work … ". *Early Childhood Research Quarterly, 19*, 355–371.

Overton, R. C. (1998). A comparison of fixed-effects and mixed (random-effects) models for meta-analysis tests of moderator variable effects. *Psychological Methods, 3*, 354–379.

Pakaslahti, L., & Keltikangas-Järvinen, L. (1998). Types of aggressive behavior among aggressive-preferred, aggressive non-preferred, non-aggressive preferred and non-aggressive non-preferred 14-year-old adolescents. *Personality and Individual Differences, 24*, 821–828.

Parke, R. D., & Slaby, R. G. (1983). The development of aggression. In P. H. Mussen (Series ed.) & E. M. Hetherington (Volume ed.), *The handbook of child psychology: Volume IV, socialization, personality, and social development* (pp. 547–641). New York: Wiley.

Phillipsen, L. C., Deptula, D. P., & Cohen, R. (1999). Relating characteristics of children and their friends to relational and overt aggression. *Child Study Journal, 29,* 269–289.

Pigott, T. D. (2009). Handling missing data. In H. Cooper, L. V. Hedges, & J. C. Valentine (Eds.), *The handbook of research synthesis and meta-analysis* (2nd ed., pp. 399–416). New York: Russell Sage Foundation.

Pigott, T. D., & Wu, M.-J. (2008). Methodological issues in meta-analyzing standard deviations: Comments on Bond and DePaulo (2008). *Psychological Bulletin, 134,* 498–500.

Popper, K. R. (1959). *The logic of scientific discovery.* New York: Harper & Row.

Prevost, A. T., Mason, D., Griffin, S., Kinmonth, A.-L., Sutton, S., & Spiegelhalter, D. (2007). Allowing for correlations between correlations in random-effects meta-analysis of correlation matrices. *Psychological Methods, 12,* 434–450.

Raudenbush, S. W. (1994). Random effects models. In H. Cooper & L. V. Hedges (Eds.), *The handbook of research synthesis* (pp. 301–321). New York: Russell Sage Foundation.

Reed, J. G., & Baxter, P. M. (2009). Using reference databases. In H. Cooper, L. V. Hedges, & J. C. Valentine (Eds.), *The handbook of research synthesis and meta-analysis* (2nd ed., pp. 73–101). New York: Russell Sage Foundation.

Rodriguez, M. C., & Maeda, Y. (2006). Meta-analysis of coefficient alpha. *Psychological Methods, 11,* 306–322.

Rosenthal, M. C. (1994). The fugitive literature. In H. Cooper & L. V. Hedges (Eds.), *The handbook of research synthesis* (pp. 85–94). New York: Russell Sage Foundation.

Rosenthal, R. (1978). Combining results of independent studies. *Psychological Bulletin, 85,* 185–193.

Rosenthal, R. (1979). The "file drawer problem" and tolerance for null results. *Psychological Bulletin, 86,* 638–641.

Rosenthal, R. (1984). *Meta-analytic procedures for social research.* Beverly Hills, CA: Sage.

Rosenthal, R. (1991). *Meta-analytic procedures for social research* (revised edition). Newbury Park, CA: Sage.

Rosenthal, R. (1994). Parametric measures of effect size. In H. Cooper & L. V. Hedges (Eds.), *The handbook of research synthesis* (pp. 231–244). New York: Russell Sage Foundation.

Rosenthal, R. (1995). Writing meta-analytic reviews. *Psychological Bulletin, 118,* 183–192.

Rosenthal, R., & DiMatteo, M. R. (2001). Meta-analysis: Recent developments in quantitative methods for literature reviews. *Annual Review of Psychology, 52,* 59–82.

Rosenthal, R., Rosnow, R. L., & Rubin, D. B. (2000). *Contrasts and effect sizes in behavioral research: A correlational approach.* New York: Cambridge University Press.

Rosenthal, R., & Rubin, D. B. (1978). Interpersonal expectancy effects: The first 345 studies. *The Behavioral and Brain Sciences, 3,* 377–415.

Rothstein, H. R., Sutton, A. J., & Borenstein, M. (2005a). Publication bias in meta-analysis. In H. R. Rothstein, A. J. Sutton, & M. Borenstein (Eds.), *Publication bias in meta-analysis: Prevention, assessment and adjustments* (pp. 1–7). Hoboken, NJ: Wiley.

Rothstein, H. R., Sutton, A. J., & Borenstein, M. (Eds.) (2005b). *Publication bias in meta-analysis: Prevention, assessment and adjustments.* Hoboken, NJ: Wiley.

Rubin, D. B. (1990). A new perspective. In K. W. Wachter & M. L. Straf (Eds.), *The future of meta-analysis* (pp. 155–165). New York: Russell Sage Foundation.

Rys, G. S., & Bear, G. G. (1997). Relational aggression and peer relations: Gender and developmental issues. *Merrill-Palmer Quarterly, 43,* 87–106.

Salmivalli, C., Kaukiainen, A., & Lagerspetz, K. (2000). Aggression and sociometric status among peers: Do gender and type of aggression matter? *Scandinavian Journal of Psychology, 41,* 17–24.

Sánchez-Meca, J., Marín-Martinez, F., & Chacón-Moscoso, S. (2003). Effect-size indices for dichotomized outcomes in meta-analysis. *Psychological Methods, 8,* 448–467.

Schafer, J. L., & Graham, J. W. (2002). Missing data: Our view of the state of the art. *Psychological Methods, 7,* 147–177.

Schmidt, F. L., & Hunter, J. E. (1977). Development of a general solution to the problem of validity generalization. *Journal of Applied Psychology, 62,* 529–540.

Schmidt, F. L., & Hunter, J. E. (1996). Measurement error in psychological research: Lessons from 26 research scenarios. *Psychological Methods, 1,* 199–223.

Schmidt, F. L., Hunter, J. E., & Raju, N. S. (1988). Validity generalization and situational specificity: A second look at the 75% rule and Fisher's z transformation. *Journal of Applied Psychology, 73,* 665–672.

Schmidt, F. L., Le, H., & Oh, I.-S. (2009). Correcting for the distorting effects of study artifacts in meta-analysis. In H. Cooper, L. V. Hedges, & J. C. Valentine (Eds.), *The handbook of research synthesis and meta-analysis* (2nd ed., pp. 317–333). New York: Russell Sage Foundation.

Schulze, R. (2004). *Meta-analysis: A comparison of approaches.* Cambridge, MA: Hogrefe & Huber.

Shadish, W. R., Cook, T. D., & Campbell, D. T. (2002). *Experimental and quasi-experimental designs for generalized causal inference.* Boston: Houghton Mifflin.

Shaffer, J. P. (1992). Caution on the use of variance ratios: A comment. *Review of Educational Research, 62,* 429–432.

Sharpe, D. (1997). Of apples and oranges, file drawers and garbage: Why validity issues in meta-analysis will not go away. *Clinical Psychology Review, 17,* 881–901.

Smith, M. L., & Glass, G. V. (1977). Meta-analysis of psychotherapy outcome studies. *American Psychologist, 32,* 752–760.

Sterne, J. A. C., Becker, B. J., & Egger, M. (2005). The funnel plot. In H. R. Rothstein, A. J. Sutton, & M. Borenstein (Eds.), *Publication bias in meta-analysis: Prevention, assessment and adjustments* (pp. 75–98). Hoboken, NJ: Wiley.

Sterne, J. A. C., & Egger, M. (2005). Regression methods to detect publication and other bias in meta-analysis. In H. R. Rothstein, A. J. Sutton, & M. Borenstein (Eds.), *Publication bias in meta-analysis: Prevention, assessment and adjustments* (pp. 99–110). Hoboken, NJ: Wiley.

Tabachnick, B. G., & Fidell, L. S. (1996). *Using multivariate statistics* (3rd ed.). New York: HarperCollins.

Tomada, G., & Schneider, B. H. (1997). Relational aggression, gender, and peer acceptance: Invariance across culture, stability over time, and concordance among informants. *Developmental Psychology, 33*, 601–609.

Valentine, J. C. (2009). Judging the quality of primary research. In H. Cooper, L. V. Hedges, & J. C. Valentine (Eds.), *The handbook of research synthesis and meta-analysis* (2nd ed., pp. 129–146). New York: Russell Sage Foundation.

Valentine, J. C., & Cooper, H. (2008). A systematic and transparent approach for assessing the methodological quality of intervention effectiveness research: The study design and implementation assessment device (Study DIAD). *Psychological Methods, 13*, 130–149.

von Eye, A., & Mun, E. Y. (2005). *Analyzing rater agreement: Manifest variable methods*. Mahwah, NJ: Erlbaum.

Werner, N. E. (2000). *Friends' influence on changes in externalizing behavior during middle childhood: A longitudinal study of relational and physical aggression*. Unpublished dissertation, University of Minnesota.

Werner, N. E., & Crick, N. R. (2004). Maladaptive peer relationships and the development of relational and physical aggression during middle childhood. *Social Development, 13*, 495–514.

White, H. D. (2009). Scientific communication and literature retrieval. In H. Cooper, L. V. Hedges, & J. C. Valentine (Eds.), *The handbook of research synthesis and meta-analysis* (2nd ed., pp. 51–71). New York: Russell Sage Foundation.

Widaman, K. F. (1993). Common factor analysis versus principal component analysis: Differential bias in representing model parameters? *Multivariate Behavioral Research, 28*, 263–311.

Widaman, K. F. (2007). Common factors versus components: Principals and principles, errors and misperceptions. In R. Cudeck & R. C. MacCallum (Eds.), *Factor analysis at 100: Historical developments and future directions* (pp. 177–203). Mahwah, NJ: Erlbaum.

Wilkinson, L., & The Task Force on Statistical Significance (1999). Statistical methods in psychology journals: Guidelines and explanations. *American Psychologist, 54*, 594–604.

Wilson, D. B. (2009). Systematic coding. In H. Cooper, L. V. Hedges, & J. C. Valentine (Eds.), *The handbook of research synthesis and meta-analysis* (2nd ed., pp. 159–176). New York: Russell Sage Foundation.

Yeaton, W. H., & Wortman, P. M. (1993). On the reliability of meta-analytic reviews. *Evaluation Research, 17*, 292–309.

Zalecki, C. A., & Hinshaw, S. P. (2004). Overt and relational aggression in girls with Attention Deficit Hyperactivity Disorder. *Journal of Clinical Child and Adolescent Psychology, 33*, 125–137.

Author Index

Aiken, L. S., 104
Alexander, R. A., 123, 142, 190
Algina, J., 123
Alliger, G. M., 142
Andreou, E., 288, 291, 293, 298
Antes, G., 277
Arbuckle, J. L., 228
Archer, J., 288
Arnold, M. E., 288, 294

B

Bagozzi, R. P., 69
Bailey, C. A., 57
Baron, R. M., 198
Barr, D. R., 139
Bauer, D. J., 246, 256
Baugh, F., 133
Bax, L., 14
Baxter, P. M., 43, 58
Bear, G. G., 81, 179, 192, 193, 194, 205, 208, 215, 235, 261, 288, 291, 332, 334
Becker, B. J., 22, 154, 169, 251, 263, 270, 271, 278, 287, 290, 291, 292, 295, 296, 297, 298, 306, 308
Begg, C. B., 266, 274, 275, 276
Berdugo-Arstark, H., 288, 294

Beretvas, S. N., 291, 292, 307
Berlin, J. A., 22, 260
Blachman, D. R., 57, 81, 179, 204, 208, 214, 220, 235, 238, 261, 288, 291, 293, 294, 299, 332, 334
Bond, C. F., Jr., 155, 170
Bonett, D. A., 119
Boorstin, D. J., 3
Borenstein, M., 14, 29, 169, 259, 276
Borman, G. D., 329, 331, 333, 336, 337, 342
Borodkin, L. J., 123, 190
Botella, J., 188, 195
Bovaird, J. A., 198
Brannick, M. T., 89, 230
Breivik, E., 69
Brendgen, M., 288, 294
Britt, D. W., 301
Brooks, J. O., III, 33
Brown, T. A., 127
Browne, M. W., 69
Bushman, B. J., 7, 15
Butovskaya, M. L., 288

C

Campbell, D. T., 19, 68, 308
Campbell, J. J., 288

357

118, 123, 124, 185, 199, 229, 230, 233, 251, 255, 274, 275

Henington, C. D., 81, 179, 204, 208, 214, 235, 253, 261, 288, 332, 334

Higgins, J. P. T., 14, 188

Hinshaw, S. P., 81, 179, 208, 235, 261, 288, 294, 295, 334

Hopewell, S., 58, 259

Howell, R. D., 69

Huedo-Medina, T. B., 188, 189, 195

Hunt, M., 8, 14

Hunter, J. E., 8, 9, 23, 84, 89, 98, 123, 126, 127, 128, 129, 133, 136, 137, 138, 139, 141, 142, 144, 145

I

Ikeda, N., 14

J

Jaccard, J., 301

Jackson, G. B., 9

Jacoby, J., 301

James, L. R., 123

Jansen, E. A., 253

Johnson, D. R., 81, 179, 205, 208, 214, 235, 261, 288, 332, 334

K

Kalaian, H. A., 308

Karlawish, J. H. T., 22

Kashy, D. A., 166

Keltikangas-Järvinen, L., 81, 179, 205, 208, 215, 235, 253, 261, 288, 332, 334

Kenny, D. A., 166, 198

Keppel, G., 203, 206, 227

Kerr, N. L., 30

Keselman, H. J., 123

Kim, J. J., 90, 122, 124

Kisamore, J. L., 230

Kline, R. B., 21, 127, 146, 219, 284, 285, 287, 307

Kovacs, M., 149

Kraemer, H. C., 22, 33

L

Le, H., 129, 139, 141, 144

Leff, S. S., 81, 179, 204, 208, 214, 235, 261, 288, 332, 334

Lerner, R. M., 308

Light, R. J., 263

Lindenberger, U., 134

Lipsey, M. W., 39, 65, 74, 77, 93, 100, 115, 116, 122, 125, 146, 150, 151, 154, 155, 164, 165, 170, 185, 199, 226

Little, T. D., 6, 12, 19, 57, 133, 134, 163, 172, 198, 284

M

MacCallum, R. C., 69, 84, 98, 136, 281, 305

Maeda, Y., 162, 169

Mallett, S., 58, 259

Marín-Martínez, F., 118, 188, 195

Maruyama, G. M., 146

Maxwell, S. E., 22

Mayeux, L., 288

McConnell, E., 19

McGrath, R. E., 125

McGraw, B., 9, 123

Meehl, P. E., 87, 300

Mehta, P. D., 246, 256

Meyer, G. J., 125

Miller, D. R., 81, 179, 204, 208, 214, 235, 261, 288, 332, 334

Miller, N., 306

Moons, K. G. M., 14

Mosteller, F., 32

Mulaik, S. A., 87, 123

Mun, E. Y., 132

Murphy, K. R., 22

Murray-Close, D., 81, 179, 205, 208, 214, 235, 261, 288, 332, 334

Muthén, B. O., 246

Myors, B., 22

N

Nangle, D. W., 288

Neale, M. C., 246, 256

Subject Index

f following a page number indicates a figure; *n* following a page number indicates a note; *t* following a page number indicates a table.

Across-time associations, 18
Aggregate analysis, 32*n*
Agreement rate, 75–76, 76*f*. *see also* Coding of studies; Reliability
Analysis of variance (ANOVA). *see also* F-ratio
  categorical moderators, 199, 203, 206, 211–216, 212*f*, 214*t*–215*t*
  computing *g* from commonly reported results and, 109, 113–114
  computing *r* from commonly reported results and, 99–100, 99*f*, 100*f*
  longitudinal change scores and, 164
  omnibus tests and, 104, 106, 113–114
  overview, 227*n*
  significance tests and, 101–103, 102*f*
Analyzing and interpreting study results, as stage of research synthesis, 9, 11, 12, 31. *see also* Data analysis; Data interpretation
Appendices in reports, 328–329. *see also* Writing the results of meta-analysis
"Apples and oranges problem," 25–26, 28
Artifact corrections. *see also* Corrections to effect sizes
  artificial dichotomization, 136–138, 136*f*, 137*f*, 138*t*
  controversy of, 127–129

  imperfect validity, 134–136, 135*f*
  overview, 126, 129–131, 130*f*, 131*f*, 144, 144*n*–145*n*
  practical matters to consider regarding, 142–144
  range restriction, 139–142, 140*f*, 141*f*, 142*f*
  recommended readings regarding, 144
  unreliability and, 131–134, 133*f*
Artificial dichotomization, 130*f*, 136–138, 136*f*, 137*f*, 138*t*
Audience
  coding and, 73
  writing results of meta-analysis and, 315–317
Average correlations matrix, 299–300

B

Backward searches. *see also* Searching the literature
  adequacy of a search and, 53–54
  overview, 49–50
  publication bias and, 259
Between-group heterogeneity, 200–201, 200*f*, 201*f*. *see also* Heterogeneity

About the Author

Noel A. Card, PhD, is Associate Professor in Family Studies and Human Development at the University of Arizona. His areas of interest include child and adolescent social developmental and quantitative research methods. He has received the Society for Research in Child Development Early Career Research Contributions Award and is an elected member of the Society of Multivariate Experimental Psychology.